# Japan–Netherlands Trade
# 1600–1800

# Japan–Netherlands Trade
# 1600–1800

## The Dutch East India Company and beyond

Suzuki Yasuko

Kyoto University Press

First published in 2012 jointly by:

Kyoto University Press
69 Yoshida Konoe-cho
Sakyo-ku, Kyoto 606-8315
Japan
Telephone: +81-75-761-6182
Fax: +81-75-761-6190
Email: sales@kyoto-up.or.jp
Web: http://www.kyoto-up.or.jp

Trans Pacific Press
PO Box 164, Balwyn North, Melbourne
Victoria 3104, Australia
Telephone: +61-3-9859-1112
Fax: +61-3-8911-7989
Email: tpp. mail@gmail.com
Web: http://www.transpacificpress.com

Set by Digital Environs, Melbourne.

## Distributors

**Australia and New Zealand**
DA Information Services/Central Book Services
648 Whitehorse Road
Mitcham, Victoria 3132
Australia
Telephone: +61-3-9210-7777
Fax: + 61-3-9210-7788
Email: books@dadirect.com
Web: www.dadirect.com

**USA and Canada**
International Specialized Book Services (ISBS)
920 NE 58th Avenue, Suite 300
Portland, Oregon 97213-3786
USA
Telephone: (800) 944-6190
Fax: (503) 280-8832
Email: orders@isbs.com
Web: http://www.isbs.com

**Asia and the Pacific**
Kinokuniya Company Ltd.

*Head office*:
38-1 Sakuragaoka 5-chome
Setagaya-ku, Tokyo 156-8691
Japan
Telephone: +81-3-3439-0161
Fax: +81-3-3439-0839
Email: bkimp@kinokuniya.co.jp
Web: www.kinokuniya.co.jp

*Asia-Pacific office*:
Kinokuniya Book Stores of Singapore Pte., Ltd.
391B Orchard Road #13-06/07/08
Ngee Ann City Tower B
Singapore 238874
Telephone: +65-6276-5558
Fax: +65-6276-5570
Email: SSO@kinokuniya.co.jp

The translation and publication of this book was supported by a Grant-in-Aid for Publication of Scientific Research Results, provided by the Japan Society for the Promotion of Science (JSPS).

ISBN    978-1-920901-51-6 (hardback), 978-1-876843-43-4 (paperback)

*Cover illustration*: From *Tōrakanzu* (Pictures of the Chinese and Dutch Trading Posts), illustrated by KAWAHARA Keiga (1786–1869), an artist well-known for his work for Dr. Philipp Franz Balthasar von Siebold, a doctor for the Dutch Factory at Dejima, Nagasaki. Courtesy of the Nagasaki Museum of History and Culture.

# Contents

# Figures

# Maps

# Tables

# Acknowledgements

Many researchers assisted me in writing this book. Particularly, I would like to thank Nakada Yasunao, Nagazumi Yōko, and J. L. Blussé. Nakada initiated me into researching the field of international trade relations in the Edo era. Nagazumi lead me to the fascinating world of the Dutch East India Company, and suggested researching the situation of exports using account books of the Dutch factory in Japan. The topic of my graduation thesis was the camphor trade between Japan and the Netherlands. This was the starting point for the book now in your hands.

I visited the Centre for the History of European Expansion, Leiden University, in 1986–87. Leonard Blussé provided much needed help there and I greatly appreciate his support and guidance during my research in the Netherlands over past years. I also thank Assistant Professor Charlotte Hille of the University of Amsterdam for teaching me Dutch habits, culture and skating during my stay in Leiden.

I would also like to thank Tashiro Kazui, Shimizu Hirokazu, Ōta Katsuya, Harada Hiroji, Nakamura Tadashi, Kato Eichi, Fujii Jōji, and W.G.J. Remmelink. Special thanks go to Tashiro, who provided me with good ideas and encouraged me to continue writing this book.

I am extremely grateful to the staff of the archives, libraries and museums where the research was undertaken: the Historiographical Institute, the University of Tokyo, Nagasaki Museum of History and Culture, National Diet Library, National Archives of Japan, Manuscript Library of Kyushu University, Chuo University Library, Keio University Library, *het Algemeen Rijksarchief* in The Hague, Lieden University Library, *Kern Instituut,* and the *Koninlijk Instituut voor taal-, land-, en volkenkunde* in Leiden. Special thanks go to Matsui Yōko and Matsukata Fuyuko of the Historiographical Institute at the University of Tokyo.

In addition, I am grateful to the colleagues and staff of Hanazono University who helped me so much, particularly Nakao Kōichi, an assistant of the Japanese history section, who examined my manuscript and tables.

This book was previously published as *Kinsei Nichiran bōekishi no kenkyū* (Shibunkaku Shuppan, Kyoto, Japan, 2004). In 2007, I stayed in Leiden during my sabbatical year and met Associate Professor Sasaki Motoe, an anthropologist at Hōsei University. She told me that many foreign researchers of

Japanese history wish to be published in English. Her words encouraged me to translate this book and I feel grateful for her suggestion.

I would like to thank Suzuki Tetsuya, editor of Kyoto University Press, who understood the importance of publishing the book in English, even though the company had never published a research book in the field of Japanese history before. Thanks are due to Ashley Davis for his conscientious, thorough and patient editorial work over two years.

I received some subsidies for writing this book from various organisations, including The Konosuke Matsushita Memorial Foundation, The Murata Science Foundation, The Ray-Key Foundation of the People's Culture, and The Resona Foundation for Asia and Oceania. I also received a Grant-in-Aid for Science Research (C) from the Japan Society for the Promotion of Science (JSPS). I wish this book would reciprocate in part their wonderful assistance.

May this book inspire others to research Japanese and world history.

Suzuki Yoko<br>
Professor<br>
Faculty of Letters<br>
Hanazono University<br>
Kyoto

# Preface

The Netherlands outfitted ships for direct voyages to Asia and started foreign trade activities from 1595. Trading companies (*voor-compagnieën*) were formed one after another in various Asian cities. One of these companies launched five ships from Rotterdam headed for Asia in 1598. The fleet set its course to sail the Atlantic southward and circumnavigate the southern tip of South America. By the time it reached the coast of Chile, however, only the primary ship, the *Hoop*, and one other, the *Liefde*, remained. There they finally decided to head for Japan.

The two ships were struck by a terrible storm. The *Liefde* lost sight of the *Hoop* and drifted for days. The ship cast up on the shore of Usuki in Chikugo Province (present-day Ōita Prefecture) in April 1600. This was the beginning of the relationship between Japan and the Netherlands. The Netherlands did not then have a stronghold in Asia at the time. The serendipitous arrival of a lone Dutch vessel in Japan, even before the Netherlands embarked on full-scale trading in Asia, evokes a sense of the deep historical bonds between the two countries.

Some of the trading companies were merged to form the Dutch United East India Company (*de Verenigde Oostindishe Compagnie*, or VOC) in 1602. The VOC set up the Board of Directors (*Heeren XVII*, or the Gentlemen Seventeen) in the Netherlands and the Governor General of the Dutch East Indies in Batavia on the Island of Java. The VOC expanded its Asia trade aggressively by opening factories in various parts of Asia. The VOC made huge profits by maintaining close communication between Europe and Asia and between Asian regions; it was able to obtain accurate information about market conditions in Asia and Europe and ship a wide variety of goods to regions where they were most profitable.

It was in 1605 that a letter sealed by Shogun Tokugawa Ieyasu was delivered to the Dutch Factory in Pattani, Indochina, allowing the VOC to travel to Japan. The Pattani factory had just opened but it was troubled by conflicts in surrounding regions that stopped the Dutch from sending ships to Japan for four years. In 1609, two Dutch ships, the *Roode Leeuw met Pijlen* and the *Griffioen*, finally arrived in Hirado with the red-sealed letter to open a factory there. Although the factory was later relocated from

Hirado to Nagasaki, the Netherlands maintained its relations with Japan until the end of the Edo period.

## Study objectives

The first objective of this study is to examine the conditions of Japanese–Dutch trade and its transitions over a long period of time. The shogunate devised and enforced one foreign policy after another according to the constantly changing state of Japan's industry and economy. Nonetheless, the VOC had its own trade policy for its factory in Japan, the VOC's stronghold in its Asia trade.

The second objective is to study how conflicts of interest between the two parties impacted on trade in Hirado and Nagasaki and led to mutual understanding or resentment. The third objective is to consider the significance of Japanese–Dutch relations from the point of view of Dutch trading policy. Finally, the fourth objective is to consider various domestic factors from within Japan that have been missing from preceding studies of Japanese–Dutch trade conducted by European scholars.

Culture has long been the main focus of the study of early modern Japanese–Dutch relations; trade has not been given much importance in the past. In particular, there have been many studies on various issues relating to *rangaku* (the learning of European knowledge, mainly medicine and science, in the Dutch language) from the latter half of the eighteenth century. *Rangaku* certainly had a major influence on Japanese culture in the late early modern period and aroused deep adulation of and curiosity about European culture and science in the mind of the Japanese.

However, a bilateral relationship between two countries is unlikely to be limited to the cultural aspect; there are always political and economic aspects to it as well. This also applies to the relationship between seclusionist early modern Japan, which forbade the Japanese people to travel overseas, and the Netherlands, the only European country that maintained contact with Japan.

The Dutch party that was directly involved in exchanges with Japan was the VOC, the state-sanctioned trading company possessing quasi-governmental power. It goes without saying that trade was of greatest interest to both the Netherlands and Japan in the seventeenth century. In the eighteenth century, however, the Netherlands actively promoted the introduction of European culture and technology into Japan at the behest of the Japanese, especially from the 1720s when the eighth shogun Yoshimune was in power. The Netherlands complied with Japan's wish for European culture as it considered this to be the best and most effective way to maintain the smooth operation of its trade with Japan.

We need to recognize anew that trade was the foundation of early modern Japanese–Dutch relations. It is impossible to grasp the significance of the early modern Japanese–Dutch relations without understanding Japanese–Dutch trade. Yet there have been very few studies of Japanese–Dutch trade over an extended period of time, even though its conditions have been discussed from various viewpoints.

To carry out the above objectives, this study follows Japanese export products from production to sale with as much context as possible. I focus on exports as there were fewer export commodities than imports. I suggest that it is possible to understand overall trade conditions by analyzing each export product in detail.

The economic and foreign policies of the shogunate were also clearly reflected in the state of export control. While imports were regulated to some extent, the shogunate's trade control measures were mostly directed at exports. An analysis of the shogunate's export regulations can reveal its foreign policy.

Analyses of the VOC's sales network for Japanese goods and the selling conditions in Europe and Southwest Asia reveal the significance of Dutch–Japanese trade to the changing conditions in the Asian and European markets at the time. The study will discuss changes in Dutch trade policy in Japan together with changes in the conditions for export products during the eighteenth century.

The study examines the state of affairs in Japan, Asia and Europe as recorded in detail from various viewpoints, especially the trade-related archival documents of the VOC and its factory in Japan. The cross-referencing of these documents paints a more vivid picture of the actual state of Japanese–Dutch trade. Trade based in Hirado and later Nagasaki was a point of contact between early modern Japan and the changing European and Asian markets; this study will examine what this trade reveals about Japanese–Durch trade more broadly.

The volume and value of principal export products—gold (koban), silver, copper and camphor—are analysed separately in terms of their export from Nagasaki into overseas markets. Please be forewarned that some statements will be repeated in multiple chapters where the export conditions of a certain product are explained in relation to another product. Some important events, like the proclamation of trade laws or the relocation of the factory from Hirado to Nagasaki in 1641, also greatly affected the trade of more than one export. For example, Chapter Six presents a sweeping analysis of copper, *koban* and camphor from export to sale over a period of twenty four years in the early eighteenth century. For this reason, it contains some topics that have already been covered in the earlier chapters that concern individual products.

## Issues in the study of early modern Japanese–Dutch trade

In the 1960s, early modern Japanese–Dutch trade was studied in the context of early modern international relations. The 1970s saw research focus on trade conditions during the Hirado period of the Dutch Factory, as this is when Japanese–Dutch trade flourished most. The translation of the diaries of the Dutch Factory began in the 1970s. These documents offer a glimpse into the state of shogunate affairs at a time when the relationship between the Dutch and leading figures in the shogunate was at its closest.

In the 1980s, research on the Hirado period was undertaken parallel to the study of individual export and import goods, trade after the Hirado period, and special forms and systems of trade like private trade and copper substitution. Some studies in the 1990s interpreted Japanese–Dutch trade in the broader context of Southeast Asian trade networks.

This study owes much to Yamawaki Teijirō's investigation of import and export volumes as they were recorded in the trade books of the Dutch Factory. It advances Yamawaki's research through detailed analysis of the domestic and foreign factors that might have affected trade volumes, in particular the amount of trade in the principal export goods of gold (*koban*), silver, copper and camphor.

There are two reasons for the focus on export volumes. First, the principal import commodity of textiles included many different types. Each type of textile was further divided into many grades for which different prices were set, making comparison and analysis extremely difficult.

Second, the variety of imported goods other than textiles increased over time. They included many different spices, minerals, pigments and medicines such as sugar, pepper, eaglewood, agallochum, benzoin, cinnamon, nutmeg, yellow sandalwood, white sandalwood, gambier, myrrh, cambogia, borneol, sappanwood, sharkskin, buckskin, lead, mercury, tin, galvanized iron, alum and amber. Private traders were active in the latter half of the early modern period, often importing expensive items like Western books, stationery goods and ornaments. These imports were, of course, not recorded in the trade books of the factory and only some of the private records still remain today. Despite these difficulties, some scholars have studied the importation of raw silk, sugar, buckskin and woolen textiles.

Most studies of trade in Nagasaki have looked at the series of trade laws and regulations starting from the seventeenth century and ending with the trade law (*Shōtoku sinrei*), introduced in 1715. These studies have revealed how the content of each law was formulated in the context of trade relations and the effectiveness of existing laws in responding to various issues. They have drawn on the archival records of the shogunate, local historical records from Nagasaki and the records of the Nagasaki trade association. There have been very few studies using Dutch or Chinese historical materials. The trade activities of the Dutch and Chinese in Nagasaki have therefore not been studied demonstratively beyond discussion of shogunate trade laws, their changes and their effects.

Chinese traders were operating in Nagasaki without formal diplomatic relations between Japan and the Qing Dynasty of China. Trade negotiations were conducted purely between visiting Chinese ships and the shogunate government. Not all Chinese ships came from mainland China; some came from various ports in Southeast Asia. Consequently, there are few documents relating to Nagasaki trade among the official archives of the Qing government; the documents that exist are unlikely to offer a full picture of the Nagasaki trade by the Chinese. Though presently underutilized, the wealth of Dutch materials are more useful in illuminating trade activities in Nagasaki at the time.

The study of the Japanese–Dutch trade began in Europe with the arrival of Kaempfer in Japan at the end of the seventeenth century, followed by Thunberg, Meijlan and Siebold. Münsterberg, Nachod and Kuiper undertook serious research from the end of the nineteenth century to the first half of the twentieth century. With the exception of Glamann's research, Japanese–Dutch trade has not been a central subject of study in recent times. Instead, Dutch trade in Japan has only been studied as part of the VOC's broader trade activities in Asia. Just like in Japan, Dutch research has tended to focus on the cultural aspects of early modern Japanese–Dutch relations.

The supplement to this book gives a full outline of research on the topic of Japanese–Dutch trade relations. It also presents the bibliographic details of sources in Japan and the Netherlands.

Bibliographic items are shown in the notes. The bibliography for the appendix is placed separately at the end of the book to list the items in the appendix only, in order to compile major preceding publications.

All names are shown with the surname first followed by the given name. In the cases of Western names, a comma is placed in between. In the cases of Japanese and other Asian names, no comma is used.

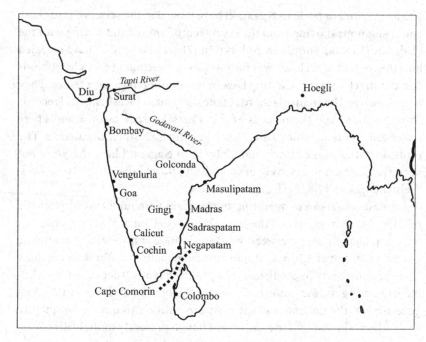

*Map 1: Map of India in the seventeenth century*

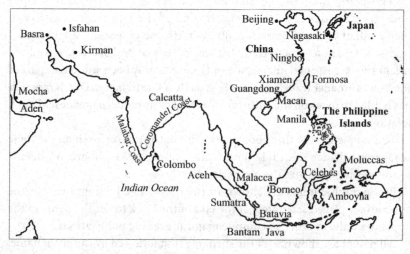

*Map 2: Map of Asia in the seventeenth century*

# Chapter One

# The Japanese–Dutch Silver Trade, 1609 to 1668

It was 1609 when the Netherlands set up a trading post in Hirado. Like Portugal, the Dutch goal was to procure as much silver as possible that could be used as capital in the Asian market. In the latter half of the 1630s, silver exports accounted for as high as 80 to 90 per cent of the total export. The Japanese trade silver for raw silk and silk fabrics, which accounted for the bulk of imports into Japan. The silver trade is therefore an important part of my investigation into the actual state of Japanese–Dutch trade at the beginning of the early modern period.

The Dutch silver trade has been researched by scholars such as Taya Hirokichi[1], Kobata Atsushi[2], Katō Ēichi, Yamawaki Teijirō, Nagazumi Yōko and Fujita Kayoko. Katō was the first person to seriously look into the Dutch trade in silver. Through a detailed analysis of the trade books of the Dutch Factory in Hirado, Katō examined silver exports during the Hirado period up to 1640.[3] Yamawaki wrote about Japanese silver exports in relation to export destinations[4] and Nagazumi discussed the role of Japanese silver in relation to trade between Hirado and Southeast Asia.[5] Fujita studied the records of the Dutch East India Company (*Verenigde Oostindische Compagnie*, hereinafter referred to as VOC) to reveal the state of silver exports from the late 1630s, until 1668 when a silver export ban was imposed.[6]

Although it is widely recognized that silver was one of the important export commodities in the beginning of the early modern period, there has been no integrated study on the development of the silver trade during the period following the opening of the Dutch Factory until the export ban. The actual state and course of the development of the silver trade is not fully understood. This chapter sheds light on the development of the silver export from the time of the Dutch Factory in Hirado to the silver export ban, addressing the problems with the trade by drawing on preceding studies.

## The Dutch Factory in Hirado (1610s)

The VOC opened a trading house in Hirado in the hope of acquiring Japanese silver, but it was not necessarily smooth sailing at the start. The Dutch were unable to procure alone Chinese raw silk which was in demand in Japan, Especially during the 1610s. Consequently, the Dutch captured Chinese junks and Portuguese ships at sea and diverted their cargos to Japan.[7] In other words, they were sending goods to Japan through piracy. The Dutch ships visited Japan on an irregular basis and the types and quantities of goods were variable. For example, an article in the *Generale Missiven* dated 15 March 1615 reports:

> The *Oude Zeeland* arrived in Bantan from Japan. Its cargos were food and weapons instead of the much awaited silver.[8]

In this way, silver exports from Japan in the 1610s were not as successful as the Dutch had hoped. As if to corroborate this, the *Diary of Richard Cocks*, which was written from 1613 by the head of the English Factory in Hirado, reports frequent use of the then international currency Real van Achten (the real of eight silver coin of Spain, hereinafter referred to as the silver real) in Hirado during the 1610s.

The Dutch and English brought silver reales to Japan as capital funds during the 1610s and the early 1620s. The silver real which Spain minted in the New World began to flow into Asia as well as Europe in large quantities from the second half of the sixteenth century. Consequently, if the Dutch and English captured Portuguese or Spanish vessels in the Asian seas, they could acquire large numbers of silver reales.

In those days, the Dutch and English in Japan exchanged the silver real with the schuit silver ingot (*chōgin*) to pay for the transactions and expenses of the trading houses.[9] The silver real itself was also used to pay Japanese tradesmen[10] and for transactions between the English and Dutch in Hirado.[11] A record shows that when the English Factory ran up a debt due to sluggish trade in the late 1610s, it received silver reales and used them to settle the debt.[12] The inflow and use of the silver real in large quantities during this period is indicative of a slump in the export of Japanese silver. Had the Dutch been able to procure and ship commodities such as much-desired Chinese raw silk to Japan, they would have acquired large quantities of silver in Japan and would not have gone to the trouble of exchanging the silver real for schuit silver.

Entries concerning the exchanging of silver reales for schuit silver are found in the trade books of the Dutch Factory until 1621.[13] No such entries are found thereafter. According to Table 1, large quantities of silver real coins were exported five years later in 1626. In the trade books after that year; 'Real' might have been used as a monetary unit but the silver real was no longer mentioned at all. According to Katō Ēichi, this was strongly influenced by *Genna no daijunkyō* (the great Genna martyrdom) of 1621. The Dutch considered that the use of the Spanish silver real might breach the religious policy of the Japanese government and stopped sending silver reales to Japan.[14] If that were the case, why was the silver real kept at the Dutch Factory in Hirado until 1626 and not taken from Japan in the years following the martyrdom?

The English voluntarily withdrew from Japan in 1623 and the Japanese government prohibited the Spanish from landing on Japanese soil in 1624. These moves left Portugal and the Netherlands as the only two European trading partners of Japan. As the conditions became more favorable for the Dutch, the Portuguese complained to the Japanese government in Edo (the shogunate capital of Japan) that the Dutch were procuring goods by the improper means of piracy and bringing them to Japan. In fact, the Dutch had been criticized by the feudal lord of Hirado and the governor of Nagasaki for their sea piracy.[15] Consequently, the Dutch were faced with an urgent need to secure a trading base in China for their trade with Japan. In 1623, they finally built Fort Zeelandia in the southwestern part of Taiwan as a base for trading in China.[16] The Dutch named this place Tayouan. This enabled the Dutch to procure large quantities of Chinese raw silk and silk fabrics that were in demand in Japan, putting the Japanese–Dutch trade on track. The conditions for the Dutch to embark on full-scale trade between Japan and China were ripening. Under these circumstances, the Dutch Factory in Hirado established strong foundations; the Dutch were able to acquire enough silver in Japan without further need for the silver real.

Although the Netherlands sent silver reales to Japan to remedy a critical shortage of capital, the Dutch refrained from using them from 1622 because, in view of the intensifying government ban on Christianity, it was Spanish money. Yet, withdrawing all the real coins from Japan risked creating shortages in the funds needed for transactions and expenses. Therefore they kept silver reales in Hirado for a while. Only in 1626, when the Japanese trade began to do well, did the Dutch finally withdraw all the remaining silver reales from Japan.

## The growth period (1620s and early 1630s)

As the trade books of the Dutch Factory from the 1620s are extant, it is possible for us to examine silver exports in detail from that period. The first entry in the trade books referring to silver exports is found in a shipping bill of the *St.Crus*, which headed for Pescadores on 25 October 1622. In the

Table 1: Silver exports, 1622–1635

|  | Month/Day | Ship name | Destination | Type | Value (tael) (1) |
|---|---|---|---|---|---|
| 1622 | 10/25 | St.Crus | Pescadores | Refined | 1,460 |
|  |  |  |  | Berg | 14,600 |
|  |  |  |  | Soma | 20,440 |
|  | 11/5 | Nieuw Bump | Pescadores | Soma | 16,060 |
|  |  |  |  | Berg | 4,380 |
|  |  |  |  | Schuit | 1,600 |
|  | 12/5 | Firando | Pescadores | Berg | 30,660 |
|  |  |  |  | Soma | 13,140 |
|  |  |  |  | Total | 102,340 |
| 1623 | 10/5 | Westkapelle | Pescadores | Soma | 14,600 |
|  | 11/10 | de Beer | Pescadores | Soma | 7,300 |
|  |  |  |  | Total | 21,900 |
| 1624 | 1/10 | Goede Hoop | Pescadores/Batavia | Soma | 43,452: 9: – |
|  |  |  |  | Berg | 3,870 |
|  | 1/18 | Goede Hoop | Batavia | Berg | 4,380 |
|  |  |  |  | Total | 51,702: 9: – |
| 1626 | 2/28 | Oranje | Taijouan | Real | 34,791: 4: 3 |
|  |  |  |  | Soma | 60,099: 2: 8 |
|  |  |  |  | Berg | 601: 3: 6 |
|  |  |  |  | Total | 95,672: 0: 7 |
| 1627 | 1/6 | Noort Holland | Taijouan | Soma | 10,000 |
|  |  |  |  | Berg | 17,993: 5: 5 |
|  | 2/26 | Erasmus | Taijouan | Soma | 37,558: 5: – |
|  |  |  |  | Berg | 2,410 |
|  | 10/22 | Vreede | Taijouan | Soma | 56,940 |
|  | 10/31 | Edam | Taijouan | Soma | 30,660 |
|  | 12/3 | Woerden | Taijouan | Soma | 52,560 |
|  |  |  |  | Total | 20,8121:10: 5 |
| 1628 | 2/20 | Westkapelle | Taijouan | Soma | 18,980 |
|  | 3/5 | Heusden | Taijouan | Soma | 73,000 |
|  | 3/23 | Chincheu | Taijouan | Soma | 6,807: 2: 5 |
|  |  |  |  | Total | 98,787: 2: 5 |
| 1633 | 1/15 | Arend | Taijouan/Batavia | Soma | 66,560 |
|  | 1/15 | Cemphaan | Taijouan/Batavia | Soma | 21,632 |
|  | 2/12 | Heusden | Taijouan | Soma | 58,240 |
|  | 2/22 | Warmont | Batavia | Soma | 52,131: 4: 9 |
|  |  |  |  | Schuit | 6,400 |

*Table 1: Continued*

|      | Month/Day | Ship name | Destination | Type | Value (tael) (1) |
|------|-----------|-----------|-------------|------|------------------|
|      | 11/13 | Wapen van Delft | Siam/Batavia | Soma | 10,750 |
|      |       |           |             | Schuit | 24,000 |
|      | 12/12 | Venloo | Taijouan | Soma | 9,750 |
|      |       |        |          | Total | 249,463: 4: 9 |
| 1634 | 2/15 | Oude Water | Taijouan/Batavia | Soma | 12,295 |
|      | 11/24 | Venloo | Taijouan | Schuit | 35,200 |
|      | 11/24 | Wapen van Delft | Siam | Soma | 8,600 |
|      |       |           |      | Schuit | 22,400 |
|      | 12/3 | Oude Water | Taijouan | Schuit | 59,200 |
|      |      |           |          | Soma | 10,500 |
|      |      |           |          | Berg | 1,300 |
|      |      |           |          | Total | 149,495 |
| 1635 | 1/23 | Venhuijsen | Taijouan | Schuit | 17,600 |
|      |      |            |          | Berg | 8401: 5: – |
|      |      |            |          | Soma | 14,600 |
|      | 2/15 | Bredamme | Taijouan | Schuit | 88,000 |
|      |      |          |          | Soma | 19,710 |
|      | 11/13 | Wapen van Delft | Siam | Schuit | 20,000 |
|      | 11/17 | Venhuijsen | Taijouan | Schuit | 10,000 |
|      | 11/17 | Grol | Taijouan | Schuit | 60,000 |
|      |      |      |          | Total | 238,569: 5: – |
|      |      |      |          | Grand total | 1,216,052: 2: 6 |

initial stage of export, silver varied in form and quality. As Figure 1 shows, silver exports at the time included the soma, schuit silver, berg silver, refined silver and the aforementioned silver real. This section will look at changes in the types and volumes of silver exported in the 1620s and the early 1630s and consider the etymology of soma silver, which was the main type of silver exported during this period.

## Types of silver exports
Schuit silver refers to the Japanese *chōgin*, which was in wide circulation within the country. It came to be commonly called schuit (a Dutch word meaning 'ship') silver because the shape of the *chōgin* ingot resembled the shape of a Dutch ship.[17] In 1622, 1,600 tael (sixteen Japanese *kan*, where one *kan* is equal to 3.75 kilograms) of schuit silver were exported, but it was

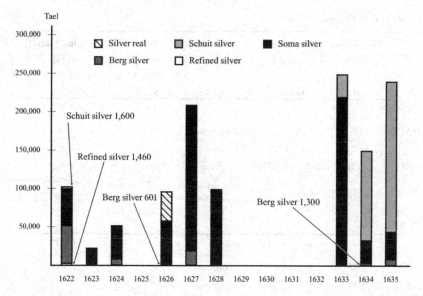

Figure 1: Annual silver export values, 1622–1635

not exported again until 1633. Refined silver was only exported in 1622; no further record of export is found in this name. However, soma silver is a kind of refined silver. Therefore it is likely that this item called refined silver was of similar quality to soma silver but of a different shape or grade.

The most notable type of silver exported in the 1620s and the early 1630s was soma silver, which had the largest share of export silver up to 1634. Soma silver was a kind of refined silver of better quality than schuit silver. In the early 1620s, the amount of exported soma silver was about the same as that of berg silver.

'Berg' is a Dutch word meaning a mountain or a lump. There was a type of silver called *yamagin* (mountain silver) which was minted at silver mines in various regions of Japan in those days.[18] Berg silver is a direct translation of the Japanese name and perhaps it had the shape of a lump of silver. Berg silver was also a kind of refined silver with the same level of purity as soma silver. In 1622, the value of berg silver exports was about the same as that of soma silver. However, berg silver was not exported in 1623. Only about 8,000 tael of berg silver was exported in 1624 compared with about 43,000 tael of soma silver. By 1626 soma silver had established its absolute dominance in the Japanese–Dutch silver trade. Berg silver was not exported from then on, except in 1634 and 1635.

In 1628, there was an armed clash between the Dutch and the Japanese at Fort Zeelandia in Tayouan; Japanese–Dutch trade was virtually stopped

Table 2: Export silver by type

|  | Total value | Proportion (%) |
|---|---|---|
| Soma silver | 746,624: 4: 2 | 61.4 |
| Berg silver | 88,596: 4: 2 | 7.3 |
| Schuit silver | 344,400 | 28.3 |
| Silver real | 34,971: 4: 3 | 2.9 |
| Refined silver | 1,460 | 0.1 |
| Grand total | 1,216,052: 2: 6 | |

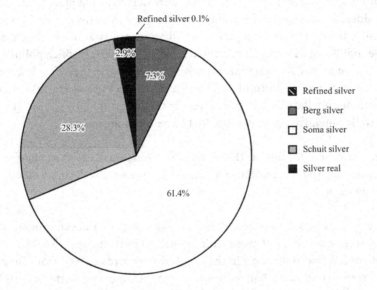

Figure 2: Silver exports by type

from 1629 to the end of 1632. Although the Dutch Factory was unable to export silver during this period, they continued to deal in silver with domestic merchants. Soma silver was the only type of silver that was traded during this period.[19] The accumulated stock of soma silver was exported at once upon resumption of trade in 1633; it amounted to about 220,000 tael. This was the last time a large quantity of soma silver was exported; the export of soma silver stopped altogether in 1635.

According to Table 1, the total silver export from 1622 to 1635 was about 1,216,000 tael. Table 2 shows a breakdown of the types of exported silver up to 1635. Figure 2 is a pie chart of this breakdown. Looking at the 1620s alone, soma accounted for almost eighty per cent of the total silver exports.[20] It is obvious that soma silver was the main commodity during the growth of silver exports until 1635.

## Etymology of the soma silver

Soma silver was exported more than any other type of silver in the 1620s and the early 1630s. There are many theories about the origin of the word 'soma' (or somma). Some people attribute it to a place name or a Chinese coin; others claim that it was derived from a word meaning a type of Chinese ship that the shape of the ingot resembled.

Kobata Atsushi was the first author who discussed the etymology of soma. He argued that soma silver was exported overseas in large quantities together with Nagito silver, Seda silver and Tajimon silver in the sixteenth century and that all these silver names were derived from place names. He considered that the soma was named after the Sama silver mine in Nima county, Iwami region, and that soma silver meant Iwami silver.[21] On the other hand, Taya Hirokichi presented historical materials which pointed to a different origin. An announcement which appeared in the *Ginza kakitome* (silver mint records) prohibited the illegal trafficking of Haifuki silver, a kind of cupellated silver produced for the Nagasaki silver mint. It was partially amended on September 1621 to read as follows:

> It is prohibited to bring the Haifuki silver to Nagasaki and export it to foreign
> countries. And it is prohibited to trade in the *souma* silver with no official
> mint stamp.[22]

It was prohibited to take away '*souma*' silver, which had been minted into the Chinese currency of sycee with no official mint stamp. A *kōjō no oboe* (note to a verbal statement) in the silver mint records of 1662 read 'Do not take *souma-fuki* in exchange for direct payment of *chōgin* [the schuit] by foreigners'.[23] '*Souma*' here could be the name of a silver refining method. Taya considers that the '*souma*' referred to here was something similar to the Chinese currency of sycee and that the '*souma-fiki*' was minted by Sycee silversmiths.[24] Taya considerd that this '*souma*' silver means soma silver.

Enomoto Sōji found mention of a kind of Chinese ship called a soma in the *Diary of Richard Cocks*. He argued that the soma ingot was called as such due to its resemblance to it.[25] While Katō Ēichi adopts the same theory about the shape of a ship, he also mentions that the Dutch archival materials merely called it 'cupellated silver'.[26] Nagazumi Yōko treats soma silver simply as the cupellated silver and makes no direct reference to its etymology.[27]

Among the different theories about the meaning of soma presented so far, the place name theory and the shape theory have been particularly strong. It is more likely in my opinion that the word was derived from the shape of the Haifuki silver (also called cupellated silver) rather than a place name in view of a range of factors. These factors are as follows.

Firstly, trade-book records of the Dutch Factory show that the soma was one of many types of silver exported in the 1620s, including berg and schuit silver. Setting aside the meaning of soma for the moment, all of these names were derived from a shape rather than a place name except for so called 'refined silver' and the silver real. There is no record of the export of Tajimon silver, Nagito silver or Seda silver by the Dutch in this period.

Secondly, a national currency system was yet to be developed in the sixteenth century; the silver ingots that were minted at individual silver mines and hallmarked as 'cupellated silver' were traded by various merchants and circulated as currency mainly in cities.[28] In the Edo period, however, the establishment of a unified currency was one of the important policy challenges for the shogunate government. It built official silver-coin mints and individual silver mines were gradually placed under their control. Under these circumstances, it would be almost impossible for the Iwami silver mine to sell large amounts of silver directly to merchants, sending them to Hirado during the 1620s and 1630s. In fact, the shogunate government set up a local silver-coin mint in Nagasaki in its attempt to regulate the export of high quality cupellated silver ingots like the soma.[29]

Thirdly, the *Diary of Richard Cocks* lists the cargo manifest of the *Sea Adventure*, 29 December 1617. It has entries about soma and Nagito silver:

- 1218: 0: 0 of 'In plate soma refined, w'th exchange'
- 11561: 1: 5 of 'In bars plate refynd lyk tyn, w'th exchange'
- 1000: 0: 0 of In plate bars of Japon, *nagites*'.[30]

Kobata argues that Iwami silver and Nagato silver were also exported at that time based on these records.[31] However, the general catalogue appended to the translated version of the *Diary of Richard Cocks* indicates that the words '*nagite*' and '*nagito*' both mean '*nagaitagin* (long plate silver)', not '*nagatogin* (silver from Nagato)'.[32] Based on this view, '*nagite*' means 'long plate' and it was named after its shape rather than a place of origin.

Fourthly, the first entry about soma silver appears in *Generale Missiven* in an article dated 8 February 1633. It describes soma silver simply as 'refined silver' and does not suggest that the name was derived from a place name.[33] Also in the *Dag-Register gehouden int Casteel Batavia* (the daily registers kept in the Castle of Batavia), soma silver is described simply and repeatedly as 'cupellated silver'.[34]

The fifth factor is somewhat related to the first one. The second largest precious metal for export in this period was copper. The types of exported copper included *tama-dō/maru-dō* (round/ball copper), *ita-dō/hira-dō* (plate/flat copper) and *sao-dō* (rod copper) which were all named after their shapes; none were named after major copper mines such as Akita.[35] Their shape was also one of the guides to their grade.

The sixth factor was that the silver mine in Iwami was the first major silver mine developed in the sixteenth century; it was said to be the largest supplier of silver exported during the same century.[36] It reached its peak production in around 1600. It is rather implausible to think that the quantity of the Iwami silver circulating domestically during the 1620s was large enough to account for the majority of silver exports to the Netherlands.

Finally and as the seventh factor, entries about a kind of small Chinese ship called a 'soma', which was smaller than the Chinese junk, are found here and there in the *Diary of Richard Cocks*, beginning with an article dated 8 August 1615: 'they of Goto 3 somos, or small junkes, theare of his, w'ch were bound for Firando, & would not let them passe'.[37] The first appearance of soma silver in *Diary of Richard Cocks* was in an article dated 10 December 1617: 'that ther wantes 4 ta.1m.oco.of wight in the 3000 tais somo plate sent p'r Niquan'.[38] This was some two years after the first appearance of the soma ship. In other words, the first half of the diary does not contain any references to soma silver. If soma silver had been widely circulating in Japan before the opening of the trading house, it should naturally have been mentioned frequently from the first year of the *Diary of Richard Cocks*. The absence of any reference to it seems very strange.

Based on these factors, I believe it is more reasonable to think that the small Chinese junk called a soma is the origin of the word for soma silver. Furthermore, the soma boat was probably another name for a sanpan boat.[39]

Prior to the development of the unified currency policy by the shogunate government, the place of production was used as a guide in determining the grade of silver. It appears that by this period the shape of silver ingots became a guide to their grade. This means that the establishment of governmental silver and gold mints to control mines across the country can help to explain the gradual fading of local colour and the changing names of export silver and copper items.

## The heyday of the silver trade (1635 to 1641)

The export of soma silver stopped in 1635 and schuit silver became the only type of silver exported from Japan from then on. There are no historical records announcing a government embargo on cupellated silver exports, including soma silver, to the Netherlands at that time. However, the following is a passage from the *Dagregister in Hirado* (daily registers kept in the factory in Hirado), dated 16 Ausgust 1635:

A letter from Junior Commercial Officer Verstegen in Nagasaki arrived late afternoon. It contained the following clauses. They are orders issued to the Portuguese by the governor of Nagasaki and they must follow it exactly and abide by it.

They may use black people to hold parasols for them but they may not use the Japanese people for this purpose. [...] Notification was given in regard to bringing in missionaries and prohibition on the export of cupellated silver, the Soma silver, swords and guns.[40]

Although these orders were reportedly issued by the magistrate of Nagasaki to the Portuguese, it is quite conceivable that they were also applied to the Dutch. The shogunate government had already issued an edict on 30 September 1609 prohibiting foreigners from taking cupellated silver out of Japan. According to the *Tōdai ki* (records of the present generation):

Silver ingots used to be minted into the Nanryō before being handed to foreigners in the past but they will remain as Japanese *chōgin-ban* [schuit silver ingots]. The order came from Sunpu and the Chinese are annoyed. But the order will be followed.[41]

The order prohibited the Chinese and other foreigners from having schuit silver recast into purer cupellated silver coins for export. However, it appears that this order was not complied with as a similar order was issued again in 1616.[42] This suggests that foreigners actually preferred high-purity cupellated silver, especially the soma, for export. One reason for their preference for cupellated silver for export would be that the grade of soma silver was almost on par with that of the silver real, an international currency in Asia and Europe, whereas the grade of schuit silver circulating in Japan was lower.

One of the main reasons for the shogunate government's issuing of this stricter ban on the exporting of cupellated silver in 1635 was that the government was using soma silver to mint large quantities of *chōgin* (schuit silver) for nationwide circulation at that time. Unfortunately, there is no historical record detailing the mintage of *chōgin*. The following passage is from a letter dated 13 November 1635 from Koeckebakker, the head of the Dutch Factory, to Governor Putmans of Formosa (Taiwan):

All the Schuit silver ingots received to date are being examined by two experienced men. They are sorted into counterfeits, poor quality, new and old. They are packed separately in boxes marked N [for New] and O [for Old] and

those which are unanimously assessed as old and top grade will be bought by
the Chinese for 25 tael in Tayouan. The lowest quality ingots may be the lowest
quality here [in Hirado] but they will be treated as the top quality there [in
Tayouan]. Since only a small quantity of old Schuit ingots are available, we will
be receiving much larger quantities of new ones this year.[43]

This tells us that the old *chōgin* and the new *chōgin* coexisted in Japan soon
after the imposition of the ban on the export of soma and other forms of
cupellated silver against the Portuguese. Since the old *chōgin* had a higher
grade and value and had become less available, it is reasonable to think
that the old schuit silver was no longer minted at this time. The shogunate
government was trying to mint large quantities of new and lower grade
*chōgin* for national circulation, so were totally regulating the use of various
silver coins as well as the old *chōgin* that were in circulation at the time.

According to the trade books of the Dutch Factory, the exchange rate
between tael (one tael is equal to ten monme of silver) and gulden used to
record the value of schuit silver exports in 1635 was one tael for 2.85 gulden
from November of the same year. This rate was established as the base
exchange rate for transactions in the whole of Japanese–Dutch trade from
then on. Although schuit silver had been in domestic circulation previously,
it was not necessarily used as a standard currency in foreign trade. By this
time, however, the newly minted and low-grade schuit silver became the
only silver available for export; the Japanese now regarded it as the base
currency to be used in transactions with the Dutch.

Regarding schuit silver, an article dated December 1637 in the *Generale
Missiven* has a supplementary note which states, 'It is a ship-shaped silver
ingot minted in Japan and worth 43 tael, that is 15 gulden. This is the
standard unit of money [in Japan]'.[44] According to the *Generale Missiven*,
from 1637 the Dutch began to perceive schuit silver as the main type of
silver exported from Japan from 1637, more so than soma silver. By the way,
the shogunate government went ahead with the mass minting of copper
coins (*kanei tsūhō*) in addition to silver coins during the 1630s. For this
reason, the government placed a ban on copper exports as well as gold
coins (*koban*).[45]

The Japanese–Dutch trade increased rapidly in value during this period;
the China trade in Tayouan went very well following a ban on the overseas
travel of Japanese traders imposed by the Japanese government in 1635.
Accordingly, the scale of Dutch trade with Japan expanded greatly.[46] This
led to a rapid rise in the value of silver exports, a trend that was promoted
further by the export bans on copper and gold coins. Silver accounted for

Table 3: Silver exports[a], 1636–1667

| | Value (tael) | | Value (tael) |
|---|---|---|---|
| 1636 | 872,000 | 1652 | 505,000 |
| 1637 | 1,133,000 | 1653 | 81,000 |
| 1638 | 1,716,000 | 1654 | 344,000 |
| 1639 | 2,508,000 | 1655 | 405,000 |
| 1640 | 1,180,000 | 1656 | 587,000 |
| 1641 | 1,112,000 | 1657 | 333,000 |
| 1642 | 399,000 | 1658 | 553,500 |
| 1643 | 473,000 | 1659 | 568,700 |
| 1644 | 686,000 | 1660 | 422,000 |
| 1645 | 763,000 | 1661 | 536,488: 7: 7 |
| 1646 | 464,000 | 1662 | 570,000 |
| 1647 | 411,000 | 1663 | (323,000) |
| 1648 | 510,000 | 1664 | (510,000) |
| 1649 | 370,000 | 1665 | 626,000 |
| 1650 | 352,000 | 1666 | 278,000 |
| 1651 | 460,000 | 1667 | (341,000) |

Source: Compiled by the author based on *Negotie Journalen* 1636–166. *Het Archief van de Nederlandse Factorij in Japan* 1609–1860, No.836–860, ARA.

Notes:

Since *Negotie Journalen* for 1661 and 1662 are missing, data in *Facturen* have been used above. (N.F.J., No. 784, 785)

Brackets indicate that data have been supplemented by *Nagasaki jikki nendairoku* (The true chronicle of Nagasaki).

A detailed table of silver exports for this period has already been prepared by Fujita Kayoko (1999a), 'Oranda Higashi Indo Gaisha shiryō ni yoru nihon gin yushutsu no sūryōteki kōsatsu (A quantitative study of Japanese silver exports according to the historical records of the VOC)' in Rekishi Bunken Kenkyūkai (ed.), and '*Iwami ginzan iseki sōgō chōsa hōkokusho*' (A comprehensive study report on the former Iwami silver mine site), Vol. 4, (Kyoto: Shibunkaku Shuppan, 1999) pp. 137–141.

a. All silver exported in this period were schuit silver (*chōgin*).

over 90 per cent of total exports in the latter half of the 1630s (1636, 1637, 1639 and 1640). This was the most prosperous period of Japanese–Dutch trade; it was later described by the Dutch as the Golden Age of Japanese–Dutch trade.

In Table 3, the total value of silver exports over six years from 1636 to 1641 can be seen. It amounted to 8,521,000 tael, about 1,420,000 tael a year on average. In particular, about 2.5 million tael of silver was exported in 1639, the highest amount in early modern history. This was the year that the Portuguese were expelled from Japan. After the withdrawal or expulsion of Japan's European trade partners (the English in 1623, the Spanish in 1624 and the Portuguese in 1639), the Netherlands became the only European country to continue to trade with the Japanese.

When the Portuguese were banned from visiting Japanese shores, their Southeast Asia trade base in Macau was severely affected; Spain's Asia trade base in Manila was also suffering from a silver real shortage in the same year.[47] This situation gave unprecedented advantage in the China trade to the Netherlands, the only country capable of procuring large quantities of Japanese silver. From this period, articles in the *Generale Missiven* started to mention shipments of silver to some Indian regions such as Coromandel and Surat.[48] The Dutch came to consider Japanese silver as useful not only as capital to conduct its China trade in Tayouan but also to cater for demand in India.[49] Thus the VOC placed great importance on Japanese silver as an important source of capital for its China and Asia trade at the time. The Japanese–Dutch trade entered the 1640s at its peak.

## The stagnation period of the silver trade (1642 to 1668)

### Changes in silver exports

After the Dutch Factory was moved from Hirado to Nagasaki by order of the shogunate government in 1641, its silver trade began to lose momentum. The amount of silver exported suddenly decreased from over one million tael per year to about 400,000 tael in 1642. The relations between the two countries were rather strained in the first half of the 1640s due to incidents such as the lodging of a protest with the Japanese government by the Dutch against the relocation of its factory to Nagasaki and the landing of a drifting Dutch ship on the shore of Nanbu in 1643.[50] When the Dutch relocated to Nagasaki, they were forced to sever their close ties with merchant groups in Hirado and Kamigata that they had nurtured since the opening of their Hirado factory. New relationships with merchant groups in Nagasaki made it difficult for the Dutch to make as much profit as before.

Japan also endured the Great Kanei Famine from 1641 to 1642, the first great famine of the Edo period. The famine prompted the proclamation of the sumptuary law[51] and sales for luxury foreign imports fell, depressing Dutch profits further. When imports were not selling well, exports decreased as well. The total export temporarily recovered to around 700,000 tael in 1645 and 1646, before dropping again in subsequent years.

Table 4 shows the total exports for five-year periods from 1636 and the annual average export for each period. The total export for the period from 1636 to 1640 was 7,409,000 tael with an annual average export of 1,481,800 tael. The total export halved during the period from 1641 to 1645: 3,433,000

*Table 4: Silver exports for five-year periods^a, 1636–1665*

|  | Total value (tael) | Annual average value (tael) |
|---|---|---|
| 1636–1640 | 7,409,000 | 1,481,800 |
| 1641–1645 | 3,433,000 | 686,600 |
| 1646–1650 | 2,107,000 | 421,400 |
| 1651–1655 | 2,295,000 | 459,000 |
| 1656–1660 | 2,464,200 | 492,840 |
| 1661–1665 | 2,565,488 | 513,097 |

Note:

a. Based on Table 3.

tael with an annual average of 686,600 tael. From then on, the total export for five years ranged between two million and 2.6 million tael with an annual average between 400,000 and 520,000 tael. Figure 3 shows that silver exports leveled off from the latter half of the 1640s and remained on the same level for a long time.

Therefore, although the Netherlands became the only European country which was able to trade with Japan in the 1640s following the expulsion of the Portuguese, it was not able to enjoy the self-described Golden Age of Japanese–Dutch trade for a very long time. Still, it is worth noting that the Dutch Factory in Japan made incomparably larger profits than the other factories according to an article in the *Generale Missiven*, dated 4 January 1644, which recorded profits of various VOC factories in Asia.[52]

## The world market and the gold–silver parity

Japanese–Dutch trade did not grow as much as the Dutch had hoped; Japanese silver exports remained sluggish as we have seen above. Domestic factors were not the only cause of this situation. Changes in the parity between gold and silver caused by changes in the distribution of gold and silver in the world markets were also deeply involved.

The first point to consider is how silver was supplied to Asia. The silver supply routes to Asia prior to the Age of Discovery included one from Europe through the Levant region and to Mocha on the southern tip of the Arabian Peninsula, and the other through Central Asia to Persia, known since ancient times.[53] From the latter half of the sixteenth century, silver real coins minted by Spain in the New World (some were minted in Spain as well) were brought out of Spain to other European countries; large quantities of these coins flowed into the Philippines via the Pacific Ocean from Mexico.[54] The Netherlands shipped large quantities of silver real to

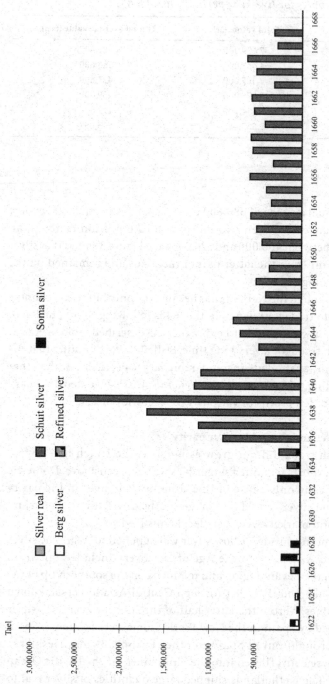

*Figure 3: Annual silver export values, 1622–1667*

Asia via the Cape route to use as capital in Asia. In these ways, the silver real was shipped by the Spanish to the Philippines via the Pacific Ocean and by the Dutch, the Portuguese and the English to various places in Asia via the Cape route in vast quantities. Subsequently, the silver real went in wide circulation in both the European and Asian markets and played the role of an international currency at that time. The quantity of the silver real supplied from the Americas to Europe peaked in around 1600 and declined gradually from then on.[55]

From the end of the sixteenth century, Amsterdam gradually replaced Antwerp as the center of European trade and finance. This enabled the Dutch to acquire ample stocks of the silver real and send large quantities of it to Asia until about 1620. However, the Dutch–Spanish war resumed in 1621 and Dutch ships were barred from accessing ports in the Spanish dominions. The silver real became scarce in the Netherlands and its value appreciated.[56] For this reason, the Netherlands began to send its foreign export currency (negotiepeningen) in addition to the silver real to Asia.[57] Once the Dutch–Spanish war ended in the 1640s, even larger amounts of silver began to flow into the Netherlands. The Dutch even lifted a ban on the export of silver bars in 1646.[58] Since various types of silver were being shipped to Asia in large quantities, the VOC no longer found it too difficult to procure silver for capital in Asia.

The parity between gold and silver had been stable until the Age of Discovery after which large quantities of the silver real flowed into Europe and Asia, causing it to fluctuate. Table 5 shows a marked downward trend in the value of silver against gold in Europe from around the 1640s.[59] The value of silver also declined in the Asian market; articles about lack of profits from the silver trade began to appear from the latter half of the 1650s. It was reported in the Generale Missiven that silver sank in price and became almost unsellable in Coromandel in 1655[60] and that silver and copper were sold in Masuliparam on the Coromandel Coast for a profit of seven per cent and 120 per cent respectively in 1659.[61] The sales margin for silver was markedly lower than that of copper during this period. This demonstrates that the value of silver was declining in India.

### The Asian market and Japanese silver

Japanese silver was an indispensable commodity in the China trade during the 1630s. The Dutch were able to procure Chinese raw silk and silk fabrics and Chinese gold by handing over Japanese silver to the Chinese. The Chinese preferred schuit silver. In 1644, an article in the Dag-Register gehouden int Casteel Batavia reported that 'The Japanese Schuit (chōgin) is

*Table 5: Gold–silver parity in Amsterdam, 1600–1699*

|  | Gold-silver parity (at mint) |
|---|---|
| 1600–04 | 1:11.21 |
| 1605–09 | 1:11.95 |
| 1610–14 | 1:12.40 |
| 1615–19 | 1:12.48 |
| 1620–24 | 1:12.17 |
| 1625–29 | 1:12.17 |
| 1630–34 | 1:12.17 |
| 1635–39 | 1:12.25 |
| 1640–44 | 1:12.35 |
| 1645–49 | 1:13.93 |
| 1650–54 | 1:13.93 |
| 1655–59 | 1:13.93 |
| 1660–64 | 1:13.20 |
| 1665–69 | 1:13.20 |
| 1670–74 | 1:13.20 |
| 1675–79 | 1:13.20 |
| 1680–84 | 1:13.09 |
| 1685–89 | 1:13.02 |
| 1690–94 | 1:13.02 |
| 1695–99 | 1:13.02 |

Source: See note 59.

the most preferred currency of the Chinese'.[62] Perhaps they liked it because Japanese silver contained copper.

In the 1640s, at the end of the Ming dynasty and the beginning of the Qing dynasty, China's domestic conditions became unstable due to civil wars that disrupted trade. In particular, Zheng Chenggong began to sabotage Dutch trade in China.[63] At the same time, many Chinese ships under the control of Zheng began to arrive in Japan to conduct active trade.[64] Since these ships brought Japanese silver directly to mainland China, the Dutch intermediary trade gradually fell into a slump.[65] The amount of Japanese silver shipped to Tonkin notably increased during the 1640s.

By the time of the relocation of the Dutch Factory to Nagasaki in 1641, the Dutch had been completely brought into the *itowappu* system (a monopsonistic system of silk purchasing). The Dutch reportedly shunned Chinese silk and opted to import raw silk and silk fabrics from Tonkin to Japan outside of the *itowappu* system, but in reality a switchover from sluggish Taiwan trade to trade with Tonkin was part of the reason as well.[66] In this way, shipments of silk products from Tonkin to Japan began in the 1640s.[67]

Large amounts of Japanese silver were shipped to Tonkin to finance the purchasing of these goods.

The VOC began to trade in the Indian region from the 1640s. It required a great amount of silver capital. As mentioned above, large amounts of silver were shipped from the Netherlands to Asia; considering the time and cost of transport from the Netherlands, the VOC's ability to procure large quantities of silver in Japan, especially when in urgent need of capital, was a great advantage for its Asia trade and its ability to make enormous profits. Shipments of Japanese silver to Coromandel and Surat in India began in around 1640. There were also one-off shipments of Japanese silver to Europe during the 1640s.[68] However, these made it very difficult for the board of the VOC (*Heren XVII*) to negotiate with American silver merchants for silver reales.[69] Therefore, Japanese silver was seldom shipped to the Netherlands after the 1640s.

Entries in the *Generale Missiven* suggest that Japanese silver played a role in Chinese trade to a certain extent during the 1640s. Reference to shipments of Japanese silver to Southwest Asia increased noticeably during the 1650s. This was the period in which large amounts of raw silk were imported into Japan from Bengal instead of Tonkin.[70] According to Fujita Kayoko, all schuit silver exports were shipped to the Indian regions or Tonkin by 1655, whereas 39 per cent of the total schuit export was sent to Coromandel in 1646.[71] In the 1650s there were entries in the *Generale Missiven* about Japanese silver shipments to Coromandel, Surat, Bengal, Persia, Siam, Tonkin and Batavia. However, the aforementioned fall in the value of silver in Asia slowed the flow of silver from Japan to the Indian regions from the latter half of the 1650s.

A shocking incident befell the VOC during the 1660s. Zheng Chenggong, whose intention to exclude the Dutch from Japanese trade had been a constant threat to the VOC's Taiwan trade[72], managed to capture Tayouan in 1662.[73] This forced the Dutch to pull out of Tayouan, which had been an important transit point for trade between Japan and China since 1623.[74] The Great Clearance was ordered in mainland China and foreign trade was placed under strict control. During this period, the value of gold appreciated in Asia and the VOC, which had been procuring Chinese gold through its China trade, suffered from gold shortages in Asia. Gold was an important capital especially in Coromandel. The Dutch asked the Japanese government to lift the ban on the export of Japanese gold (*koban*) and the request was readily accepted. The Dutch began to export Japanese gold mainly to Coromandel from 1664 and made enormous profits. This authorization of Japanese gold export was to have severe repercussions for the Japanese silver trade.

## The ban on silver exports

The Japanese government pushed ahead with the policy to curb silver exports in the 1660s.[75] It placed a ban on the importation of many foreign goods in 1668[76] and went on to prohibit the export of silver and copper in the same year. The *Kiyō gundan* (collection of records of the Nagasaki region) contains the following passage about the ban on silver exports:

> In 1668 while Matsudaira Jinzaburō and Kōno Gonemon were the governors of Nagasaki, silver was in short supply as only silver had been exported to foreign countries year after year. For this reason, the senior government councilor issued an order to export *koban* [gold] as well in trading with the Chinese and the Dutch. Since the exchange rate for selling the *koban* to the Chinese and the Dutch is set at 1 *ryō* to 56 monme, there will be no *aidakin* [exchange gain] for a period of four years from now on.[77]

According to this passage, silver exports were banned in an attempt to stop the decline in the domestic reserves of schuit silver.

The *Koshūki* (collection of historical records) has the following passage about the declining domestic reserves of silver:

> In 1668 while Kōno Gonemon and Matsudaira Jinzaburō were the Governor of Nagasaki, the Dutch and the Chinese were directed to be fully aware when they visited Japan that various goods imported from foreign countries would be purchased by Japanese merchants at low prices from the coming year. In the following year, governor Kōno studied the amounts of silver handed over to the Chinese and the Dutch in the twenty years up to that year and found that the total amount of silver exported over the twenty years reached 600,000 kanme, which was about 30,000 kanme per year. The amount of *chōgin* refined at the silver mint from silver mined at various places in Japan was approximately 7,000 kanme. This meant that the continuation of unregulated overseas export year after year would result in a gradual decline in Japan's silver reserves.[78]

More silver was exported during this period than was made at the silver mint. Consequently, it was obvious that the continuation of unregulated silver exports would reduce domestic stocks of schuit silver markedly. This was why silver exports were banned according to the record. Table 6 shows the details of silver exports on Dutch ships reported in the records of Nagasaki (*Nagasaki-ki*). Table 7 shows comparisons between Dutch and Japanese records of Japanese silver exports per year. There are no extreme discrepancies between the records despite some variations depending on the source.

Table 6: *Silver exports on Dutch ships, 1648–1667*

|  | Number of ships | Total export value in silver (kanme) | Exports in goods (kanme) | Exports in *chōgin* and silver products (kanme) | Other (kanme) |
|---|---|---|---|---|---|
| 1648 | 6 | 6,987.547 | 556.765 | 6,221.400 | 209.382 |
| 1649 | 7 | 7,076.169 | 775.634 | 5,343.300 | 960.235 |
| 1650 | 7 | 5,472.540 | 1,025.086 | 3,940.600 | 506.855 |
| 1651 | 8 | 6,656.157 | 1,294.425 | 4,895.600 | 466.132 |
| 1652 | 9 | 7,052.273 | 1,062.021 | 5,538.900 | 451.352 |
| 1653 | 5 | 7,423.915 | 786.763 | 6,190.200 | 446.961 |
| 1654 | 4 | 5,190.776 | 900.324 | 3,848.200 | 442.251 |
| 1655 | 4 | 5,102.594 | 703.971 | 4,011.500 | 387.123 |
| 1656 | 8 | 8,435.482 | 1,668.747 | 6,190.250 | 576.484 |
| 1657 | 8 | 5,873.300 | 2,017.373 | 3,444.237 | 411.690 |
| 1658 | 9 | 7,961.833 | 1,811.937 | 5,640.547 | 509.348 |
| 1659 | 8 | 8,066.364 | 1,422.050 | 5,960.395 | 683.918 |
| 1660 | 5 | 6,545.258 | 1,715.557 | 4,268.385 | 561.315 |
| 1661 | 11 | 9,128.688 | 2,958.166 | 5,543.590 | 626.932 |
| 1662 | 8 | 9,204.090 | 2,068.044 | 5,960.010 | 1,176.036 |
| 1663 | 6 | 6,410.993 | 2,259.850 | 3,671.400 | 479.742 |
| 1664 | 9 | 11,014.226 | 4,138.785 | 5,602.473 | 1,272.968 |
| 1665 | 12 | 10,620.537 | 2,573.851 | 7,045.600 | 1,001.086 |
| 1666 | 7 | 8,699.768 | 1,995.610 | 2,040.000 | 876.858 |
| 1667 | 8 | 10,430.334 | 2,145.152 | 6,978.840 | 1,306.341 |

Source: 'Nagasaki ki (Official records of Nagasaki)' in Hayashi Fukusai (ed.), *Tsūkō ichiran* (Records of dealings with foreign countries), Vol. 4 (Tokyo: Kokusho Kankōkai, 1913), pp. 332–335.

Note: Each total export value above is the sum total of the three items on the right side.

Like the *Kiyō gundan*, the *Koshūki* states as follows:

In 1668 when Matsudaira Jinzaburō was the governor of Nagasaki, it was decided that the export of silver to the Dutch and the Chinese should be prohibited for four years up to 1671 and *koban* should be exported instead because the continuous export of silver would gradually deplete the amount of silver within Japan.[79]

It is clear that the Japanese government intended to prohibit the export of silver for four years and not permanently. In other words, the silver export ban was a temporary measure; it was not a government policy to ban silver export permanently and totally in 1668. Accordingly, the government readily authorized the resumption of silver export when it received a request from

*Table 7: Comparison of export values, 1648–1667*

| | Trade books[a] (kanme) | Nachod[b] (kanme) | Silver exports[c] (kanme) | Chōgin and silver products[d] (kanme) |
|---|---|---|---|---|
| 1648 | 5,100 | 3,800 | 5,600 | 6,221.400 |
| 1649 | 3,700 | 3,700 | 3,200 | 5,343.300 |
| 1650 | 3,520 | 3,520 | 3,520 | 3,940.600 |
| 1651 | 4,600 | 4,600 | 4,600 | 4,895.600 |
| 1652 | 5,050 | 4,800 | 5,050 | 5,538.900 |
| 1653 | 5,810 | 5,810 | 5,810 | 6,190.200 |
| 1654 | 3,440 | 3,440 | 3,440 | 3,848.200 |
| 1655 | 4,050 | 4,050 | 4,050 | 4,011.500 |
| 1656 | 6,770 | 5,870 | 5,870 | 6,190.250 |
| 1657 | 3,330 | 3,330 | 3,330 | 3,444.237 |
| 1658 | 4,135 | 5,037.600 | 5,540 | 5,640.547 |
| 1659 | 5,437 | 5,687 | 5,680 | 5,960.395 |
| 1660 | 4,220 | 4,220 | 4,220 | 4,268.385 |
| 1661 | 5,364.488 | 6,164.480 | 5,370 | 5,543.590 |
| 1662 | 5,700 | 5,710 | 5,700 | 5,960.010 |
| 1663 | — | 3,238.550 | 3,230 | 3,671.400 |
| 1664 | — | — | 5,100 | 5,602.473 |
| 1665 | 6,260 | 5,680 | 6,260 | 7,045.600 |
| 1666 | 2,780 | 2,500.500 | 2,780 | 2,040.000 |
| 1667 | — | 800 | 3,410 | 6,978.840 |

Notes:
a. Calculated from Table 3.
b. Tominaga Makita (tr.), *17-seiki nichiran kōshō shi* (A history of the Japanese–Dutch relations in the 17th century), (Nara: Yōtokusha, 1956), p. 455, which is a translation of Oskar Nachod (1897), *Die Beziehungen der Niederländischen Ostindischen Kompagnie zu Japan im siebzehnten Jahrhundert*.
c. Kyushu Bunkashi Kenkyūjo Shiryōshū Kankōkai (ed.), *Nagasaki jikki nendairoku* (The true chronicle of Nagasaki), pp. 66–86.
d. Based on Table 6.

the Chinese four years later in 1672[80], but authorization to resume silver export to the Dutch was never issued after that time. This was because the Dutch chose not to ask the Japanese government to lift the ban, not because of continued enforcement on the part of the Japanese government.

Commentaries in historical records on the Dutch side are confined to simple statements about the imposition of a ban on silver export in Japan.[81] An article in the *Generale Missiven* dated 31 January 1672 stated that 'the ban on silver export from Japan has been a great blessing for the VOC and it is hoped this will continue for a long time'.[82] The silver export ban was not a significant hindrance to the Dutch because the VOC could easily ship large quantities of silver from Europe to Asia and in fact it sent more silver to Asia after this ban was imposed.[83]

Therefore, the Chinese and the Dutch had completely different reactions to the lifting of the silver export embargo in 1672. For the Chinese, there was no profit in the export of Japanese gold to China because the value of gold was low relative to the value of silver within China. This is why they asked the Japanese government to lift the ban and began to import silver again. On the other hand, the Dutch had trouble procuring enough gold to use as capital in Asia at the time. Moreover, since the value of silver had been depressed in the Asian market and it was easy to procure silver from Europe, the Dutch were hoping to acquire from Japan as much gold as possible rather than silver. For this reason, Japanese silver had already stopped playing its role in the Dutch–Asia trade by the latter half of the 1660s.

## Conclusion

What was the role of Japanese silver for the VOC? When the Dutch set up their trading post in Hirado, they expected to acquire as much Japanese silver as possible to use as capital in Asia. To achieve this, it was absolutely necessary for the Dutch to procure large quantities of Chinese raw silk and silk fabrics that were in demand in Japan. They established their base in Tayouan during the 1620s and began to trade extensively in China. They established a foundation for the further development of their trade with Japan.

When the Portuguese dropped out of trade with Japan in the latter half of the 1630s, the Dutch operated full-scale intermediary trade between the neighboring countries of China and Japan. This enabled the Dutch to make enormous profits. The Hirado/Nagasaki–Tayouan–China route of the Dutch had replaced the Nagasaki–Macau trade route of the Portuguese which was once called the Golden Route. The prosperity of the Japanese–Dutch trade in the latter half of the 1630s was driven by the strength of the Tayouan-based trade. Japanese silver certainly played the role of capital for Dutch–Chinese trade; the Dutch ability to procure local capital efficiently increased their gains from trade further.

This state was realized under the following conditions. Firstly, the Japanese government prohibited Japanese merchants from going overseas to conduct trade in 1635. Secondly, the Ming dynasty in China was reluctant to get involved in overseas trade and prohibited foreign trade in principle. Due to their respective foreign policies, it was not easy for these two neighboring countries to trade with each other directly. These conditions facilitated the successful functioning of Dutch intermediary trade.

The circumstances changed in the 1640s, however. The Dutch–Chinese trade went into a difficult phase due to the chaotic transition from the Ming dynasty to the Qing dynasty and disruption of the Dutch trade by Zheng Chenggong. As the Qing took over China from the Ming, more Chinese ships began to arrive in Japan directly. If Chinese merchants became directly involved in the trade with Japan, the Dutch-Japanese trade would face a predicament. Consequently, the Dutch gradually switched to exporting raw silk from Tonkin and Bengal to Japan as its China trade in Tayouan went into a slump. In other words, the Dutch began to change their focus from the 1640s from intermediary trade between China and Japan to intermediary trade between Asia and Japan. For this reason, the Dutch began to ship Japanese silver as capital to the Southeast Asian regions including Tonkin, and the Indian regions including Surat, Coromandel and Bengal, and Persia.

From the 1640s, the value of silver began to depreciate in the European market and the Dutch were able to acquire large quantities of the silver real from Spain and ship them to Asia. This led to a gradual depreciation in the value of silver in the Asian market in the latter half of the 1650s. Japanese silver, a necessity at the time of the opening of the Dutch Factory in Hirado, gradually lost its importance as capital in Asia due to the sluggish China trade, the depreciation in the value of silver in the European and Asian markets and the availability of large quantities of the silver real to the Dutch.

The active trade in Japanese silver by the Dutch lasted for only a short period, about six decades from 1609 to 1667. The volume of exports was small in the first twenty years due to instability in the Japanese–Dutch trade. In view of this, the real period of active Japanese–Dutch silver trade was about forty years or so. It was only in the five years from 1637 to 1641 that the volume of silver exports exceeded one million tael per year. The annual average fell to about 680,000 tael in the first half of the 1640s, falling further to between 400,000 and 500,000 tael in the latter half of the same decade. It then stayed at the same level for a long time.

Raw silk and Japanese silver have been regarded as the principal import and export commodities of the Japanese–Dutch trade in the early modern period. Yet the period in which the silver trade was conducted and flourished was limited to the early part of this period; the silver trade would have declined faster if the export of copper and gold (koban) had been authorized in the early part of the 1640s. The export of silver continued although sluggishly because there was an embargo on the export of other potentially profitable Japanese commodities.

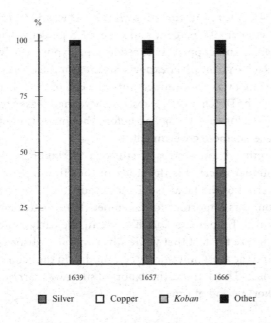

Figure 4: Export commodities by per cent, 1639–1666

Note: The amount of export of silver is based on Table 2. Regarding the total amount of export, we referred to 'Memorie der in Japan geregeerd hebbende Opperhoofden, mitsgaders den tijd van hun op- en afreijse na en van Jedo ...', tabel met opgave van de namen der Opperhoofden, de data van de hofreise, bedragen van invoer, omzet, verlies, en winst, het aantal verongelukte schepen, etc. met een tienjaarlijkse samenvatting, over 1620-1808. *Archief Japan* No. 664. ARA.

The embargo on the export of copper was lifted in 1646; copper was exported as far as the European market in the latter half of the 1650s. At the same time, Japan moved from the *itowappu* system of trade to a freer direct-dealing system of trade which pushed up the prices of imports and rapidly increased the amount of silver exports in return. However, this applied only to dealings with the Chinese; it was the export of copper rather than silver which increased substantially in the case of Dutch trade.

Figure 4 shows that the total silver export accounted for 98 per cent of the total export in 1639, when the export of Japanese silver by the Dutch reached its peak. However, in 1657, after the changeover from the *itowappu* system to the direct-dealing system, 63.6 per cent of the total export was in silver, 31.1 per cent was in copper and 5.3 per cent was in other commodities. It is obvious that the proportion of silver decreased and the export of copper increased. In 1666, following the authorization

of *koban* exports, the proportion of silver exports was 42.9 per cent, *koban*
31.4 percent, copper 19.9 percent and others 5.8 percent. The combined
exports of *koban* and copper far exceeded the export of silver. In 1668,
the Japanese embargo on silver exports meant that the export of Japanese
silver by the Dutch was not resumed until the end of the Edo period. This
did not trouble the Dutch greatly; Japanese silver had ceased to be a sought
after commodity for the Dutch well before the imposition of the export
embargo by the Japanese government.

Since the only advanced area of study of the Japanese–Dutch trade
in the early modern period is the study of the Hirado period, the most
prosperous period of the Japanese–Dutch trade, the silver trade tends to
draw attention. It is important to remember that this tendency obscures
the long history of Japanese–Dutch trade in the early modern period.
We must recognize the fact that while silver was an indispensable export
commodity and the most noteworthy commodity in the beginning of early
modern Japanese–Dutch trade, the export of silver was carried out for only
a relatively short period of time.

# Chapter Two

# Copper Trade during the Hirado Era

This chapter looks at the types of export copper reported in the trade books of the Dutch factory from the Hirado era till the 1650s. It investigates copper exports in the context of relations between the Netherlands and the shogunate government of the time, especially the ban on copper export promulgated by the shogunate government in 1637.

Although large quantities of copper were exported from Japan onboard Dutch and Chinese fleets in the early modern period, no detailed accounts of the conditions of copper exports during the Hirado era, when the Dutch factory operated in Hirado, are available. By examining the issues from the viewpoints of both Japan and the Netherlands, this chapter will clarify the circumstances surrounding the export of copper during the Hirado era.

## Copper exports during the Hirado era

### The 1610s

Very little information is available about the opening of the Dutch factory in Hirado and the export of copper is no exception. Jacques Specx and Hendrick Brouwer headed up the trading post and set trading conditions from 1609 to 1620. Records kept by the English factory—set up in Hirado four years after the opening of the Dutch Factory—indicate that the Dutch factory was already purchasing copper at the time. For example, one article from 6 August 1615 says, 'Capt. Speck tould me he receaved a barks landing of copp'r this day frō Sackay'.[1] Another letter dated 23 February 1616 and posted in Hirado by Richard Wickham to Commander John Jourden in Bantam says, '[The Dutch] shipped part of this gold away, used another part to purchase copper and used the rest to purchase food, brass-plated iron most needed for copper arms manufacturing and ship operation, and ironwork'.[2] According to a report by Richard Cocks about copper prices at the time, 'there were three types of copper: one was 90 or 100 monme per 100 kin and the other two were 80 to 90 monme per 100 kin'.[3]

These English records confirm that the Dutch were already procuring copper in the 1610s. One article among the Dutch archives suggests the ongoing export of copper by the Dutch. On 4 September 1622, the Dutch Factory was notified by the lord of the Hirado domain of an order of the shogun containing five clauses. The second clause stipulated the prohibition of 'the export of short swords, pistols, other small arms and military supplies'. In response, Jacques Specx, the first head of the Dutch Factory, prepared a 'letter of explanation', saying:

> It poses few obstacles to us as long as it allows us to supply enough military supplies to our forts, ships and war in the East Indies. But as there is a risk that the export of iron and copper will be banned if they come to be regarded as military supplies in the future and therefore we must give due consideration to this matter.[4]

## 1621 to 1636

Copper and silver export figures from 1621 to 1636, calculated from the trade books of the Dutch Factory *Negotie Journalen*, are shown in Table 8. After 1625, the value of copper exports hovered from about one quarter to one fifth of that of silver exports. Silver exports did not completely dominate other export commodities in value terms during the 1620s. It was from 1636 that the value of silver exports increased dramatically over everything else.

Table 9 is another table of copper exports. It shows the annual total copper export value based on the calendar year, while Table 8 shows the total amount of copper exported per shipping year. The shipping year was used to calculate export values during the Hirado era because Dutch ships usually sailed for home during the period from October to February.[5] Table 9 shows the importance of setting a clear basis for the tabulation period when demonstrating changes in trade quantities.

Katō Ēichi analysed the account books of Dutch ships to estimate the amount of silver exports for each shipping year in his discussion of silver exports during the Hirado era.[6] On the other hand, a table prepared by Oskar Nachod[7] and referred to in the historical records (*Senoku sōko*) of the Izumiya copper refinery in Osaka is based on the calendar year instead of the shipping year. Table 9 has been prepared for comparison with this table.

In 1637, there was a rapid fall in the price of copper to 288,395 kin, not even one half of the level for the previous year. According to the records of the Izumiya copper refinery, this was due to the dramatic increase in the domestic demand for copper that resulted from the copper coin minting

Table 8: Copper and silver exports based on shipping year, 1621–1636

| | Number of ships that exported copper | Volume of copper exports (catty) | Value of copper exports (gulden) | Value of silver exports (gulden) |
|---|---|---|---|---|
| 1621 (1621/10–1622/2) | 2 | 50,000 | 16,170: 12: – | — |
| 1622 (1622/10–1622/12) | 2 | 97,455 | 30,831: 17: 11 | 410,600: –: – |
| 1623 (1623/10–1624/1) | 1 | 1,970 | 305: 3: 5 | 252,064: 14: 7 |
| 1624 (1624/12–1625/2) | — | — | — | — |
| 1625 (1625/11–1626/2) | 2 | 288,418 | 91,077: 3: 12 | 338,513: 15: |
| 1626 (1626/10–1627/2) | 2 | 197,618 | 62,547: 15: 5 | 236,207: 14: 13 |
| 1627 (1627/10–1628/3) | 2 | 517,740 | 162,986: 18: 12 | 851,045; –: – |
| 1632 (1633/1–1633/2) | 4 | 362,184 | 112,171: 17: 8 | 643,273: 16: – |
| 1633 (1633/11–1634/2) | 3 | 274,419 | 77,644: 8: 12 | 194,803: 14: – |
| 1634 (1634/11–1635/2) | 7 | 615,835 | 182,979: 7: 14 | 849,579: 14: – |
| 1635 (1635/11–1636/2) | 7 | 802,799 | 238,636: 11: 14 | 1,403,119: 2: – |
| 1636 (1636/11–1637/2) | 8 | 667,434 | 198,436: 19: 10 | 3,012,450: –: – |

Source: *Negotie Journalen* 1620–37, *Archief Japan* No.829–837, ARA.

Table 9: Copper exports based on calendar year, 1621–1637

| | Number of ships that exported copper | Volume of copper exports (catty) | Value of copper exports (gulden) |
|---|---|---|---|
| 1621 | 1 | 11,600 | 3,480 |
| 1622 | 3 | 135,855 | 43,522 |
| 1623 | — | — | — |
| 1624 | 1 | 1,970 | 305 |
| 1625 | 1 | 98,242 | 30,701 |
| 1626 | 1 | 190,176 | 60,377 |
| 1627 | 4 | 715,358 | 225,535 |
| 1628 | — | — | — |
| 1629 | — | — | — |
| 1630 | — | — | — |
| 1631 | — | — | — |
| 1632 | — | — | — |
| 1633 | 6 | 519,755 | 156,489 |
| 1634 | 7 | 556,644 | 160,169 |
| 1635 | 5 | 579,069 | 169,822 |
| 1636 | 6 | 753,592 | 229,170 |
| 1637 | 4 | 313,611 | 94,216 |

Source: Same as Table 8.

project that was commenced in June 1636 and expanded to eight locations throughout Japan in August 1637.[8]

This is correct in a broad sense, but copper exports in the calendar year 1637 were the cargos of ships that left Japan in January and February 1637. They should therefore be included in the exports for the shipping year 1636, so no copper was exported in the shipping year 1637. Although the export of copper was going well at the beginning of 1637, it completely stopped from May in the same year when a ban on copper export was promulgated.

This situation can be somewhat misunderstood if only the calendar years are taken into account. After the relocation of the Dutch factory to Nagasaki in 1642, visiting Dutch ships departed between September and December. This observation matched the shipping year with the calendar year, making tabulation and analysis of copper exports easier.

## Types of export copper

Types of copper exported during the Hirado period included *usuitadō* (called *bladt coper* by the Dutch), *gokidō* (*gocqie coper*), *tamadō* (*broot coper*), which appears to be of the same quality as *gokidō*, *itadō* (*plaet coper*), and *saodō* (*staef coper*). Table 10 shows that there were subtle variations in export copper in terms of type and quality as some products were divided further into fine (*fijn*) and crude (*grof*) categories. A trial shipment of Japanese commodities on board the *Leiden* left Batavia for the Netherlands in April 1621. It contained four types of Japanese copper: copper bars of fine quality, *usuitadō* (sheet copper), round *akadō* (red copper) and *sodō* (crude copper).[9]

Let us discuss each of these types with reference to Table 10.

### Usuitadō
Sheet copper was exported in 1622, 1624 and 1627. This expensive copper was traded in the price range of 15.5 tael (155 monme) to 17.5 tael (175 monme) per picol (100 kin) and exported in small volumes of up to 2,000 kin or so. The finest quality copper, shipped on the *Nieuw Zeeland* on 10 February 1622, is likely to have been of similar quality judging from the high price it commanded (17.5 tael per picol).

### Gokidō[10]
A research report on the Chikuzen, Chikugo, Hizen and Higo regions (*Chikuzen Chikugo Hizen Higo tansakusho*), which is considered to have been written in around 1627 and is held in the University of Tokyo Historiographical Institute Archive, contains the following passage:

The ship owned by someone called Doi Jōho sails to Cochinchina every year with a red seal certificate, which is a license from the shogunate government to trade outside of Japanese waters. When he was asked what goods the ship usually carried, he answered that it carried Noh fans and *gokidō*. When he was asked what *goki* was used for, he answered that the Chinese bought it to turn it into cups or goblets.

It states that the Chinese bought *goki* to use as cups, but it is unclear whether *goki* was a cup-shaped copper or if it was used as a raw material for the manufacturing of cups. According to an entry in the *Generale Missiven* of the VOC dated 9 December 1637, 50 picol of *goki* (*gogy*), or crude copper, was shipped from Hirado to Tayouan together with high-grade copper. A note to this entry states that the meaning of the word *goki* was unknown.[11]

Gokidō first appears in the trade books of the Dutch factory in an entry dated 26 February 1627; the *Erasmus*, returning to Tayouan, carried 6,000 kin of *gokidō*, priced at 8.5 tael (85 monme) per picol. It seems that *gokidō* was a low quality copper. It traded at the lowest price level among the aforementioned types of copper, ranging from 7.8 tael (78 monme) to 9 tael (90 monme) per picol. The last report of *gokidō* export was dated 14 February 1636, when 35,061 kin was shipped on board the *Rarop*.

## Tamadō

Tamadō seems to have been identical to *gokidō* or of similar quality. In the cargo list of the *Oude Water*, 3 November 1634, it was described as *gouckies offte broot coper* (*goki*, namely *tamadō* copper).[12] There is no record of its export in 1635, but it reappears from November 1636. It is likely that the difference between *gokidō* and *Tamadō* was in name only; they both referred to round crude copper.

## Itadō (hiradō)

Itadō (plate copper) first appeared in trade books when the *Wapen van Zeeland* exported 98,242 kin for 10 tael per picol on 17 November 1625. It subsequently appeared in the shipping bills of the *Groll*, dated 24 November 1634, the *Swaen*, and the *Wapen van Delft*. The price stayed the same on these occasions, but there were times when small amounts were traded at lower prices, such as 8.5 tael (85 monme) and 9.5 tael (95 monme) per picol.

## Saodō[13]

The first appearance of this type of copper in trade books was the description 'bar-shaped copper of fine quality' in a shipping bill of the *Bredamme*

*Table 10: Copper exports by ship, 1621–1637*

| | Ship name | Destination | Item | Note | Quantity (catty) | Unit price (picol/tael) | Export value (rael) | Export value (gulden) |
|---|---|---|---|---|---|---|---|---|
| 1621/10/10 | Zwaan | Jaccatra | Coper | Fijn coper | 11,600 | 10 | 1,160: –: – | 3,480: –: – |
| 1622/ 2/10 | Nieuw Zeeland | Jaccatra | Coper | Fijn coper | 25,900 | 10 | 2,590: –: – | – |
| | | | | Fijnder | 10,000 | 11.8 | 1,180: –: – | – |
| | | | | Coper heel fijn | 2,500 | 17.5 | 437: 5: – | – |
| | | | | Expenses | – | – | 22: 7: – | – |
| | | | | Total | 38,400 | | 4,230: 2: – | 12,690:12: – |
| 1622/10/25 | St. Crus | Pescadores | Coper | Bladt coper | 636 | 17.5 | 111: 3: – | 333:18: – |
| 1622/12/ 5 | Firando | Pescadores/ Batavia | Coper | Fijn root Jappans coper | 96,819 | 10.5 | 10,165: 9: 9 | 30,497:19:11 |
| 1624/1/10 | Goede Hope | Pescadores/ Batavia | Coper | Bladt coper | 1,970 | 15.5 | 305: 3: 5 | 916: 1: – |
| 1625/11/17 | Wapen van Zeeland | Batavia | Coper | Root coper in plaeten | 98,242 | 10 | 9,824: 2: – | 30,700;12: 8 |
| 1626/1/ 8 | Zierickzee | Batavia | Coper | Root coper | 175,031 | 10 | 17,503: 1: – | – |
| | | | | Root coper heel fijn | 15,145 | 12 | 1,817: 4: – | – |
| | | | | Total | 190,176 | | 19,320: 5: – | 60,376:11: 4 |
| 1627/2/10 | Holland | Batavia | Coper | Root coper | 177,355 | 10 | 17,735: 5: – | – |
| | | | | Root coper heel fijn | 12,968 | 12 | 1,556: 1: 6 | – |
| | | | | Bladt coper ofte geslaegen coper | 1,295 | 16.5 | 213: 6:21/2 | – |
| | | | | Total | 191,618 | | 19,505: 2:81/2 | 60,954: –: 5 |

| Date | Ship | Origin | | Type | Quantity | Rate | Price | Total |
|---|---|---|---|---|---|---|---|---|
| 1627/2/26 | *Erasmus* | Taijouan[a] | *Coper* | *Root coper genaempt Gocqie* | 6,000 | 8.5 | 510: -: - | 1,593:15: - |
| 1627/10/22 | *Vreede* | Taijouan/Batavia | *Coper* | *Groff root coper* | 319,803 | 10 | 31,980: 3: - | – |
| | | | | *Fijn coper* | 2,432 | 12 | 291: 8: 4 | – |
| | | | | Total | 322,235 | | 32,272: 1: 4 | 100,850: 8:12 |
| 1627/10/31 | *Edam* | Taijouan/Siam | *Coper* | *Groff root coper* | 168,786 | 10 | 16,878: 6: - | – |
| | | | | *Fijn coper* | 16,499 | 12 | 1,979: 8: 8 | – |
| | | | | *Coper genaempt gockij* | 10,220 | 8 | 1,025: 2: - | – |
| | | | | Total | 195,505 | | 19,883: 6: 8 | 62,136:10: - |
| 1633/1/15 | *Zwarte Arend* | Taijouan Batavia | *Coper* | *Root coper* | 163,086 | 10 | 16,308: 6: - | 50,964: 7: 8 |
| | | – | | – | – | – | – | – |
| 1633/1/15 | *Cemphaan* | Taijouan/Batavia | *Coper* | – | 41,259 | 10 | 4,125: 9: - | – |
| | | | | – | 29,939 | 9 | 2,694: 5: 1 | – |
| | | | | Total | 71,198 | | 6,820: 4: 1 | 21,313:15:10 |
| 1633/2/12 | *Heusden* | Taijouan/Batavia | *Coper* | *Fijn coper* | 9,342 | 12 | 1,121: -: 4 | – |
| | | | | *Groff coper* | 37,459 | 10 | 3,745: 9: - | – |
| | | | | *Groff coper* | 21,085 | 9 | 1,897: 6: 5 | – |
| | | | | Total | 67,886 | | 6,764: 5: 9 | 21,139:6:14 |
| 1633/2/22 | *Warmont* | Siam | *Coper* | *Groff coper* | 60,014 | 10 | – | 18,754: 7: 8 |
| 1633/11/13 | *Wapen van Delft* | Batavia | *Coper* | – | 136,262 | 9 | – | 38,323:13:12 |
| 1633/12/12 | *Venloo* | Taijouan | *Coper* | *Groff root coper* | 21,309 | 9 | 1,917: 8: 1 | 5,993: 3: 2 |

*Table 10: Continued*

| | Ship name | Destination | Item | Note | Quantity (catty) | Unit price (picol/tael) | Export value (rael) | Export value (gulden) |
|---|---|---|---|---|---|---|---|---|
| 1634/2/15 | Oude Water | Taijouan | Coper | – | 14,851 | 10 | – | 4,640:18:12 |
| | | Batavia | | | 101,997 | 9 | – | 28,686:13: 2 |
| | | | Total | | 116,848 | | | 33,327:11:14 |
| 1634/11/ 3 | Oude Water | Taijouan | Coper | Broot coper | 122,973 | 8.3 | – | 31,896: 1:14 |
| 1634/11/24 | Groll | Batavia | Coper | 1,450 plaeten | 67,798 | 10 | – | 21,186:17: 8 |
| 1634/11/24 | Zwaan | Batavia | Coper | 1,070 plaeten | 50,021 | 10 | – | 15,631:11: 4 |
| 1634/11/24 | Venloo | Taijouan | Coper | | 52,388 | 8.3 | – | 13,588: 2: 8 |
| 1634/11/24 | Wapen Van Delft | Siam | Coper | Gockies coper | 20,100 | 8.3 | – | 5,213: 8:12 |
| | | | | Plaet coper | 59,600 | 10 | – | 18,625: –: – |
| | | | | Plaet coper | 13,500 | 9 | – | 4,007:16: 4 |
| | | | Total | | 93,200 | | – | 27,846: 5: – |
| 1634/12/ 4 | Schagen | Batavia | Coper | 1,112 plaeten | 53,416 | 10 | – | 16,692:10: – |
| 1635/ 2/15 | Bredamme | Taijouan/ Batavia | Coper | Plaet coper | 118,352 | 9.5 | 11,243: 4: 4 | – |
| | | | | Plaet coper | 10,087 | 10 | 1,008: 7: – | – |
| | | | | Fijn coper in staeffkens | 47,600 | 12 | 5,712: –: – | – |
| | | | Total | | 176,039 | | 17,904: 1: 4 | 56,137:18:12 |

| Date | Ship | Origin | | Description | Quantity | | Price | Guilders |
|---|---|---|---|---|---|---|---|---|
| 1635/11/12 | Wapen van Delft | Siam | Coper | Rood coper, 2307 plaeten | 47,835 | | 9 | 13,453:11:14 |
| | | | | | 29,404 | — | 9.5 | 8,729: 6: 4 |
| | | | | | 26,385 | — | 10 | 8,245: 6: 4 |
| | | | | | 7,738 | — | 8.5 | 2,055: 8: 2 |
| | | | | Total | 111,362 | — | | 32,483:12: 8 |
| 1635/11/13 | Nieuw Amsterdam | Batavia | Coper | 2534 plaeten | 22,522 | — | 10 | 7,038: 2: 8 |
| | | | | | 48,836 | — | 9.5 | 14,498: 3:12 |
| | | | | | 51,638 | — | 8.5 | 13,716: 6:14 |
| | | | | Total | 112,996 | — | | 35,252:13: 2 |
| 1635/11/17 | Venhuijsen | Taijouan | Coper | Gockies coper | 11,587 | — | 8.3 | 3,005: 7: 8 |
| | | | | Gockies coper | 7,465 | — | 7.8 | 1,819:11:14 |
| | | | | Total | 19,052 | — | | 4,824:19: 6 |
| 1635/12/31 | Wassenaer | Batavia | Coper | 3,117 plaeten | 112,644 | — | 8.5 | 29,921: 1: 4 |
| | | | | | 22,541 | — | 9.5 | 6,691:16:14 |
| | | | | | 14,435 | — | 10 | 4,510:18:12 |
| | | | | Total | 149,620 | — | | 41,123:16:14 |
| 1636/1/19 | Warmont | Taijouan/ Batavia | Coper | Plaet coper | 25,289 | — | 10 | 7,902:16: 4 |
| | | | | Plaet coper | 16,931 | — | 9.5 | 5,026: 7: 8 |
| | | | | Fijn staefges coper | 40,000 | — | 11.5 | 14,375: -: - |
| | | | | Gockies coper | 44,897 | — | 8.5 | 11,925:15: - |
| | | | | Gockies coper | 5,226 | — | 7.8 | 1,273:16: 4 |
| | | | | Total | 132,343 | — | | 40,503:15: - |

*Table 10: Continued*

| | Ship name | Destination | Item | Note | Quantity (catty) | Unit price (picol/tael) | Export value (rael) | Export value (gulden) |
|---|---|---|---|---|---|---|---|---|
| 1636/1/27 | Huijsduinen | Taijouan/Batavia | Coper | Plaet coper | 31,119 | 9.5 | — | 9,238:8:12 |
| | | | | Plaet coper | 6,540 | 8.5 | — | 1,737:3:12 |
| | | | | Staefges coper | 40,000 | 11.5 | — | 14,375: -: - |
| | | | | Sockies coper | 28,643 | 8.5 | — | 7,608:5:10 |
| | | | | Total | 106,302 | | — | 32,958:18: 2 |
| 1636/2/14 | Rarop | Taijouan/Batavia | Coper | Staefges coper | 74,200 | 11.5 | — | 26,665:12: 8 |
| | | | | Staefges coper | 17,900 | 10 | — | 5,593:15: - |
| | | | | Plaet coper | 22,876 | 10 | — | 7,148:15: - |
| | | | | Plaet coper | 11,087 | 8.5 | — | 2,944:19: 6 |
| | | | | Gockies coper | 26,955 | 8.5 | — | 7,159:18: 2 |
| | | | | Gockies coper | 8,106 | 7.8 | — | 1,975:16: 4 |
| | | | | Total | 161,124 | | — | 51,488:16: 4 |
| 1636/11/2 | Wassenaar | Batavia | Coper | 1,566 plaeten | 70,160 | 10 | — | 19,995:12: - |
| | | | Staefges coper | — | 30,000 | 12 | — | 10,260: -: - |
| 1636/11/2 | Galliasse | Taijouan/Batavia | Plaet coper | | 12,525 | 10 | — | 3,569:12: 8 |
| 1636/11/17 | Noordwijk | Taijouan | Staefges coper | — | 6,000 | 13 | — | 2,223: -: - |
| | | | Broot coper | 1,295 plaeten | 13,030 | 9 | — | 3,342: 3:14 |

| Date | Ship | Destination | Coper | | | | | |
|---|---|---|---|---|---|---|---|---|
| 1636/12/31 | Petten | Taijouan/ Batavia | Broot coper | — | 60,398 | 10 | — | 17,213:8:10 |
| | | | Staefges coper | — | 76,314 | 9 | — | 19,574:10:13 |
| | | | Plaet coper | — | 65,000 | 12 | — | 22,230: –: – |
| | | | Plaet c oper | — | 20,396 | 10 | — | 5,812:17: 3 |
| 1637/1/29 | Groll | Taijouan | Broot coper | — | 50,000 | 9 | — | 12,825: –: – |
| | | | Staefies coper | — | 30,000 | 12 | — | 10,260: –: – |
| 1637/1/29 | Groll | Tonquin | Broot coper | — | 30,000 | 9 | — | 7,695: –: – |
| 1637/2/9 | Rarop | Taijouan | Plaet coper | — | 67,436 | 10 | — | 19,219: 5: 3 |
| | | | Broot coper | — | 50,891 | 9 | — | 13,053:10:13 |
| | | | Staeffies coper | — | 20,000 | 13 | — | 7,410: –: – |
| 1637/2/16 | Zwaan | Taijouan | Staeffies coper | — | 60,200 | 13 | — | 22,304: 2: – |
| | | | Broot coper | — | 5,084 | 10 | — | 1,448:18:13 |

Source: *Negotie Journalen* 1620–37, *Archief Japan* No.829–837, ARA.

Note:

a. This destination was spelt either Taijouan, Taijwan or Taijouwan: Taijouan is used in the table above for consistency.

dated 15 February 1635. It seems that the quality of *saodō* was much higher than that of *gyokudō* or *itadō*; it was always traded at high price levels.

## Changes in the description of copper in trade books

Table 10 shows that the recording format of trade books was changed in 1633. Until an entry dated 12 February 1633 for the *Heusden*, copper exports were recorded by type or quality in units of tael and the total value was converted into gulden and recorded in the books. After that date all shipments were calculated in units of gulden except for those of the *Venloo*, dated 12 December 1633, and the *Bredamme*, dated 15 February 1635.

Looking at the itemized entries before and after February 1634, the entries before that time emphasized the quality of copper and whether or not it was red copper (*root coper*). Yet the descriptions of quality and price were not established clearly. For example, an item described as fine quality copper (*fijn coper*) might be priced at 10 tael (100 monme) per picol at one point and 12 tael (120 monme) at another; the description of quality and the price varied from year to year. Some entries had descriptions such as *usuitadō* or *gokidō*, but most were simply described as either fine or crude. In November 1634, emphasis shifted from qualitative distinctions to shape distinctions, namely distinguishing between *itadō*, *gokidō*, *tamadō* and *saodō*.

A shipping bill dated 19 January 1636 that was contained in the journal of the *Warmont*, returning to Tayouan and Batavia, has the following entry:

A 11  coper voor  132343 cattij te weten,

| | | | | | |
|---|---|---|---|---|---|
| 25,289 cattij | plaetcoper | a | T.10 | 't picol | f. 7,902: 16: 4 |
| 16,931 cattij | do | a | T.9.5 | 't picol | f. 5,026: 7: 8 |
| 40,000 cattij | fijn staefges coper | a | T.11.5 | 't picol | f. 14,375: -: - |
| 44,897 cattij | Gockieis coper | a | T. 8.5 | 't picol | f. 11,925: 15: - |
| 5,226 cattij | do | a | T.7.8 | 't picol | f. 1,273: 16: 4 |
| 132,343 cattij | cooper cost | | | total | f. 40,502: 15[14] |

A shipping bill of the *Noortwijck*, dated 17 November 1636, returning to Tayouan, has the following:

B 50: aen staefges coper voor 6,000 cattij fijn do a T.13.''t picol    f.2,223: -: -
    57: aen broot coper voor 13,030 cattij do a T.9 't picol         f.3,342: 3: 14
    11: aen coper voor 60,398 cattij do bestaende in 1,295 stx
        aten a T.10 'tpicol                                        f.17,213: 8: 10[15]

In format A, copper was recorded on page 11 of the ledger, regardless of its type and quality. Format A was used until February 1636. From November

1636 journals were recorded using format B, in which different types of copper were recorded as separate items and had separate pages in the ledger. In format A, copper was originally a single item recorded on page 11 of the ledger. When the recording format was changed from A to B, page 11 of the ledger was assigned to *itadō* (*plaet coper*) and pages 50 and 57 were newly assigned to *saodō* and *tamadō* respectively.

At the same time, previously varying descriptions of type and quality were gradually standardized and eventually only three types of copper remained: *tamadō*, *itadō* and *saodō*. There was little variation of quality within each type. The price for each type of copper stabilized; *tamadō* was traded at 9 tael (90 monme) per picol (100 kin), *itadō* at 10 tael (100 monme) and *saodō* at 12–13 tael (120–130 monme). These three types of copper shared a similar proportion of the total copper export in the 1636 shipping year (from November 1636 to February 1637). *Tamadō* accounted for 33.8 per cent of the total copper export for this period at 224,319 kin, *itadō* 34.8 per cent at 230,915 kin and *saodō* 31.6 per cent at 211,200 kin.

These changes in the descriptions of copper which took place from 1633 and 1636 were part of an overall review of the Dutch Factory's trade book recording method. Cornelis van Neijenroode, who had been the head of the Dutch Factory since 1623, died in January 1633. He developed a mental problem towards the end of his tenure and his book keeping became quite disorganized.[16] His disorderly accounting practices came to light after his death and caused a serious problem. Pieter van Santen was temporarily appointed acting head of the Dutch Factory to replace van Neijenroode in January 1633. Nicolaes Coukebacker arrived from Batavia and officially took up the position of head factor in September of the same year.

Coukebacker swiftly embarked on the reform of accounting practices in the factory. According to Katō, the following two major changes were made. Firstly, the calendar year was adopted as its accounting year. Secondly, the profit and loss account and the balance account were set up as summaries to assist with term-end settlements, enabling the profits and losses of individual items to be calculated and carried forward to the next term. This established the procedure for the annual closing of trade books, with one calendar year representing one accounting term in a strict sense.[17] For this reason, the practice of periodic accounting in a strict sense began at around this time; the *Negotie Journalen* came to fulfill its original function as an accounting journal rather than a type of commercial diary or daily trade journal as it used to be. This trade book reform resulted in the reorganization of export copper descriptions and the adoption of a new format.

As will be shown later, the export of copper was banned from 1637 to 1646. After the embargo was lifted, *tamadō* was no longer exported and *itadō* and *saodō* became the only types of export copper. The export of *itadō* was subsequently stopped from 1649; *saodō* became the only type of copper exported in regular trade. Crude copper, *itadō* and other types were exported occasionally after that time but only in small quantities. *Itadō* (*hiradō*) was temporarily exported during the eighteenth century in private trade, but there was no comparison between that and *saodō* in terms of export quantity. With regard to the export of *itadō*, records of transactions during the Hōreki (1751–1763) era can be found in *Nagasaki okaiire hiradō chakudaka narabini kaiukedaka ukegaki (utsushi)* (Receipts for deliveries and purchases of plate copper at Nagasaki buying agent [duplicate]), which is in the possession of the Nagasaki Museum of History and Culture, but the transactions in the remaining period are not known as they was conducted outside of regular trade.

The description of *saodō* also changed from 1646 to the early 1650s. In around 1646, it was simply described as 'Coper voor 100000 cattij staaff do (100,000 catty of copper in copper bars)'.[18] A description in 1649 reads, 'Coper voor 64000 cattij zuijver gewicht fijngerafineert do in staven (net weight 64,000 catty of fine refined copper in bars)'.[19] The description of *saodō* in the trade books became more standardized in the 1650s: for example, '600 picol suijver gewich geraffineert staafcoper (net weight 600 picol of refined Japanese copper bars)'[20] or 'Japans coper voor 80000 catij gerafineert staeff coper (80,000 catty of Japanese fine refined copper in bars)'[21]. This standard format was more or less followed from then on.

## The copper export ban of 1637

When the Tayouan incident was resolved and the export of copper began to run smoothly following the resumption of Japanese–Dutch trade in 1633, there were already moves to ban copper exports. An article dated 6 November 1633 in the *Hirado Oranda shōkan no nikki* (Diary of the Dutch Factory in Hirado) reads as follows:[22]

Official interpreter Riuemon said he had heard the following from Lord Hirado himself. The town governor of Osaka had asked the Bakufu to forbid the Dutch from sending copper and copper coins to Cochinchina. The pressure was coming not from himself but from Mr Hirano Tōjirō—the shogun's purveyor living in Kyoto—and Mr Chaya Shinkurō—the shogun's kimono fabric supplier—and it would become difficult for these merchants to dispose of and sell copper in Cochinchina. Lord Hirado was very surprised and replied: how could he forbid the Dutch from exporting copper and other commodities when they have been authorized by the shogun to conduct trade freely? The town governor replied: he had received such a request from these merchants but it was not feasible and there was no need to worry.

Since the Dutch established Tayouan as the base for their trading activity in China and its vicinity in 1623, conflicts between them and Japan's authorized trade ships that had been using Tayouan before then were unavoidable. After the Tayouan incident happened in 1628, Japanese–Dutch trade was temporarily suspended until it resumed in 1633. This also meant the resumption of obstruction and smear tactics against the Dutch by Japan's authorized traders. However, the pleas of the Japanese traders were not enough to secure a ban on the export of copper by the Dutch.

By the way, the shogunate government was planning to set up a unified currency system from its inception. It minted *Keichō-tsūhō* in 1606 and *Genna-tsūhō* in 1619 as part of its plan. It also banned the use of old currency coins such as *Eiraku-sen*.[23] However, the ban could not be enforced too strictly as there were insufficient newly minted coins.[24] In order to resolve this situation and achieve the unified currency system, the government began a mass mintage project of *Kanei-tsūhō* coins.

According to a letter from the head of Ayutthaya Factory, the *Kanei-tsūhō* was already accepted in Siam by 1634; copper coins made in Sakamoto, Oumi, were the finest quality.[25] Large quantities of copper coins were exported from 1633.[26] Since *Kanei-tsūhō* coins were reportedly in production at the Mito domain in as early as 1625, it is not unreasonable to imagine that the production of *Kanei-tsūhō* coins was being trialed in various places from the beginning of the Kanei era. The government must have made the decision to mass-produce the Kanei-tsūho in view of the reputation of the trial mintage. In any case, the shogunate government officially issued an order to commence large scale minting of Kankei-tsūhō coins on 1 June (old lunar calendar date) 1636. The following article is found in *Tokyo shi shikō* (Historical materials for the city of Tokyo):[27]

> On 1 June, the shogunate government began minting the *Kanei-tsūhō* as the new coin to be used as a currency for a long time in an effort to create a unified currency. Copper mints (*zeniza*) were opened at Shiba and Asakusa in Edo and at Sakamoto in Oumi for this purpose. It established a currency system for the minting and circulating of the new coins on this day. It also prohibited the previous practice of selective use of coins (*erizeni*).

On the same date, an article in the *Tokugawa jikki* (Official chronicles of the Tokugawa Shogunate) reads, 'New coins are to be minted in Edo and

Sakamoto, Oumi, and no other coins, including bad quality coins, shall be minted at any place other than these'.[28] This was the start of the mass minting of *Kanei-tsūhō* coins by the government for currency unification.

An embargo on copper export was proclaimed in the following year. The Netherlands received a report on the embargo on 8 April 1637 prior to the proclamation: 'the shogun has forbidden the Dutch and other foreigners from exporting copper from Japan'.[29] On 1 May (old intercalary 7 March), 'The copper export ban was confirmed today by a letter from Commercial Officer Verstegen'.[30] The Dutch Factory was officially notified on 30 May 1637:[31]

> The head factor was summoned to the house of Magistrate Daigaku in the Hirado domain. He was verbally notified by this magistrate and Magistrate Daizen of a new order from Edo regarding copper export and shown the document. He was given a letter from Lord Hirado addressed to him and a copy of a letter from a senior shogunate councilor (*Rojū*) addressed to Lord Hirado. The letters said strictly that no one was permitted to export copper from Japan. Please refer to the following translation for more details. The aforementioned magistrates advised the head factory to abide by the ban strictly. He accepted and promised to adhere to it closely.

The following is a translation of the letter from the councilor to Lord Hirado:

> This is to notify you that the shogun has issued an order to ban the export of copper out of Japan. You are hereby directed to transmit this strict order throughout your domain and stop the export of copper accordingly.
>     The first day of the fourth month.
>
> |  |  |
> |---|---|
> | From | Abe Bingo-no-kami |
> |  | Matsudaira Izu-no-kami |
> |  | Sakai Sanuki-no-kami |
> |  | Doi Ōi-no-kami |
> | To | Matsura Iki-no-kami |

The date of the letter falls on 24 May according to the new calendar (1 April 1637, according to the old calendar).

Copper exports were banned thereafter under this order. The order was communicated to Batavia in December of 1637. An article dated 26 February 1637 in the *Generale Missiven* reads as follows:[32]

> The shogun ordered to ban copper exports. This was instigated by complaints made by those who were in charge of coin minting. When they were asked

why the new coinage project by order of the shogun was not making much
progress, they replied that it was because foreigners exported copper. Due to
this embargo, we will not be able to export even a catty of copper from Japan
for the next several years. It is uncertain when this order will be revoked.

As mentioned here, it is highly likely that this ban was issued for the purpose
of securing domestic reserves of copper for the coinage project that had
began in the previous year. However, according to Oskar Nachod, 'the
Dutch were not overly upset by this. It was because this interdict did not
play a large part for them at the time; the bulk of their exports was in silver
and silver was the source of profit and the necessity for the procurement
of Chinese goods'.[33] Despite this, the Dutch persistently petitioned Lord
Hirado and senior shogunate councilors for permission to export copper
after the promulgation of this embargo.

The *General Missiven* has some articles regarding Japanese copper. It was
reported in December 1639 that the price of copper in Persia reached 35–40
larinen per 30 pond; the volume of orders amounted to 200,000 man, or
600,000 pond.[34] Copper prices in Persia in 1637 are known: 28–30 larinen for
crude copper and 30–32 larinen for fine bar copper.[35] The Dutch managed to
ship only half of the volume of orders for Japanese copper from Batavia to
Coromandel in that year.[36] In 1642, the price rose to 50 larinen per 30 pond
at the Dutch Factory in Gamron, Persia; they could only raise 25,635 pond
of the 150,000 pond that was ordered.[37] Since most of the copper used by the
VOC in Asia was obtained from Japan, the company had to bring Swedish
or Hungarian copper from Europe to Asia to make up for the shortfall
created by the embargo.[38] In view of its Hirado-based trade alone, it was
silver that generated a lot of profit. Nonetheless, the embargo on Japanese
copper export was not an insignificant situation from the viewpoint of the
overall Asia trade of the VOC.

By the way, in 1636, the *Kanei-tsūhō* coinage project was expanded from
the aforementioned locations—Shiba and Asakusa in Edo and Sakamoto
in Oumi—to Mito in Hitachi and Sendai in Mutsu. In the following year,
minting also started at Yoshida in Mikawa, Matsumoto in Shinano, Takada
in Echigo, Okayama in Bizen, Hagi in Nagato and Taketa in Bingo. Minting
at Inomiya in Suruga began in 1639, but the coinage projects in all these
locations ended in 1640.[39]

Although the embargo on copper export was not lifted when the minting stopped, it is worth noting that there was a subtle change of tone in the
responses of Lord Hirado and senior shogunate councilors to the petitions
for the lifting of the copper embargo made by the Dutch Factory. When the

Dutch petitioned Lord Hirado for authorization to export copper in 1639, he replied, 'It can only become possible once the minting of copper coins is completed and the country has a sufficient amount of copper coins; it is not possible until then'.[40] In 1640, the Dutch asked Makino Takumi-no-kami Nobushige, a senior statesman in the shogunate government, about the possibility of gaining authorization to export a small quantity of copper every year, he replied, 'At your wish, I have spoken to senior councilors for a few times regarding your request about copper. From what I have heard from them, you will not be given authorization so easily. It is because of its implications (as a strategic material)'.[41] In the same year, Lord Hirado consulted Matsudaira Izu-no-kami Nobutsuna, a senior shogunate councilor, about copper. He later told the Dutch, 'The export of copper from Japan is prohibited by an officially decreed order of the shogun. There is no prospect of removal of this interdict because it is a material needed for war'.[42]

In 1639, Lord Hirado said that the reason for the copper export embargo was the production of coinage; this was also recorded in archival materials of the Dutch. Couckebacker, the head of the Dutch Factory, wrote on 11 February 1639 that the export of copper would not be permitted until after the completion of the coinage project.[43] However, in 1640, senior shogunate councilors explained that export authorization could not be granted because copper was a military material.

Although the end of the *Kanei-tsūhō* mintage project in 1640 removed a major obstacle to copper export, the shogunate government was reluctant to lift the embargo at that point. In that year, there was a close link between the stated reason for the embargo on the grounds that copper was a military material and the demolition of the Dutch Factory building in Hirado and its relocation to Nagasaki by order of the government. The *Hirado Oranda shōkan no nikki* (Diary of the Dutch factory in Hirado) has the following passage with regard to this relocation:[44]

> Various reports are circulating about our relocation and the demolition of the warehouse. Senior councilors, their stewards, high-ranking Edo officials and other people who visit us everyday say as follows. It came about for the important reason of stabilization of Japan and so that a rebellion such as the one happened recently in Arima (so called the conflict of Simabara) would not happen again with support from foreigners.
>
> Because Christianity is the reason and the shogun realized a while ago that 'the Dutch and the Portuguese are of the same race' (...) he ordered us to move to Nagasaki where town governors would scrutinize our lives and behavior closely to examine whether our presence would be good or bad for him and would decide how to treat us in the future based on the result.

When the Shimabara conflict broke out in October 1637, the Dutch participated in order to demonstrate their allegiance to the shogunate government and caused great damage to the insurgents of Shimabara with shelling from their ships. While this action confirmed their obedience to the shogunate government, it also inspired some sense of fear of the Dutch on the part of the shogunate. Matsudaira Nobutsuna, who had been sent to Shimabara to suppress the uprising, headed for Hirado to inspect the Dutch Factory after Shimabara was pacified. After witnessing the power of Dutch ships and canons, it was quite natural for the shogunate to try to relocate the Dutch Factory to a domain under its direct control in order to monitor their every move.[45]

The government's misgivings about the Dutch prompted it to not only adopt a measure to relocate the Dutch Factory from Hirado to Nagasaki under its direct control, but also to continue the ban on copper export even after the completion of the coinage project on the grounds that it was a military material. The second clause of the 1621 five-clause decree of the shogun imposed a ban on the export of military supplies. The Dutch Factory's first Head Factor Jacques Specx had expressed his concern that copper and iron might be regarded as military supplies and placed under an embargo. His concern became a reality at this time.

## Conclusion

Although the records of the *Generale Missiven* that are extant since 1610 refer to copper in various places, the only time that copper is clearly described as 'Japanese copper' is in the record of 982.5 picol (98,250 catty) of Japanese red copper (*Japan root coper*) that was among the goods onboard a ship arriving in Batavia on 3 February 1626.[46] There are not many detailed descriptions of Japanese copper in the *Generale Missiven* after that date. References to Japanese copper appear much earlier in historical records in Persia, to which large quantities of Japanese copper were shipped. Japanese copper appears in *Bronnen tot de Geshiedenis der Oostindische Compagnie in Perzie 1611–1638* (Resources for the history of the East India Company in Persia 1611–1638) in 1623. Shipping bills dated 10 November of the *Vreede* and the *Weesp* leaving Surat for Persia contain one hundred boxes of Japanese copper; among the cargo of spices, coins, non-coin silver and other goods were 5,765 catty of Japanese copper valued at 35 gulden per picol, a total of 2,017 gulden, 15 stuiver.[46]

In Asia, there was a strong demand for Japanese copper in Persia until the 1640s.[48] This was perhaps because copper coins were used in this region and copper was also needed for military use as the region experienced incessant conflicts. Other than Persia, copper was shipped to Surat, a copper transit point to Persia, and to Coromandel. It was also occasionally shipped to the Netherlands.

Copper accounted for smaller proportions of the total export than silver during the Hirado era. Still, Japanese copper was an indispensable commodity for the Dutch in its Asia trade, including Persia. The revision of the trade book description of copper in particular suggests that its importance increased during the second half of the 1630s. However, the export of copper was banned in 1637. This measure was put in place so that the nationwide *Kanei-tsūhō* coinage project that had started in the previous year would operate smoothly. The embargo was not lifted after the coinage project ended in 1640, when government officials began to state that copper could not be exported because it was a military resource.

In the past, Kobata Atsushi, Oskar Nachod, Nagazumi Yōko and Yamawaki Teijirō thought that the coinage project that began in the previous year was the reason for the copper export ban of 1637.[49] On the other hand, Kristof Glamann considered that it was because copper was a military material.[50] The coinage project was the initial reason but the copper export ban was maintained even after the completion of the coinage project based on the view that copper was a military material. In other words, the embargo was continued for a reason that was different from the initial intent as the domestic situation changed.

In the history of the early modern period, this was the only time that the shogunate government proclaimed and enforced a copper export ban for as long as nine years. Although the government carried out coinage projects frequently from the latter half of the 1660s, it was extremely difficult to place an embargo on copper because it had become the most important export commodity by then.

# Chapter Three

# The Copper Trade of the Dutch Factory in Nagasaki

Japanese copper accounted for a large proportion of copper marketed in Asia by the VOC.[1] Copper was primarily used in Asia for military supplies (small arms, etc.). It was also used for coinage in Japan, India and the Moluccas, and for making temple ornaments, Buddhist statues and various household utensils.[2]

The VOC initially procured Japanese copper to supply its trading posts in various parts of Asia[3], but it began to export large quantities of Japanese copper to Europe from the latter half of the 1650s. Between 1672 and 1676, the amount of Japanese copper exports sometimes reached about one third or even one half of the total amount of copper and brass from Sweden, which was a major supplier of copper in the European market.[4] Adam Smith, the eighteenth century economist, observed in *An Inquiry into the Nature and Causes of the Wealth of Nations*, 'The copper of Japan makes an article of commerce in Europe [...]. The price of copper in Japan must have some influence upon its price at the copper mines in Europe'.[5] The fact that Japanese copper was circulating as a commodity in Europe and influencing the European copper market must have been a phenomenon that European economists at the time could not overlook.

This chapter will examine copper in the Japanese–Dutch trade from a quantitative point of view, based mainly on the trade books of the Dutch Factory and *Nagasaki jikki nendairoku* (The true chronicles of Nagasaki), and consider the actual state of the copper trade from various angles. This exercise covers important issues over a number of phases from 1646, when the copper embargo was lifted, to the end of the eighteenth century.

## The copper trade in the mid- to late-seventeenth century

### Changes in the copper trade after the lifting of the embargo
The copper export embargo promulgated in 1637 was lifted in September 1646.[6] A rumor began to circulate from 1643 that the export of copper

would be authorized. In May of that year the Dutch received credible
information from Shirōuemon, the *otona* (civilian supervisor) of Dejima,
about the impending authorization of copper export.[7] Yet, an article dated
6 February 1645 in *Nagasaki Oranda shōkan no nikki* (The diaries of the
Dutch factory at Nagasaki) shows that the Dutch saw little prospect of
obtaining permission to export copper at this time.[8]

It was not until May 1645 that the situation began to improve. An article
dated 19 May in the diaries of the Dutch Factory in Nagasaki reports that
the governor of Nagasaki hinted at a possible resumption of copper export
during a conversation with the Dutch about trading conditions on the
Coromandel coast:

> Nagasaki governor Baba Saburōzaemon came to the Factory on horseback
> [...] I was asked how our trade in Coromandel coast was and replied it was
> flourishing just as in Japan. Baba said that we would not be exporting as much
> money from Coromandel coast as from Japan. I replied that unlike in Japan
> we not only sold goods but also purchased considerable amounts of goods in
> Coromandel and hence we needed a lot of money. I said that this was why the
> VOC wished to export copper from Japan. His Honor said to the interpreter
> before leaving that he wondered why his superiors continued to ban the export
> even though there was an abundance of copper in Japan and that he would
> discuss it with his fellow governor Yamazaki Gonpachirō on his return and
> he expected to have an (export) authorization.[9]

The Dutch again petitioned Inspector General Inoue Chikugo-no-kami
and Nagasaki governor Baba Saburōzaemon for permission to export
copper during their annual visit to Edo in February 1646.[10] The export
of copper was finally authorized in September of that year.[11] News of the
lifting of the copper export embargo reached Batavia in January 1647:

> The long awaited permission to export copper was given this year at last. The
> prices for 4,000 picol of it have already gone down considerably—9 tael per
> picol for fine *saodō* (bar copper) and 8 tael for *itadō* (plate copper). These
> were desirable deals.[12]

It is clear from this report that Batavia was very satisfied with the low
prices of copper in Japan when the export ban was lifted. In 1637, when
the export of copper was banned, the price of bar copper was between 12
and 13 tael per picol (100 kin) and the price of plate copper was 10 tael.
Copper prices lowered considerably after the lifting of the ban. One major

reason for this was that some commission merchants who dealt with the Dutch Factory in Hirado were excluded when the factory was relocated to Nagasaki in 1641; the factory was able to deal directly with the *dōfukiya* in Osaka.[13] The *dōfukiya* were copper smelting works in Osaka which refined crude copper from various parts of Japan and then sold it as refined copper. In addition, an oversupply of copper in Japan after the completion of all the *Kanei-tsūhō* coinage projects in 1640 would have contributed to the lowering of copper prices.[14]

In 1646, approximately 220,000 kin of bar copper and 200,000 kin of plate copper were exported; these two types of copper were exported in almost equal quantities. In the following year, however, the export quantity jumped to a total of 532,305 kin, 11,776 kin of which were in high grade bar copper at 9.2 tael per picol, 464,898 kin were in standard bar copper and 55,631 kin were in plate copper. The volume of plate copper export dropped dramatically. 1647 was the last year that a large quantity of plate copper was exported as part of the VOC's regular trade. As Table 11 shows, although the bulk of copper exported from then on was bar copper, other types of copper were exported in 1659, 1660 and 1672.[15]

Copper prices were fixed to the market value price in 1646 and 1647, but they increased in 1648 as Inspector General Inoue Chikugo-no-kami and the governors of Nagasaki ordered copper merchants to sell copper to the Dutch at higher prices.[16] Moreover, there had been a significant drop in the quality of copper which made copper trade negotiations difficult. The Dutch were unable to purchase copper and there was no copper exported in 1648.[17] From 1649, the price rose from 9 tael per picol to 11.6 tael per picol. The price kept copper exports down to about 300,000 kin in 1649 and 320,000 kin in 1650. When the price went down marginally to 11 tael per picol in 1651, the export quantity increased temporarily to 710,000 kin. The export quantity settled at around 300,000 kin per year from then on. It appears that this was according to the Dutch Factory's policy; its council met and resolved in 1653 to 'sign contracts with Japanese merchants for the purchase of a total of 275,800 kin of copper and 46,300 kin of camphor and, [thereafter, purchase] 300,000 kin of copper and 40,000 kin of camphor annually at firm fixed prices for the next three years'.[18]

Circumstance surrounding the export of copper began to change from 1656–1657; the export quantity gradually increased albeit with some fluctuations. This was a so-called *aitai-baibai* (direct dealings/free trade) period which followed the abolition of the *itowappu* system in 1655. The *itowappu* system was instituted in 1604; under it Chinese raw silk, which accounted for the bulk of imports at that time, was purchased *en bloc*, the prices fixed

## Table 11: Copper exports, 1646–1805

| Month/date | | Vessel name [a] | Destination | Unit price [b] | Export quantity (catty) [c] | Export quantity (gulden) [d] |
|---|---|---|---|---|---|---|
| 1646 | 10/22 | Koninck van Polen | Taijouan | 8 | 111,424 | 25,404: 13: 7 |
| | 10/22 | Zeerob | Taijouan | 9 | 100,000 | 26,560: –: – |
| | 10.22 | Meerman | Taijouan | 9 | 60,000 | 15,390: –: – |
| | 10.25 | Swarten Beer | Taijouan/Tonquin | 9 | 5,000 | 1,282: 10: – |
| | | | | 8 | 15,005 | 3,421: 2: 12 |
| | 10.25 | Hillegersberg | Taijouan | 8 | 75,317 | 17,172: 5: 8 |
| | 10.25 | Goulden Gans | Taijouan | 9 | 57,500 | 14,748: 15: – |
| | | | | Total | 424,246 | 103,069: 6: 11 |
| 1647 | 10.12 | Yongen Prins | Batavia | 9 | 70,000 | 17,955: –: – |
| | 10.16 | Beer | Taijouan | 9 | 300,442 | 77,063: 7: 7 |
| | | | | 9.2 | 3,824 | 1,002: 13: – |
| | 10.16 | Berckhout | Taijouan | 9 | 29,089 | 7,461: 6: 9 |
| | | | | 8 | 20,028 | 4,566: 7: 10 |
| | 10.31 | Hillegersberg | Taijouan | 9 | 65,367 | 16,766: 12: 11 |
| | | | | 9.2 | 7,952 | 2,085: –: 4 |
| | | | | 8 | 35,603 | 8,117: 9: 10 |
| | | | | Total | 532,305 | 135,017: 17: 3 |
| 1648 | – | – | – | – | – | – |
| 1649 | 10.25 | Witte Valck | Taijouan | 11.6 | 64,000 | 21,158: 8: – |
| | 10.28 | Griffioen | Siam/Batavia | 11.6 | 120,000 | 39,672: –: – |
| | 10.31 | Gekroonde Liefde | Taijouan | 11.6 | 80,000 | 26,448: –: – |
| | 10.31 | Witte Paard | Taijouan | 11.6 | 41,500 | 13,719: 18: – |
| | | | | Total | 305,500 | 100,998: 6: – |
| 1650 | 10.25 | Vreede | Batavia | 11.6 | 220,000 | 72,732: –: – |
| | 10.13 | Witte Valck | Taijouan | 11.6 | 60,000 | 19,836: –: – |
| | 10.20 | Hulst | Taijouan/Tonquin | 11.6 | 39,500 | 13,058: 14: – |
| | | | | Total | 319,500 | 105,626: 14: – |
| 1651 | 10.18 | Campen | Taijouan | 11 | 60,000 | 18,810: –: – |
| | 10.18 | Vergulde Pelikaan | Taijouan | 11 | 100,000 | 31,350: –: – |
| | 10.18 | Hillegersberg | Taijouan | 11 | 100,000 | 31,350: –: – |
| | 10.25 | Gekroonde Liefde | Taijouan | 11 | 100,000 | 31,350: –: – |
| | 10.25 | Taijouan | Taijouan | 11 | 20,000 | 6,270: –: – |
| | 10.28 | Jongen Prins | Batavia | 11 | 80,000 | 25,080: –: – |
| | | | | 10.5 | 250,000 | 74,812: 10: – |
| | | | | Total | 710,000 | 219,022: 10: – |
| 1652 | 10.17 | Vergulde Pelikaan | Taijouan | 11 | 80,000 | 25,080: –: – |
| | 10.17 | Zaandijk | Taijouan | 11 | 70,000 | 21,945: –: – |
| | 10.19 | Smient | Taijouan | 11 | 40,000 | 12,540: –: – |

*Table 11: Continued*

| | Month/date | Vessel name [a] | Destination | Unit price [b] | Export quantity (catty) [c] | Export quantity (gulden) [d] |
|---|---|---|---|---|---|---|
| | 10.22 | *Morgenster* | Taijouan | 11 | 60,000 | 18,810: –: – |
| | 10.22 | *Trouw* | Taijouan | 10 | 150,000 | 42,750: –: – |
| | 11.4 | *Koning van Polen* | Taijouan | 10 | 50,000 | 14,250: –: – |
| | | | Total | | 450,000 | 135,375: –: – |
| 1653 | 11.6 | *Baars* | Taijouan | 10.3 | 48,598 | 14,265: 18: 10 |
| | 11.6 | *Liefde* | Taijouan | 10.3 | 94,000 | 27,593: 14: – |
| | 11.7 | *Witte Paard* | Taijouan | 10.3 | 94,000 | 27,593: 14: – |
| | 11.10 | *Witte Valk* | Taijouan | 10.3 | 28,200 | 8,278: 2: 3 |
| | 11.10 | *Campen* | Taijouan | 10.3 | 37,600 | 11,037: 9: 9 |
| | | | Total | | 302,398 | 88,768: 18: 6 |
| 1654 | 10.25 | *Breda* | Taijouan | 10.5 | 60,000 | 17,955: –: – |
| | 10.25 | *Witte Paard* | Taijouan | 10.5 | 90,000 | 26,932: 10: – |
| | 10.31 | *Witte Valk* | Taijouan | 10.5 | 70,000 | 20,947: 10: – |
| | 10.31 | *Kalf* | Taijouan | 10.5 | 80,000 | 23,940: –: – |
| | | | | 10.3 | 30,000 | 8,806: 10: – |
| | | | Total | | 330,000 | 98,581: 10: – |
| 1655 | 10.19 | *Arnemuiden* | Taijouan | 11.1 | 100,000 | 31,635: –: – |
| | 10.19 | *Zoutelande* | Taijouan | 10.9 | 91,300 | 28,362: 6: 14 |
| | 10.19 | *Vlieland* | Taijouan | 10.9 | 120,000 | 37,278: –: – |
| | 10.20 | *Angelier* | Taijouan | 11.1 | 100,000 | 31,635: –: – |
| | | | Total | | 411,300 | 128,910: 6: 14 |
| 1656 | 10.17 | *Arnhem* | Batavia | 11.4 | 250,000 | 81,987: 7: 8 |
| | 10.17 | *Cabo de Jasques* | Tonquin | 11.4 | 40,000 | 13,117: 19: 10 |
| | 10.22 | *Koning David* | Taijouan | 11.4 | 160,000 | 52,471: 18: 7 |
| | 10.22 | *Zoutelande* | Taijouan | 11.4 | 130,000 | 42,633: 8: 11 |
| | 10.22 | *Charlois* | Taijouan | 11.4 | 30,000 | 9,838: 9: 11 |
| | 10.27 | *Arnemuiden* | Taijouan | 11.4 | 130,000 | 42,633: 8: 11 |
| | | *Kalf* | Taijouan | 11.4 | 110,000 | 36,074: 8: 14 |
| | 10.31 | *Avondster* | Taijouan | 11.4 | 39,300 | 12,888: 8: 4 |
| | | | Total | | 889,300 | 291,645: 9: 12 |
| 1657 | 10.12 | *Koudekerke* | Batavia | 11.4 | 160,000 | 52,499: 5: 10 |
| | 10.12 | *Ulysses* | Batavia | 11.4 | 350,000 | 114,842: 3: 8 |
| | 10.12 | *Groene Molen* | Taijouan | 11.4 | 100,000 | 32,812: 1: – |
| | 10.12 | *Haas* | Taijouan | 11.4 | 50,000 | 16,406: –: – |
| | 10.20 | *Erasmus* | Taijouan | 11.4 | 200,000 | 65,624: 2: – |
| | 10.20 | *Hercules* | Taijouan | 11.4 | 300,000 | 98,436: 3: – |
| | 10.26 | *Domburg* | Taijouan | 11.4 | 200,000 | 65,624: 2: – |
| | 10.26 | *Bloemendaal* | Taijouan | 11.4 | 50,000 | 16,406: –: 8 |
| | | | Total | | 1,410,000 | 462,649: 17: 10 |

*Table 11: Continued*

| Month/date | | Vessel name [a] | Destination | Unit price[b] | Export quantity (catty)[c] | Export quantity (gulden)[d] |
|---|---|---|---|---|---|---|
| 1658 | 10.12 | *Venenburg* | Taijouan | 11.4 | 160,000 | 52,417: 4: – |
| | 10.12 | *Arnemuiden* | Taijouan | 11.4 | 140,000 | 45,865: 1: – |
| | 10.12 | *Haas* | Taijouan | 11.4 | 60,000 | 19,665: –: – |
| | 10.12 | *Breukelen* | Taijouan | 11.4 | 60,000 | 19,665: –: – |
| | 10.16 | *Bloemendaal* | Taijouan | 11.4 | 60,000 | 19,665: –: – |
| | 10.16 | *Zeeridder* | Taijouan | 11.4 | 60,000 | 19,665: –: – |
| | 10.16 | *Vink* | Taijouan | 11.4 | 40,000 | 13,110: –: – |
| | 10.20 | *Kalf* | Taijouan | 11.4 | 90,000 | 30,161: 16: 11 |
| | 10.22 | *Trouw* | Batavia | 11.4 | 330,000 | 108,750: –: – |
| | 10.22 | *Domburg* | Batavia | 11.4 | 300,000 | 98,863: 13: – |
| | | | | Total | 1,300,000 | 427,828: 14: 11 |
| 1659 | 10.17 | *Vogelenlank* | Batavia | 12 | 150,000 | 51,727: 10: – |
| | | | | 9.8 | 19,425 | 5,457: 17: 13 |
| | 10.25 | *Brouwershaven* | Taijouan | 12 | 150,000 | 51,727: 10: – |
| | 10.25 | *Spreeuw* | Taijouan | 12 | 150,000 | 51,727: 10: – |
| | 10.25 | *Breukelen* | Taijouan | 12 | 50,000 | 17,242: 10: – |
| | 10.30 | *Nieuw Poort* | Taijouan | 12 | 150,000 | 52,582: 10: – |
| | | | | 11.5 | 5,000 | 1,662: 10: 15 |
| | 10.30 | *Ulysses* | Taijouan | 12 | 150,000 | 52,582: 10: – |
| | | | | Total | 824,425 | 284,710: 8: 12 |
| 1660 | 10/15 | *Venenburg* | Batavia | 11.8 | 400,000 | 136,800: –: – |
| | 10/24 | *Spreeuw* | Malacca | 11.8 | 100,000 | 34,122: –: – |
| | 10/24 | *Ooievaar* | Malacca | 11.8 | 355,000 | 121,136: 16: 9 |
| | | | | 11 | 29,000 | 9,240: 5: – |
| | | | | 9.8 | 14,935 | 4,171: 6: – |
| | 10/24 | *Kalf* | Malacca | 11.8 | 240,000 | 81,895: 6: 7 |
| | | | Batavia | 11 | 1,000 | 318: 12: – |
| | | | | Total | 1,139,935 | 387,684: 13: – |
| 1661 | 10/21 | *'s-Graveland* | Batavia | 11.8 | 340,000 | 116,280: –: – |
| | ☉[e]10/21 | *Diemermeer* | Batavia | 11.8 | 350,600 | 119,905: 4: – |
| | 11/10 | *Buienskerke* | Malacca | 11.8 | 360,000 | 123,120: –: – |
| | 11/10 | *Boodschap* | Malacca | 11.8 | 80,000 | 27,360: –: – |
| | 11/10 | *Goeree* | Malacca | 11.8 | 100,000 | 34,200: –: – |
| | 11/10 | *Nieuw Poort* | Malacca | 11.8 | 168,900 | 57,763: 16: – |
| | 11/11 | *Vollenhoven* | Batavia | 11.8 | 200,000 | 68,039: 3: 4 |
| | | | | Total | 1,599,500 | 546,668: 3: 4 |
| 1662 | 11/4 | *Kleverskerke* | Batavia | 11.9 | 150,000 | 52,582: 10: – |
| | ☉ 11/4 | *Vollenhoven* | Batavia | 11.9 | 100,000 | 35,055: –: – |
| | 11/4 | *Buienskerke* | Batavia | 11.9 | 250,000 | 87,637: 10: – |

*Table 11: Continued*

| Month/date | Vessel name [a] | Destination | Unit price[b] | Export quantity (catty)[c] | Export quantity (gulden)[d] |
|---|---|---|---|---|---|
| 11/4 | Vogelzang | Malacca | 11.9 | 300,000 | 105,165: –: – |
| 11/4 | Dolphin | Malacca | 11.9 | 260,000 | 91,143: –: – |
| 11/4 | 's-Graveland | Malacca | 11.9 | 100,000 | 35,055: –: – |
| 11/4 | Loosduinen | Malacca | 11.9 | 70,000 | 24,538: 10: – |
| | | | Total | 1,230,000 | 431,176: 10: – |
| 1663 – | No N. J.[f] | ①p. 81. | 11.8 | (1,511,160) | (624,109: 1: 9) |
| | | | 10 | (99,621) | (34,867: –: –) |
| | | | Total | (1,610,780) | (658,976: 1: 9) |
| 1664 | No N. J. | ①p. 83. | | (2,440,200) | (1,007,802: 12: –) |
| 1665 10/18 | Buienskerke | Batavia | 12.4 | 200,000 | 72,390: –: – |
| 10/18 | Elburg | Batavia | 12.4 | 100,000 | 36,195: –: – |
| 10/18 | Waterhoen | Combodia | 12.4 | 10,000 | 3,619: 10: – |
| 10/28 | Sparendam | Malacca | 12.4 | 293,400 | 106,614: 4: 8 |
| 10/28 | Alphen | Malacca | 12.4 | 300,000 | 109,012: 10: – |
| 10/28 | Spreeuw | Tonquin | 12.4 | 5,000 | 1,816: 17: 8 |
| | | | Total | 908,400 | 329,648: 2: – |
| 1666 10/18 | Kattenburg | Malacca | 12.4 | 400,000 | 179,342: 16: – |
| 10/18 | Loosduinen | Malacca | 12.4 | 200,000 | 89,774: 13: – |
| 10/18 | Kleverskerke | Malacca | 12.4 | 200,000 | 89,600: –: – |
| 10/18 | Nieuw Poort | Malacca | 12.4 | 207,000 | 92,876: –: – |
| | | | Total | 1,007,000 | 451,593: 9: – |
| 1667 | No N. J. | ①p,86. | (12.5) | (1,034,800) | (452,725) |
| 1668 10/25 | Pauw | Malacca | 13.4 | 41,400 | 19,923: 15: – |
| 10/25 | Rammekens | Malacca | 13.4 | 100,000 | 48,125: –: – |
| 10/25 | Nieuw Poort | Malacca | 13.4 | 210,000 | 101,062: 10: – |
| 10/25 | Victoria | Malacca | 13.4 | 200,000 | 96,250: –: – |
| 10/25 | Buienskerke | Batavia | 13.4 | 350,000 | 168,437: 10: – |
| | | | Total | 901,400 | 433,798: 15: – |
| 1669 10/5 | Eendracht | Batavia | 12.8 | 350,000 | 161,087: 10: – |
| 10/14 | Goude Leeuw | Malacca | 12.8 | 155,000 | 71,338: 15: – |
| 10/14 | Hilversum | Malacca | 12.8 | 100,000 | 46,025: –: – |
| 10/14 | Gooiland | Malacca | 12.8 | 240,000 | 110,460: –: – |
| 10/14 | Overveen | Malacca | 12.8 | 120,000 | 57,505: –: – |
| | | | Total | 965,000 | 446,416: 5: – |
| 1670 10/19 | Schermer | Batavia | 12.7 | 400,000 | 182,700: –: – |
| 11/2 | Pouleron | Malacca | 12.7 | 450,000 | 205,537: 10: – |

Table 11: *Continued*

| Month/date | | Vessel name [a] | Destination | Unit price[b] | Export quantity (catty)[c] | Export quantity (gulden)[d] |
|---|---|---|---|---|---|---|
| | 11/2 | *Alphen* | Malacca | 12.7 | 340,000 | 155,295: –: – |
| | 11/2 | *Buienskerke* | Malacca | 12.7 | 373,000 | 170,367: 15: – |
| | 11/2 | *Noordwijk* | Malacca | 12.7 | 700,100 | 319,770: 13: 6 |
| | | | Total | | 2,263,100 | 1,033,670: 18: 6 |
| 1671 | 10/18 | *Hazenberg* | Malacca | 12.6 | 450,000 | 204,750: –: – |
| | 10/18 | *Pijnacker* | Malacca | 12.6 | 200,000 | 91,000: –: – |
| | 10/19 | *Goude Leeuw* | Malacca | 12.6 | 142,000 | 64,610: –: – |
| | 10/19 | *Papenburg* | Malacca | 12.6 | 150,000 | 68,250: –: – |
| | 10/21 | *Pauw* | Batavia | 12.6 | 200,000 | 91,000: –: – |
| | | | | 12.6 | 58,000 | 26,390: –: – |
| | 10/22 | *Tulpenburg* | Malacca | 12.6 | 399,500 | 181,772: 10: – |
| | | | Total | | 1,599,500 | 727,772: 10: – |
| 1672 | 10/23 | *Stermeer* | Batavia | 12.5 | 550,000 | 250,250: –: – |
| | 11/12 | *Voorhout* | Malacca | 12.5 | 150,000 | 68,250: –: – |
| | 11/12 | *Beemster* | Malacca | 12.5 | 400,000 | 182,000: –: – |
| | 11/12 | *Pijnacker* | Malacca | 12.5 | 246,700 | 112,248: 10: – |
| | 11/12 | *Buijren* | Malacca | 12.5 | 303,306 | 132,696: 7: 6 |
| | 11/12 | *Udam* | Malacca | 12.5 | 7,676 | 3,198: 1: 1 |
| | | | | 12.5 | 250,000 | 113,750: –: – |
| | 11.12 | *Spanbroek* | – | 12.5 | 346,600 | 157,703: –: – |
| | | | Total | | 2,254,282 | 1020,095: 18: 7 |
| 1673 | 10/29 | *Nuissenburg* | Batavia | 12.35 | 325,000 | 146,168: 15: – |
| | 10/29 | *Experiment* | Batavia | 12.35 | 200,000 | 89,950: –: – |
| | 10/29 | *Beemster* | Batavia | 12.35 | 325,000 | 146,168: 15: – |
| | 10/29 | *Spanbroek* | Batavia | 12.35 | 325,000 | 146,168: 15: – |
| | 10/29 | *Buiren* | Batavia | 12.35 | 329,400 | 148,147: 13: – |
| | | | Total | | 1,504,400 | 676,603: 18: – |
| 1674 | – | No N. J. | ②p. 450 | 12.2 | (1,792,000) | (765,184: –: –) |
| 1675 | – | No N. J. | ①p. 98 | 12.1 | (1,020,900) | (432,351: 3: –) |
| 1676 | – | No N. J. | ①p. 100 | 12 | (2,056,100) | (863,562: –: –) |
| 1677 | – | No N. J. | ②p. 460 | 11.9 | (1,703,500) | (691,621: –: –) |
| 1678 | – | No N. J. | ②p. 462 | 11.9 | (1,608,800) | – |
| 1679 | 10/24 | *Huis te Spijk* | Malacca | 11.9 | 600,000 | 260,400: –: – |
| | 10/24 | *Betuwe* | Malacca | 11.9 | 550,000 | 238,700: –: – |
| | 10/24 | *Meeuw* | Batavia | 11.9 | 650,000 | 282,100: –: – |

*Table 11: Continued*

| Month/date | Vessel name [a] | Destination | Unit price[b] | Export quantity (catty)[c] | Export quantity (gulden)[d] |
|---|---|---|---|---|---|
| 10/24 | Kronen | Malacca | 11.9 | 550,000 | 238,700: –: – |
|  |  |  | Total | 2,350,000 | 1019,900: –: – |
| 1680 | – | No N. J. | ① p. 104 | – (2,685,200) | – |
| 1681 | – | No N. J. | ② p. 469 | – (2,400,000) | – |
| 1682 | – | No N. J. | ② p. 472 | – (2,500,000) | – |
| 1683 | – | No N. J. | ② p. 481 | – (1,600,000) | – |
| 1684 | – | No N. J. | ② p. 481 | – (2,280,000) | – |
| 1685 | – | No N. J. | ② p. 489 | – (2,100,000) | – |
| 1686 | 11/2 | Pijlswaart | Batavia | 11.9 | 350,000 | 151,900: –: – |
|  | 11/2 | Bovenkarspel | Malacca | 11.9 | 470,000 | 203,980: –: – |
|  | 11/4 | Waalstroom | Malacca | 11.9 | 650,000 | 282,100: –: – |
|  | 11/5 | Maas | Malacca | 11.9 | 600,000 | 260,400: –: – |
|  |  |  | Total | 2,070,000 | 898,380: –: – |
| 1687 | 10/21 | Huis te Spijk | Batavia | 11.9 | 600,000 | 260,400: –: – |
|  | 10/22 | Mastenbos | Batavia | 11.9 | 400,000 | 173,600: –: – |
|  | 10/25 | Moerkapelle | Malacca | 11.9 | 500,000 | 217,000: –: – |
|  |  |  | Total | 1,500,000 | 651,000: –: – |
| 1688 | 10/9 | Lek | Malacca | 11.9 | 500,000 | 217,000: –: – |
|  | 10/10 | Boswijk | Malacca | 11.9 | 250,000 | 108,500: –: – |
|  | 10/13 | Oostenburg | Batavia | 11.9 | 500,000 | 217,000: –: – |
|  |  |  | Total | 1,250,000 | 542,500: –: – |
| 1689 | 10/28 | Wijk op Zee | Malacca | 11.9 | 300,000 | 130,200: –: – |
|  | 10/29 | Montfoort | Malacca | 11.9 | 550,000 | 238,700: –: – |
|  | 10/30 | Castricum | Malacca | 11.9 | 560,000 | 243,040: –: – |
|  | 11/1 | Prinseland | Batavia | 11.9 | 550,000 | 238,700: –: – |
|  |  |  | Total | 1,960,000 | 850,640: –: – |
| 1690 | 10/19 | Waalstroom | Malacca | 11.9 | 700,000 | 307,800: –: – |
|  | 10/21 | Ridderschap | Batavia | 11.9 | 750,000 | 325,500: –: – |
|  |  |  | Total | 1,450,000 | 629,300: –: – |
| 1691 | 11/6 | Boswijk | Batavia | 11.85 | 250,000 | 108,062: 10 |
|  | 11/7 | Wijk op Zee | Batavia | 11.85 | 300,000 | 129,675: –: – |
|  | 11/9 | Walenburg | Batavia | 11.85 | 350,000 | 151,287: 10: – |
|  |  |  | Total | 9,000,000 | 389,025: –: – |

*Table 11: Continued*

| Month/date | | Vessel name [a] | Destination | Unit price[b] | Export quantity (catty)[c] | Export quantity (gulden)[d] |
|---|---|---|---|---|---|---|
| 1692 | 10/25 | *Berkel* | Malacca | 11.85 | 450,000 | 194,512: 10 |
| | 10/26 | *Handboog* | Malacca | 11.85 | 500,000 | 216,125: –: – |
| | 10/27 | *Oosthuizen* | Batavia | 11.85 | 400,000 | 172,900: –: – |
| | 10/29 | *Pampus* | Malacca | 11.85 | 450,000 | 194,512: 10 |
| | | | | Total | 1,800,000 | 778,050: –: – |
| 1693 | 10/16 | *Hobre* | Malacca | 11.85 | 250,000 | 108,062: 10: – |
| | 10/16 | *Langewijk* | Malacca | 11.85 | 250,000 | 108,062: 10: – |
| | 10/16 | *Ittersheim* | Batavia | 11.85 | 250,000 | 108,062: 10: – |
| | 10/17 | *Standvastigheid* | Batavia | 11.85 | 150,000 | 64,837: 10: – |
| | 10/19 | *Huis te Loo* | Malacca | 11.85 | 300,000 | 129,675: –: – |
| | | | | Total | 1,200,000 | 518,700: –: – |
| 1694 | 11/2 | *Belois* | Malacca | 11.85 | 370,000 | 159,932: 10: – |
| | 11/3 | *Langewijk* | Batavia | 11.85 | 500,000 | 216,125: –: – |
| | 11/4 | *Huijs te Dieren* | Batavia | 11.85 | 360,000 | 155,610: –: – |
| | 11/4 | *Spierdijk* | Malacca | 11.85 | 370,000 | 159,932: 10: – |
| | | | | Total | 1,600,000 | 691,600: –: – |
| 1695 | 10/22 | *Prinseland* | Batavia | 11.85 | 500,000 | 216,125: –: – |
| | 10/23 | *Langewijk* | Batavia | 11.85 | 400,000 | 172,900: –: – |
| | 10/24 | *Oosthuizen* | Batavia | 11.85 | 400,000 | 172,900: –: – |
| | 10/27 | *Huis te Dieren* | Batavia | 11.85 | 400,000 | 172,900: –: – |
| | | | | Total | 1,700,000 | 734,825: –: – |
| 1696 | 10/11 | *Nierop* | Mallacca | 11.85 | 375,000 | 162,093: 15: – |
| | 10/12 | *Langewijk* | Mallacca | 11.85 | 375,000 | 162,093: 15: – |
| | 10/13 | *Schoonderloo* | Mallacca | 11.85 | 450,000 | 194,512: 10: – |
| | 10/15 | *Jerusalem* | Batavia | 11.85 | 168,700 | 72,920: 11: 8 |
| | | | | (11.85) | 281,300 | 121,590: 12: – |
| | | | | Total | 1,650,000 | 713,211: 3: 8 |
| 1697 | 10/28 | *Nieuwland* | Mallacca | 11.85 | 390,000 | 168,577: 10: – |
| | 10/29 | *Huis te Duine* | Mallacca | 11.85 | 450,000 | 194,512: 10: – |
| | 10/31 | *Schulp* | Mallacca | 11.85 | 300,000 | 129,675: –: – |
| | 10/31 | *Etersheen* | Mallacca | 11.85 | 460,000 | 198,835: –: – |
| | 11/1 | *Voetboog* | Batavia | (11.85) | 171,943 | 74,323: 8: 8 |
| | | | | 11.85 | 208,100 | 89,951: 4: 8 |
| | 11/3 | *Karthago* | Batavia | (11.85) | 488,050 | 210,840: 14: – |
| | | | | 11.85 | 31,950 | 13,811: 5: 3 |
| | | | | Total | 2,500,043 | 1,080,526: 12: 7 |
| 1698 | – | No N. J. | ②p. 542 | – | (2,937,900)[g] | – |

## Table 11: Continued

| Month/date | Vessel name [a] | Destination | Unit price[b] | Export quantity (catty)[c] | Export quantity (gulden)[d] |
|---|---|---|---|---|---|
| 1699 | — | No N. J. | ②p. 545 | — | (2,250,000) | — |
| 1700 | — | No N. J. | ②p. 550 | — | (1,496,900) | — |
| 1701 | — | No N. J. | ①p. 142 | — | (1,658,700) | — |
| 1702 | 11/5 | Diemen | Malacca | 12.84 | 300,000 | 140,070: –: – |
| | 11/6 | Westhoven | Malacca | (12.84) | 500,000 | 233,450: 13: 8 |
| | 11/7 | Concordia | Malacca | (12.84) | 123,053 | 57,453: 11: 8 |
| | | | | 12.84 | 361,247 | 168,665: 8: 12 |
| | 11/9 | Berkenrode | Batavia | 12.84 | 260,000 | 121,394: –: – |
| | | | Total | | 1,544,300 | 721,033: 13: 12 |
| 1703 | 10/26 | Taxisboom | Mallacca | 12.84 | 250,000 | 116,725: –: – |
| | 10/27 | Kiefhoek | Mallacca | (12.84) | 133,053 | 62,122: 11: 8 |
| | | | | 12.84 | 356,900 | 166,636: 12: 3 |
| | 10/28 | Brandenburg | Batavia | 12.84 | 400,000 | 186,760: –: – |
| | 10/30 | Ellemeet | Batavia | (12.84) | 490,000 | 228,781: 12: 8 |
| | | | Total | | 1,629,953 | 761,025: 16: 3 |
| 1704 | 10/14 | Lokhorst | Mallacca | 12.84 | 325,000 | 151,742: 10: – |
| | 10/15 | Popkenburg | Mallacca | 12.84 | 550,000 | 256,795: –: – |
| | 10/16 | Waarde | Mallacca | 12.84 | 550,000 | 256,795: –: – |
| | 10/18 | Kattendijk | Batavia | 12.84 | 404,422 | 188,825: 16: 8 |
| | | | Total | | 1,829,422 | 854,158: 6: 8 |
| 1705 | 11/2 | Bon | Batavia | 12.8 | 440,000 | 204,820: –: – |
| | 11/3 | Bredenhof | Batavia | 12.8 | 440,000 | 204,820: –: – |
| | 11/5 | Nieuwburg | Batavia | 12.8 | 400,000 | 186,200: –: – |
| | 11/6 | Prins | Batavia | 12.8 | 550,000 | 256,025: –: – |
| | | | Total | | 1,830,000 | 851,865: –: – |
| 1706 | 10/21 | Abbekerk | Malacca | 12.8 | 300,000 | 139,650: –: – |
| | 10/22 | Bredenhof | Malacca | 12.8 | 300,000 | 139,650: –: – |
| | 10/23 | Lokhorst | Malacca | 12.8 | 300,000 | 139,650: –: – |
| | 10/24 | Bellvliet | Batavia | 12.8 | 300,000 | 139,650: –: – |
| | 10/26 | Sloten | Batavia | 12.8 | 300,000 | 139,650: –: – |
| | | | Total | | 1,500,000 | 698,250: –: – |
| 1707 | 10/11 | Zoelen | Malacca | 12.8 | 400,000 | 186,200: –: – |
| | 10/12 | Venhuisen | Malacca | 12.8 | 400,000 | 186,200: –: – |
| | 10/13 | Haring | Malacca | 12.8 | 400,000 | 186,200: –: – |
| | 10/15 | Zuiderburg | Batavia | 12.8 | 300,000 | 139,650: –: – |
| | | | Total | | 1,500,000 | 698,250: –: – |

## Table 11: Continued

| Year | Month/date | Vessel name [a] | Destination | Unit price[b] | Export quantity (catty)[c] | Export quantity (gulden)[d] |
|---|---|---|---|---|---|---|
| 1708 | 10/30 | Haak | Malacca | 12.8 | 240,000 | 111,720: –: – |
| | 10/31 | Zoelen | Batavia | 12.8 | 290,000 | 134,995: –: – |
| | 11/2 | Baarzande | Batavia | 12.8 | 297,200 | 138,346: 12: – |
| | | | | Total | 827,200 | 385061: 12: – |
| 1709 | 10/12 | Korssloot | Malacca | 12.8 | 350,000 | 162,925: –: – |
| | 10/19 | Standvastigheid | Malacca | 12.8 | 400,000 | 186,200: –: – |
| | 10/20 | Berg | Batavia | 12.8 | 400,000 | 186,200: –: – |
| | 10/22 | Arion | Batavia | 12.8 | 350,000 | 162,925: –: – |
| | | | | Total | 1,500,000 | 698,250: –: – |
| 1710 | 11/10 | Lokhorst | Batavia | 12.8 | 350,000 | 162,925: –: – |
| | 11/10 | Nederhoven | Malacca | 12.8 | 350,000 | 192,925: –: – |
| | 11/10 | Bon | Batavia | 12.8 | 350,000 | 192,925: –: – |
| | 11/10 | Samson | Malacca | 12.8 | 450,000 | 209,475: –: – |
| | | | | Total | 1,500,000 | 698,250: –: – |
| 1711 | 10/31 | Lokhorst | Batavia | 12.8 | 250,000 | 116,375: –: – |
| | 10/31 | Bredenhof | Batavia | 12.8 | 250,000 | 116,375: –: – |
| | 10/31 | Raadhuis | Batavia | 12.8 | 250,000 | 116,375: –: – |
| | 10/31 | Rijnestein | Batavia | 12.8 | 250,000 | 116,375: –: – |
| | | | | Total | 1,000,000 | 465,500: –: – |
| 1712 | 10/20 | Nederhoven | Malacca | 12.85 | 200,000 | 93,450: –: – |
| | 10/20 | Abbekerk | Malacca | 12.85 | 200,000 | 93,450: –: – |
| | 10/20 | Ouwerkerk | Malacca | 12.85 | 198,600 | 92,795: 17: – |
| | 10/20 | Charlois | Batavia | 12.85 | 148,300 | 69,293: 3: 8 |
| | | | | Total | 746,900 | 348,989: –: 8 |
| 1713 | | No N. J. | ④Vol. 7. p. 50 | 13.15 | (1,000,000) | (47,750: –: –) |
| 1714 | 10/25 | Strijkebolle | Malacca | 13.25 | 270,000 | 129,937: 10: – |
| | 10/26 | Zanderhoef | Batavia | 13.25 | 390,000 | 187,687: 10: – |
| | 10/28 | Arion | Batavia | 13.25 | 390,000 | 187,687: 10: – |
| | | | | Total | 1,050,000 | 505,312: –: – |
| 1715 | 10/14 | Risdam | Malacca | 13.25 | 385,000 | 185,281: 5: – |
| | 10/15 | Sleewijk | Batavia | 13.25 | 385,000 | 185,281: 5: – |
| | 10/17 | Zanderhoef | Batavia | 13.25 | 380,000 | 182,875: –: – |
| | | | | Total | 1,150,000 | 553,437: 10: – |
| 1716 | 11/2 | Rijksdorp | Batavia | 14.84 | 650,000 | 348,985: –: – |
| | 11/3 | Ternisse | Batavia | 14.84 | 650,000 | 348,985: –: – |
| | | | | Total | 1,300,000 | 697,970: –: – |

## Table 11: Continued

| Year | Month/date | Vessel name [a] | Destination | Unit price[b] | Export quantity (catty)[c] | Export quantity (gulden)[d] |
|---|---|---|---|---|---|---|
| 1717 | 10/23 | Noordbeek | Batavia | 14.84 | 650,000 | 350,350: −: − |
| | 10/24 | Luchtenburg | Batavia | 14.84 | 450,000 | 242,550: −: − |
| | | | | | 200,000 | 107,697: 6: 8 |
| | | | | Total | 1,300,000 | 700,597: 6: 8 |
| 1718 | 10/12 | Meeroog | Batavia | 14.84 | 450,000 | 242,550: −: − |
| | | | | (14.84) | 200,000 | 108,117: 6: 8 |
| | 10/13 | Ternisse | Batavia | 14.84 | 450,000 | 242,500: −: − |
| | | | | (14.84) | 200,000 | 108,117: 6: 8 |
| | | | | Total | 1,300,000 | 701,334: 13: − |
| 1719 | | No ships | − | − | − | − |
| 1720 | | No N. J. | ④Vol. 7. p. 526 | (14.84) | (1,300,000) | − |
| 1721 | 11/7 | Bantveld | Batavia | 14.84 | 140,000 | 75,460: −: − |
| | | | | (14.84) | 510,000 | 275,699: 4: − |
| | 11/8 | Boekenrode | Batavia | 14.84 | 100,000 | 53,900: −: − |
| | | | | (14.84) | 550,000 | 297,322: 13: 8 |
| | 11/9 | Valkenbos | Batavia | 14.84 | 160,000 | 86,240: −: − |
| | | | | (14.84) | 490,000 | 264,887: 9: − |
| | | | | Total | 1,950,000 | 1,053,509: 6: 8 |
| 1722 | 10/29 | Hillrgonda | Batavia | 14.84 | 50,000 | 26,950: −: − |
| | | | | (14.84) | 600,000 | 324,828: −: − |
| | | | | Total | 650,000 | 351,778: −: − |
| 1723 | 10/17 | Cornelia | Batavia | 14.84 | 400,000 | 215,600: −: − |
| | | | | (14.84) | 120,000 | 65,094: 17: 8 |
| | 10/18 | Appollonia | Batavia | | 518,400 | 281,209: 17: − |
| | | | | Total | 1,038,400 | 561,904: 14: 8 |
| 1724 | 11/4 | Kasteel van Woerden | Batavia | 14.84 | 430,200 | 231,877: 16: − |
| | | | | (14.84) | 170,000 | 92,339: 16: 8 |
| | | | | Total | 600,200 | 324,217: 12: 8 |
| 1725 | 10/24 | Wapen van Hoorn | Batavia | 14.84 | 525,000 | 282,975: −: − |
| | 10/25 | Kasteel van Woerden | Batavia | 14.84 | 525,000 | 282,975: −: − |
| | | | | Total | 1,050,000 | 565,950: −: − |
| 1726 | 10/14 | Wapen van Hoorn | Batavia | 14.84 | 420,000 | 226,380: −: − |
| | 10/15 | Adelaar | Batavia | 14.84 | 440,000 | 237,160: −: − |
| | | | | Total | 860,000 | 463,540: −: − |

Table 11: Continued

| Month/date | | Vessel name [a] | Destination | Unit price[b] | Export quantity (catty)[c] | Export quantity (gulden)[d] |
|---|---|---|---|---|---|---|
| 1727 | 11/2 | Meerlust | Batavia | 14.84 | 450,000 | 242,550: –: – |
| | 11/3 | Jacoba | Batavia | 14.84 | 550,000 | 296,450: –: – |
| | | | Total | | 1,000,000 | 539,000: –: – |
| 1728 | – | No N. J. | ④Vol. 8. p. 227 | – | (960,000) | – |
| 1729 | – | No N. J. | ④Vol. 9. p. 78 | – | (1,000,000) | – |
| 1730 | – | No N. J. | ④Vol. 9. p. 210 | – | (830,000) | – |
| 1731 | 10/20 | Blijdorp | Batavia | 14.84 | 444,000 | 239,316: –: – |
| 1732 | 11/6 | Landskroon | Batavia | 14.84 | 490,600 | 264,433: 8: – |
| | 11/7 | Huis te Marquette | Batavia | 14.84 | 500,200 | 269,607: 16: – |
| | | | Total | | 990,800 | 534,041: 4: – |
| 1733 | 10/26 | Huis te Foreest | Batavia | 14.84 | 450,200 | 286,512: 17: – |
| | 10/27 | Huis te Marquette | Batavia | 14.84 | 361,120 | 230,389: 18: 1 |
| | | | – | | 100,000 | 52,274: 5: – |
| | | | Total | | 911,320 | 569,177: –: 1 |
| 1734 | 10/15 | Huis den Eult | Batavia | 14.84 | 520,000 | 300,209: 1: 9 |
| | 10/16 | Popkensburg | Batavia | 14.84 | 500,000 | 288,663: 5: 8 |
| | | | Total | | 1,020,000 | 588,872: 7: 1 |
| 1735 | 11/4 | Popkensburg | Batavia | 14.84 | 630,000 | 382,785: 12: 13 |
| 1736 | – | No N. J. | ④Vol. 9. p. 816 | | (1,070,000) | – |
| 1737 | 10/12 | Abbekerk | Batavia | 14.84 | 520,000 | 280,416: 7: 7 |
| | 10/13 | Enkhuizen | Batavia | 14.84 | 530,000 | 285,808: 19: 15 |
| | | | Total | | 1,050,000 | 566,225: 7: 6 |
| 1738 | – | No N. J. | ⑤ p. 303 | – | (1,050,000) | – |
| 1739 | 10/21 | Popkensburg | Batavia | 14.84 | 500,000 | 269,500: –: – |
| | 10/22 | Arnestijn | Batavia | 14.84 | 500,000 | 269,500: –: – |
| | | | Total | | 1,000,000 | 539,000: –: – |
| 1740 | 11/8 | Arnestijn | Batavia | 14.84 | 450,000 | 242,550: –: – |
| | 11/8 | Krabbendijke | Batavia | 14.84 | 550,000 | 296,450: –: – |
| | | | Total | | 1,000,000 | 539,000: –: – |
| 1741 | 10/28 | Krabbendijke | Batavia | 14.84 | 500,000 | 269,500: –: – |
| | 10/29 | Reigersdaal | Batavia | 14.84 | 500,000 | 269,500: –: – |
| | | | Total | | 1,000,000 | 539,000: –: – |

*Table 11: Continued*

| Month/date | | Vessel name [a] | Destination | Unit price[b] | Export quantity (catty)[c] | Export quantity (gulden)[d] | | |
|---|---|---|---|---|---|---|---|---|
| 1742 | 10/17 | *Gunterstijn* | Batavia | 14.84 | 550,000 | 296,450: | –: | – |
| | 10/18 | *Westhoven* | Batavia | 14.84 | 450,000 | 242,550: | –: | – |
| | | | | Total | 1,000,000 | 539,000: | –: | – |
| 1743 | 11/4 | *Beukesteijn* | Batavia | 14.84 | 400,000 | 215,600: | –: | – |
| | 11/5 | *Polanen* | Batavia | 14.84 | 400,000 | 215,600: | –: | – |
| | | | | Total | 800,000 | 431,200: | –: | – |
| 1744 | 11/1 | *Ruyven* | Batavia | 12.35 | 300,000 | 76,381: | 12: | – |
| | 11/2 | *Heuvel* | Batavia | 12.35 | 300,000 | 76,381: | 16: | – |
| | | | | Total | 600,000 | 152,763: | 8: | – |
| 1745 | 12/28 | *Kleverskerk* | Batavia | 12.35 | 340,000 | 86,565: | 16: | 4 |
| | 12/29 | *Hofwegen* | Batavia | 12.35 | 330,000 | 83,487: | 4: | – |
| | 12/30 | *Vrijheid* | Batavia | 12.35 | 330,000 | 83,487: | 4: | – |
| | | | | Total | 1,000,000 | 253,540: | 4: | 4 |
| 1746 | 11/1 | *Nieuwstad* | Batavia | 12.35 | 370,000 | 94,174: | –: | – |
| | 11/2 | *Westhoven* | Batavia | 12.35 | 370,000 | 94,174: | –: | – |
| | 11/3 | *Vrijheid* | Batavia | 12.35 | 360,000 | 91,704: | –: | – |
| | | | | Total | 1,100,000 | 280,052: | –: | – |
| 1747 | 10/21 | *Westkapelle* | Malacca/ Negapatnam | 12.35 | 600,000 | 151,618: | –: | – |
| | 10/22 | *Batavier* | Batavia | 12.35 | 200,000 | 51,182: | –: | – |
| | 10/23 | *Maarsseveen* | Batavia | 12.35 | 300,000 | 76,282: | –: | – |
| | | | | Total | 1,100,000 | 279,082: | –: | – |
| 1748 | 10/11 | *Schellag* | Malacca/ Negapatnam | 12.35 | 330,000 | 87,110: | –: | – |
| | | | | 12.35 | 220,000 | 54,340: | –: | – |
| | 10/12 | *Jager* | Batavia | 12.35 | 550,000 | 141,450: | –: | – |
| | | | | Total | 1,100,000 | 282,900: | –: | – |
| 1749 | 10/28 | *Witsburg* | Malacca/Houglij | 12.35 | 200,000 | 49,400: | –: | – |
| | 10/29 | *Oudkarspel* | Malacca/ Negapatnam | 12.35 | 600,000 | 148,200: | –: | – |
| | 10/30 | *Geldermalsen* | Batavia | 12.35 | 300,000 | 74,100: | –: | – |
| | | | | Total | 1,100,000 | 271,700: | –: | – |
| 1750 | 10/17 | *Deunisveld* | Malacca/Bengal | 18 | 230,000 | 82,800: | –: | – |
| | 10/18 | *Haarlem* | Malacca/ Negapatnam | 18 | 570,000 | 205,200: | –: | – |
| | 10/19 | *Zuiderburg* | Batavia | 18 | 300,000 | 108,000: | –: | – |
| | | | | Total | 1,100,000 | 396,000: | –: | – |

## Table 11: Continued

| Month/date | Vessel name[a] | Destination | Unit price[b] | Export quantity (catty)[c] | Export quantity (gulden)[d] |
|---|---|---|---|---|---|
| **1751** 11/5 | Sloten | Malaca /Coromandel | 18 | 500,000 | 180,000: –: – |
| 11/6 | Elswoud | Batavia | 18 | 300,000 | 108,000: –: – |
| 11/7 | Pasgeld | Batavia | 18 | 300,000 | 108,000: –: – |
| | | | Total | 1,100,000 | 396,000: –: – |
| **1752** 10/25 | Hof D'uno | Malacca/ Negapatnam | 18 | 450,000 | 162,000: –: – |
| 10/26 | Bosschenhove | Batavia | 18 | 100,000 | 36,000: –: – |
| | | | | 550,000 | 198,000: –: – |
| | | | Total | 1,100,000 | 396,000: –: – |
| **1753** 10/15 | Vlietlust | Batavia | 18 | 550,000 | 198,000: –: – |
| 10/15 | Witsburg | Batavia | 18 | 550,000 | 198,000: –: – |
| | | | Total | 1,100,000 | 396,000: –: – |
| **1754** 11/3 | Ruiteveld | Batavia | 18 | 550,000 | 198,000: –: – |
| 11/4 | Vlietlust | Batavia | 18 | 550,000 | 198,000: –: – |
| | | | Total | 1,100,000 | 396,000: –: – |
| **1755** 10/– | Radermacher | Batavia | 18 | 550,000 | 198,000: –: – |
| 10/– | Amelisweert | Batavia | 18 | 550,000 | 198,000: –: – |
| | | | Total | 1,100,000 | 396,000: –: – |
| **1756** 10/12 | Radermacher | Batavia | 18 | 550,000 | 198,000: –: – |
| 10/13 | Keukenhof | Batavia | 18 | 550,000 | 198,000: –: – |
| | | | Total | 1,100,000 | 396,000: –: – |
| **1757** 10/31 | Admiraal de Ruyter | Batavia | 18 | 550,000 | 198,000: –: – |
| 11/1 | Tulpenburg | Batavia | 18 | 550,000 | 198,000: –: – |
| | | | Total | 1,100,000 | 396,000: –: – |
| **1758** 10/15 | Leimuiden | Batavia | 18 | 700,000 | 252,000: –: – |
| **1759** 11/7 | Drie Papegaaien | Batavia | 18 | 500,000 | 180,000: –: – |
| 11/8 | Zuid Beveland | Batavia | 18 | 500,000 | 180,000: –: – |
| 11/9 | Leimuiden | Batavia | 18 | 500,000 | 180,000: –: – |
| | | | Total | 1,500,000 | 540,000: –: – |
| **1760** 10/27 | Keukenhof | Batavia | 18 | 550,000 | 198,000: –: – |
| 10/28 | Zuid Beveland | Batavia | 18 | 550,000 | 198,000: –: – |
| | | | Total | 1,100,000 | 396,000: –: – |
| **1761** 10/16 | Boschenhove | Batavia | 18 | 550,000 | 198,000: –: – |
| 10/17 | Duinenburg | Batavia | 18 | 550,000 | 198,000: –: – |
| | | | Total | 1,100,000 | 396,000: –: – |

## Table 11: Continued

| | Month/date | Vessel name [a] | Destination | Unit price[b] | Export quantity (catty)[c] | Export quantity (gulden)[d] |
|---|---|---|---|---|---|---|
| 1762 | 11/4 | *Overnes* | Batavia | 18 | 550,000 | 198,000: –: – |
| | 11/5 | *Burg* | Batavia | 18 | 550,000 | 198,000: –: – |
| | | | | Total | 1,100,000 | 396,000: –: – |
| 1763 | 10/25 | *Enkhuizen* | Batavia | 18 | 550,000 | 198,000: –: – |
| | 10/26 | *Leimuiden* | Batavia | 18 | 550,000 | 198,000: –: – |
| | | | | Total | 1,100,000 | 396,000: –: – |
| 1764 | 10/14 | *Enkhuizen* | Batavia | 18 | 550,000 | 198,000: –: – |
| | 10/15 | *Zuid Beveland* | Batavia | 18 | 550,000 | 198,000: –: – |
| | | | | Total | 1,100,000 | 396,000: –: – |
| 1765 | 11/3 | *Burch* | Batavia | 18 | 600,000 | 216,000: –: – |
| 1766 | 10/22 | *Burch* | Batavia | 18 | 500,000 | 180,000: –: – |
| | 10/23 | *Landskroon* | Batavia | 18 | 500,000 | 180,000: –: – |
| | | | | Total | 1,000,000 | 360,000: –: – |
| 1767 | 10/12 | *Verdenhof* | Batavia | 18 | 650,000 | 234,000: –: – |
| 1768 | – | No N. J. | ①[h] | – | (697,500) | – |
| | | | ⑤ | – | (627,500) | – |
| 1769 | – | No N. J. | ① | – | (1,322,500) | – |
| | | | ⑤ | – | (1,322,500) | – |
| 1770 | – | No N. J. | ① | – | (697,500) | – |
| | | | ⑤ | – | – | – |
| 1771 | – | No N. J. | ① | – | (1,242,500) | – |
| | | | ⑤ | – | (1,142,500) | – |
| 1772 | – | No N. J. | ① | – | (600,000) | – |
| | | | ⑤ | – | (530,000) | – |
| 1773 | – | No N. J. | ① | – | (1,340,000) | – |
| | | | ⑤ | – | (1,270,000) | – |
| 1774 | 10/23 | *Blijenburg* | Batavia | 18 | 450,000 | 133650: –: – |
| | 10/24 | *Geinwens* | Batavia | 18 | 450,000 | 133650: –: – |
| | | | | Total | 900,000 | 267300: –: – |
| 1775 | 10/14 | *Stavenisse* | Batavia | 18 | 600,000 | 178200: –: – |
| 1776 | 11/15 | *Zeeduin* | Batavia | 18 | 600,000 | 178200: –: – |
| | 11/15 | *Stavenisse* | Batavia | 18 | 600,000 | 178200: –: – |
| | | | | Total | 1,200,000 | 356400: –: – |

64

*Table 11: Continued*

| Month/date | | Vessel name [a] | Destination | Unit price[b] | Export quantity (catty)[c] | Export quantity (gulden)[d] |
|---|---|---|---|---|---|---|
| 1777 | 10/17 | Rodenrijs | Batavia | 18 | 450,000 | 133650: -: - |
| | 10/20 | Zeeduin | Batavia | 18 | 450,000 | 133,650: -: - |
| | | | | Total | 900,000 | 267,300: -: - |
| 1778 | 11/7 | Huis te Spijk | Batavia | 18 | 450,000 | 133,650: -: - |
| | | | | | 25,000 | 5,177: 19: - |
| | 11/8 | Rodenrijs | Batavia | 18 | 450,000 | 133,650: -: - |
| | | | | | 25,000 | 5,177: 19: - |
| | | | | Total | 950,000 | 277,655: 18: - |
| 1779 | 10/28 | Rodenrijs | Batavia | 18 | 450,000 | 133,650: -: - |
| | 10/29 | Huis te Spijk | Batavia | 18 | 450,000 | 133,650: -: - |
| | | | | Total | 900,000 | 267,300: -: - |
| 1780 | 10/16 | Kanaän | Batavia | 18 | 450,000 | 133,650: -: - |
| | 10/17 | Mars | Batavia | 18 | 450,000 | 133,650: -: - |
| | | | | Total | 900,000 | 267,300: -: - |
| 1781 | 11/5 | Mars | Batavia | 18 | 650,000 | 193,050: -: - |
| 1782 | - | No ships | - | - | - | - |
| 1783 | 10/25 | Trompenburg | Batavia | 18 | 560,000 | 166,320: -: - |
| 1784 | 11/21 | Ouwerkerk | Batavia | 18 | 500,000 | 148,500: -: - |
| 1785 | 10/22 | Schelde | Batavia | 18 | 630,000 | 187,110: -: - |
| 1786 | 10/10 | Arenhorn | Batavia | 18 | 565,000 | 167,805: -: - |
| | 10/11 | Albasserdam | Batavia | 18 | 685,000 | 203,445: -: - |
| | | | | Total | 1,250,000 | 371,250: -: - |
| 1787 | 10/29 | Rozenburg | Batavia | 18 | 515,000 | 152,955: -: - |
| | 10/30 | Zeeland | Batavia | 18 | 615,000 | 182,655: -: - |
| | | | | Total | 1,130,000 | 335,610: -: - |
| 1788 | 11/20 | St. Laurens | Batavia | 18 | 615,000 | 182,655: -: - |
| | 11/20 | Rozenburg | Batavia | 18 | 515,000 | 152,955: -: - |
| | | | | Total | 1,130,000 | 335,610: -: - |
| 1789 | 11/10 | Recht door Zee | Batavia | 18 | 515,000 | 152,955: -: - |
| | 11/10 | St. Laurens | Batavia | 18 | 615,000 | 182,655: -: - |
| | | | | Total | 1,130,000 | 335,610: -: - |
| 1790 | 11/6 | Zuiderburg | Batavia | 18 | 580,000 | 172,260: -: - |

## Table 11: Continued

| Year | Month/date | Vessel name [a] | Destination | Unit price[b] | Export quantity (catty)[c] | Export quantity (gulden)[d] |
|---|---|---|---|---|---|---|
| 1791 | — | No ships | — | — | — | — |
| 1792 | 11/3 | Erfprins | Batavia | 18 | 600,000 | 178,200: —: — |
| 1793 | 10/23 | Erfprins | Batavia | 18 | 552,000 | 163,944: —: — |
| 1794 | 11/1 | Erfprins | Batavia | 18 | 600,000 | 178,200: —: — |
| 1795 | — | No ships | — | — | — | — |
| 1796 | 11/1 | Westkappelle | Batavia | 18 | 540,000 | 160,380: —: — |
| 1797 | — | Eliza | Batavia | 18 | 140,000 | 41,500: —: — |
| 1798 | — | Eliza[i] | Batavia | 18 | 300,000 | 89,100: —: — |
| 1799 | 10/18 | Franklin | Batavia | 18 | 250,000 | 74,250: —: — |
| 1800 | 11/1 | Massachusetts | Batavia | 18 | 630,000 | 187,110: —: — |
| 1801 | 10/20 | Margaretta | Batavia | – | 228,200 | 68,269: 12: — |
| 1802 | 10/12 | Mathilda Maria | Batavia | 18 | 150,000 | 44,550: —: — |
| | 10/12 | Samuel Smith | Batavia | 18 | 620,000 | 184,140: —: — |
| | | | | Total | 770,000 | 228,690: —: — |
| 1803 | 10/19 | Rebecca | Batavia | 18 | 730,000 | 216,810: —: — |
| 1804 | – | No N. J. | – | – | (852,000)[j] | — |
| 1805 | 11/9 | Resolutie | Batavia | 18 | 630,000 | 187,110: —: — |

Notes:

a. Vessel names have been drawn from the *Generale Missiven* (See f. ④ below for the full title of this document) and Bruijn, J. R., F. S. Gaastra and I. Schoffer (eds) (1979), *Dutch–Asiatic Shipping in the 17th and 18th Centuries*, 3 vols, The Hague: Nijhoff. Some of them are spelt differently from those recorded in shipping bills of the *Negotie Journalen*. For example, 's' becomes 'z', 'ck' becomes 'k', 'c' becomes 'k' and so on.

b. The unit price is in tael per picol (100 kin).

1 tael = 10 monme in silver, 1 picol = 100 kin = 100 catty

c. The quantity is expressed in catty. 1 catty = 1 kin, 1 picol = 100 kin.

The quantity is expressed in pond in the *Negotie Journalen* of the Dutch Factory from 1666 but figures have been converted and expressed in catty in the above list for the purpose of comparison.

| | |
|---|---|
| 1666–1697 | 1 picol = 125 pond |
| 1698–1781 | 1 picol = 120 pond |
| 1783 onward | 1 picol = 120 7/8 pond |

*Table 11: Continued*

d. 1 gulden = 20 stuiver, 1 stuiver = 16 pening
   Before 1665        1 tael = 57 stuiver
   1666 –1743       1 tael = 70 stuiver
   1744–circa 1773   1 tael = 40 stuiver
   1774 onward     1 tael = 33 stuiver

Export quantities in the above list are net exports from 1646 to 1655, total exports from 1656 to 1749, and net exports from 1750 to 1805.

e. ⊙ denotes that the figure is based on an extant shipping bill (*facturen*) as the relevant *Negotie Journalen* are missing.

f. "No N. J." denotes that the relevant *Negotie Journalen* are missing and other historical materials/documents have been relied upon.

The historical materials/documents referred to are shown by circled numbers and page numbers in the 'Destination' column. The circled numbers correspond to the following reference materials/documents.

Unit prices and export quantities in brackets ( ) have been calculated by the author.

① Kyushu Bunkashi Kenkyūjo Shiryōshū Kankōkai (ed.), *Nagasaki jikki nendairoku* (The true chronicles of Nagasaki).

② Van Dam, p. , *Beschryvinge van de Oostindische Compagnie,* Tweede boek, deel I, F.W. Stapel (ed.), The Hague: Martinus Nijhof, 1931.

③ Tominaga Makita (tr.), *17-seiki nichiran kōshō shi* (A history of the Japanese–Dutch relations in the 17th century), Nara: Yōtokusha, 1956, which is a translation of Oskar Nachod (1897), *Die Beziehungen der Niederländischen Ostindischen Kompagnie zu Japan im siebzehnten Jahrhundert,* 1897.

④ *Generale Missiven van Gouverneurs-Generaal en Randen aan Heren XVII der Vernigde Oostindishe Compagnie,* Vol. 1-8, Coolhaas, W. Ph. (1965-85), Vol. 9, Van Goor, J. (ed.), Vol. 11, Schooneveld-Oosterling, J. E. (ed.), The Hague. 1997.

⑤ Kuiper,J. F., *Japan en de Buiteuwereld in de 18e Eeuw,* The Hague: Martinus Nijhof, 1921.

⑥ Saitō Agu, *Zūfu to Nihon* (H. Doef and Japan): Kōbunkan, 1923.

g. Of which 437,900 kin were received prior to this year. The actual quantity transacted in this year was 2.5 million kin.

h. 70,000 kin of copper substituted for gold were included in the quantity of regular copper export in 1768 and from 1770 in *Nagasaki jikki nendairoku.* Consequently, there is no separate data in the *Negotie Journalen.*

For copper export quantities from 1768 to 1773, figures from both ① *Nagasaki jikki nendairoku* (pp. 235–238) and ⑤ *Japan en de Buiteuwereld in de 18e Eeuw* (pp. 304–305) are listed here.

i. After this year, the *Negotie Journalen* in some years have no record of vessel names. This is probably because the company chartered and dispatched American vessels to Japan. For this reason, some of the vessel names have been drawn from ⑥ Saitō Agu, *Zūfu to Nihon* (H. Doef and Japan).

j. In this year, The *Maria Susanna* and the *Gezina Antoinette* arrived and exported the amount of copper listed here.

⑥ Saitō Agu, *Zūfu to Nihon,* pp. 41–42.

Table 12: *Average copper export and import over five-year periods, 1646–1680*

| | Export from Japan (pond) | Import to the Netherlands (pond) | Sales in Surat (pond) |
|---|---|---|---|
| 1640–50 | 469,784[a] | 28,648 | 39,974 |
| 1651–55 | 445,925 | 14,488 | 151,253 |
| 1656–60 | 1,368,315 | 378,816 | 272,168 |
| 1661–65 | 2,060,925 | 336,000 | 408,493 |
| 1666–70 | 1,447,713 | 383,450 | 326,930 |
| 1671–75 | 2,040,800 | 618,753 | 545,534 |
| 1676–80 | 2,554,600 | 257,922 | 660,267 |

Source: Glamann, *Dutch–Asiatic Trade 1620–1740*, The Hague: Martinus Nijhof, 1958, p. 175.

Note:

a. Period average excluding 1648.

by the Japanese. The Portuguese, Japan's main trading partner at that time, called it the *pankado* system.

According to *Kiyō gundan* (a collection of records of the Nagasaki region), imported goods were purchased by direct dealings (i.e. by auction) after the abolition of the *itowappu* system; the resultant rise in the prices of imports inevitably increased the value of transactions. Since silver was the primary export commodity exchanged for these imports, this situation led to a major outflow of silver from Japan. It is said that the *shishō kamotsu shishō* was established in 1672 partly in order to stop this silver drain.[19] Under this system, which was applicable to all imports, Nagasaki offered to buy imports at certain prices *en bloc* if their offers were accepted by foreign merchants. The Dutch called this system *taxatie handel* (appraisal trade).

By the way, much of the outflow of silver during the direct dealings period was carried by the Chinese fleet; the amount of silver exported by the Dutch fleet was relatively small. Rather than silver, it was the amount of copper exports that increased notably during this period. Table 12 and Figures 5–1 and 5–2 show the rapid increase in the volume of copper exports from the latter half of the 1650s. This was due to the Dutch policy of exporting more copper than silver.

The export of gold (*koban*) was authorized in 1664, while the export of silver, a principal export commodity at the time, was banned four years later in 1668. Permission to resume silver exports was given to the Chinese fleet in 1672[20], but the Dutch declined the shogunate's offer for resumption and did not export silver from Japan again for the rest of the

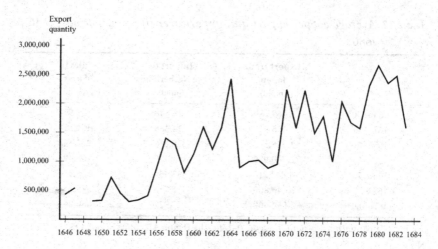

*Figure 5-1: Copper export quantities, 1646–1683*

Source: See note 17.

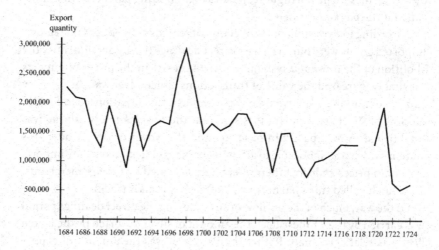

*Figure 5-2: Copper export quantities, 1684–1724*

early modern period. The export of copper was also banned at the same time as the proclamation of the silver export embargo in 1668.[21] This was because the copper coin (*Kanei-tsūhō*) mintage project was commenced again in that year. However, as soon as the ban order was issued, copper merchants petitioned the government to allow copper exports. The ban was removed in the following year without actually being enforced.[22] The petition of copper merchants to the government was certainly one reason for the removal of the ban, but there were other major factors. One of these factors was the dramatic increase in domestic copper production from the booming copper mining industry in contrast to the declining gold and silver mining industry in the latter half of the seventeenth century.[23] There was also a lack of export commodities that could replace silver and copper if the export of both of them were banned; the Dutch strongly hoped to export a lot of copper rather than silver at that time.

Table 11 shows two trends in the price movement of copper from the 1650s. In one trend, the price of copper reached 11.4 tael per picol in 1656, gradually rose from then on and peaked at 13.4 tael per picol in 1668, when the Kanbun-era coinage project commenced. The price then declined until the end of the seventeenth century. The other trend shows that the price fluctuated subtly every year till 1675, then stabilized from 1676, maintaining a certain level for several years at a time. The reason for this stabilization was that the shogunate government officially appointed sixteen merchants to engage in the copper trade in 1678, establishing for these merchants a monopolistic system of copper export.[24] As domestic copper production expanded in the latter half of the seventeenth century, new players began to enter the copper trade. A group of existing copper merchants, led by Izumiya, who had previously been selling copper to foreigners, petitioned the government to bar these irregular traders from doing business.[25] The government obliged. This system was convenient for the government as it was able to control the copper trade through these official merchants.

The shogunate government increased its control of foreign trade by instituting the aforementioned *shishō kamotsu shishō* in 1672. Faced with a profit slide, the Dutch submitted a petition for improving the system to the government in 1675. The petition did not produce any results, so the governor general of the Dutch East Indies sent a letter to the shogun asking for trade reform; it was sent to Japan in 1683 and delivered to the shogunate when the Dutch visited Edo in the following year.[26] The *shishō kamotsu shishō* was abolished and replaced by the *gojōdaka* system in 1685. The *itowappu* system was revived at the same time, but the conditions of this round of the *itowappu* system were quite different from those prior to its abolishment in 1655. Since raw silk was no longer a major import commodity, its pricing did not influence the prices of other imported goods. On the other hand, the *gojōdaka* system introduced annual limits for foreign trade transactions and set the annual trade limit for the Chinese fleet to 6,000 kanme in silver and the limit for the Dutch fleet to 50,000 *ryō* in gold.[27] The Dutch limit of 50,000 *ryō* translates to about 1,050,000 gulden. Nachod estimates that the volume of

Dutch trade under the *shishō kamotsu shishō* was between 1.3 million and 1.5 million gulden.[28] Based on these figures, Dutch trade would have decreased by a further 450,000 to 250,000 gulden under the *gojōdaka* system.

There are many theories about how these maximum values were set by the government. One argues that they were worked out according to exportable quantities of copper.[29] Another argues that they were based on past values of silver exports by the Chinese and gold exports by the Dutch during the *shishō kamotsu shishō* period (1672–1685).[30] Looking at the history of copper exports by the Dutch around that time, the total quantity of copper exports for the thirteen years under the *shishō kamotsu shishō* system was 26,583,326 kin, which equates to an annual average of 2,044,871 kin. From 1679 to 1686, the quantity of copper exports remained over 2 million kin per year and declined to around 1.5 million kin per year from 1687. On the other hand, camphor was not exported in 1686 and the volume of export from then on remained lower than the pre-1685 level. Gold (*koban*) exports fluctuated independently of the *gojōdaka* system; while 40,000 *ryō* of *koban* were exported temporarily in 1684, the volume of export from then on was quite small.

This comparison of exports shows that the export volume of major commodities declined after the introduction of the *gojōdaka* system. A reduction in the volume of the copper export was especially notable. It appears that the export of copper was regulated, or rather that the volume of the copper export that had increased in the latter half of the *shishō kamotsu shishō* period was brought down to the previous level.

## The copper trade at the end of seventeenth century

Copper exports from Japan were at their highest level at the end of the seventeenth century. This was because Japan's copper production peaked at that time. As the domestic copper production expanded, copper prices began to exhibit a downward trend from the 1670s.[31] The *gojōdaka* system introduced in 1685 placed limits on the value of the trade that the Chinese and Dutch fleets could conduct per year. It led both to rising prices of imported goods due to short supply and an increase in the incidence of the *nukeni* (smuggling) of imports between foreigners and the Japanese through illegal channels.[32] It was hoped that provision would be made for legal transactions outside of the *gojōdaka* system. An oversupply of copper to Nagasaki also became a problem at the end of the seventeenth century.

For these reasons, a *dō-shiromono-gae* (copper substitution trade) system was set up in 1695. It allowed all payments for imported goods outside of the *gojōdaka* limits to be settled in copper. This resulted in a rapid increase in

*Table 13: Copper substitution trade recorded in trade books, 1696–1703*

| | Vessel name | | Export quantity (pond) | Export quantity (kin) | Export value (gulden) |
|---|---|---|---|---|---|
| 1796 | Jerusalem | | 351,625 | 281,300 | 121,590: 12: – |
| 1697 | Karthgo | | 214,928¾ | 171,943 | 74,323: 8: 8 |
| | | | 610,062½ | 488,050 | 210,840: 14: – |
| | | Total | 824,991¼ | 659,993 | 285,164: 2: 8 |
| 1702 | Westhoven | | 600,000 | 500,000 | 233,450: 13: 8 |
| | Concordia | | 147,663½ | 123,053 | 57,453: 11: 8 |
| | | Total | 747,663½ | 623,100 | 290,904: 5: – |
| 1703 | Kiefhoek | | 159,663½ | 133,053 | 62,122: 11: 8 |
| | Ellement | | 588,000 | 490,000 | 228,781: 12: 8 |
| | | Total | 747,663½ | 613,053 | 290,904: 4: – |

Source: *Negotie Journalen* 1620–37, *Archief Japan*, No.880–883, ARA.

copper exports. A petition for the authorization of copper substitution was initially submitted to the government by Chaya Kyūka, a Kyoto merchant, in 1694.[33] However, authorization was actually issued to Fushimiya Shirobē, an Edo merchant with a strong connection to Yanagisawa Yoshiyasu, the grand chamberlain (*sobayōnin*).[34] The grand chamberlain was an assistant to the shogun who acted as a liaison between the shogun and senior councilors (*rodū*); this role gradually came to have a great political influence within the shogunate government.

Fushimiya was granted exclusive permission for copper substitution worth 1,000 kanme of silver in exchange for the payment of 1,500 *ryō* of gold as a levy to the government.[35] This authorization was given in August 1695 on the old calendar, October on the new calendar. Fushimiya began to negotiate with the Dutch in Nagasaki in December on the new calendar. Accordingly, there were no copper exports under the copper substitution system in 1695.

Fushimiya's substitution allowance of 1,000 kanme of silver was about 844,000 kin of copper, based on the then market price of 11.85 tael per picol. Two thirds of this allowance were allocated to Chinese trade and the remaining one third was allocated to Dutch trade.[36] The allocation to the Dutch trade amounted to about 280,000 kin of substitution copper. Table 13 shows the amounts of copper substitution recorded in the shipping bills of the Dutch ships. It shows that the amount exported in 1696 was almost the same as the allocated amount. Copper exports under the *gojōdaka* system and under the *dō-shiromono-gae* system were recorded separately in the Dutch shipping bills until 1703. Table 14 shows the amounts of copper substitution recorded in *Nagasaki jikki nendairoku* from 1695 to 1715. It also shows the quantities of substitute copper that were higher than the actual amounts of substitution.

In 1696, Fushimiya was again granted an exclusive allowance for 5,000 kanme of silver, but one third of this allowance was subsequently given to the town of Nagasaki. In the following year, authorization for trade worth 5,000 kanme in silver was awarded to the town of Nagasaki instead of Fushimiya. Of a total profit of about 45,000 *ryō* in gold, 10,000 *ryō* was distributed to Nagasaki and the rest was collected by the shogunate government.[37]

The shogunate government commenced the coinage of the Genroku *koban* in 1695, the year in which copper substitution was introduced, and, from 1697, tried to export this *koban* of lower grade than the Keichō *koban* at the same price as the Keichō *koban*. The Dutch adopted a policy to minimize the export of the new *koban* and encourage the export of more copper.[38] For this reason, the Dutch bought as much copper as was possible in 1696 and 1697, temporarily storing it in the factory of Dejima.[39] In 1698, the Dutch exported 2,937,900 kin of copper on board eight vessels.[40] It was the highest amount of copper exports per year by the Dutch in the history of the early modern period.

In 1698, the shogunate government limited annual copper exports to 6,402,000 kin for the Chinese and 2,500,000 kin for the Dutch, a total of 8,902,000 kin, as if to stop Japan's export from becoming too dependent on copper.[41] These limits were based on copper exports in the previous year. They aimed to stop the outflow of copper beyond those amounts.[42] However, as 1697 was the year in which exceptionally large amounts of copper were exported, it would have been very difficult to even reach these quotas from then on. The 1698 limits were aggregate quantities of copper exports under *gojōdaka* and copper substitution.[43] The nature of the copper substitution system changed at that point from a system which added an extra amount of copper to the *gojōdaka* limit of copper export to a system by which Nagasaki raised funds to pay levies to the shogunate government or to distribute silver to its citizens. Copper substitution was no longer attractive to the Dutch at all.

Transactions worth the Dutch's allocated annual limit of 800 kanme were carried out until 1703, but on the basis of 12.8 tael per picol (100 kin), which was the same price as the *gojōdaka* copper price (see Table 14). The copper substitution quota of 800 kanme was reached only three times after that: in 1707, 1709 and 1710. Conversely, there was no copper substitution at all in

Table 14: Breakdown of copper exports, 1695–1715

| | Copper exports under gojōdaka quota (kin) | Copper exports under shiromono-gae substitution (kin) | Total[a] |
|---|---|---|---|
| 1695 | 1,700,000.00 | 308,638.89 | 2,008,639 |
| 1696 | 1,370,000.00 | 462,962.96 | 1,832,963 |
| 1697 | 1,766,055.05 | 733,944.95 | 2,500,000 |
| 1698 | 1,795,154.19 | 704,845.81 | 2,500,000 |
| 1699 | 1,798,245.61 | 701,754.39 | 2,500,000 |
| 1700 | 574,065.69 | 672,834.31 | 1,246,900 |
| 1701 | 985,865.69 | 672,834.31 | 1,658,700 |
| 1702 | 873,921.63 | 670,578.37 | 1,544,500 |
| 1703 | 959,421.63 | 670,538.37 | 1,630,000 |
| 1704 | 1,829,421.63 | No substitution due to silver shortage | 1,829,422 |
| 1705 | 1,430,504.63 | 399,495.37[a] | 1,830,000 |
| 1706 | 1,500,000.00 | No substitution due to silver shortage | 1,500,000 |
| 1707 | 827,165.69 | 672,834.31 | 1,500,000 |
| 1708 | 827,166.00 | No substitution due to silver shortage | 827,166 |
| 1709 | 827,165.69 | 672,834.31 | 1,500,000 |
| 1710 | 827,165.69 | 672,834.31 | 1,500,000 |
| 1711 | 831,791.42 | 168,208.58[b] | 1,000,000 |
| 1712 | 696,648.74 | 50,251.26[c] | 746,900 |
| 1713 | 918,300.65 | 81,699.35[d] | 1,000,000 |
| 1714 | 928,444.84 | 121,555.95[e] | 1,050,000 |
| 1715 | 1,028,444.84 | 121,555.92[f] | 1,150,000 |

Source: Tabulated based on Kyushu Bunkashi Kenkyūjo Shiryōshū Kankōkai (ed.), Nagasaki jikki nendairoku (The true chronicles of Nagasaki) (1999), pp. 123–161.

Notes:

Decimal numbers have been rounded off in the total column.

a. Only 475 kanme of silver were substituted with copper due to a silver shortage in this year.

b. Only 200 kanme were substituted with copper due to a decrease in the amount of substitution copper.

c. Only 60 kanme were substituted with copper due to a substitution copper shortage.

d. Only 100 kanme were substituted with copper due to a substitution copper shortage.

e. Only 150 kanme were substituted with copper due to a substitution copper shortage.

f. Only 150 kanme were substituted with copper due to a substitution copper shortage.

1704, 1706 and 1708. This suggests that the copper substitution trade with the Dutch was no longer an important part of trade from 1704 onward.

One of the major factors in the introduction of the annual copper export limits in 1698 was the resumption of the coinage project in the previous year. The coinage project began at Kameido, Edo in 1697.[44] Another *zeniza* (copper mint) was established in Kyoto in 1700.[45] Large quantities of copper were supplied to these mints. The *dōza* was set up in 1701 under these circumstances for the purpose of collecting Nagasaki *kaidō* or *goyōdō* (export copper). The *dōza* was a government agency which placed all copper refineries under its umbrella and controlled the whole process from copper collection to refining and exporting.[46]

In 1701, Izumiya, a leading copper refinery, submitted to the *dōza* an estimate of copper consumption for handiwork and coinage for one year, calculated by all copper refineries as a group. According to the estimate, about 1.7 million kin of copper were allocated to handiwork and about 2.3 million kin were allocated to coinage per year. It is clear that the amount of copper consumed by copper mints each year was virtually equivalent to that exported to the Netherlands.[47] Tables 11 and 14 suggest that the establishment of the *dōza* did not necessarily resulted in a substantial increase in the amount of Nagasaki export copper. The first reason why the *dōza* failed to facilitate in the collection of Nagasaki export copper was the gradual decline of Japan's copper production that began around this time. This meant that the combined annual quota for copper exports by the Chinese and Dutch fleets put into effect from 1698 was unrealistic.[48] The second reason was the shortage of funds on the part of the *dōza*. The *dōza* continued to pay the same prices to refineries, although the cost of copper mining increased year by year.[49] The *dōza* tended to be behind in its payments to refineries.[50]

The third reason is somewhat related to the second reason: price differences appeared between the so called *jiuridō* (copper for domestic consumption) and the Nagasaki *kaidō* (copper for export). From 1711 in particular, it became difficult to procure copper for export below the market price as the Osaka copper market rose substantially.[51] A series of large earthquakes in 1703, 1704, 1706 and 1707 also contributed to the rise in copper prices. When castles, temples, shrines, samurai houses and some civilian houses were destroyed by earthquakes, there would be a sudden jump in the demand for copper as it was used to make roof tiles. In fact, Izumiya's records contain entries relating to the receipt and delivery of orders for roof tiles from the shogunate government.[52] An earthquake in October 1707 destroyed about 10,000 civilian homes in Osaka.[53] Because a majority of refineries were based in Osaka at the time, it is certain that some refineries suffered direct damage in this earthquake. Copper exports decreased dramatically in the following year.

The fourth reason was that copper refineries were paid for copper in gold from 1702 and suffered a loss from exchange rates between gold and silver. At the time, Japan had a currency system based on the three-tier metal standard. The gold coin (*koban*) was used in Edo and the eastern part of Japan and the silver coin (*chōgin*) was used in Osaka and the western part of Japan. The copper coin (*zeni*, or *Kanei-tsūhō*) was used as a small denomination coin throughout Japan. Many money changers were located in major cities in order to exchange between gold, silver and copper coins. Since most of copper refineries were located in Osaka, within the silver coin zone, they had to change the gold coins they received from the government into silver coins. They had trouble getting their gold coins changed if the amounts were very large.[54] These factors made the procurement of copper by the *dōza* very difficult.[55] It was consequently abolished in 1712.

## Asian and European markets in the seventeenth century

### The European situation and Japanese copper

As mentioned above, it was the basic policy of the VOC to consume Japanese copper within Asia. However, changes in the European situation from the latter half of the 1650s increased the importance of Japanese copper. The Netherlands experienced rapid economic growth as it avoided direct involvement in the Thirty Years' War, which was fought primarily in Germany during the first half of the seventeenth century. After the war, a new conflict arose between England and the Netherlands over control of the North Sea. The First Anglo–Dutch War broke out in 1652 and hostilities between the two countries continued even after peace was temporarily declared in 1654. This situation had an impact on decisions concerning return shipments from Asia to the Netherlands as well.

The price of sugar began to rise in the Amsterdam market from the second half of the 1640s and large amounts of sugar were shipped as ballast on return voyages from Asia.[56] However, the price of sugar dropped from 45–50 gulden per 100 pond at the beginning of the 1650s to 35 gulden by 1654 and further to 26 gulden by 1655.[57] After the outbreak of the First Anglo–Dutch War, however, the demand for sugar as a luxury item plunged. By contrast, the demand for copper as a military material increased and pushed up the copper price. It soared from 36 gulden to 56 gulden per 100 pond in the Amsterdam market from about 1655.[58] Although small quantities of Japanese copper had been shipped to Europe prior to that time, the board of the VOC (*Heren XVII*) decided at the end of 1655 to include copper in the list of priority goods to be carried by its ships returning from Asia to Europe.[59]

The number of entries in the *Generale Missiven* about the inclusion of copper in returning shipments increased from around 1657. An article dated 31 January 1657 reads, 'Purchased only 8,893 picol of bar copper at 11.4 tael (per picol) out of orders for 15,000–20,000 picol; 3,143 picol to be shipped'.[60] This was a report on the procurement of Japanese copper in 1656, when Batavia asked the factory in Japan to export large quantities of Japanese copper following the board's decision back in the Netherlands. However, the Dutch Factory in Japan was unable to respond to the request immediately and only managed to export 8,893 picol, about one half of the requested quantity. Still, it was more than twice the amount of copper exported in the previous year.

Copper exports from Japan increased rapidly from then on and reached about 1.41 million kin in 1658. A *Generale Missiven* article dated 6 January 1659 reports that 14,100 picol (1.41 million kin) were to be shipped to the Netherlands and 4,160 picol (416,000 kin) to West Asia.[61] In December of the same year, 1.3 million kin of copper were exported from Japan, 720,000 kin of which were shipped to the Netherlands.[62] In 1660, 10,000 picol (1 million kin) of fine bar copper were purchased at 11.5 tael per picol, 2,700 picol (270,000 kin) of which were carried on returning vessels as ballast and the remaining 7,300 picol (730,000 kin) were allotted for sale in Asia because copper was highly profitable in Asia.[63] In this way, shipments of Japanese copper that had previously been consumed in Asia to the Netherlands was were frequently reported in the *Generale Missiven* from the latter half of the 1650s.

According to Table 12, the amount of copper imported to the Netherlands exceeded the amount of copper sold in Surat by about 7,300 pond in the period from 1671 to 1675. An article dated 31 January 1673 reads, 'Part of Japanese copper is designated as ballast for home, therefore cannot be sent to Surat.'[64] This suggests that priority was given to the Netherlands over Asia as a destination for Japanese copper exports. Japanese copper was included in the price list at the Amsterdam market in 1669 and continued to be listed until 1688.[65]

One background factor of this was the outbreak of the aforementioned First Anglo–Dutch War in 1652; the Netherlands was intermittently involved in wars up to the Third Anglo–Dutch War in the first half of the 1670s. Denmark and Sweden were also at war from 1658 to 1660[66]; as Sweden was a major supplier of copper, a shortage of copper in the European market emerged. This copper shortage pushed up the price of copper in the European market. This is why large shipments of Japanese copper to Europe began in the second half of the 1650s.

However, the import of Japanese copper to Europe was a secondary measure and only carried out when it was considered beneficial in view of the condition of the Asian market, cost differentials between the Dutch and Japanese markets, and fluctuations in the prices of other ballast goods.[67] When copper prices fell in Europe in around 1680, entries about copper shipment to the Netherlands disappeared from the *Generale Missiven*. An article in 1686 reads, 'The Board expressed displeasure with high numbers of private cargos on return voyages to the Netherlands and voiced dissatisfaction with small quantities of Japanese copper shipments'.[68] This indicates that the VOC returned to a policy of importing Japanese copper into the Netherlands; entries about shipments of copper on homeward ships began to appear in the *Generale Missiven* again in the 1690s.[69]

## Japanese copper export destinations in Asia
Japanese copper was sold to different regions, with large sales going to the region of Southwest Asia. These regions are discussed below.

### Persia
As we have seen in Chapter Two, Japanese copper had been shipped to Persia since 1620. The highest volume of orders came from this region during the period of the copper export ban in the latter half of the 1630s. According to Table 15, the allocated amount of copper to Persia in 1654 (2,000 picol/200,000 kin) was much larger than that to Coromandel or Surat. Soon after this allocation was decided, 29,312 gulden of copper were shipped from Surat to Persia[70], worth about 100,000 kin based on the purchase price in Japan in the previous year. The Japanese bar copper sales in Persia generated a profit of 119 per cent in 1657.[71] Orders in 1658 amounted to 200,000 pond (160,000 kin at 125 pond per 100 kin). However, copper shipments to Persia declined after an article about a shipment from Tayouan to Persia in 1659.[72] Table 15 shows that the allocation of copper to Persia gradually decreased.

### Bengal
Bengal refers to the whole region along the lower reaches of the Ganges River in eastern India. A *Generale Missiven* article dated 31 December 1649 reports shipments of copper and sugar[73]; Japanese bar copper was sold in the next year at 27 ropia per 1 man (68 pond).[74] The price rose to 44 ropia by

*Table 15: Allocation of copper within Asia in the seventeenth century*

| Year | Region | Quantity | Note |
|------|--------|----------|------|
| 1654 | Coromandel | 538 picol | Vol. 2, p. 707 |
|  | Surat | 559 picol |  |
|  | Persia | 2,000 picol |  |
| 1669 | Surat | 3,000 picol | Vol. 3, p. 665 |
|  | Coromandel | 1,500 picol |  |
|  | Bengal | 600 picol |  |
|  | Malabar | 414 picol |  |
| 1674 | Bengal | 1,000–1,500 kisten[a] | Vol. 3, p. 921 |
|  | Colombo (Ceijlon)[c] | 8,000 kisten[b] |  |
| 1675 | Cochin (Malabar), Vengulurla (Konkan) | 4,620 kisten | Vol. 4, p. 5 |
| 1677 | Surat, Gamron (Persia) | 7,500 kisten | Vol. 4, p. 200 |
| 1679 | Coromandel | 1,500 picol | Vol. 4, p. 284 |
|  | Bengal | 10,000 picol |  |
|  | Ceijlon | 2,000 picol |  |
|  | Surat | 5,000 picol |  |
|  | Persia | 300 picol |  |
|  | Mocha | 200 picol |  |
| 1683 | Surat | 4,000 kisten | Vol. 4, p. 619 |
|  | Bengal | 1,000 kisten |  |
| 1684 | Ceijlon | 600 kisten | Vol. 4, p. 724 |
|  | Surat | 7,000–7,500 kisten |  |
|  | Persia | 600 kisten |  |
|  | Coromandel, other | 8,300 kisten |  |
| 1685 | Coromandel | 6,000 kisten | Vol. 4, p. 816 |
| 1697 | Surat | 6,000 kisten | Vol. 5, p. 857 |

Source: W. Ph. Coolhaas (ed), *Generale Missiven van Gouverneurs Generale en Raden aan Heren XVII der Verenigde Ootindische Compagnie,* Vol. 2–5, (The Hague: Martinus Nijhof, 1964–1975).

Notes:

Only the copper allocation figures that are clearly reported in the *Generale Missiven* are listed above.

Relevant page numbers are listed in the "Note" column.

These allocations might or might not represent the total amount of copper available for allocation each year.

a. One kisten means one box that is equivalent to one picol (1 picol = 100 catty = 1 kin).

b. 5,000 of these 8,000 kisten were sent to Surat.

c. Regions in which these cities were situated are given in brackets.

1671 and sales at this price produced a profit of 150 per cent.[75] Table 16 shows the sales of Japanese copper at the Dutch Factory in Hoegli (see Map 1), which was the center of the Bengal region. The Hoegli factory sold nearly ten times more Japanese copper in 1671 than previously. According to the end-of-year report, the sale price of copper at Hoegli had dropped due to oversupply.[76] For this reason, the volume of sales in the following year fell to almost one twentieth of the previous year's volume.

The annual sales volume fluctuated considerably year by year during the 1670s. 10,000 picol (1 million kin) of copper were allocated to Bengal in 1679. Copper enjoyed steady sales during the 1680s, except in 1688. However, the price was floating around 30 ropia per man (68 pond), which was not very high. There are articles in the *Generale Missiven* reporting higher copper prices in Coromandel.[77] The 1680s was a decade when only small quantities of copper were shipped to Europe. Consequently, the amounts of copper sold in Bengal were larger than those in the previous decade even though prices were slightly lower as shown in Table 16 and Figure 6. Europeans engaged in an intense sales competition in this region and the British gradually gathered strength in the eighteenth century. Consequently, the Dutch had a hard time with the sale of copper and other products in this region from the early stages.

## Coromandel coast

Coromandel refers to the whole southeastern coastal area of India. According to Table 15, 538 picol (53,800 kin) of copper were allocated to this region in 1654. A profit rate of 120 per cent from copper sales was recorded at Masulipatam, which was an important trade post on the Coromandel coast for the Dutch.[78] Although copper was shipped to the Coromandel coast after that on an ongoing basis[79], the number of entries in the *Generale Missiven* about copper shipments to the Coromandel coast decreased from 1672; an article from this time expressed a desire for more copper.[80]

Entries about copper sales on the Coromandel coast reappeared in 1676; a profit of 104 per cent from the sale of Japanese copper in Sadraspatam was reported in 1677.[81] However, a comment was made in 1681 that the sale of Japanese copper on the Coromandel coast was no longer very profitable. Although it was true that the selling of copper was interrupted by belligerency around Golconda, this slump in sales was mainly brought on by oversupply.[82]

The copper price in Masulipatam in 1677 was 75 pagoda for one bar (520 pond).[83] A profit of 13.5 pagoda was made for every bar of copper sold in Golconda in 1679.[84] Each bar of copper was sold for 69 pagoda in 1683.[85]

*Table 16: Japanese copper sales at the Dutch Factory in Heogli, 1667–1690*

| Year | Quantity (pond) | Quantity (kin) |
|------|-----------------|----------------|
| 1667 | 100,283 | 80,226.4 |
| 1668 | 20,468 | 16,374.4 |
| 1669 | 29,627 | 23,701.6 |
| 1670 | 28,919 | 23,135.2 |
| 1671 | 263,762 | 211,099.6 |
| 1672 | 12,400 | 9,920.0 |
| 1673 | 199,551 | 159,640.8 |
| 1674 | 231,336 | 185,068.8 |
| 1675 | 23,800 | 19,040.0 |
| 1676 | 170,484.5 | 136,387.6 |
| 1677 | 25,840 | 20,672.0 |
| 1678 | 149,872 | 119,897.6 |
| 1679 | 156,400 | 125,120.0 |
| 1680 | 140,719.5 | 112,575.6 |
| 1681 | 449,636 | 359,708.8 |
| 1682 | 226,327 | 181,061.6 |
| 1683 | 451,792 | 361,433.6 |
| 1684 | 212,024 | 169,619.2 |
| 1685 | 276,352 | 221,081.6 |
| 1686 | 217,600 | 174,080.0 |
| 1687 | 631,176 | 504,940.8 |
| 1688 | 17,000 | 13,600.0 |
| 1689 | 365,895 | 292,716.0 |
| 1690 | 312,676 | 250,140.8 |

Source: Yearly sales figures have been drawn from Iwao Seiichi, 'Sakoku jidai ni okeru Nihon dō hanbairo (Japanese copper sales channels in the seclusion period)', *Nihon rekishi* (Japanese history), 2–5, p. 4 (Tokyo: Yoshikawa Kōbunkan, 1947). Figures in kin (catty) have been converted from them.

Large quantities of copper flowed into Coromandel from the latter half of the 1670s. This was because of escalating hostilities between the Kingdom of Golconda, which controlled this region at that time, and the Mughal Empire, which was expanding southward from its power base in the north. Copper was an indispensable commodity for military purposes and demand soared. It was reported that there was demand for copper, although it was impossible to conduct business in Golconda, the capital of the kingdom, due to war. Another factor in the concentration of copper sales on the Coromandel coast during the 1680s was a slump in copper prices in Bengal situated to the north.

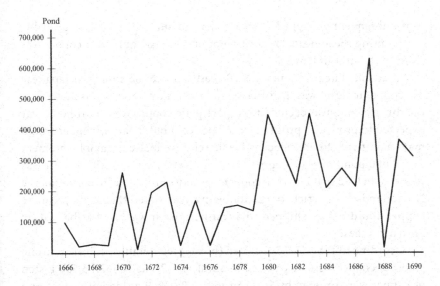

Figure 6: *Japanese copper sales at the Dutch Factory in Hoegli, 1667-1690*

Note: Yearly sales figures have been drawn from Iwao Seiichi (1947), '*Sakoku jidai ni okeru Nihon dō hanbairo* (Japanese copper sales channels in the seclusion period)', *Nihon rekishi* (Japanese history), 2–5, p. 4; figures in *kin* (catty) have been converted from them.

A profit of 80 per cent was made from the sale of 13,000 picol (1.3 million kin) of Japanese copper in 1684.[86] At one point in this year, the VOC even decided 'not to ship Japanese copper to Bengal because prices [were] going up in Coromandel coast'.[87] In the same year, a profit of 101 per cent was gained from the sale of 2,786 bars of Japanese copper at 61 pagoda per 480 pond in Golconda.[88] The Mughal Empire subjugated the Golconda Kingdom in 1687 and placed the Coromandel region under its control. However, the demand for copper still remained as copper coins were used in the region.

## Surat
Surat was a trading port in the western Indian region of Gujarat, situated near the mouth of the Tapti River that flowed into the Gulf of Cambay (see Figure 6). Surat was the largest consumer of Japanese copper in Asia during this period. It is said that only cloves were more profitable than Japanese copper among the forty items traded by the Dutch Factory in Surat at that time.[89] Table 12 shows a rapid increase in the volume of copper sales in Surat from the 1660s. According to the *Generale Missiven*, a profit of 82 per cent was made from the sale of 219,600 pond of Japanese copper in 1652.[90] Table 15 shows that Surat was allocated 559 picol (55,900 kin) of copper in 1654; cargos worth 23,014 gulden, mostly comprised of copper,

were subsequently shipped from Tayouan to Surat via Malacca, probably representing the allocated copper amount.[91] 100,000 gulden of copper was shipped to Surat in 1659.[92]

An article dated 31 January 1670 reads, 'Since the supply of Japanese bar copper to Surat was insufficient and the future outlook was uncertain, the director in Surat decided to import plate copper from Europe. It was expected to produce a profit of 70–80 per cent but Japanese copper would make a profit of 136–138 per cent. He therefore requested a sample shipment of 150,000 pond of plate copper from the Netherlands'.[93] Although it was reported in 1672 that Japanese copper was more profitable in Surat than the Netherlands[94], an article in the following year stated that some Japanese copper could not be shipped to Surat because it was used as ballast on return voyages.[95]

According to Table 15, 7,500 kisten (boxes each roughly equivalent to one picol) of copper were dispatched to Surat and Persia in 1677. 5,500 kisten of copper were ordered by Surat in 1681[96]; 226,869 gulden of copper and tin were shipped from Japan to Surat via Malacca at the end of 1681 and 352,532 gulden of mostly copper were shipped on the same route at the end of 1682.[97] It was reported in 1691 that the 110,400 pond of copper made a profit of 94 per cent.[98]

Surat replaced Persia as Asia's largest copper consuming region from the 1660s. This was because this region completed the trade route to Agra, the capital of the Mughal Empire. Surat was therefore the coastal gateway of northern India. Large quantities of copper were consumed in northern India; copper was used to manufacture military weapons, domestic products and copper coins. The Gujarat region in which Surat is situated also played the role of a trading port for the region of present-day Pakistan and Afghanistan. In fact, the trade route from Agra reached as far as Lahore and Kabul. Another route extended from Surat to Jodhpur, Multan and Qandahar.[99] It is quite possible that Japanese copper reached not only northern India but also other distant provinces such as Afghanistan.

### Other regions

Other export destinations included Malabar in the southern region of India, which extended from Ceylon to the southwestern coast, and Konkan in the north. These places appeared in the *Generale Missiven* only infrequently and usually together with other places. Copper and tin were shipped to Malabar and Vengulurla, a city in Konkan, in 1669.[100] Gold coins and copper bars were sent to Ceylon and Vengulurla in 1670[101], and in 1675 a total of 4,620 kisten were allocated to Cochin in Malabar and Vengulurla, as shown in Table 15. Copper and tin were sent from Ceylon to Malabar in 1676.[102] 1,500 kisten and 700 kisten of copper were sold in Vengulurla and Malabar respectively in 1680.[103] Cargos worth 68,428 gulden, mostly in copper, were shipped to Malabar in 1681.[104] 600 kisten of copper were sent to Ceylon in 1684 for trade with the city of Madure in the south of India.[105] A shipment of copper and tin to Malabar via Malacca in 1685 was reported in 1686.[106] Copper and tin were sent from Malacca to Ceylon; only copper was sent to Malabar in 1688.[107] 134,881 gulden of cargos mostly in copper were shipped to Ceylon in 1690.[108]

Copper shipments for Ceylon were not necessarily for consumption in the Ceylon region. There were some instances when copper shipped to Bengal was sent to Coromandel due to low prices, or copper was dispatched from Surat to Bengal or Persia. However, Ceylon served as a transit point for the whole Indian subcontinent and a place for the temporary storage of goods more than any other region. Direct return voyages were operating between Ceylon and the Netherlands. For this reason, it is important to consider company policies behind each shipment of copper to Ceylon.

## The purchase and sale of Japanese copper by the Dutch

### Channels for the procurement of Japanese copper by the VOC

It goes without saying that the VOC was able to conduct its trade in Southwest Asia on better terms than other Europeans because of its copper exports from Japan. However, Japan was not the only source of Japanese copper for the Dutch. It was possible to procure Japanese copper in Southeast Asia as Chinese vessels also brought it to this region for trade. Not all Chinese vessels came from mainland China. Any vessel owned and crewed by the Chinese was able to conduct trade in Nagasaki as a Chinese vessel (tōsen). In other words, not all Chinese ships trading in Nagasaki were under the control of the Ming or Qing Dynasty of China; where a vessel was based was largely irrelevant.[109] While copper was certainly in demand as a raw material for coinage in mainland China, it was not uncommon for some Chinese vessels to purchase copper for reselling to Europeans. The Dutch conducted its copper trade with Chinese vessels in Siam, Bantan and Batavia at that time (see Map 2).

The Dutch also sold copper in Southeast Asia when they anticipated profits. For example, a Dutch ship left Siam and sold 300 picol (30,000 kin) of bar copper in Malacca for a profit of 50 per cent in 1677.[110] A Chinese junk carrying 1,000 kisten (100,000 kin) of copper sailed from Japan to Batavia in 1679. The VOC bought up all of them at 18 rixdaalder per picol.[111] Chinese junks carrying 2,400 kisten (240,000 kin) of copper sailed from Japan to

Bantan in 1680 and inflicted considerable losses to the VOC.[112] The reason for this was either because the 240,000 kin of copper caused copper prices in Bantan to fall or because they were sold to the British or the French instead of the Dutch. In the same year, a Chinese junk brought 900 kisten (90,000 kin) of copper from Canton (Guangdong) to Bantan.[113] Although it is unclear if the copper was of Japanese origin, this is an example of copper shipment from mainland China to Bantan for the purpose of selling it to Europeans.

The Dutch were keen on the copper trade in Siam. The Dutch Factory in Siam opened in 1613 and subsequently closed down several times before reopening in 1665 for continuous operation. In 1681, it was reported in the *Generale Missiven* that four junks sailing from Siam for Japan would return with 5,000 kisten (500,000 kin) of copper[114], but there was no report on how much of this shipment the Dutch managed to acquire. The amount procured by the Dutch in Siam in 1684 was reported in the *Generale Missiven* as follows, 'Five Siamese vessels returned to Siam from Japan with 10,000 kisten (1 million kin) of Japanese copper. The VOC purchased 821 kisten at 6.5–7 tael or 16.25–17.5 rixdaalder per kisten and 282 kisten at 8 tael per kisten in exchange for cloves (of equivalent value). The remaining copper would be transported to India by Islamic merchants. One kisten is equivalent to 28 pond'.[115]

The Dutch paid attention to the movements of their European rivals in Siam. It was reported in 1685 that twelve or thirteen British, Portuguese and French vessels purchased bar copper at high prices in Siam and sailed westward.[116] In the same year, the Dutch conducted a survey of vessels arriving in Siam over the period from 5 October 1683 to 30 November 1684. They found that there were forty-two incoming vessels, twelve of which came from Japan, eleven were British, three were French and three were Portuguese.[117] The remaining thirteen were probably Dutch vessels. A report in the *Generale Missiven* 1693 reads, 'The [Siam] Kingdom dispatched four junks to Japan and nine junks headed for China in 1692. Two British vessels and one Surat vessel arrived in Siam and purchased 1,400 bars of tin and 400 picol of copper'.[118]

As described above, the major trade ports of Southeast Asia, except Batavia, were visited by not only the Dutch but also the British, the French, the Danish and the Portuguese. Islamic merchants who had been active in this region prior to the Age of Discovery were also still around. Various merchants traded with one another in this region and Japanese copper was one of the commodities they bought and sold. In this sense, there was a complex sales network for Japanese copper operated by the

Chinese in parallel with the simple trade route of the Dutch, who exported copper from Japan and sold it in Southwest Asia and Europe. The Dutch even bought some Japanese copper from this network. In fact, Japanese copper was an indispensable commodity in the complex trade network in Southeast Asia.

## Copper sales in India

The Dutch were able to secure an advantageous position in their Indian trade thanks to their ability to procure certain amounts of copper at low prices each year in Japan. However, the Dutch were not the only supplier of copper to India; the British in particular represented a threat. They not only brought copper to the Indian region from Europe but also supplied India with copper from the Chinese in Canton (Guangdong), Siam, Bantan and Malacca. The impact of their activity was already felt in the latter half of the 1650s. An article in the *Generale Missiven* in 1660 reported on the situation in Surat as follows, '[the] Japanese bar copper they [the British] possessed [in Surat] in 1658 [was] probably bought from Chinese junks in Bantan'.[119] The British sent European copper to India, particularly Surat, which was their base during the seventeenth century. Although the *Generale Missiven* reported in 1674 that European plate copper was not preferred in Surat[120], an article in 1676 complained that they gained little profit from Japanese copper because the British had sent 3.5 million pond of plate copper to Surat.[121]

The British gradually developed an advantage in their Indian trade based on copper from Europe and Southeast Asia. The *Generale Missiven* reported in 1692 that copper prices had fallen in Golconda in the Coromandel region, stating that, 'The VOC's monopoly of copper has no practical meaning. Large quantities of copper are brought out of Japan every year by the Chinese and the Siamese. They give favors to the British and the Portuguese by providing them with copper. This is why the British and the Portuguese can supply certain amounts of copper to Coromandel and other regions in India'.[122] Of course it would not have been a problem had the Dutch been able to procure an ample amount of Japanese copper and pour it into their trade with India. But the shogunate government strengthened its restrictive policy on the export of Japanese copper during the eighteenth century and made it difficult for the Dutch to acquire as much copper as it wanted in Japan. Consequently, the aforementioned report sounds like a sigh of frustration let out by the Dutch who were tired of the keen competition with their European rivals over copper sales in India. In addition to hindrances to trade created by other Europeans, the Netherlands could not underestimate internal obstruction by the VOC officers who stole profits from the company through private trade.

Although the Dutch did not have a totally advantageous position in copper sales in India during the latter half of the seventeenth century, they were still able to trade on considerably favorable terms due to their ability to secure large quantities of copper in Japan. After the turn of the eighteenth century, however, Japan's restrictive copper export policy and aggressive copper sales activities by the VOC's competitors dealt heavy blows to the Dutch.

## Dutch policies for trade with Japan in the eighteenth century

### The copper trade in the early eighteenth century

Although the volume of copper exports never reached 2.5 million kin in the eighteenth century, more than 1.5 million kin of copper were exported annually until 1710 (except in 1708). The volume decreased to around 1 million kin from 1711 to 1715 and remained at that level. The price was 12.8 tael per picol until 1711, and increased to 12.85 tael in 1712 and to 14.84 tael by 1716. The price was lifted because it was difficult to collect copper if the selling prices to the Chinese and the Dutch were considerably lower than the domestic market price in Osaka. The refineries that took over the task of copper collection after the abolishment of the dōza copper administration agency stated that they would be able to 'send much more copper to Nagasaki every year if copper could be sold to the Chinese and the Dutch in Nagasaki at the Osaka market prices'.[123]

A new decree called Shōtoku shinrei was issued in 1715. The following provisions are particularly notable:

• For trade with the Chinese, the number of incoming vessels per year was limited to thirty and the value of trade per year was limited to 6,000 kanme in silver, of which the amount of export copper was limited to 3 million kin.
• For trade with the Dutch, the number of incoming vessels per year was limited to two and the value of trade per year was limited to 3,000 kanme, of which the amount of export copper was limited to 1.5 million kin.[124]

Chinese vessels exported about 40,000 picol (4 million kin) of copper in 1714. However, the amount of copper exports decreased dramatically in 1715, the year in which the Shōtoku shinrei was promulgated, to about 7,637 picol (763,700 kin)[125], far lower than the prescribed volume of 3 million kin. By contrast, Table 11 and Figure 5 show that the amount of copper exported on the Dutch fleet increased from 1.05 million kin in 1714 to 1.15 million kin in 1715 and 1.3 million kin in 1716. *Koban* (gold), not copper, became the export item that experienced a marked fall in volume in Dutch trade after the promulgation of the *Shōtoku shinrei*. Details of the export of *koban* are discussed in the next chapter.

The setting of the annual copper export volume at 1.5 million kin under these trade regulations actually increased the copper exports of the Dutch, rather than limiting them. However, the limit on the number of incoming vessels to two a year posed a difficult problem to the Dutch. They exported 1.3 million kin of copper annually for several years from 1716 but, as shown in Table 17, the Dutch Factory actually bought the government-prescribed quota of 1.5 million kin of copper in Japan every year from 1716 to 1718. The difference between the export volume and the purchase volume was created by the limit on the number of incoming vessels to two a year under the *Shōtoku shinrei*. The maximum load capacity of a Dutch vessel was 650,000 kin.[126] Two vessels could only carry 1.3 million kin of copper even though the Dutch Factory bought 1.5 million kin each year. The remaining 200,000 kin were stored in their warehouse at Dejima. This anomalous situation was only resolved when three Dutch vessels arrived in 1721 as an exception.

The shogunate government, on the other hand, had great difficulty collecting copper for Nagasaki. Under the government policy for the collection of Nagasaki *kaidō* (export copper) after the promulgation of the *Shōtoku shinrei*, the amount of copper for overseas export was set at 4.5 million kin. This amount was apportioned to copper mines throughout Japan as their export copper quotas in 1715.[127] This policy was an attempt by the government to secure enough copper for export and to facilitate collection, but it was aborted in 1722 due to a lack of funds for the purchase of copper.[128] Under these circumstances, the Dutch were told in 1720 that the previous annual quota of 50,000 *ryō* of Kenji *koban* would be recalculated on the basis of Kyōhō *koban* from the next year. Since the value of Kyōhō *koban* was twice as much as that of Kenji *koban*, the annual quota would be halved to 25,000 *ryō*, with export copper being limited to 1 million kin. Further, a new decree issued in 1721 provided that the annual limit for copper exports would be varied according to variations in copper production from Japan's copper mines.[129]

It is apparent from changes in the copper export volumes shown in Table 11 that the annual quota for copper exports for the Dutch of around 1 million kin was an absolute maximum; it was all that could be supplied to the Dutch because of the constant copper shortages in the eighteenth century produced by decreasing copper production and increased domestic copper consumption for coinage projects.

*Table 17: Breakdown of copper exports, 1716–1741*

| | Exported quantity (kin) | Purchased quantity (kin) | Stored in Dejima (kin) | Note |
|---|---|---|---|---|
| 1716 | 1,300,000 | 1,500,000 | (A) 200,000 | |
| 1717 | 1,300,000 | 1,500,000 | (B) 200,000 | |
| 1718 | 1,300,000 | 1,500,000 | (C) 200,000 | |
| 1719 | No arrival | ① 750,000 | – | |
| 1720 | 1,300,000 | ② 750,000 | (D) 200,000 | Export = (① + ②) – D |
| 1721 | 1,950,000 | ③ 1,150,000 | – | Export = A + B + C + D + ③ |
| 1722 | 650,000 | 688,400 | (E) 38,400 | |
| 1723 | 1,038,400 | ④ 1,000,000 | – | Export = E + ④ |
| 1724 | 600,000 | 430,200 | – | Aid 170,000 kin |
| 1725 | 1,050,000 | 1,000,000 | – | Temporary 50,000 kin |
| 1726 | 860,000 | 800,000 | – | Temporary 60,000 kin |
| 1727 | 1,000,000 | 1,000,000 | – | |
| 1728 | 960,000 | 960,000 | – | |
| 1729 | 1,000,000 | 1,000,000 | – | |
| 1730 | 830,000 | 780,000 | – | Temporary 50,000 kin |
| 1731 | 444,000 | 444,000 | – | |
| 1732 | 990,800 | 990,800 | – | |
| 1733 | 911,320 | 811,320 | – | Gift 100,000 kin |
| 1734 | 1,020,000 | 1,000,000 | – | Temporary 20,000 kin |
| 1735 | 630,000 | 600,000 | – | Temporary 100,000 kin (30,000 kin this year) |
| 1736 | 1,070,000 | 1,000,000 | – | (70,000 kin from the previous year) |
| 1737 | 1,050,000 | 1,000,000 | – | Temporary 35,000 kin Gift 15,000 kin |
| 1738 | 1,050,000 | 1,000,000 | – | Gift 50,000 kin |
| 1739 | 1,000,000 | 1,000,000 | – | |
| 1740 | 1,000,000 | 1,000,000 | – | |
| 1741 | 1,000,000 | 1,000,000 | – | |

Source: Tabulated based on Kyushu Bunkashi Kenkyūjo Shiryōshū Kankōkai (ed.), *Nagasaki jikki nendairoku* (The true chronicles of Nagasaki) (1999), pp. 164–197.

## The copper trade from the 1720s

According to Tables 11 and 17, the export of copper was in a state of insta-bility from 1722; the volume of copper export fluctuated wildly from one year to another. This was because the number of incoming Dutch vessels was limited to two a year under *Shōtoku shinrei*. It was not uncommon for one of them to become wrecked on its way to Japan; in that case only one vessel might arrive to export copper that year. For example, only one ship arrived in 1722, 1724, 1731 and 1735 and the amount of copper export fell to 400,000–600,000 kin in these years as a matter of course.

A succession of trade restriction laws enforced by the shogunate government from the end of the seventeenth century gradually reduced the profitability of trade with Japan and drove the Dutch into a difficult position. When the *Shōtoku shinrei* was issued in 1715, it was proposed at the council of the Dutch East Indies in Batavia that a special envoy should be sent to petition the shogun to improve trade conditions, but the proposal was rejected for fear of the severance of Japanese–Dutch trade relations.[130] However, the Dutch began to actively seek improvements in trade conditions in the 1720s. In 1723, the governor general of the Dutch East Indies sent the governors of Nagasaki a questionnaire about a decree on foreign trade issued in the previous year. In 1724, Durven, the then head of the Dutch Factory, halted a decline in import prices by insisting that he would not allow the unloading of cargos from a newly arrived Dutch vessel until import prices reached a reasonable level in the eyes of the Dutch.[131]

In order to improve Japanese–Dutch trading relations in the eighteenth century, the Dutch sought higher import prices and more copper exports. Japan had the authority to determine the prices of imports since the promulgation of the *Shishō kamotsu shishō* in 1672. The shogunate government began to collect export levies from Nagasaki in 1699. Since Nagasaki was supposed to distribute part of its foreign trade profits in silver to its citizens first and pay the remainder to the shogunate[132], the amount of levy fluctuated year by year. Although the levy was set at 50,000 *ryō* per year from 1723[133], the scale of foreign trade at Nagasaki continued to shrink and therefore profits continued to decline.[134] As a result Nagasaki had to generate profits to pay for the levy by purchasing imports at low prices and selling them to domestic merchants at higher prices to increase profit margins.

Moreover, the gap between the aforementioned Osaka market copper price and the Nagasaki export copper price began to widen in the eighteenth century. While the domestic copper price appreciated as domestic copper production declined and the domestic copper consumption for coinage increased, the price of Nagasaki export copper remained fixed. In the eighteenth century, copper refineries began to receive compensation for export copper after the abolishment of the *dōza*. They petitioned the government for compensation for export copper in 1712. According to the records of Izumiya, the representative of copper refiners in Osaka, refineries asked for compensation for losses incurred from rising prices:

It was envisioned that copper production at various copper mines could be accelerated so that more copper could be refined because the Osaka copper prices were rising. With the market rising since last year, however, sending copper to Nagasaki and selling it to the Chinese and the Dutch this year at last year's prices would result in a significant loss. [The refineries] would like to be compensated for this loss.[135]

The shogunate government agreed in 1713 to pay the refineries compensation for export copper in silver.[136] According to Table 18, the unit price of copper in the trade books of the Dutch Factory was found to be higher than the domestic market price as early as 1678. The price gap widened from the 1710s.

The cost of copper for the Dutch became 61.75 monme (6.175 tael) per 100 kin in 1721 and remained at this level for a long time. Compensation at the time was about 146 per cent. This compensation for copper was paid from profits made by setting the purchase prices of imports at low levels. These factors were behind the setting of import prices at considerably lower levels than the Dutch had hoped for. The Japanese never explained to the Dutch that this was the system on which Japan's foreign trade operated. When the shogunate government issued new trade decrees or amended existing trade laws, it issued a notice of their contents only and never explained reasons behind them. As a result, the Dutch constantly puzzled over orders issued by the Japanese, uncertain about the reasons for them. It was as if they were walking in a fog.

According to Table 17, in the 1720s and 1730s an extra 20,000–100,000 kin of exported copper was classified as 'aid' (gojosei), 'temporary' (rinji) and 'gift' (hairyō). The 'aid' copper was exported in 1722 and 1724, generally when one of the Dutch vessels was shipwrecked. The copper authorized for export under the 'aid' category was purchased by the Dutch and not given by the shogunate for free.[137] The 'temporary' copper was authorized for export when export quantities were relatively small, even though two vessels did arrive. Like 'aid', it was purchased by the Dutch and was not given by the shogunate for free. The 'gift' copper was given in 1733 and 1738; 100,000 kin of copper were given by the government in reward for the import of Persian horses in 1733[138] and 1738.[139]

The Dutch received orders for the import of Persian horses from Shogun Yoshimune during the 1720s, but they declined as it was too difficult to transport them. When Japan promised to increase the annual export quota by 50 per cent and the number of vessels to three a year in exchange for the importation of Persian horses, the Dutch agreed and imported two Persian horses for the first time in 1725. However, Japan reneged on the promise. In protest against this breach, the Dutch adopted a policy to actively petition the government in Edo for trade improvement from then on. Van der Bel, who took up the post of the head of the Dutch Factory in Japan in 1732, had a mandate to abandon the Japan factory if necessary.[140] In other words, the governor general of the Dutch East Indies and the council in Batavia considered that it would be desirable to temporarily suspend the company's trade in Japan in order to review its terms of trade if the shogunate government would not agree to the Dutch's demand for trade improvement.[141]

In 1735, the board of the VOC (*Heren XVII*) back in the Netherlands ordered the governor general in Batavia to abandon the Dutch Factory in Japan if no improvement could be made to its trade in Japan.[142] However, they made it a condition that alternative sources of copper and camphor should be found to replace their Japanese sources. The Batavia administrators seriously considered their options if they were to terminate their trade in Japan, but the prospects were discouraging.[143] They came to the view that their withdrawal from Japan and termination of the Japan trade simply because of a deteriorating trade balance could have an enormous negative impact on the VOC's Asia trade as a whole. Consequently, in 1737, the board of the VOC revoked its approval for the termination of trade in Japan.[144]

The shogunage government began another coinage project in 1736 and set up a new *dōza* (the second-round copper agency) in 1738. This time the government adopted a system by which the *dōza* purchased copper from individual copper mines according to the ratio of Nagasaki export copper and the domestic copper designated for each copper mine.[145]

The second-round *dōza* operated until 1746. In the meantime, the shogunate government set out an even harsher trade reduction policy. It decreed in 1743 that the annual foreign trade should be halved.[146] The Kanpō decree cut the Dutch's annual trade to 550 kanme and its copper exports to 500,000 kin.[147] The decision to reduce the copper export quota resulted from an adjustment made to the quantity of export copper in consideration of the quantity of copper required for coinage projects that commenced in various locations between 1736 and 1741, as well as a decrease in the domestic production of copper. For example, the largest copper producing mine at the time in Akita received a reduction of its Nagasaki export copper quota to 1.05 million kin in 1745. However, after the coinage project in Akita was shut down later that year, the quota was increased to 1.25 million kin.[148]

The export of copper by the Dutch fell to 800,000 kin in 1743 and 600,000 kin in 1744, returning to the standard quantity set in 1720 of 1 million kin in 1745. The shogunate authorized an increase of 100,000 kin to the Dutch in

*Table 18: Comparison of Dutch and Japanese unit prices of copper, 1665–1757*

| | Negotie Journalen | Nagasaki jikki nendairoku | Difference |
|---|---|---|---|
| 1665 | 12.4 | 12.4 | 0 |
| 1666 | 12.4 | 12.4 | 0 |
| 1667 | 12.5 | – | – |
| 1668 | 13.4 | 13.4 | 0 |
| 1669 | 12.8 | 12.8 | 0 |
| 1670 | 12.7 | 12.7 | 0 |
| 1671 | 12.6 | 12.6 | 0 |
| 1672 | 12.5 | 12.5 | 0 |
| 1673 | 12.35 | 12.35 | 0 |
| 1674 | 12.2 | 12.2 | 0 |
| 1675 | 12.1 | 12.1 | 0 |
| 1676 | 11.9 | 12.1 | (0.2) |
| 1677 | 11.9 | 12 | (0.1) |
| 1678 | 11.9 | 11.6 | 0.3 |
| 1679 | 11.9 | 11.5 | 0.4 |
| 1680 | – | 11.5 | – |
| 1681 | 11.9 | 11.3 | 0.6 |
| 1682 | 11.9 | 11.2 | 0.7 |
| 1683 | 11.9 | 11.1 | 0.8 |
| 1684 | 11.9 | 10.9 | 1.0 |
| 1685 | 11.9 | 10.9 | 1.0 |
| 1686 | 11.9 | 10.9 | 1.0 |
| 1687 | 11.9 | 11 | 0.9 |
| 1688 | 11.9 | 10.95 | 0.95 |
| 1689 | 11.9 | 11 | 0.9 |
| 1690 | 11.9 | 11 | 0.9 |
| 1691 | 11.85 | 11 | 0.85 |
| 1692 | 11.85 | 10.9 | 0.95 |
| 1693 | 11.85 | 10.9 | 0.95 |
| 1694 | 11.85 | 10.9 | 1.05 |
| 1695 | 11.85 | 10.8 | 0.95 |
| 1696 | 11.85 | 10.8 | 0.95 |
| 1697 | 11.85 | 10.9 | 1.05 |
| 1698 | – | 11.35 | – |
| 1699 | – | 11.4 | – |
| 1700 | 12.34 | 11.89 | 0.45 |
| 1701 | – | 11.89 | – |
| 1702 | 12.84 | 11.93 | 0.91 |
| 1703 | 12.84 | 11.93 | 0.91 |
| 1704 | 12.84 | 11.93 | 0.91 |

*Table 18: Continued*

| 1705 | 12.8 | 11.89 | 0.91 |
|---|---|---|---|
| 1706 | 12.8 | 11.89 | 0.91 |
| 1707 | 12.8 | 11.89 | 0.91 |
| 1708 | 12.8 | 11.89 | 0.91 |
| 1709 | 12.8 | 11.89 | 0.91 |
| 1710 | 12.8 | 11.89 | 0.91 |
| 1711 | 12.8 | 11.89 | 0.91 |
| 1712 | 12.85 | 11.94 | 0.91 |
| 1713 | – | 12.24 | – |
| 1714 | 13.25 | 12.34 | 0.91 |
| 1715 | 13.25 | 12.33 | 0.92 |
| 1716 | 14.84 | 12.34 | 2.5 |
| 1717 | 14.84 | 12.34 | 2.5 |
| 1718 | 14.84 | 12.35 | 2.49 |
| 1719 | – | 12.35 | – |
| 1720 | – | 12.35 | – |
| 1721 | 14.84 | 3.875 | 10.965 |
|  | 14.84 | 6.175 | 8.665 |
| 1722 | 14.84 | 6.175 | 8.665 |
| 1723 | 14.84 | 6.175 | 8.665 |
| 1724 | 14.84 | – | 8.665 |
| 1725 | 14.84 | 6.175 | 8.665 |
| 1726 | 14.84 | 6.175 | 8.665 |
| 1727 | 14.84 | 6.175 | 8.665 |
| 1728 | – | 6.175 | – |
| 1729 | – | 6.175 | – |
| 1730 | – | 6.175 | – |
| 1731 | 14.84 | 6.175 | 8.665 |
| 1732 | 14.84 | 6.175 | 8.665 |
| 1733 | 14.84 | 6.175 | 8.665 |
| 1734 | 14.84 | 6.175 | 8.665 |
| 1735 | 14.84 | 6.175 | 8.665 |
| 1736 | – | 6.175 | – |
| 1737 | 14.84 | 6.175 | 8.665 |
| 1738 | – | 6.175 | – |
| 1739 | 14.84 | 6.175 | 8.665 |
| 1740 | 14.84 | 6.175 | 8.665 |
| 1741 | 12.84 | 6.175 | 6.665 |
| 1742 | 12.84 | 6.175 | 6.665 |
| 1743 | 12.84 | 6.175 | 6.665 |
| 1744 | 12.35 | 6.175 | 6.175 |
| 1745 | 12.35 | 6.175 | 6.175 |
| 1746 | 12.35 | 6.175 | 6.175 |

*Table 18: Continued*

| | | | |
|------|-------|-------|--------|
| 1747 | 12.35 | 6.175 | 6.175  |
| 1748 | 12.35 | 6.175 | 6.175  |
| 1749 | 12.35 | 6.175 | 6.175  |
| 1750 | 18    | 6.175 | 11.825 |
| 1751 | 18    | 6.175 | 11.825 |
| 1752 | 18    | 6.175 | 11.825 |
| 1753 | 18    | 6.175 | 11.825 |
| 1754 | 18    | 6.175 | 11.825 |
| 1755 | 18    | 6.175 | 11.825 |
| 1756 | 18    | 6.175 | 11.825 |
| 1757 | 18    | 6.175 | 11.825 |

Notes:

Prices are shown in tael (1 tael = 10 monme in silver).

The difference is calculated by subtracting the unit price in *Nagasaki jikki nendairoku* from the unit price in *Negotie Journalen*.

a. According to *Nagasaki jikki nendairoku* (p. 171), 1.15 million kin of export copper were sold in 1721, of which 750,000 kin were sold at 3.8175 tael per 100 kin as a shortfall from the previous year and 400,000 kin were sold at 6.175 tael as the current year's allocation.

1746. This annual copper export quota of 1.1 million kin was maintained for nineteen years until 1764.[149] On this basis, it would be reasonable to conclude that the copper export restriction in 1743 was a government response to decreasing domestic copper production and the sudden increase in the domestic demand for copper for coinage projects.

## The copper trade in the late eighteenth century

In 1761, the annual copper quota was 1.1 million kin. A passage in the Dutch records about the distribution of domestically produced copper at this time reads as follows:

> Japanese mines produce about 360,000–400,000 picol (3.6–4 million kin) of refined copper annually. 11,000 picol (1.1 million kin) of them are allocated to the Dutch. 900 picol (90,000 kin) are allocated to private trade to remunerate the governors of Nagasaki. 15,000 picol (1.5 million kin) are allocated to the Chinese and 10,000–13,000 picol (1–1.3 million kin) are allocated to domestic consumption.[150]

This means that about 30 per cent of the total domestic production of copper was exported to the Netherlands at this time. After nineteen consecutive years at the 1.1 million kin level, the Akita copper mine was unable to send 800,000 kin of its allocated 1.8 million kin export copper to Nagasaki due to a fall in production in 1764. The annual quota of Nagasaki export copper was reallocated between Akita (1 million kin), Nanbu (730,000 kin) and Besshi/Tachikawa (720,000 kin).[151]

A decree for a reduction of copper exports to the Dutch was issued in the same year:

> Due to a reduction in production at Akita copper mine in 1764, the quota of copper sold to the Netherlands is to be cut by 300,000 kin to 800,000 kin from next year for some time. The Netherlands is requested to respond in writing upon arrival next year whether it wishes to purchase substitute goods to the value of this cut or reduce its import shipments on incoming vessels to the said value.[152]

The decree restricted the annual export of copper by the Dutch to 800,000 kin from 1765.[153] A third-round dōza was set up in 1766.[154] This dōza regulated all copper production from regional copper mines and controlled the supply of both domestic consumption copper and Nagasaki export copper.[155] It continued to operate until the end of the Edo period.

In 1764, the Dutch were ordered to cut the quantity of copper export and reduce the number of incoming ships to one every second year so that just three ships could arrive every two years. The Dutch petitioned the shogunate government in 1767 to maintain the number of annual arrivals at two vessels, saying that they might become short of gifts to present to the shogun if a ship was lost on its way in the year earmarked for a single arrival. This petition appeared to have been received favorably by the government as it was accepted; the government increased the annual copper export quota by 100,000 kin to 900,000 kin as well.[156]

According to Table 11, the quantity of copper export fluctuated greatly after this trade restriction of 1764, but it averaged out at around the annual quota. The copper export rose to 1.2–1.3 million kin for the period between 1786 and 1789. The period from the latter half of the 1760s to the latter half of the 1780s was called the Tanuma era. During this era, the reins of the shogunate government were in the hands of Tanuma Okitsugu, who rose from the grand chamberlain of the tenth shogun Ieharu to become senior councilor (rodū). Unlike his predecessors, Tanuma administered the affairs of state emphasizing mercantilist policies and economics. He had his eyes on gains from foreign trade and devised measures to maximize profits within the limits of overseas trade. He even adopted a policy to import gold and silver from foreigners to make up for the shortage of gold and silver in Japan.

Isaac Titsingh, the then head of the Dutch Factory, remarked that Japan might open up to the outside world if Tanuma remained in power.[157] However, Tanuma was overthrown in 1786 and power was seized by Matsudaira Sadanobu, a grandson of the eighth shogun Yoshimune and a senior councilor who had been dissatisfied with Tanuma's policies. Matsudaira began to implement new austerity measures and embarked on the reform of the Nagasaki trade in 1790 by issuing a strict trade reduction order.[158] The order provided that due to a decline in domestic copper production in recent years the annual trade quota for that year would be halved, the number of incoming vessels would be limited to one a year and the annual copper export quota would be reduced to 600,000 kin. Under this order, the export of copper was destined to diminish and the Dutch trade as a whole followed a path of further decline.

## Conclusion

Gustaaf Willem van Imhoff became the governor general of the Dutch East Indies in 1743.[159] Van Imhoff, who enjoyed a good reputation for his clear-sightedness among the governors general, endeavored to revitalize the waning VOC. Around the same time, the eighth shogun Yoshimune was called the restorer of the Edo shogunate. It was an amazing coincidence that these two figures appeared on the scene at the same time. As soon as van Imhoff took up the governor general's office, he submitted a report entitled *Considerations on the Japan Trade* to the council of the East Indies in Batava.[160] It was the export of copper that van Imhoff devoted most space to in his report. At that time, the VOC considered the procurement of the largest possible amount of Japanese copper, which was in demand in India, as the most important part of their trade in Japan. In 1744, orders from the Coromandel region of India alone amounted to 1.5 million pond.[161] Yet the export from Japan was around 1 million pond per year only. At the same time, the British and other Europeans began to bring large quantities of European copper to copper consuming regions in India, so any reduction in the quantity of copper exports from Japan was a severe blow to the VOC's India trade.

'[Copper] is the bride round whom we all dance'[162]; this remark made by van Imhoff symbolizes the importance of Japanese copper to the VOC. The VOC derived great prosperity from its Asia trade in the latter half of the seventeenth century. It was able to acquire large quantities of copper through its trade with Japan, feeding it to its India trade. In the eighteenth century, however, the reorganized British East India Company actively made roads into Asia, squeezing out the Dutch. The British gradually gained domination over trade in India; this domination was finally established at the Battle of Plassey in 1757. Moreover, the shogunate government set out a series of policy measures to limit the outflow of copper from Japan in the eighteenth century as domestic copper production declined and the domestic economy flourished, increasing the consumption of copper for coin minting and other uses. Unable to secure large amounts of Japanese copper, the VOC profits were eroded; internal corruption, private trade and strong advances into the Asia trade by European countries such as Britain, France and Denmark all pushed the Netherlands towards a path of decline. The VOC was ultimately disbanded at the end of the eighteenth century.

The tracings of the rise and fall of the VOC strangely coincide with the ups and downs of its trade in Japan. The groom forsaken by the bride was destined to stop dancing and to leave the bright stage quietly.

# Chapter Four

# The *Koban* Trade and the Asian Market

Japan imported coins from China from ancient times to the medieval period. In ancient times, Japanese coins were minted on the model of Chinese coins. In the medieval period, the Ashikaga shogunate of Japan did not actively pursue the minting of coins. Large quantities of Chinese coins were imported instead, forming the foundation of Japan's monetary economy as they circulated throughout the country, greatly promoting the growth of the Japanese economy.

After foreign mining technologies were introduced into Japan in the sixteenth century, the production of gold, silver and copper increased at mines in various parts of the country. When the Tokugawa shogunate came to power in the beginning of the seventeenth century, it developed Japan's own monetary system by flushing foreign and privately minted coins out of circulation. From the Warring States period in the late sixteenth century, gold production began to increase at mines in the Izu and Kai domains. Mines on Sado Island and at Yamagano in Satsuma later began production.[1] The Sado mines were particularly prolific producers of gold and silver, so the shogunate placed the island under its direct control, appointing the governor and pressing forward with mine development.

The minting of *koban* (a kind of gold coin) began during the Warring States period under the regime of Oda Nobunaga and Toyotomi Hideyoshi (1570–1590). The *ōban* and *koban* were initially used to reward their subordinates rather than for market circulation. Most precious metal coins used in the medieval and early modern periods were minted into circular shapes of various sizes. The near oval shape of the *koban*, as shown in Figure 7, must have been considered a great novelty by foreigners. In reality, oval-shaped gold coins were much easier to store in a box than round coins.

The shogunate in Edo began to mint official coins. They included *koban*, *chōgin* (silver ingot/coin) and *dōsen* (copper coin). These Japanese coins were carried out of the county by the Chinese and Dutch fleets as export products during the Edo period.

*Figure 7: Keichō* koban

This chapter will discuss the export of *koban* by the Dutch. The first scholar who tackled this subject seriously was Yamawaki Teijirō, who studied the market conditions of the VOC's Japanese gold exports.[2] My discussion here will focus on topics that have not been addressed in the past, such as the issues surrounding the export of *koban* by the VOC, changes in *koban* exports, and the role of *koban* in the Asian market, especially on the Coromandel coast.

## Export of *koban* in the seventeenth century

### The *koban* export embargo of 1641
Although the Dutch might have imported some gold to pay for Japanese goods in the 1620s and 1630s[3], *koban* was very rarely exported from Japan. It was shortly before the relocation of the Dutch to Nagasaki in 1640 that they made a serious attempt to export *koban* for the first time.

An article dated 10 November in the *Diary of the Dutch Factory in Hirado* reads as follows:

Senior Commercial Officer Carel Hartsingh and Commercial Officer Augustin Muller returned from Kamigata with 159,000 tael. 125,373 tael of them were in gold and the rest were in silver. They reported that although it was a small amount, they did their utmost in Kyoto, Osaka and Sakai and borrowed some at interest of 2 percent per month and the rest at 2.5 percent per month. The

prices of *koban* and *ōban* (large gold coins) were reasonable. The *koban* price
was 6 tael 2 maas per piece and the *ōban* price was 45 tael 5 maas per piece.[4]

According to this article, the Dutch Factory borrowed 159,000 tael of gold
and silver; it did not acquire the gold and silver as payment for imported
goods. At that time, Batavia had received orders from Surat and Coromandel
for 20 ton (2,000,000 gulden) of gold.[5] Since Batavia had only about 210,000
gulden of gold in stock, the Dutch urgently needed large quantities of the
Japanese *koban* and Chinese gold. They acquired between 400,000 and
500,000 gulden of gold from Chinese merchants in Tayouan and hoped to
procure a larger amount of *koban* in Japan.[6]

In response to this urgent need for *koban*, the Dutch Factory in Japan
borrowed it as mentioned above. A journal of the factory contains the
shipping bills of Dutch vessels departing Japan on 20 November 1640.[7] Table
19 shows entries about *koban* exports that were recorded on shipping bills.
The *Witte Olifant*, *Pauw* and *Lis* exported 6,000 *ryō* of *koban* each at 6.2
tael per piece. Records show that the *Lis* carried a total of 3,000 *ryō* (2,000
*ryō* at 6.2 tael and 1,000 *ryō* at 6.4 tael) in addition to the 6,000 *ryō*. When
the 3,000 *ryō* on the *Lis* are excluded and 300 *ōban* coins on the *Broekoord*
are added, these shipments roughly add up to the 125,000 tael mentioned
in the above article. Therefore, it is likely that the 3,000 *ryō* on the *Lis* were
acquired trough another deal.

This was the first time that the export of *ōban* was entered in the factory's
journal; *ōban* was rarely exported as part of the company's regular official
(*motokata*) trade after that time.[8] Approximately 410,542 gulden of *koban*
and *ōban* were exported in this year, close to the amount of gold Batavia
had expected to procure from China. The expansion of the VOC's trade in
Bengal and Coromandel was one of the reasons that the company decided
to export not only silver but also gold from Japan (*koban*) as orders for
gold were received from Surat. For this reason, the volume of imports from
Bengal to Japan increased year by year from the latter half of the 1630s.[9]
Bengali raw silk, which subsequently became a major Japanese import, was
imported for the first time in 1640.[10]

However, it was not smooth sailing for *koban* exports. Upon hearing a
rumor about the export of *koban* and *ōban* by the Dutch on 4 December
1640, Inspector General Inoue Chikugo-no-kami wrote to Lord Hirado:

> I have heard that the Dutch were shipping gold out of Japan and would like
> you to stop them if it is true. This has never happened before. I shall inform
> the shogunate government of this matter and ask if the top councilor objects

*Table 19: The export of* koban *and* ōban *in 1640*

| D/M/Y | Vessel name | Type | Unit price (tael) | Quantity | Tael (T.) | Gulden (fl.) |
|-------|-------------|------|-------------------|----------|-----------|--------------|
| 20/11/1640 | Witte Olifant | Koban | 6.2 | 6,000 | 37,200 | 10,6020 |
| | Pauw | Koban | 6.2 | 6,000 | 37,200 | 10,6020 |
| | Lis | Koban | 6.2 | 6,000 | 37,200 | 10,6020 |
| | | | 6.2 | 2,000 | 12,480 | 3,5340 |
| | | | 6.4 | 1,000 | 6,400 | 1,8240 |
| | Broekoord | Ōban | 45.5 | 300 | 13,650 | 3,8802.5 |
| | Total | | | | 144,050 | 41,0542.5 |

Source: *Negotie Journalen* 1640, *Archief Japan* No. 840, ARA

to it. In the meantime, you are requested not to give them permission to do so until you receive a directive from Edo.[11]

Written instructions dated 15 February 1641 from the head of the Dutch Factory, François Caron, who was returning to the Netherlands, to his officers at the factory stipulated that the export of gold (minted or otherwise) was prohibited until a directive was received from the shogunate.[12] The Dutch were formally notified by the shogunate of a ban on gold exports on 11 August 1641, after their relocation to Nagasaki. That day, the Dutch were summoned to the official residence of the Nagasaki governor by Inoue Chikugo-no-kami and told to stop the export of gold and goldwork.[13] Since the Dutch were making enormous profits from silver and the export of *koban* was only a trial at that stage, the gold export embargo was not a major blow to them. It is also possible that small quantities of *koban* were exported off-the-book, even during the embargo period because *koban* was used on a daily basis as money at the factory.

### The lifting of the *koban* export embargo

The export of *koban* resumed in the mid-1660s. A background factor for this was the gradual decline in the value of silver from the 1640s in Europe as well as in Asia. The relative value of gold rose and gold became a much more profitable commodity than silver from the 1660s in Asia.[14]

The governor general and council of Batavia sought gold as well as silver from the Netherlands prior to the 1660s and asked the board (*Heren XVII*) for larger quantities of Ducaten gold coins and gold ingots from Europe in the 1660s.[15] Sources of gold in Asia included China, the Indonesian archipelago (the west coast of Sumatra in particular) and Malacca. There had been gold and silver trade routes from Europe in the southwestern region of India from ancient times. One of them originated from the Levant and Asia Minor, passed through Arabia and Persia, and followed the trade route of Islamic merchants to Gujarat, Malabar Coast and Ceylon.[16] However, it was not easy for the VOC to acquire gold through these trade routes.

In addition to this difficulty, the VOC's China trade, which used to be a great source of gold supply for the company, was obstructed by the Zheng clan after the transition from the Ming dynasty to the Qing dynasty in the 1640s. In 1662, Zheng Chenggong captured Tayouan, forcing the the Dutch to surrender this important trading base.[17] This made it extremely difficult for the Dutch to acquire large amounts of Chinese gold.

The Dutch suffered an acute shortage of gold required for their trade activity in Asia and needed to find a new supply. The VOC considered Japanese gold coins and reportedly began to export *koban* from Japan, albeit unofficially, in 1663, which was only a year after they lost Tayouan.[18]

In 1664, the shogunate authorized the Netherlands to export *koban*. A history of Nagasaki (*Nagasaki kongen ki*) reported, 'The export of gold was prohibited prior to 1664. The governors of Nagasaki in that year were Kurokawa Yohei and Shimada Kyūtarō. The Dutch asked for permission to export 500 *ryō* of *koban*. They gave them permission to export at an exchange rate of 68 monme to 1 piece (*ryō*) of *koban*'.[19]

The Dutch continued to petition the shogunate frequently, but the shogunate very rarely took the circumstances of the Dutch into consideration through the Edo era. Therefore, it is natural that the shogunate's readiness to meet the Dutch request to lift the ban on *koban* export in 1664 points to a domestic situation that favored the reception of the Dutch request.

This brings the domestic silver problem to the foreground. Silver was produced in abundance in the first half of the 1640s, when the export of *koban* was banned, but domestic silver production began to decline in the 1650s.[20] After the abolishment of the *itowappu* system in 1655, however, foreign and Japanese merchants in the Nagasaki trade began to deal with one another directly, resulting in large quantities of silver, a principal export commodity, flowing out of the country during this period.[21] During the 1660s, the shogunate took measures to prevent large outflows of silver and implemented a ban on the importation of non-essential luxury goods in 1668.[22] Their intention was to minimize imports and thereby minimize the amount of silver to be exported in exchange as much as possible.[23] That was when the Dutch asked to reduce silver exports and start *koban* exports instead. Since their request suited the existing silver export restriction policy, it was readily accepted by the shogunate.

At the time of the lifting of the *koban* export embargo in 1664, the Dutch negotiated the terms of export with Nagasaki governor Kurokawa Yohei and *Machi-doshiyori* (Head Official) Takashiam Shirobē.[24] The Dutch initially offered to export 5,000–6,000 *ryō* of *koban* at 6.2 tael per piece, but the head official told them that anything under 6.6 tael was unacceptable. In the end, they agreed to a trial export 500 *ryō* at the price of 6.8 tael per *ryō*. On 5 November 1664 on the new calendar, the Dutch acquired 500 *ryō* at a unit price of 6.8 tael, but the Dutch vessels had already left Nagasaki by the time the negotiation took place.[25] This lot was subsequently shipped in 1655 with a further 2,000 *ryō* at 6.6 tael, as shown in Table 20. *Koban* was exported every year from then on.

## The *aidakin*

After the lifting of the *koban* export ban in 1664 and until 1667, the Dutch acquired *koban* but at a considerably higher price than in the local market. This price discrepancy was a result of a kind of margin called the *aidakin*. The historical records of Nagasaki report:

> Since the Dutch wished to export *koban* regardless of price, their wish was granted. That is, the export of 500 *ryō* was authorized as requested for the first time in that year. Exports from the next year were as follows:
> - 1665: 500 *ryō* at 68 monme (6.8 tael) per *ryō*
> - 1666: 30,000 *ryō* at the same price as above
> - 1667: 50,075 *ryō* at the same price as above
>
> The Dutch exported the above and since the export price was 68 monme while the Nagasaki market price was 57–58 monme per *ryō*, a profit of about 10 monme was made for every *ryō*. This profit was called *aidakin* (margin or brokerage fee) and used as subsidies for Nagasaki officials and the town.[26]

Various descriptions of the *aidakin*[27] are contained in the historical records of Nagasaki. Engelbert Kaempfer, who arrived in Japan in 1690, also wrote about the *aidakin*, describing it as '*aidakin*, a margin for company' assigned to Nagasaki.[28] Kaempfer's comments suggested that the Dutch were concerned about disadvantages created by *aidakin* in their *koban* trade.

A major reason for the establishment of the *aidakin* by the shogunate was the great fire of Nagasaki in 1663. The fire started in Chikugo-chō, Nagasaki, on 8 March and, fanned by a strong wind, spread to sixty three neighborhoods; fifty-seven were totally destroyed and six partially destroyed. Only two neighborhoods and Dejima escaped the blaze.[29]

Table 20: Koban exports, 1665-1752

| Year | Month /Date | Vessel name[1] | Unit price (tael)[2] | Export quantity (ryō) | Export value (tael)[3] | Export value (gulden)[4] | Note |
|---|---|---|---|---|---|---|---|
| 1665 | 10.28 | Alplen | 6.6 | 2,000 | 13,200 | 37,620 | [5] |
| | | | 6.8 | 500 | 3,400 | 9,690 | |
| | | Total | | 2,500 | 16,600 | 47,310 | |
| 1666 | 10.18 | Cattenburg | 6.8 | 6,400 | 43,520 | 152,320 | |
| | 10.18 | Loosduinen | 6.8 | 6,400 | 43,520 | 152,320 | |
| | 10.18 | Spreeuw | 6.8 | 6,000 | 40,800 | 142,800 | |
| | 10.18 | Claverskerk | 6.8 | 2,000 | 13,600 | 47,600 | |
| | 10.18 | Nieuw Poort | 6.8 | 6,400 | 43,520 | 152,320 | |
| | 10.18 | Esperance | 6.8 | 2,678 | 18,210.4 | 63,736: 8 | |
| | | Total | | 29,878 | 203,170.4 | 711,096: 8 | |
| 1667 | No N. J. | [6] | (6.8) | 44,814 | (304,735.2) | (1,066,573: 4) | ③ p. 86 |
| 1668 | 10.25 | Buiksloot | 5.6 | 18,900 | 105,840 | 370,440 | |
| | 10.25 | Goude Leeuw | 5.6 | 18,900 | 105,840 | 370,440 | |
| | 10.25 | Pauw | 5.6 | 18,900 | 105,840 | 370,,440 | |
| | 10.25 | Rammekens | 5.6 | 18,900 | 105,840 | 370,440 | |
| | 10.25 | Nieuw Poort | 5.6 | 18,900 | 105,840 | 370,440 | |
| | 10.25 | Victoria | 5.6 | 12,000 | 67,200 | 235,200 | |
| | 10.25 | Buyenskerke | 5.6 | 7,465 1/2 | 41,806.8 | 146,323: 16 | |
| | | Total | | 113,965 1/2 | 638,206.8 | 2,233,723: 16 | |
| 1669 | 10.14 | Goude Leeuw | 5.6 | 24,000 | 13,440 | 470,400 | |
| | 10.14 | Hilversum | 5.6 | 18,000 | 100,800 | 352,800 | |
| | 10.14 | Goikant | 5.6 | 24,000 | 134,400 | 470,400 | |
| | 10.14 | Overveen | 5.6 | 35,284 | 197,590.4 | 691,566: 4 | |
| | | Total | | 101,284 | 567,190.4 | 1,985,166: 4 | |
| 1670 | 11.2 | Pouleron | 5.8 | 18,900 | 109,620 | 383,670 | |
| | 11.2 | Alphen | 5.8 | 14,700 | 85,260 | 298,410 | |
| | 11.2 | Buyenskerke | 5.8 | 21,000 | 121,800 | 426,300 | |
| | 11.2 | Noortwijk | 5.8 | 22,733 | 131,851.4 | 461,470: 9 | |
| | | Total | | 77,333 | 448,531.4 | 1,569,859: 9 | |
| 1671 | 10.18 | Hazenberg | 5.8 | 21,000 | 121,800 | 426,300 | |
| | 10.18 | Pijnacker | 5.8 | 21,000 | 121,800 | 426,300 | |
| | 10.19 | Goude Leeuw | 5.8 | 21,000 | 121,800 | 426,300 | |
| | 10.19 | Papenburg | 5.8 | 21,000 | 121,800 | 426,300 | |
| | 10.20 | Wijting | 5.8 | 42,000 | 24,360 | 852,600 | |
| | 10.22 | Tulpenburg | 5.8 | 19,041 | 110,437.8 | 386,532: 3 | |
| | | Total | | 107,241 | 6,219,977.8 | 2,176,992: 3 | |
| 1672 | 11.12 | Beemster | 6.8 | 16,800 | 114,240 | 399,840 | |
| | 11.12 | Pijnacker | 6.8 | 21,000 | 142,800 | 499,840 | |
| | 11.12 | Udam | 6.8 | 14,607 | 99,327.6 | 347,646: 12 | |
| | 11.12 | Buijren | 6.8 | 16,800 | 11,4240 | 3,99840 | |
| | | Total | | 69,207 | 470,607.6 | 1,647,126: 12 | |
| 1673 | 10.29 | Nuisenburg | 6.8 | 12,600 | 85,680 | 2,99880 | |

|      |       |                |       |           |            |                |              |
|------|-------|----------------|-------|-----------|------------|----------------|--------------|
|      | 10.29 | *Laren*        | 6.8   | 8,400     | 57,120     | 199,920        |              |
|      | 10.29 | *Experiment*   | 6.8   | 12,600    | 85,680     | 299,880        |              |
|      | 10.29 | *Beemster*     | 6.8   | 12,600    | 85,680     | 299,880        |              |
|      | 10.29 | *Spanbrock*    | 6.8   | 12,600    | 85,680     | 299,880        |              |
|      | 10.29 | *Buiren*       | 6.8   | 11,905    | 80,954     | 283,339        |              |
|      |       | Total          |       | 70,705    | 480,794    | 1,682,779      |              |
| 1674 | No N. J. |             | 6.8   | 50,657 1/2 | (343,859) | (1,203,506: 10) | ① p. 450    |
| 1675 | No N. J. |             | (6.8) | 41,073    | (279,296.4) | (977,537: 8)  | ② Vol. 4, p. 88 |
| 1676 | No N. J. |             | 6.8   | 19,989    | (135,925.2) | (475,738: 4)  | ① p. 459    |
| 1677 | 10.16 | *Huis Te Spijck* | 6.8 | 8,400     | 57,120     | 199,920        |              |
|      | 10.16 | *Middelburg*   | 6.8   | 8,400     | 57,120     | 199,920        |              |
|      | 10.16 | *Schieland*    | 6.8   | 12,960    | 88,128     | 308,448        |              |
|      |       | Total          |       | 29,760    | 202,368    | 70,8288        |              |
| 1678 | No N. J. |             | 6.8   | 25,070    | (170,476)  | (596,666)      | ② Vol. 4, p. 252 |
| 1679 | 10.24 | *Huis te Spijck* | 6.8 | 4,200     | 28,560     | 99,960         |              |
|      | 10.24 | *Betuwe*       | 6.8   | 8,400     | 57,120     | 199,920        |              |
|      | 10.24 | *Cronen*       | 6.8   | 8,527     | 57,983.6   | 202,942: 12    |              |
|      |       | Total          |       | 21,127    | 143,663.6  | 502,822: 12    |              |
| 1680 | No N. J. |             | 6.8   | 7,331     | (49,850.8) | (174,477: 16)  | ① p. 468    |
| 1681 | No N. J. |             | 6.8   | 16,677 1/2 | (11,340)  | (396,924: 10)  | ① p. 469    |
| 1682 | *7    |                |       |           |            |                |              |
| 1683 | No N. J. |             | 6.8   | 13,392    | (91,065.6) | (318,729: 12)  | ① p. 469    |
| 1684 | No N. J. |             | (6.8) | 41,432    | (281,737.6) | (98,6081: 2)  | ① p. 486    |
| 1685 | No N. J. |             | (6.8) | 127       | (863.6)    | (3,022: 12)    | ③ p. 111    |
| 1686 | 11.2  | *Pijlswaart*   | 6.8   | 143       | 972.4      | 3,404: 4       |              |
| 1687 | 10.21 | *Spijk*        | 6.8   | 6,644     | 45,185.2   | 158,127: 2     |              |
|      |       | *Mastenbosch*  | 6.8   | 4,200     | 28,560     | 99960          |              |
|      |       | Total          |       | 10,844    | 73,739.2   | 258,087: 2     |              |
| 1688 | 10.9  | *Leck*         | 6.8   | 11,397    | 77,499.6   | 271,248: 12    |              |
|      |       | *Boswijck*     | 6.8   | 4,200     | 28,560     | 99,960         |              |
|      |       | Total          |       | 15,597    | 106,059.6  | 371,208: 12    |              |
| 1689 | 10.30 | *Castricum*    | 6.8   | 1,823 1/2 | 12,399.8   | 43,399: 6      |              |
| 1690 | 10.21 | *Ridderschap*  | 6.8   | 12,261    | 83,374.8   | 291,811: 16    |              |
| 1691 | 11.6  | *Boswijk*      | 6.8   | 4,200     | 28,560     | 99,960         |              |
|      | 11.7  | *Wijk op Zee*  | 6.8   | 14,357 3/4 | 97,632.7  | 341,714: 9     |              |
|      | 11.9  | *Walenburg*    | 6.8   | 4,200     | 28,560     | 99,960         |              |
|      |       | Total          |       | 22,757 3/4 | 154,752.7 | 541,634: 9     |              |

*Table 20: Continued*

| Year | Month /Date | Vessel name*1 | Unit price (tael)*2 | Export quantity (ryō) | Export value (tael)*3 | Export value (gulden)*4 | Note |
|------|-------------|---------------|---------------------|----------------------|----------------------|------------------------|------|
| 1692 | 10.27 | Oosthuiizen | 6.8 | 3,753 1/2 | 25,523.8 | 89,333: 3 | |
| 1693 | 10.16 | Itershem | 6.8 | 8,400 | 57,120 | 199,920 | |
| | 10.17 | Standvastigheid | 6.8 | 9,437 1/4 | 64,173.3 | 224,606: 11 | |
| | | Total | | 17,837 1/4 | 121,293.3 | 424,526: 11 | |
| 1694 | 11.3 | Langewijk | 6.8 | 9,783 | 66,524.4 | 232,835: 8 | |
| 1695 | 10.27 | Huijs te Dieren | 6.8 | 7,277 | 49,483.6 | 173,192: 12 | |
| 1696 | 10.15 | Jerusalem | 6.8 | 13,026 1/2 | 88,580.2 | 310,030: 4 | |
| 1697 | | - | - | - | - | - | - |
| 1698 | No N. J. | | | 7,537 1/2 | (51,255) | (179,392: 10) | ① p. 542 |
| 1699 | No N. J. | | | 2,385 1/2 | (16,221.4) | (56,774: 18) | ① p .545 |
| 1700 | No N. J. | | | 25,394 | (172,679.2) | (604,377: 4) | ① p. 550 |
| 1701 | No N. J. | | | 1,816 1/4 | (12,353.9) | (43,238: 13) | ③ p. 142 |
| 1702 | 11.9 | Berkenroode | 6.8 | 21,111 1/2 | 143,558.2 | 502,453: 14 | |
| 1703 | 10.28 | Brandenburg | 6.8 | 19,245 1/2 | 130,869.4 | 458,042: 18 | |
| 1704 | 10.18 | Cattendijk | 6.8 | 2,427 | 16,503.6 | 57,762: 12 | |
| 1705 | 11.5 | Nieuwburg | 6.8 | 5,000 | 34,000 | 119,000 | |
| | 11.6 | Prince Eugenius | 6.8 | 4,290 1/4 | 29,173.7 | 102,107: 19 | |
| | | Total | | 9,290 1/4 | 63,173.7 | 221,107: 19 | |
| 1706 | 10.24 | Bellevliet | 6.8 | 3,000 | 20,400 | 71,400 | |
| | 10.24 | stoten | 6.8 | 1,978 1/2 | 13,453.8 | 47,088: 6 | |
| | | Total | | 4,978 1/2 | 33,853.8 | 118,488: 6 | |
| 1707 | 10.11 | Zoelen | 6.8 | 2,110 | 14,348 | 50,218 | |
| | 10.12 | Venhuijsen | 6.8 | 2,110 | 14,348 | 50,218 | |
| | 10.13 | Haringtuijn | 6.8 | 2,110 | 14,348 | 50,218 | |
| | 10.15 | Zuijderburgh | 6.8 | 13,296 3/4 | 90,417.9 | 316,462: 13 | |
| | | Total | | 19,626 3/4 | 133,461.9 | 467,116: 13 | |
| 1708 | 10.30 | Haak | 6.8 | 4,500 | 30,600 | 107,100 | |
| | 10.31 | Zoelen | 6.8 | 4,500 | 30,600 | 107,100 | |
| | 11.2 | Barsande | 6.8 | 11,468 1/4 | 77,984.1 | 272,944: 7 | |
| | | Total | | 20,468 1/4 | 139,184.1 | 487,144: 7 | |
| 1709 | 10.20 | Berg | 6.8 | 5,000 | 34,000 | 119,000 | |
| | 10.22 | Arion | 6.8 | 15,228 | 103,550.4 | 36,242: 4 | |
| | | Total | | 20,228 | 137,550.4 | 481,426: 4 | |

| | | | | | | | |
|---|---|---|---|---|---|---|---|
| 1710 | 11.10 | *Lokhorst* | 6.8 | 4,000 | 27,200 | 95,200 | |
| | 11.10 | *Nederhoven* | 6.8 | 4,000 | 27,200 | 95,200 | |
| | 11.10 | *Bon* | 6.8 | 7,596 | 51,652.8 | 180,784: 16 | |
| | 11.10 | *Samson* | 6.8 | 4,500 | 30,600 | 107,100 | |
| | | Total | | 20,096 | 136,652.8 | 478,284: 16 | |
| 1711 | | – | – | – | – | – | |
| 1712 | 10.20 | *Nederhoven* | 6.8 | 10,400 | 70,720 | 247,520 | |
| | 10.20 | *Abbekerk* | 6.8 | 10,400 | 70,720 | 247,520 | |
| | 10.20 | *Charlois* | 6.8 | 13,616 1/2 | 92,592.2 | 324,072: 7 | |
| | | Total | | 34,416 1/2 | 234,032.2 | 819,112: 7 | |
| 1713 | No N. J. | | (6.8) | 19,845 | (134,946) | (472,311) | ② Vol. 7, p. 50 |
| 1714 | 10.25 | *Strijkebolle* | 6.8 | 5,000 | 34,000 | 119,000 | |
| | 10.26 | *Sanderhoef* | 6.8 | 5,000 | 34,000 | 119,000 | |
| | 10.28 | *Arion* | 6.8 | 9,236 | 62,804.8 | 219,816: 16 | |
| | | Total | | 19,236 | 130,804 | 457,816: 16 | |
| 1715 | 10.14 | *Risdam* | 6.8 | 6,000 | 40,800 | 142,800 | |
| | 10.15 | *Sleewijk* | 6.8 | 6,000 | 40,800 | 142,800 | |
| | 10.17 | *Sanderhoef* | 6.8 | 5,556 | 37,780.8 | 132,232: 16 | |
| | | Total | | 17,556 | 11,9380.8 | 417,832: 16 | |
| 1716 | 11.2 | *Rijsdorp* | 6.8 | 2,700 | 18,360 | 64,260 | |
| | 11.3 | *Terninsse* | 6.8 | 2,612 | 17,761.6 | 62,165: 12 | |
| | | Total | | 5,312 | 36,121.6 | 126,425: 12 | |
| 1717 | 11.23 | *Noordbeek* | 6.8 | 2,000 | 13,600 | 47,600 | |
| | 11.24 | *Luchtenburg* | 6.8 | 1,736 | 11,804.8 | 41,316: 16 | |
| | | Total | | 3,736 | 25,404.8 | 88,916: 16 | |
| 1718 | 10.12 | *Meeroogh* | 6.8 | 2,000 | 13,600 | 47,600 | |
| | 10.13 | *Terninsse* | 6.8 | 2,660 | 18,088 | 63,308 | |
| | | Total | | 4,660 | 31,688 | 110,908 | |
| 1719 | | No ships | – | | – | – | |
| 1720 | No N. J. | | (6.8) | 5,406 | (36,760.8) | (128,662: 16) | ② Vol. 7, p. 526 |
| 1721 | 11.7 | *Bentvelt* | 6.8 | 2,400 | 32,640 | 57,120 | |
| | 11.8 | *Berkenrode* | 6.8 | 2,400 | 32,640 | 57,210 | |
| | 11.9 | *Valkenbos* | 6.8 | 2,422 | 32,939.2 | 57,643: 6 | |
| | | Total | | 7,222 | 98,219.2 | 171,973: 6 | |
| 1722 | 10.29 | *Hillegonda* | 13.6 | 3,538 | 48,116.8 | 168,408: 8 | |
| 1723 | 10.17 | *Cornelia* | 13.6 | 6,400 | 87,040 | 304,640 | |
| | 10.18 | *Appollonia* | 13.6 | 6,422 | 87,339.2 | 305,687: 4 | |
| | | Total | | 12,822 | 174,379.2 | 610,327: 4 | |

Table 20: Continued

| Year | Month /Date | Vessel name[1] | Unit price (tael)[2] | Export quantity (ryō) | Export value (tael)[3] | Export value (gulden)[4] | Note |
|------|------|------|------|------|------|------|------|
| 1724 | 11.4 | Casteel van Woerden | 13.6 | 3,187 | 43,343.2 | 151,701: 4 | |
| 1725 | 10.24 | Wapen van Hoorn | 13.6 | 3,712 1/2 | 50,490 | 176,715 | |
|      | 10.25 | Casteel van Woerden | 13.6 | 3,800 | 51,680 | 180,880 | |
|      |      | Total | | 7,512 1/2 | 102,170 | 357,595 | |
| 1726 | 10.14 | Wapen van Hoorn | 13.6 | 1,420 | 19,312 | 67,592 | |
|      | 10.15 | Adelaar | 13.6 | 1,422 3/4 | 19,349.4 | 67,722: 18 | |
|      |      | Total | | 2,842 3/4 | 38,661.4 | 135,314: 18 | |
| 1727 | 11.2 | Meerlust | 13.6 | 4,800 | 65,280 | 228,480 | |
|      | 11.3 | Jacoba | 13.6 | 5,082 1/4 | 69,118.6 | 241,915: 2 | |
|      |      | Total | | 9,882 1/4 | 134,398.6 | 470,395: 2 | |
| 1728 | No N. J. | | (13.6) | 9,437 | (128,343.2) | (449,201: 4) | ② Vol. 8, p. 227 |
| 1729 | No N. J. | | 13.6 | 8,630 | (117,368) | (410,788) | ② Vol. 9, p. 78 |
| 1730 | No N. J. | | – | 5,168 | – | – | ② vol .9 p. 210 |
| 1731 | 10.20 | Blijdorp | 8.57 1/7 | 1,641 | 14,065.71 | 49,229: 19 | |
| 1732 | 11.6 | Landskroon | 8.57 1/7 | 3,810 | 32,657.14 | 114,300 | |
|      |      | Huis te Marquette | 8.57 1/7 | 4,303 1/4 | 36,885 | 129,097: 10 | |
|      |      | Total | | 8,113 1/4 | 69,542.14 | 243,397: 10 | |
| 1733 | 10.20 | Huis te Foreest | 8.57 1/7 | 2,270 | 19,457.14 | 68,100 | |
|      | 10.27 | Huis te Marquette | 8.57 1/7 | 3,338 | 28,611.43 | 100,140 | |
|      |      | Total | | 5,608 | 48,068.2 | 168,240 | |
| 1734 | 10.15 | Huis den Eult | 8.57 1/7 | 2,587 | 22,174.28 | 77,610 | |
|      | 10.16 | Popkensburg | 8.57 1/7 | 2,629 | 22,534.28 | 78,870 | |
|      |      | Total | | 5,216 | 44,708.57 | 156,480 | |
| 1735 | 11.4 | Popkensburg | 8.57 1/7 | 5,393 1/2 | 46,232.49 | 161,813: 4 | |
| 1736 | No N. J. | | (8.57 1/7) | 6,993 | (59,939.99) | (209,790) | ② Vol. 9, p. 816 |
| 1737 | – | Enkhuijsen | 84.613 4/5[8] | 38 | | | |
| 1738 | No N. J. | | | | | | |
| 1739 | 10.22 | Arnestijn | 8.57 1/7 | 579 | 49,628.5 | | |
| 1740 | – | – | – | – | – | – | |
| 1741 | – | – | – | – | – | – | |

| | | | | | | | |
|---|---|---|---|---|---|---|---|
| 1742 | – | – | | – | – | – | – |
| 1743 | – | – | | – | – | – | – |
| 1744 | 11.1 | *Ruyven* | | 1,000 | (A)[*9] | | |
| | | | | 1,146 1/2 | (B) | | |
| | 11.2 | *Heuvel* | | 1,000 | (A) | | |
| | | | | 1,255 1/2 | (B) | | |
| | | Total | | 4,402 | | | |
| 1745 | 12.29 | *Hofwegen* | 13.6 | 1,400 | (B) | 19,040 | 38,080 |
| | 12.30 | *Vrijheid* | 13.6 | 1,300 | (B) | 17,680 | 35,360 |
| | | Total | | 2,700 | | 36,720 | 73,440 |
| 1746 | 11.1 | *Niew Stad* | | 300 | (B) | 4,080 | 8,160 |
| | 11.2 | *Westhoven* | | 300 | (B) | 4,080 | 8,160 |
| | 11.3 | *Vrijheid* | 13.6 | 700 | (B) | 9,520 | 19,040 |
| | | Total | | 1,300 | | 17,680 | 35,360 |
| 1747 | 10.2 | *Westcappel* | 13.6 | 5,000 | (B) | 68,000 | 136,000 |
| 1748 | 10.11 | *Schellag* | 13.6 | 1,700 | (B) | 23,120 | 46,240 |
| 1749 | | | | | | | |
| 1750 | 10.18 | *Haarlem* | 12 | 1,000 | (B) | 12,000 | 24,000 |
| | | | 7 | 1,000 | (A) | 7,000 | 14,000 |
| | 10.19 | *Zuyderburg* | 12 | 354 | (B) | 4,248 | 8,496 |
| | | Total | | 2,354 | | 23,248 | 46,496 |
| 1751 | | | | 0 | | | |
| 1752 | 10.25 | *Hof d'Uno* | *10 | 824 1/2 | (A) | 5,820 | 11,640 |
| 1753 | 10.15 | *Witsburg* | | 172 | (A) | 1,206.7 | 2,413.8 |

Source: *Negotie Journalen* 1665–1752, *Archief Japan* No.860–924, ARA, The Hague, 1931.

*1: Vessel names have been drawn from the *Generale Missiven* and Bruijn, J. R., F. S. Gaastra and I. Schoffer (eds) *Dutch-Asiatic Shipping in the 17th and 18th Centuries*, 3 vols, The Hague: Martinus Nijhoff, 1979. Some of them are therefore spelt differently from those recorded in shipping bills of the *Negotie Journalen*. For example, 's' becomes 'z', 'ck' becomes 'k', 'c' becomes 'k' and so on.

*2: The unit price is in tael per picol (100 kin). 1 tael = 10 monme in silver, 1 picol = 100 kin = 100 catty.

*3: The quantity is expressed in catty. 1 catty = 1 kin, 1 picol = 100 kin. The quantity is expressed in pond in the *Negotie Journalen* from 1666, but figures have been converted and expressed in catty in the above list for the purpose of comparison.

    1666–1697         1 picol = 125 pond

    1698–1781         1 picol = 120 pond

    1783 onward     1 picol = 120 7/8 pond

*4: 1 gulden = 20 stuiver, 1 stuiver = 16 pening

    Before 1665      1 tael = 57 stuiver

    1666–1743       1 tael = 70 stuiver

    1744–circa 1773  1 tael = 40 stuiver

    1774 onward     1 tael = 33 stuiver

*Table 20: Continued*

Export quantities in the above list are net exports from 1646 to 1655, total exports from 1656 to 1749, and net exports from 1750 to 1805.

*5: The total of 2,500 *ryō* includes 500 *ryō* procured in the previous year (6.6 tael per *ryō*) and 2,000 procured in the current year (6.8 tael per *ryō*).

*6: No N. J. denotes that a relevant *Negotie Journalen* is missing and other historical materials have been relied upon.

The historical materials referred to are shown by circled numbers and page numbers in the 'Note' column. The circled numbers correspond to the following reference materials.

① Van Dam, p. , *Beschryvinge van de Oostindische Compagnie*, Tweede boek, deel I, F .W. Stapel (ed.), The Hague: Martinus Nijhoff, 1931.

② *Generale Missiven van Gouverneurs-Generaal en Randen aan Heren XVII der Vernigde Oostindishe Compagnie*, Vol. 1–8, Coolhaas, W. Ph. (1965–85), Vol. 9 (The Hague: Martinus Nijhoff, 1965–85), Van Goor, J. (ed.), Vol. 11, Schooneveld-Oosterling, J. E. (ed.), The Hague: Bureau der Rijkscommissie voor Vaderlandse Geschiedenis, 1997.

③ Kyūshū Bunkashi Kenkyōjo Shiryōshō Kankōkai (ed.), *Nagasaki jikki nendairoku* (The true chronicles of Nagasaki), 1999.

*7: *Negotie Journalen* is missing and no record is found in ①, ② or ③ above, or in the list of gold exports from Nachod.

*8: Only Kyōhō *koban* were exported up to the previous year; the newly minted Genbun *koban* were exported in this year. They were probably samples as the quantity was small.

*9: Two types of *koban* were exported from this year. For reasons of expediency, the Genbun *koban* is labelled (A) and the Kyōhō *koban* is labelled (B) in the list from this year.

*10: Although the recorded unit price is 12 tael, it should be around 7 tael based on 5,820 tael for 824.5 *ryō*.

The shogunate loaned 2,000 kanme of silver to Nagasaki to be repaid in installments over ten years.[30] A Portuguese ship that had been burned and was sunk by the Japanese when it came to Nagasaki to ask for the resumption of trade in 1640 was salvaged. Its cargos of 60 kanme of silver were recovered. Some of the silver was distributed to the residents of Nagasaki.[31] It is likely that the *aidakin* was also introduced for distribution in the town of Nagasaki for the purpose of reconstruction after the fire in the previous year, as the shogunate assigned the whole of 3 kanme of *aidakin* to the town of Nagasaki instead of collecting it in 1664.[32]

From 1668 to 1671, the export price was temporarily reduced to the local market price and *koban* was traded at low prices (between 5.6 and 5.8 tael per *ryō*). One reason for the price reduction in 1668 was that the Dutch asked the shogunate to reduce the *koban* price in order to compensate for losses they would suffer as a result of the silver export ban proclaimed in that year.[33] Gold also replaced silver as the standard base currency for Japanese–Dutch trade, making the *koban* the basis for accounting for the amount of trade. In addition, the shogunate had decided that Nagasaki had largely recovered from the fire of 1663 and so ended the collection of *aidakin* which subsidized Nagasaki's reconstruction efforts. Due to these factors, *koban* was exported at the local market price at that time.

Circumstances surrounding *koban* exports from 1668 are explained in the 'Nagasaki-shū (Nagasaki collection)':

> Due to a gradually declining production at domestic silver mines, it was decided in 1668 that foreign trade accounts were going to be settled in *koban* from then on. *Koban* would be handed to the Dutch at the current market price, which was 57–58 monme per *ryō*, and hence the Dutch and the Chinese began to export *koban*. The market price of *koban* in the home country was around 90 monme per *ryō* and they would make considerable profits.[34]

While the information on 'the market price in the home country' was probably obtained from the Chinese, no *koban* was exported to the Netherlands at this time. Since *koban* was circulating in Batavia as money, it is likely that the information refers to a benchmark price there.

According to Table 20, large quantities of *koban* were exported during this period of market-price based transactions. Even though the *koban* export was merely a substitute for silver, the Dutch reaped enormous profits from the desirable trade terms. However, this favorable situation for the Dutch did not last long; the shogunate revised the Nagasaki trade law by introducing the *shishō kamotsu shishō* (appraisal trade, or *taxatie handel* in Dutch) system in 1672. Under this system, the export price of *koban* was increased to the pre-1667 level of 6.8 tael per *ryō*.[35] The Dutch were forced to trade *koban* at this price until the early Kyōhō era, despite changes in weight and purity of the coins as a result of re-minting.

The introduction of the *shishō kamotsu shishō* in 1672 began to generate a discrepancy between the export price of *koban* and its local market price, like that created by the earlier *aidakin*. This time, however, all the *aidakin* were delivered to the government treasury in Osaka; that is, they were collected by the shogunate.[36] Table 21 shows the amounts of *aidakin* over a period of thirteen years under the *shishō kamotsu shishō*. The total amount for the period was about 100,727 *ryō*. During the *shishō kamotsu shishō* period, an office was set up for merchants operating under the system where the purchase prices of imports to be paid to the Chinese and the Dutch and the selling prices to be charged to the specified domestic merchants were decided. Substantial profits were generated from the large differences between the purchase prices and the selling prices of imports. These profits were called *shishō mashigane* (trade profit margins); they were mostly assigned to the town of Nagasaki and never collected by the shogunate.[37]

The amounts of *aidakin* in Table 21 are disproportionately high compared with the volumes of *koban* exports. For example, in 1672, 69,207 *ryō* of *koban* exports with the *aidakin* of 8 monme per *ryō* resulted in 555 *kan*, 656 monme. When this is converted at a rate of 60 monme per *ryō*, the *aidakin* for this year would be about 9,228 *ryō*. The difference between this amount and the amount in the table is as much as 10,000 *ryō*. It is likely that the figures in Table 21 include the *aidakin* placed on not only *koban* exports in regular trade, but also *koban* exports in private trade by the VOC officers. If that is the case, the *aidakin* would have caused considerable losses and imposed a heavy strain on not only the export of *koban* but also the operation of the factory in Japan. However, a further review of archival materials and conversion methods would be needed before this can be confirmed.

The *shishō kamotsu shishō* was abolished in 1685 and replaced by the *gojōdaka* (trade value cap) system. *Aidakin* was again distributed to the town of Nagasaki as a subsidy.[38] This was intended to lessen the financial strains caused by the restriction of Nagasaki trade to prescribed annual caps under the *gojōdaka* system. Table 22 shows the amounts of *aidakin* that were given to Nagasaki over a period of twelve years after the introduction of the *gojōdaka* system to the imposition of a ban on the export of the Keichō *koban*. The Nagasaki trade association was formed in 1698 and the shogunate began to collect levies from Nagasaki in 1699. It is known that the *aidakin* was distributed for the common benefit of the Nagasaki people at the time.[39]

## *Koban* exports after the Genroku re-coinage

The shogunate began minting a new type of *koban* known as the Genroku *koban* from 1695.[40] An official notice about the re-coinage reads:

> Since the existing gold and silver coins are old, the minting of the new coins will commence. Due to a gradual decrease in production at our gold and silver mines in recent years, the standard of the new coins shall be adjusted so that gold and silver coins will circulate widely in society.[41]

One reason for this perceived gold and silver coin shortage was the development of the nationwide market at the time.[42] The shogunate was motivated to lower the standard of gold and silver coins in order to gain enormous profits from the debasement of coinage while alleviating the coin shortage at the same time.[43] It was trying to use profits from this re-coinage to fill its coffers and escape its financial straits. However, the Genroku re-coinage created great turmoil in not only the domestic economy but also in the Dutch trade with Japan.

Table 21: Aidakin paid, 1672–1684

| Year | Aidakin |
|------|---------|
| 1672 | 19,545 *ryō*, silver 2 monme |
| 1673 | 16,381 *ryō*, silver 9 monme |
| 1674 | 9,025 *ryō* 1 bu, silver 13 monme |
| 1675 | 2,847 *ryō* 2 bu, silver 2 monme |
| 1676 | 3,881 *ryō* 1 bu, silver 3 monme |
| 1677 | 5,951 *ryō* 1bu |
| 1678 | 4,933 *ryō*, silver 9 monme |
| 1679 | 4,894 *ryō* 3 bu, silver 3 monme |
| 1680 | 1,871 *ryō* 1 bu |
| 1681 | 5,813 *ryō* 3 bu, silver 9 monme |
| 1682 | 9,207 *ryō* 3 bu, silver 10 monme |
| 1683 | 5,450 *ryō* 3 bu, silver 7 monme |
| 1684 | 10,923 *ryō* 2 bu, silver 9 monme |
| Total | 100,727 *ryō* 2 bu, silver 3 monme |

Source: *Nagasaki kongen ki*, pp. 131–132

Table 22: Aidakin paid, 1685–1696

| Year | Aidakin |
|------|---------|
| 1685 | 343 *ryō*, silver 1 monme |
| 1686 | 1,835 *ryō* 1 bu, silver 10 monme |
| 1687 | 3,308 *ryō* 1 bu |
| 1688 | 3,912 *ryō* 1 bu, silver 12 monme |
| 1689 | 2,000 *ryō* 2 bu, silver 4 monme |
| 1690 | 3,185 *ryō* 2 bu, silver 14 monme |
| 1691 | 4,360 *ryō*, silver 9 monme |
| 1692 | 2,410 *ryō* 2 bu, silver 4 monme |
| 1693 | 3,349 *ryō*, silver 14 monme |
| 1694 | 2,410 *ryō* 1 bu, silver 4 monme |
| 1695 | 2,121 *ryō* 3 bu, silver 14 monme |
| 1696 | 2,802 *ryō*, silver 11 monme |
| Total | 33,039 *ryō* 3 bu, silver 7 monme |

Source: *Nagasaki kongen ki*, pp. 132–133

Note: The figures in Tables 21 and 22 are also recorded in 'Koshūki'(in *Tsūkō ichiran*, Vol. 4, p. 281) with minor variations.

According to van Imhoff, who became the governor general of the Dutch East Indies in the 1740s, the purity of the Keichō *koban* was 20 carat 8.5–9 grain (86.28–86.46 per cent gold content). The Genroku *koban* weighed almost the same as the Keichō *koban* but had a much lower purity of 13 carat 6–7 grain (56.25–56.59 per cent gold content).[44] This means that the Genroku *koban* was debased by about 35 per cent from the Keichō *koban*. The shogunate ordered the Dutch to export this lower quality Genroku *koban* at the same price as the Keichō *koban* from 1697.[45] The order to treat the Genroku *koban* as if it was of the same value as the Keichō *koban* was applicable not only to foreign countries but also within Japan. The Dutch in Batavia estimated that paying the price for the Keichō *koban* to buy the Genroku *koban* would result in a loss of 15–16 per cent.[46] It was unlikely that the new *koban* would be traded at the same price as the Keichō *koban* in Coromandel, a major destination for Japanese *koban* exports, and even less likely in Bengal or Surat where silver coins were primarily traded.[47]

In response to the shogunate's order, the governor general and council in Batavia sought to avoid the new *koban* as much as possible, instead exporting *saodō* (copper bars), camphor and copper coins.[48] Copper exports were encouraged because copper was profitable in all regions of India at that time. In fact, the volume of copper exports jumped to 2.5 million kin in 1697, about 1 million kin more than usual. However, it was impossible to avoid the export of *koban* completely unless some alternative export goods were found. As an article in *Nagasaki jikki nendairoku* in 1696 reports, the shogunate ordered the cutting of *koban* exports, saying that more copper should be transported from then on.[49] It was a government policy at the time to reduce *koban* exports and increase copper exports.

Under these circumstances, the Dutch seriously considered whether they could expect any profits by exporting *chōgin* (silver coins), which the Dutch were prohibited from exporting at the time, instead of the inferior Genroku *koban*. In 1696, they sent samples of *chōgin* to Batavia for examination and concluded that, because *chōgin* had also been debased by as much as 18 per cent at that time, the export of *chōgin* would return 5.3 per cent less profit than *koban*.[50]

According to the *Dagregister* (Diary of the Dutch Factory), the board in the Netherlands (*Heren XIII*) asked in a 1703 letter if it was possible to export silver instead of *koban*. The factory in Japan replied that there was no prospect of profit from it.[51] In an article dated 30 November 1707 in the *Generale Missiven*, the board in the Netherlands again asked for the export of silver instead of *koban* from Japan.[52] The fact that the possible resumption of silver exports from Japan was discussed several times at board meetings in the Netherlands suggests the enormity of the burden imposed on the Dutch by the export of the low quality Genroku *koban*.

The minting of another new *koban* started in 1710. The Dutch saw the Kenji *koban* as even worse than the Genroku *koban*. The Kenji *koban* had almost the same purity as the Keichō *koban*, but it was much lighter. While the Genroku *koban* weighed 47 condrijn, the Kenji *koban* was around 25 condrijn, only about half the weight of the former.[53] Yet, the Dutch were ordered to export the Kenji *koban* from 1713 at the same price as the Keichō and Genroku *koban*.[54] The Dutch resisted strongly as never before. The Dutch Factory protested to the Nagasaki governor, saying that it was given a strict order by the governor general of the Dutch East Indies in Batavia to reject transactions if it had to receive the Kenji *koban* at that price.[55] Although the Dutch ultimately yielded to the shogunate order and accepted the Kenji *koban* at the that price, they continued to annoy the Japanese by making representations to the Nagasaki governor, such as a questionnaire about *koban* from the head of the Dutch Factory. The export of the Kenji *koban* aggravated the loss rate by around 35 per cent.[56]

As successive adverse conditions confronted the Dutch's Japan trade, a new shogunate decree about foreign trade terms called *Shōtoku shinrei* was promulgated in 1715. An article in the *Generale Missiven* describes five clauses comprising this decree:

Clause 1:  No more than two vessels per year shall be permitted to arrive.

Clause 2:  An annual turnover up to 300,000 tael shall be permitted. Gold and silver are (counted) as before.

Clause 3:  Copper may be exported up to 1.5 million kisten (boxes) at 120 pond (per picol). However, at least 12,000 tael must be comprised of camphor, lacquer ware, ceramic ware, foodstuffs and other products. Moreover, 14,000 tael, or 10,000 tael according to a Chinese translation, of the annual turnover of 300,000 tael must be retained (at Dejima). The rest may be exported in *koban*.

(Clauses 4 and 5 omitted).[57]

In the actual text of the *Shōtoku shinrei*, Clause 3 contains an order to the Dutch concerning *koban*. It says, 'The amount of *koban* exported in the trade with the Dutch should be reduced'.[58] It is apparent from this that the real intention of the shogunate for the *Shōtoku shinrei* with regard to Dutch trade was the restraint of *koban* exports rather than restraint of annual copper exports. It is possible to surmise that the shogunate adopted this policy in order to reduce *koban* exports and increase Japanese copper exports on the back of strong protests by the Dutch against the light-weight Kenji *koban*. There was a deep concern on the part of the shogunate that outflows of *koban* might exacerbate the already serious gold coin shortage in Japan caused by the growth of the domestic economy. In addition, the shogunate government wanted to prevent mass outflows of *koban*, which was to be used for the re-minting of the new Shōtoku *koban*. The Shōtoku *koban* had the same weight and purity as the Keichō *koban* in order to normalize the domestic economy that had been confused since the appearance of the Genroku *koban*.

The minting of the Shōtoku *koban* began in 1715, but it ended after a short period. It was followed by the minting of the Kyōhō *koban* under the administration of Shogun Yoshimune. These two coins had almost the same purity and weight as the Keichō *koban*.[59] The extremely unpopular Kenji *koban* was exported up to 1721 and the Shōtoku and Kyōhō *koban* were exported from 1722. Yet, the change did not alleviate Dutch losses caused by the export of *koban* from Japan because the shogunate ordered them to export these fine *koban* at twice the price of the Kenji *koban* (13.6 tael per *ryō*).[60] In fact, the government order to treat the Shōtoku and Kyōhō *koban* as twice as valuable as the Kenji *koban* was applicable not only to exporters but also within Japan; therefore the Dutch had no prospect of reducing their losses.

A Dutch trade decree was issued in 1733 for the primary purpose of restricting *koban* exports again. According to the *Nagasaki jitsuroku taisei* (Compendium of authentic records of Nagasaki), the following decree was issued:

In September this year, the annual trade turnover of 1,700 kanme is reduced by 600 kanme from now on. The copper export quota remains at 1 million *kin* and the *koban* export quota is reduced.[61]

However, trade books of the Dutch show that this decree had little effect. Table 20 indicates that, although *koban* exports were low, there was no sudden drop from this year. Ultimately, the re-coinage of the low purity Genbun *koban* in 1736 delivered a fatal blow to the export of *koban* by the Dutch. According to Dutch records, the value of the previous Kyōhō *koban* was 66 per cent higher than the newly minted Genbun *koban*.[62]

According to the *Nagasaki jikki nendairoku*, the export of *koban* continued steadily even after 1736, but only 38 *ryō* of the Genbun *koban* were exported in 1737 according to the *Negotie Journalen* of the Dutch Factory. The amount of *koban* exports in 1738 is unknown as the *Negotie Journalen* entry for that year is missing. 579 *ryō* of the Kyōhō *koban* were exported in 1739 and no *koban* exports were recorded in any of the shipping bills from 1740 to 1743. 1,000 *ryō* of the Genbun *koban* and 1,146.5 *ryō* of the Kyōhō *koban* were listed on the shipping bill of the *Ryuven* headed for Batavia; 1,000 *ryō* of the Genbun *koban* and 1,255.5 *ryō* of the Kyōhō *koban* were exported on the *Heuvel* in 1744. This means that 2,000 *ryō* of the Genbun *koban* and 2,402 *ryō* of the Kyōhō *koban* were exported in that year.

A total of 2,700 *ryō* of the Kyōhō *koban* were exported in 1745: 1,400 *ryō* on the *Hofwegen* and 1,300 *ryō* on the *Vrijheid*. 1,300 *ryō* of the Kyōhō *koban* were exported on board three vessels in 1746: 300 *ryō* on the *Nieuwstad*, 300 *ryō* on the *Westhoven* and 700 *ryō* on the *Vrijheid*. The *Westkapelle* exported 5,000 *ryō* of the Kyōhō *koban* in 1747, but the rest of the page is missing. According to the *Generale Missiven*, the 5,000 *ryō* on the *Westkapelle* were the only export of *koban* for that year. The cargo was shipped to Coromandel together with 11,921 pond of camphor.[63] The *Schellag* exported 1,700 *ryō* of the Kyōhō *koban* to Coromandel via Malacca in 1748.[64] There are no records of *koban* exports in 1749. A total of 2,354 *ryō* (1,354 *ryō* of the Kyōhō *koban* and 1,000 *ryō* of the Genbun *koban*) were exported by two ships in 1750. No export was recorded for 1751. 824.5 *ryō* of the Genbun *koban* were exported on the *Hof* in 1752 and 172 *ryō* were shipped on the *Witsburg* in 1753. This was the last record of *koban* exports in the *Negotie Journalen*.

In fact, it is difficult at this stage to present accurate figures for exports over the period from 1736 to 1752 as historical records present a number of problems. For example, Table 23 shows the amounts of *koban* exports reported in *Nagasaki jikki nendairoku*. These figures did not deviate very much from the amounts of *koban* exports recorded in shipping bills contained in the *Negotie Journalen* of the Nagasaki factory (see Table 20) until 1735. For this reason, some of the copper export figures in Table 20 were based on figures from *Nagasaki jikki nendairoku* when relevant *Negotie Journalen* records were unavailable. *Koban* export figures in these two archival materials began to differ widely from 1736. The list of *koban* exports in Kuiper's *Japan en de Buiten wereld in de 18e Eeuw* (Japan and the outside world in the 18th century) has many blanks in this period.[65]

According to *Nagasaki jikki nendairoku*, the Genbun *koban*, which was recorded as *bunkin*, was exported by the Dutch from 1746. However, the *Negotie Journalen* of the Dutch Factory shows that the Kyōhō *koban* (*groote goude kobang*), which was called *kokin*, was the main export *koban* up to 1750. Although *Nagasaki jikki nendairoku* reports that as much as 1,000–3,000 *ryō* of *koban* were exported every year from 1736, only several hundred *ryō* of *koban* exports can be confirmed in the *Negotie Journalen*; there is no record of *koban* exports in some years. It is conceivable that this was because part of the *koban* exports were already being treated as goods of private trade then. These questions about *koban* exports during this period need to be investigated further in the future.

*Table 23:* Koban *exports according to* Nagasaki jikki nendairoku, *1664-1762*

| Year | Quantity | Year | Quantity | Year | Quantity |
|---|---|---|---|---|---|
| 1664 | 500 ryō | 1700 | 2,385 ryō 2 bu | 1736 | New koban 2,200 ryō |
| 1665 | 1,500 ryō | 1701 | 1,816 ryō 1 bu | 1737 | Genbun 3,000 ryō*² |
|  |  |  |  |  | Old koban 2,000 ryō |
| 1666 | 29,878 ryō | 1702 | - | 1738 | 3,000 ryō |
| 1667 | 44,814 ryō | 1703 | - | 1739 | 3,000 ryō |
| 1668 | 103,165 ryō 2 bu | 1704 | - | 1740 | 3,000 ryō |
| 1669 | 119,284 ryō | 1705 | - | 1741 | 3,000 ryō |
| 1670 | 77,333 ryō | 1706 | - | 1742 | 3,000 ryō |
| 1671 | 107,204 ryō | 1707 | - | 1743 | - |
| 1672 | - | 1708 | - | 1744 | Genbun 1,500 ryō- |
| 1673 | 46,200 ryō | 1709 | - | 1745 | Genbun 2,700 ryō |
| 1674 | 50,567 ryō 2 bu | 1710 | - | 1746 | Genbun 1,000 ryō |
| 1675 | - | 1711 | - | 1747 | Genbun 1,000 ryō |
| 1676 | - | 1712 | - | 1748 | Genbun 1,000 ryō |
| 1677 | - | 1713 | - | 1749 | Genbun 1,000 ryō |
| 1678 | - | 1714 | - | 1750 | Genbun 1,000 ryō |
| 1679 | - | 1715 | 17,556 ryō | 1751 | Genbun 1,000 ryō |
| 1680 | - | 1716 | 5,312 ryō | 1752 | Genbun 1,000 ryō |
| 1681 | - | 1717 | 3,736 ryō | 1753 | Genbun 1,000 ryō |
| 1682 | - | 1718 | 4,660 ryō | 1754 | Genbun 1,000 ryō |
| 1683 | - | 1719 | - | 1755 | Genbun 1,000 ryō |
| 1684 | 41,432 ryō | 1720 | 5,406 ryō | 1756 | Genbun 1,000 ryō |
| 1685 | 127 ryō | 1721 | 7,222 ryō | 1757 | Genbun 1,000 ryō |
| 1686 | 143 ryō | 1722 | 3,588 ryō | 1758 | Genbun 500 ryō |
| 1687 | 10,844 ryō | 1723 | 13,822 ryō | 1759 | - |
| 1688 | - | 1724 | - | 1760 | Genbun 1,500 ryō |
| 1689 | - | 1725 | - | 1761 | Genbun 1,500 ryō |
| 1690 | - | 1726 | - | 1762 | Genbun 1,500 ryō |
| 1691 | - | 1727 | - |  |  |
| 1692 | - | 1728 | - |  |  |
| 1693 | - | 1729 | - |  |  |
| 1694 | - | 1730 | - |  |  |
| 1695 | 7,277 ryō | 1731 | 1,641 ryō |  |  |
| 1696 | 13,026 ryō 2 bu | 1732 | 8,114 ryō 1 bu |  |  |
| 1697 | - | 1733 | 5,608 ryō |  |  |
| 1698 | 7,537 ryō 2 bu | 1734 | New koban 1,770 ryō 3 bu*¹ |  |  |
|  |  |  | Old koban 2,627 ryō |  |  |
| 1699 | - | 1735 | New koban 490 ryō 3 bu |  |  |

Notes:
*1: 'New koban' means Genbun koban. 'Old koban' means Kyōhō koban.
*2: 'Genbun' means Genbun koban.

The export of *koban* continued until 1753, but the actual transactions ceased in the previous year. Annual exports of up to 1,000 *ryō* were treated as private trade rather than regular trade from 1753. *Koban* exports recorded for 1753 had been acquired prior to that year. According to *Nagasaki jikki nendairoku*, the export of 1,000 *ryō* of the Genbun *koban* was permitted annually from 1753 to 1762. Although the quantity fluctuated from year to year, 10,000 *ryō* (1,000 *ryō* per annum on average) were exported as private trade shipments over a period of ten years. *Koban* exports stopped from 1763. According to *Nagasaki kaisho gosatsumono* (Five-volume books of the Nagasaki trade association), 'The export of *koban* was banned in 1763; ordered to export 70,000 kin of copper as a replacement for 1,000 *ryō* of export *koban*'.[66] In this way, 70,000 kin of copper were exported instead of 1,000 *ryō* of *koban* from 1763. *Koban* was never exported after that.

## Distribution routes for *koban*

This section examines the various sales channels for exported *koban* within the Asian market from the second half of the seventeenth century to the first half of the eighteenth century (see Maps 1 and 2 for place locations).

### Coromandel
The Indian subcontinent of the latter half of the seventeenth century can be divided into three regions according to the prevailing monetary system:
  1. The northern region from Surat and Gujarat to Bengal that primarily used silver coins,
  2. The central region from Bombay to Golconda that used both gold and silver coins,
  3. And the southern region from the Malabar coast to the coast of Coromandel that primarily used gold coins.[67]
These regions were not completely separate economically. For example, silver coins were still accepted in Coromandel even though gold coins were dominant there, and copper coins were accepted throughout India. The above divisions are simply based on the primary money used in each region.[68]

The Japanese *koban* was the preferred gold coin in Coromandel in the latter half of the seventeenth century.[69] Coromandel had two gold coins: the pagoda and fanum. According to purity testing conducted in Negapatam in 1720, the purity of the pagoda coin was about 20 carat 8.5 grain, almost the same as the Keichō *koban*. The fanum had a purity of 7 carat 10 grain.[70] Conversion rates used from 1676 to around 1691 were 1 pagoda to 6 gulden and 12 fanum to 1 pagoda.[71] The VOC first obtained permission to set up a mint in Pulicut on the Coromandel coast and later built another mint in Negapatam in 1658.[72] The Dutch sent imported foreign gold coins and bullions to these mints and re-coined them into local coins. Much of the Japanese *koban* were re-coined into the pagoda and fanum at these mints and some were sold as they were.

According to the *Generale Missiven*, 6.5 ton (650,000 gulden) were sent to Coromandel in 1669.[73] This figure would amount to about 33,163 *ryō* at the previous year's purchase price in Japan of 5.6 tael per *ryō*. Articles about *koban* shipments to Coromandel appear here and there in the *Generale Missiven* from then on.[74] While it is apparent from these articles that *koban* were mostly shipped to Coromandel, it is difficult to find accurate accounts of the amounts of *koban* shipped there in the latter half of the seventeenth century when *koban* was making a profit of about 30 per cent. Trade books of the Dutch Factories in Coromandel, especially the one in Negapatam, need to be examined further in the future.

As mentioned earlier, the Dutch were forced to trade different kinds of *koban* at the same price as the fine quality Keichō *koban*, in spite of the debasement and weight changes that resulted from frequent re-coinages in Japan during the eighteenth century. The frequent *koban* re-coinages only led to greater losses every time they were re-minted into local coins in Coromandel. Table 24 shows the annual losses incurred in Coromandel by *koban* imports. The figures are based on a survey of the *koban* market conditions in Coromandel from 1702 to 1724 conducted by van Heiningen in 1726. Van Heiningen's survey will be analysed in detail in Chapter Six.[75]

According to Table 24, a total of 291,582 *ryō* of *koban* were sent to Coromandel in this period with an annual average of 12,677 *ryō*. The losses incurred from *koban* debasement in Japan reached around 1.5 million gulden.[76] The losses continued to increase every time a new *koban* was re-minted in Japan and exported. More than one type of *koban* was exported to Coromandel by the VOC and the amount of loss varied depending on the type of *koban*. For example, the export of the Keichō *koban* from Japan had already been banned in the early eighteenth century, but the Dutch were able to continue shipping it to Coromandel from stock in Batavia for a while.

It was reported in the *Generale Missiven* that 372,077 *ryō* of the Genroku *koban* were re-minted at Negapatam in a period from 1 January 1709 to 31 August 1716 at a cost of 2,446,376 gulden. It generated a profit of 61,980 gulden, or about 2.5 per cent.[77] By contrast, the re-minting of the Kenji *koban* took place in Negapatam over a period from 17 May 1714 to 19 February 1717. It cost 985,368 gulden and resulted in a loss of 337,686 gulden, or 34.5 per

Table 24: Koban sales in Coromandel, 1702-1724

| | Koban sales in Coromandel (ryō) | Loss (gulden) | Loss per piece (gulden) | Type of koban imported from Japan |
|---|---|---|---|---|
| 1701/02 | 22514 | 71,477 | 3.17 | Genroku koban |
| 1702/03 | 17940.3125 | 54,370 | 3.03 | " |
| 1703/04 | 11034 | 34,085 | 3.1 | " |
| 1704/05 | 8455 | 26,764 | 3.17 | " |
| 1705/06 | 24864.25 | 81,979 | 3.7 | " |
| 1706/07 | 13500 | 41,319 | 3.06 | " |
| 1707/08 | 5168.75 | 16,736 | 3.24 | " |
| 1708/09 | 22121.75 | 72,311 | 3.27 | " |
| 1709/10 | 12468.25 | 41,296 | 3.31 | " |
| 1710/11 | 16228 | 52,451 | 3.23 | " |
| 1711/12 | 21996 | 73,168 | 3.33 | " |
| 1712/13 | 3920 | 10,907 | 2.78 | Kenji koban |
| 1713/14 | 29538.25 | 205,701 | 6.96 | " |
| 1714/15 | 15200 | 98,392 | 6.47 | " |
| 1715/16 | 2000 | 6,152 | 3.08 | " |
| 1716/17 | 17556 | 143,853 | 8.19 | " |
| 1717/18 | 5312 | 46,166 | 8.69 | " |
| 1718/19 | 3714 | 32,274 | 8.69 | " |
| 1719/20 | 4660 | 39,677 | 8.51 | " |
| 1720/21 | 8400 | 30,003 | 3.57 | " |
| 1721/22 | 5406 | 46,998 | 8.69 | Kyōhō koban |
| 1722/23 | 8828 | 157,225 | 17.81 | " |
| 1723/24 | 10760 | 183,284 | 17.03 | " |

Notes:
*Koban* sales and losses in Coromandel have been calculated based on *De archieven van de Verenigde Oostindische Compangie* No.2039, ARA. Fractions less than a gulden have been disregarded in the loss column.
1 gulden = 20 stuiver. 1 tael = 70 stuiver.

cent.[78] The Genroku *koban* generated little profit and the Kenji and Kyōnō *koban* incurred losses of around 35 per cent. The loss rate rose to around 38 per cent in the 1730s and reached 39 per cent in 1736.[79]

The Coromandel region, a major destination for *koban* exports, came under the control of the Mughal Empire when the Golconda Kingdom was annexed in 1687. Mughal's official silver coins became dominant in this region and the economy gradually shifted from a gold standard to a silver standard. This led to a fall in the value of gold in Coromandel. Moreover, Coromandel suffered severe economic damage under Mughal control and followed a course of decline without recovering its prosperity of the past years. On the other hand, Bengal in northern India came to establish superiority and enjoyed prosperity.[80]

## Bengal

Bengal appeared in the *Generale Missiven* from 1669 after the export ban on *koban* was effectively lifted in 1664. According to the records, a 1669 trial of re-minting *koban* into local coins in Bengal generated a profit of around 43 per cent.[81] 18,900 *ryō* were sold to the Nawab (viceroy of a province of the Mughal Empire) at 18.75 ropia per *ryō*, producing a profit of about 34 per cent.[82] In 1671, 31,333 *ryō* were shipped, 14,000–15,000 *ryō* of which were sold to the Nawab at the 1669 price and the remainder were sold at 19.5 ropia for a profit of 35 per cent.[83] *Koban* shipments in 1672 were worth as much as 1,108,380 gulden[84], but only 299,880 gulden worth of *koban* were allocated to Bengal in 1673 due to a higher demand in Batavia.[85] As the *koban* price in Bengal was on the rise during this period, 16,800 *ryō* were sent from Malacca in 1675.[86] A profit of 67,833 gulden was made from the sale of 19,036 *ryō* of *koban* in that year.[87] After fetching 19.5 ropia per *ryō* in 1674, *koban* did not rise above 18–18.25 ropia in 1675.[88] The market deteriorated at the beginning of 1676 with the price falling to 17.5 ropia and sales slowing.[89] Large shipments of *koban* to Bengal stopped at around this time.

Further falls in the price of *koban* were reported after 1676. The amount of *koban* allocated to Bengal from Batavia and Malacca gradually became smaller and shipments less frequent. An article in the *Generale Missiven* in 1680 reads, 'While silver is very popular and highly valued in Bengal, there is little demand for gold and therefore Japanese *koban* is currently priced at no more than 16.5 ropia per *ryō* or 8.25 rixdaalder in Bengal'.[90] After this article, the *koban* and Ducaten gold coins were shipped only when silver could not be obtained from the Netherlands, but *koban* were mostly sent to Coromandel rather than Bengal.[91]

As seen above, large quantities of *koban* were sent to Bengal from around 1670, giving the impression that these shipments were given priority until around 1675. However, Bengal's economy was originally silver coin-based; the export of *koban* to Bengal was limited to times when the value of gold appreciated temporarily. When the gold price fell, most *koban* exports were directed to Coromandel, which was a primary market for gold.[92]

## Other regions

*Koban* was circulating as money in key VOC trading bases such as Batavia and Malacca. It was also shipped to Jepara and Bantan at a low price of 8 rixdaalder per *ryō* in the 1670s.[93] As it was usually traded at 9 rixdaalder in Batavia at the time, it is obvious that *koban* did not fetch a good price in these areas.

*Koban* was shipped to Ceylon in the 1680s.[94] Ceylon had close economic links with Coromandel, where gold coins were used primarily. Ceylon was the place from which the VOC managed and controlled its India trade. It is quite possible that *koban* was circulated as money in Ceylon as it was in Batavia. One reason for the export of *koban* to Ceylon was political instability in Coromandel. As mentioned earlier, the Mughal Empire was gradually extending its influence to the southern part of the Deccan Plateau during this period. Ceylon probably served as a temporary storage place of *koban* until an appropriate time for shipment to Coromandel or as a transit point for shipment to regions to the west such as Surat. Vessels bound for the Netherlands from Ceylon probably carried some *koban* as well. Accordingly, shipments to Ceylon must be studied with care as they could have been sent to various destinations from there.

Orders for *koban* were received from Surat as well as Coromandel in 1640[95], but no large shipments were made as *koban* exports were banned in Japan in the following year. It appears that *koban* were also shipped to Macassar and other destinations, but in small quantities.

Now let us summarize changes in the Asian *koban* trade after the lifting of the *koban* export embargo in Japan.

In 1665 and 1666, there were no notable records of activity in the Asia market as *koban* prices were still high in Japan and export quantities were small. Articles about *koban* began to appear in the *Generale Missiven* from around 1667. One dated 23 December of the same year reads as follows:

The Company is likely to be able to procure sufficient amounts of *koban* in Japan from now on. Gold procured in Andragiry, the west coast [of Sumatra] and Japan are available at much more reasonable prices than back home. Hence there are no plans to place orders [for gold] with the headquarters; [rather] it is hoped that more silver coins will be sent here.[96]

In the first half of the 1660s, the governor general and council in Batavia asked the board in the Netherlands to send large shipments of gold to Asia almost every year, but these requests stopped until the mid-1670s, when moderately priced *koban* became available in large quantities in Japan. Since no coins were available in the home country for shipment to Asia, the board directed Batavia in a correspondence dated 5 September 1672 to use the Japanese *koban* as money worth 9 rixdaalder.[97] The government general and council in Batavia followed the directive by proclaiming a formal exchange rate for currency at 9 rixdaalder, or 60 stuiver to 1 ryō of koban in 1673.[98] The board in the Netherlands expected that koban could relieve the constant gold shortage in Asia.

However, from 1672 koban export prices rose in Japan and the company adopted a policy minimizing koban exports and giving priority to copper exports that were expected to be more profitable. This led to not only a decline in koban exports but also large fluctuations in the volume of koban exports from one year to another. As a result, the availability of koban in the Asia market became unstable. In fact, many articles in the Generale Missiven during the 1680s reported that koban were not available; '10,000 ryō of koban are needed as Batavia has run out of coins' or, 'Koban from Japan should be shipped to Batavia; cannot be sent to Coromandel'.[99] The value of koban in Batavia appreciated under these circumstances; the exchange rate was lifted to 10 rixdaalder per ryō on 8 June 1690.[100]

Although koban had brought the Dutch a profit of around 30 per cent in Coromandel until then, the value of koban was debased in a succession of re-coinages in Japan from the late seventeenth century. This led to mounting losses for the VOC when koban were re-minted into local coins in Coromandel. Brazilian gold began to flow into Europe in large quantities from the early eighteenth century and its arrival in the Asia market also diminished the importance of Japanese koban. Moreover, copper and silver became more important than gold in the Asia market during the eighteenth century.[101] These internal and external factors accelerated the decline of the Japanese koban in the trade of the eighteenth century.

## Conclusion

Fluctuations in the gold–silver parity in the European and Southwest Asian markets from the seventeenth century had a major impact on the Asia trade of the VOC. The company was in need of enormous capital for its transit trade within Asia because there was little demand for European goods in Asia in those days. It therefore watched fluctuations in the gold–silver parity closely, procuring necessary capital in the form of gold or silver based on their profitability. The goods that the Dutch wished to procure in Japan varied accordingly.

The relative importance of gold, silver and copper as Japanese export products also changed according to domestic economic conditions. The combination of these internal and external factors led to the lifting of the koban export embargo in 1664.

However, the prosperity of the koban trade did not last long. Various internal and external factors were again at work. The internal factors included

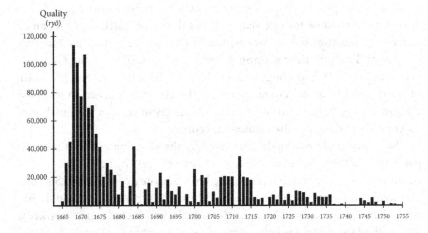

*Figure 8:* Koban *exports, 1665–1752*

a decline in domestic gold production, a *koban* shortage due to domestic economic growth, *koban* debasement through re-coinages to cover the shortages, and the withdrawal of old *koban* for re-coinages. A fall in the value of gold in the Southwest Asian market in the eighteenth century was a major external factor.

From a microscopic viewpoint, the *koban* trade flourished from 1668 to 1679. According to Figure 8, the quantity of *koban* exports was particularly large during a seven year period from 1668 to 1675, amounting to a total of 582,837 *ryō* with an annual average of 83,262 *ryō*. About 400,000 *ryō* were exported in the period of four years from 1668 to 1671, when *koban* could be exported at the local market price. The VOC set a formal exchange rate for *koban* as currency in Batavia in 1673. It made profits of around 30 per cent in the main gold consuming region of Coromandel in the latter half of the seventeenth century.

From a macroscopic viewpoint, the *koban* trade prospered until the fine-quality Keichō *koban* became unavailable for export at the end of the seventeenth century (1664–1696). Although large quantities of *koban* were exported on a few occasions during the eighteenth century, the Dutch were suffering great losses as a result of *koban* debasement from re-coinages and the freezing of the price at previously high levels.

Table 20 shows *koban* exports over seventy years around the turn of the eighteenth century. About 1 million *ryō* of *koban* were shipped out by the Dutch fleet during the first thirty-five years and about 380,000 *ryō* during the second thirty-five years. The annual revenue of the Tokugawa shogunate from the late 1680s to the 1690s was approximately 1.17 million *ryō*.[102] The total *koban* export in the seventeenth century was almost equal to the government revenue for one year in those days; the outflow of this much currency from the country was bound to have an impact on its domestic economy. The Japanese economy was growing well over the Genroku years (1688–1703). The shogunate could not afford to overlook the drain of important domestic currency out of the country forever under these circumstances. It began to signify its intensions to restrict the outflow of *koban* after the turn of the eighteenth century.

The *koban* trade was again frustrated by the shogunate, which promulgated the *Shōtoku shinrei* in 1715 to cut *koban* exports by the Dutch. To add insult to injury, the Dutch were ordered to trade the newly minted Shōtoku and Kyōhō *koban* at double the price of the Keichō *koban*, even though they were identical in purity and weight. These unfavorable trade terms markedly diminished the desire for *koban* exports on the part of the Dutch. The VOC eagerly looked for alternative Japanese exports such as copper and camphor that might be profitable overseas, but to no avail. The Dutch therefore could not afford to stop *koban* exports completely. They had to continue trading some *koban* at a loss in order to maintain their trade with Japan.

On the other hand, Japan needed to export *koban* in addition to copper despite the decline in production during the eighteenth century in order to acquire foreign goods, technology, knowledge and information. The negative side of Japanese–Dutch trade gradually cast a dark shadow over both countries.

In 1736, Shogun Yoshimune commenced the mintage of the much debased Genbun *koban* with the intention not to export them. This made the decline of the *koban* trade definite. The last time *koban* exports were entered in the trade journal of the Dutch Factory was in 1753. The export of *koban* continued as part of private trade until 1762, but even that was stopped from 1763 because the shogunate wanted to secure raw material for the minting of new coins. The shogunate also took the drastic step of importing gold and silver, commodities Japan used to export.[103] In this way, the *koban* trade came to its end after nearly a century. Having served their purpose, the odd-shaped Japanese gold coins quietly disappeared from Asian countries.

# Chapter Five

# Camphor Production and Sale

The word 'camphor (kampfer, kamfer)' is said to have been derived from the Arabic word 'kafur', which is said to have originated with a Sanskrit word meaning 'pure white'.[1] The peoples of the three great ancient cultures— Indian, Islamic and Chinese—discovered how to extract borneol from the *dryobalanops camphora* growing on the Malay Peninsula and the Island of Sumatra in Southeast Asia. It is said to have been as valuable as or even more valuable than gold due to its rarity; only a minute amount of the substance could be extracted from each tree.[2] Since camphor had a similar aroma to borneol, even though it was not as elegant or sublime, and since it was available at lower prices, it was welcomed as a borneol substitute in the southern regions and India.[3]

Camphor has been studied vigorously from the angle of the spice trade by Yamada Kentarō.[4] Miyashita Saburō's study is noteworthy from a pharmacopoeial point of view.[5] The production of Satsuma camphor has been studied by Suzuki Hajime and Murano Moriharu.[6] There have been some studies of Tosa camphor as well.[7]

Camphor was exported by the Chinese and Dutch fleets throughout the early modern period until the end of the Edo period. Although the volume of camphor exports was much smaller than metal exports (gold, silver and copper), it was the largest non-metal export. Studies of the foreign trade in camphor have been undertaken by Iwao Seiichi and Yamawaki Teijirō[8], but few studies have dealt with the camphor trade by the Dutch over a long period of time.

This chapter will mainly focus on the trade books of the Dutch Factory (*Negotie Journalen*) and the *Generale Missiven* of the VOC. It will shed light on the production, trade and sale of camphor.

## Camphor production

Chinese camphor production began in the twelve or thirteenth century in the Fujian and Canton (Guangdong) provinces, where camphor trees grew in abundance.[9] It appears that Chinese camphor was brought to Japan on Ryūkyū ships and exported to Korea by the early fifteenth century.[10] Camphor production in Japan started by the latter half of the sixteenth century at the latest. Since the *Nippo jisho* (Japanese–Portuguese dictionary) published in 1603–1604 contains the phrase 'Xonou Yaqu (burn camphor): to produce camphor'[11], it is likely that camphor production was spreading in the Kyūshū region to a certain extent by the early seventeenth century.

Camphor production began in Satsuma Province when Lord Shimazu Yoshihiro of the Satsuma domain brought back some Korean potters on his return from Toyotomi Hideyoshi's Korean campaign in 1590s. The potters settled in the Naeshirogawa district and introduced camphor production to the area.[12] Murano Moriharu argues that camphor production was imported from Korea based on this record.[13] On the other hand, Yamada Kentarō suggests that it is rather baffling that camphor production came from Korea when there was no camphor trees there.[14] Abe Keiji considers that the camphor production method employed by the potters was very similar to the sulfur production technique used in Korea at the time; it might have been applied to camphor production.[15] In any case, there is no historical record of the existence of camphor production in Korea in those days.

The abovementioned *Nippo jisho* was published at the beginning of the seventeenth century. Since it would have taken several years to compile the dictionary, the phrase meaning 'to produce camphor' must have been already known to a certain extent in Nagasaki and other parts of Kyūshū by 1600. In that case, camphor production could have been imported from Korea in the 1690s and quickly spread to the whole of Kyūshū within a decade or so. However, such information about a new excellent method of manufacture would have been secret and not easily spread. Consequently, it is more reasonable to think that camphor production came from China, which had an established method of production by the latter half of the sixteenth century at the latest.

Korean potters in Naeshirogawa increased camphor production by applying their advanced ceramic manufacturing skill to improve the production bowl. 'Meiji 5 nen Shōnō seihō hatsumei no negaisho' emphasizes the importance of bowl making in camphor production by stating, 'Formation of camphor crystals depends on the quality of the bowl. Camphor crystals do not adhere to the bowl if low-quality clay is used to make the bowl or the bowl was fired poorly and therefore this requires utmost care'. This probably led to the incorrect view that the method of camphor production was imported from Korea.

The camphor production method was recorded in the *Wakan sansai zue* (Illustrated Sino–Japanese encyclopedia), published in 1722.[16] 'Nihon

*Figure 9: The 'burn out' method of camphor production*

Source: See note 17.

sankai meibutsu zue (Illustrated encyclopedia of notable Japanese products)'
published in 1754 has the following description and the illustration shown
in Figure 9:

> Camphor trees' roots are cut into small chips and boiled in a pot. (...) The
> pot is covered with a bowl and the gap between the pot and the bowl is sealed
> with clay so that vapor does not escape. Dew drops forming inside the cover
> are camphor crystals.[17]

The method was somewhat improved in the nineteenth century, as reported
in *Jūtei honzō Kōmoku keimō* (Revised edition botanical classification)[18],
published in 1803, but the basic process remained the same. This method
of camphor production, which was common in the early modern period,
was introduced to Europe by a foreign scholar in the latter half of the
eighteenth century. C. p. Thunberg, a Swedish botanist who visited Japan
in 1775, wrote:

> The camphor tree grows wild in abundance in Satsuma Province and Gotō
> Islands. Almost all of the camphor consumed in Europe comes from these

two places. The Japanese chop the trunk and roots of the camphor tree into small pieces and boil them in an iron pot full of water with a wooden lid in the shape of a very high dome. This dome section is filled with straws or hay which capture camphor contained in the rising vapor. Camphor adheres to straws and comes off in the form of powder. The powder is collected in a tub, which is bought by the VOC by weight.[19]

The camphor production method described in these historical records was called the 'burn out method' (also known as the sublimation or earthen pan method). Camphor tree trunks and roots were finely chopped, put in a pot filled with water, covered and boiled. Sublimated camphor, which would collect on the inside of the lid or on straws inside the lid, is harvested later.

The volume of camphor exports gradually increased from the latter half of the eighteenth century; the annual average volume reached around 70,000 kin in the 1830s–1840s. The export of camphor flourished toward the end of the Edo period, so much so that most camphor trees were cut down and, in Satsuma, the original stock was depleted. Shimazu Nariakira, the lord of the Satsuma domain at the end of the Edo period, regarded camphor as the third most important product of his domain after sugar and Japan wax[20] and encouraged research to improve its quality. Yamamoto Sōbei, a retainer of the Satsuma domain, took efforts to cultivate camphor and camphor seedlings.[21] These and other efforts were taken in Satsuma in response to the expanding overseas exports.

Satsuma was the primary camphor producing region in the early modern period; 'camphor' and 'camphor tree' were listed as its notable products in *Kefukigusa* (Reference book for the study of poetry, Haiku), published in 1647.[22] Camphor also appears in *Satsusshū sanbutsu roku* (Catalogue of products from the Satsuma Province), published in 1792.[23] It was also produced in Ōsumi Province and Hyūga Province, as reported in *Wakan sansai zue* (see note 16). According to *Sangoku meishō zue*, published in 1843, camphor producing districts in those days included Hiwaki, Nakagō and Hazuki in Satsuma, Ōnejime, Kanoya and Tanegashima in Ōsumi, and Yoshida, and Kakutō and Masaki in Hyūga.[24] Most early modern export camphor were produced in these areas.

In the trade journals of the Dutch Factory, camphor was called 'Japansche campher (Japanese camphor)' until 1661; on some occasions, 'Satsumase campher (Satsuma camphor)' was used. The two descriptions coexisted until 1671, when 'Satsumase campher' became the only description for camphor. This suggests that most export camphor was produced in the Satsuma domain. Satsuma camphor was brought to the offices of the Satsuma domain

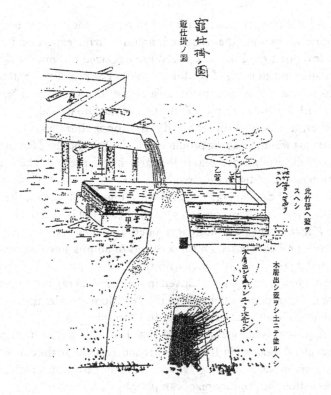

*Figure 10: The distillation method of camphor production*

Source: Nihon sangyō shi shiryō (Archival resources for
the history of Japanese industry), Vol. 4, p. 454.

government, transferred to the Satsuma government warehouse in Nagasaki, and dispatched to Dejima by camphor merchants.[25]

Another camphor producing region outside of the Satsuma domain was Tosa, to be discussed later. Camphor was also produced on the Gotō Islands and on Tsushima Island, but in much smaller amounts than in the Satsuma domain.[26] The 'burn out method' was introduced to the Tosa domain and camphor production started in the 1750s and 1760s. Camphor production in Tosa expanded to the extent that the product was sold outside of the domain in the 1830s.[27]

A more efficient camphor production process, called the 'distillation method', was developed in the latter half of the 1850s.[28] The new method increased the production volume dramatically and improved the quality of the camphor. The mechanism used in the distillation process is shown in Figure 10. One of the main features of this distillation method was a wooden cooling tub called the 'vessel', invented to replace the ceramic bowl used in the burn out method that required manufacturing expertise. It was an epochal invention for Tosa; it replaced the unglazed ceramic bowl, which was very difficult to make if not for the skill of a specialized potter. Tosa began to produce large quantities of camphor for export from Nagasaki together with Satsuma camphor at the end of the Edo period.[29]

However, it is doubtful that the distillation method was invented in Tosa. Satsuma was the leading producer of camphor and the Satsuma name represented the product overseas in the early modern period. The 'camphor production method (distillation method)' is found in various texts such as the *Nihon nōgyō zensho* (agricultural encyclopedia of Japan), the *Nihon sangyō shi shiryō* (archival resources for the history of Japanese industries) and the *Kagaku kogyō zensho* (encyclopedia of chemical industry); this method was probably based on the writings of an unknown author on an unknown date on sheets of paper with the Kōchi prefectural government letterhead. These writings are archived in the Shirai Library of the National Diet Library. Camphor production in the Tosa domain from the end of the Edo period has been studied earnestly in Kōchi prefecture.

Although it is widely considered that the distillation method was independently developed in Tosa, there are some articles in the diaries of the Dutch Factory in Nagasaki (*Dagregisters*) from the early nineteenth century that suggest that the production of camphor by the distillation process was also practiced in Satsuma at that time. An article dated 4 April 1803 reports, 'Duty chief interpreter Sukezaemon came and told me that Lord Satsuma intended to have the maximum amount of camphor distilled'.[30] Another article dated 29 April 1804 reads as follows:

> Some distilleries have been built again in Satsuma and he, the contractor, thinks he can secure all the camphor ordered this year, but it is not yet certain because although the camphor distillers of Satsuma have certainly set up distilleries again, they are still very cautious about building up their stock.[31]

It is therefore apparent that camphor was produced by distillation in Satsuma at the beginning of the nineteenth century, even though the specific method is unknown. It is likely that this method was introduced to Tosa.

## The camphor trade in the seventeenth century

This section will examine in detail the production of camphor in Satsuma and the impacts that changes in the demand for camphor in Asia had on the purchasing of camphor in Nagasaki.

## The camphor trade during the Hirado factory era

The Dutch Factory was set up in Hirado in 1609, but there are no extant journals (*Negotie Journalen*) prior to 1620, or general ledgers (*Groot boeken*) prior to 1624. Subsequently, we can only glean the fact that some camphor was exported from Japan by the red seal ships that were authorized by the shogun and by the Dutch feet during the 1610s, after the opening of the factory.[32]

In 1621 and 1622, camphor was bought from Hirado merchants, Hiranoya Sakubei ('Sackobij' in the Dutch records) and Taniya Rihyōe ('Riffioije'), in cash or as payment for various goods. As shown in Table 25, camphor deals were often handled by these two merchants jointly. Camphor was not exported from 1623 to 1626, but the Dutch Factory bought 31,962 kin of camphor from someone called Shinre and exported all of them in 1626.

A memorandum dated 15 November 1632 stated that camphor was one of the 'goods not to be taken out abroad without authorization' in the Satsuma domain.[33] It is therefore likely that camphor dealers in Satsuma were selling camphor to merchants in Nagasaki or Hirado, or directly to the Dutch Factory on the authority of the Satsuma domain government. In January 1633 the Dutch Factory bought 13,986 kin of camphor at 8.5 tael per picol from a Hirado merchant named Sukēmon ('Sckemon') after the resolution of the Tayouan incident. An article dated 15 September 1633 in the diary of the Dutch Factory in Hirado (*Dagregister*) reports the contents of a correspondence from a freeman (a Dutch person other than the Dutch Factory officers) in Nagasaki named Carel Laurense:

*Table 25: Camphor transactions, 1621–1622*

| Date | Quantity (catty) | Tael | Merchant |
|---|---|---|---|
| 1621. 8.22 | 1,970 | 167: 4: 5 | Sackobij *1 |
| 9. 9 | 5,362 | 455: 7: 7 | Sackobij *1 |
| 9.23 | 16,914 | 1,437: 6: 9 | Sackobij *1 |
| 10.23 | 3,882 | 329: 9: 7 | Riffioij Sackobij *2 |
| 10.25 | 20,124 | 1,710: 5: 4 | Riffioij Sackobij *2 |
| 11.2 | 15,257 | 1,296: 8: 4 | Sackobij Rffieij |
| 12.2 | 21,661 | 1,841: 1: 8 | Riffioije Sackobij |
| 1622. 1.27 | 14,866 | 1,263: 6: 1 | Riffioije Sackobij |
| 8. 9 | *3 | *4 | Riffioije Sackobij |

Source: *Negotie Journalen* 1620–24, *Archief Japan*, No.829, ARA.

*1: Sackobij: Hiranoya Sakubei.

*2: Riffioij(e) Sackobij or Sackobij Rjffeij: the transaction with the Dutch Factory was conducted between Taniya Rihyōe and Hiranoya Sakubei jointly.

*3: The quantity of neither copper nor camphor is recorded.

*4: 3611: 7: 9 tael in payment for copper and camphor.

The Lord of Satsuma has forbidden camphor production. It is because large
finest-quality trees have been used for this purpose. (...) We used be able to
buy camphor at 5 tael 5 maas (per picol) but now we have to pay at least 6 tael
or 6 and a half tael (per picol).[34]

The difference in the unit price between January and September was due
to the Dutch Factory buying camphor from merchants in Hirado at higher
prices, not because the camphor price dropped in that period. Directives
dated 31 May 1633 from the Governor General of the Dutch East Indies in
Batavia to the Dutch Factory in Hirado stated that it was very ignominious
to purchase camphor at 8 tael per picol in Hirado when a freeman was able
to buy it at 6 tael in Nagasaki in 1631.[35] Nonetheless, the situation persisted
even in the latter half of 1633.

An article dated 21 September 1633 reports that 'Carel in Nagasaki said
camphor was not available at any price below 7 tael there'.[36] Although the
price of camphor was lower in Nagasaki than in Hirado, the prohibition of
camphor production in Satsuma was pushing the price up there as well.

Trade books between 1633 and 1635 do not name camphor merchants
other than Sckemon in 1633; they merely state the factory's dealings with
several merchants ('verscheijde personen'). For four years from 1636 to
1639, the factory purchased camphor exclusively from a Hirado merchant
named Harimaya Kurōzaemon ('Farima Croseijmon'). An article dated 13
June 1636 of the diary reads:

> The Hirado citizen Harimaya Kurōzaemon signed a contract with the head of
> the factory to deliver 500 picol of camphor in the coming November but the
> delivery has now become impossible. It is because Lord Satsuma has banned
> the production of camphor again.[37]

Faced with another camphor production ban, the Dutch Factory dispatched
an envoy bearing a letter and gifts to Satsuma and sent people to other
regions to investigate the availability of camphor.[38] Harimaya Kurōzaemon
headed for Satsuma in February 1637 by order of the head of the factory,
Nicolaes Couckebacker, to deliver letters to three Satsuma councilors:
Shimazu Danjō Daihitsu Hisayoshi ('Simazu Daijsio'), Niiro Kaga-no-kami
Tadakiyo ('Nijro Canganocamij') and Kawakami Sakon Shōgen Hisakuni
('Caiwacami Chiougin').[39,40] Harimaya was a sole dealer, handling the
transaction process from the purchase of camphor to the sale of camphor
to the Dutch Factory and playing a greater role than Carel Laurense, who
acted as a successful camphor dealer in 1633 and 1634.

The volume of camphor exports for 1636 was only 20,067 kin due to the camphor production ban issued in that year. The volume dropped dramatically to 1,100 kin in 1637.[41] The price of camphor rose in the second half of the 1630s as a result of the ban, from 6–7 tael per picol prior to 1635 to 7–8.5 tael in 1636 and 10 tael from 1637.

Camphor production in Satsuma was banned again in 1639. The *Diary of the Dutch Factory in Hirado* reads as follows:

> Today I heard the following from Harimaya Kurōzaemon, a merchant and citizen of Hirado. It came to Lord Satsuma's knowledge that some tenants of the camphor forest were attempting to cut the camphor trees earmarked for official uses in order to produce camphor for private gain despite various interdicts. (…) The Lord prohibited the production of camphor under penalty of death. (…) By all indications, no camphor could be procured from Satsuma in the next few years.[42]

No camphor was exported in 1640 as a result of this prohibition. The recurring prohibitions on camphor production in Satsuma in 1633, 1636 and 1639 were measures taken against a spate of illegal logging incidents in which camphor trees that were earmarked for official purposes such as construction of the domain buildings were cut down for camphor production.

## The camphor trade in the mid- to late-seventeenth century

The price of camphor was stable from 1641, the year the Dutch Factory was relocated from Hirado to Nagasaki, to 1644. In the duration, the Dutch expressed dissatisfaction with the small volume of camphor exports. Batavia was receiving large orders mainly from the southwestern Asian regions at the time and needed more camphor from Japan. An article in the *Diary of the Castle of Batavia 1644–1645* reads as follows:

> The head of the Factory in Japan only managed to procure 30,155.5 catty of camphor, which has arrived here on board the *Den Zwaan*. We expected that a greater amount of camphor would be obtained (due to a lower camphor price) as the prices of rice and other foodstuffs had dropped by about one third in the last 4–5 years but our expectation was not fulfilled despite the sufficient effort made by the factory head. The lord of Satsuma prohibited logging in the forest which has a dense growth of camphor trees and has been producing the greatest quantity of camphor. Since food prices remain low, camphor merchants did not demand more than 12 tael per picol (100 kin). They promised us to procure as much camphor as possible next year.[43]

The volume of exports in 1644 was small due to the abovementioned situation in Satsuma. The Dutch tried to increase the volume in 1645 in order to make up for shortfalls in the previous years[44], but orders from Surat alone reached 800 picol with additional orders for 100 picol received from the Netherlands.[45] In response to such large orders, the volume of camphor exports in 1645 was a record amount of 104,002 kin.

It would have been difficult to fill these orders after Lord Satsuma issued a partial ban on the logging of camphor trees in 1644. The record-breaking export volume suggests that the prohibition was not adhered to thoroughly in Satsuma. About 25,000 kin of camphor were obtained from merchants in Higo and exported in 1645. However, the large exports resulted in overstocking in Batavia when orders from Surat were later cancelled.[46] Consequently, the export volume was reduced in 1646 to the previous annual export level. In that year, however, the camphor price which had stayed at 12 tael per picol since 1641 fell considerably to 7 tael.

The names of the camphor merchants who had business with the Dutch Factory in the 1640s are found in the Dutch factory's trade books. The Dutch Factory generally bought camphor from one or two exclusive merchants during the 1620s and 1630s. It began to enter into purchase contracts with several camphor merchants through *otona* (civilian supervisors in Dejima) and interpreters during the 1640s. They included the Higo-based merchants mentioned above.

There are some articles about camphor from Higo in the *Diary of the Dutch Factory* from around that time. For example, an article dated 30 June 1643 reports that '22,900 kin of camphor were received'.[47] There is a corresponding entry in the *Negotie Journaal* of 3 July which reads, 'About 2,753 tael were paid in cash for a purchase of 22,946 kin of camphor from Higo merchant Mr Toraya Shōbei ('Torraija Sieubeij')'.[48] Another article dated 13 June 1644 reports that a large ship carrying 570 *hyō* (bales) of camphor from Higo arrived but poor weather prevented it from unloading.[49] An article dated 17 November 1644 reports that '210 *hyō* of camphor from Higo were received and immediately weighed'.[50] There is a corresponding entry in a *Negotie Journaal* dated 20 November that states, 'About 664 tael were paid in cash for a purchase of 120 barrels of camphor, net weight 5,538 kin (gross weight 6,858 kin), from Higo merchant Mr Taroya Sebyōe'.[51]

In this way, camphor was delivered from Higo to the Dutch Factory during the 1640s. It is unclear whether the camphor was actually produced in Higo, or if it was Satsuma camphor procured by Higo merchants through illegal channels despite frequent camphor production bans in Satsuma. The appearances of the merchant names in the *Negotie Journalen* were limited to a period from 1643 to 1645; business dealings between them and the Dutch Factory were obviously not permanent. For this reason, it is probably more reasonable to think that it was Satsuma camphor delivered via Higo rather than camphor produced in Higo.

Camphor production was banned again in Satsuma from 1647 to 1651. The diary of the Dutch Factory reported, 'No camphor is produced in Satsuma'[52] and 'Very little camphor will be produced for export for several years'.[53] Consequently, only 200 kin of camphor were exported in 1647 and none were exported in 1648. In 1650, the Dutch met their immediate needs by purchasing old camphor that had been stored in warehouses for five to six years at prices higher than 6.5 tael per picol.[54] The Dutch Factory reluctantly took the advice of its interpreters in February 1650 that it should refrain from buying camphor as the price was as high as 8 tael per picol at that stage.[55]

The procurement of camphor continued to be extremely difficult in 1651. Interpreters explained that camphor production had been largely suspended in the previous year due to the failure of the rice crop; it would be impossible to obtain more than 10,000 kin of camphor and the price would also be higher.[56] True to their expectations, the price rose even higher than the price at the end of the previous year that had kept the factory from buying. The factory paid 9 tael per picol and managed to procure only 224 picol (22,400 kin).[57]

In 1652, the Dutch Factory entered a contract with the only camphor producer authorized by Lord Satsuma to purchase camphor at 9 tael per picol, but the seller declared that he would not produce any in the next year as he would incur a loss at that price.[58] Still, the Dutch managed to export 31,588 kin in 1652. It was decided at the council of the factory on 17 September 1653 that it would sign contracts with Japanese merchants to purchase 46,300 kin of camphor and continue to buy 40,000 kin annually for three years at a fixed price.[59] Nevertheless, it was unable to export any camphor in that year because the Japanese side failed to deliver camphor in time for the departure of the Dutch ships.[60] This suggests that the delay was caused by the difficulty of price negotiations.

In 1654, the factory officers came to a decision to purchase from 40,000 to 50,000 kin of camphor at 9 tael per picol[61] and held negotiations with a camphor merchant from 3 July to 11 August. In the end, the price was set at 10.5 tael per picol, higher than the factory had hoped.[62] 15,125 kin were delivered on 3 September and 21,517.5 kin were delivered on 7 September. The seller later agreed to discount the price of these lots to 9 tael per picol as they were old stock produced a year before.[63] The remaining 18,691 kin were delivered on 20 September, making up a total of 55,333.5 kin. That accounts for almost all the exports for that year. According to trade books, all three deliveries were purchased at 9 tael per picol although the initial contract price was 10.5 tael per picol.

No camphor was exported in 1655 and 1656 at all. An article dated 31 January 1657 in the *Generale Missiven* reports as follows:

> We could not buy camphor this season. The Chinese bought small quantities of camphor at 14 tael per picol. Satsuma never burns (produces) camphor in large quantities. According to some Satsuma people, (camphor production) does not bring a lot of profits and it is generally more advantageous to work in a gold mine than in camphor production. We are therefore unable to secure much of the medicine from now on in this situation.[64]

Since the camphor production ban pushed the camphor price up to 14 tael per picol, the Dutch were unable to procure enough camphor and only 11,600 kin were exported in 1657. The Dutch again had trouble procuring camphor as the price rose to 15 tael per picol in 1658[65]; they only managed to export 9,267 kin. It appears that this slump in camphor exports in the latter half of the 1650s was caused by the resumption of mining at Nagano and Yamagano gold mines in Satsuma by the authority of the shogunate in 1656.[66] The major Satsuma gold mines were at the height of their activity from 1657 to around 1665.[67] There was a much greater influx of workers to these gold mines than in any other periods. The camphor price rose from 10 tael per picol in 1657 to 14 tael in 1666 to pay for the increasingly higher wages of camphor producers in order to stop them from leaving for work in the gold mines.[68]

The export of camphor was generally sluggish during the 1650s; no camphor was exported for three years and very small quantities were exported in 1657 and 1658. Table 26 shows camphor exports from 1633 on a five-yearly basis. The volume of exports in the latter half of the 1650s was only about 75,000 kin; it had exceeded 100,000 kin in the five-year periods immediately before and after that period.

The 1660s was the *aitai* (direct dealings) period, during which the Dutch Factory made enormous profits; its total export value exceeded 2 million gulden per year and the export of camphor went without a hitch. However, no camphor was exported for a few years from 1670, perhaps due to the issuing of another camphor production ban in Satsuma.[69] The trade books from the latter half of the 1670s to the first half of the 1680s are missing so there is no detailed data for that period, but the price was stable in the 13 to 13.5 tael range. The annual export volume remained quite low at around 20,000 kin from the latter half of the 1680s to the 1690s.

*Table 26: Camphor exports, 1631–1665*

| Period | Number of years in which camphor was exported | Quantity exported |
|---|---|---|
| 1631–35 | 3 | 139,444 |
| 1636–40 | 4 | 100,421 |
| 1641–45 | 5 | 241,429 |
| 1646–50 | 4 | 113,930 |
| 1651–55 | 3 | 109,399 |
| 1656–60 | 4 | 75,171 |
| 1661–65 | 3 | 100,882 |

Source: Tabulated based on Table 30.

# Destinations of Japanese camphor exports in the seventeenth century

Camphor was used as a precious medicine in Arabia and also for Islamic rituals in ancient times because of its borneol-like aroma. It was brought to India and used as incense by Hindus. Buddhists and Hindus sometimes applied camphor to statues of their gods and the Buddha at religious services. It was also used as a refrigerant, mainly by nobles who rubbed it on their skin or took it by mouth to enjoy its cooling effect in hot weather. It was in demand as an insect repellent in the tropics. As a medicine, it was believed to have analgesic and antipyretic effects. The demand for camphor increased as its uses expanded over time. This section will discuss the regions to which Japanese camphor was exported in the seventeenth century.

## Persia

Persia was one of the major destinations of Japanese camphor exports in Asia. Goods were often shipped to Persia via Surat; there remains a number of letters addressed to the Dutch Factory in Surat. The first record of camphor shipment to Persia was an entry in the shipping bill of the *Vrede* and the *Weesp* sailing from Surat to Persia, dated 10 November 1623. It reads, '13 boxes of camphor (…) total weight 3,360 (catty), 25 gulden per picol, total 840 gulden'.[71] The price in 1623 was 25 gulden per picol, whereas in 1622 75,800 catty of camphor were exported from Japan at 8.5 tael per picol, or 24.23 gulden. Based on this price, the camphor shipped to Persia is likely to have been of Japanese origin. It was sold in Persia for 7,565 gulden, about nine times higher than the original price.[72]

A more specific account of Japanese camphor ('Japansche campher') can be found in a correspondence dated 9 November 1627 from the governor general to shareholders in the Netherlands. It lists the cargos on board seven ships which included '120 picol of Japanese camphor'.[73] Part of the cargos were to be sent to Surat and another part to Persia.

70 picol of Japanese camphor were shipped from Surat to Persia in 1629.[74] A shipping bill from February 1634 contains 10,293 catty of Japanese camphor at 18.75 gulden per picol.[75] This lot came on board the *Venloo*, which departed Japan in the previous December. Half of the 20,190 catty of camphor exported by the *Venloo*[76] was dispatched to Persia.

In 1636, 9,000 pond of camphor were included in an order prepared by the Dutch Factory in Gamron, Persia, based on the sales forecasts for the next year.[77] Some camphor was shipped from Tayouan in 1643, but the quantity is unknown.[78] Selling camphor was reasonably profitable for the Dutch; the estimated profit from the sale of camphor in 1651 was about 147 per cent.[79] It is apparent that there was a considerable demand for camphor in Persia as 15,000 pond and 12,000 pond were shipped from Batavia in 1650 and 1656 respectively.[80]

The export of camphor continued over the years. A shipment was recorded in 1669[81] and 4,000 pond (3,200 catty) were allocated to Persia in 1679.[82] That year, it was said that Japanese camphor and porcelain china were profitable in Persia.[83] Table 27 shows that 28,301 pond (22,608 catty) of camphor were shipped to Persia between 1691 and 1697. According to the *Generale Missiven*, Camphor was quite profitable at the end of the seventeenth century; the rate of return in Persia was 347 per cent in 1682, 298.5 per cent in 1683 and 233 per cent in 1698.

## Surat

Like Persia, Surat was a major camphor consuming region. Camphor was sent there from as early as 1636. The *Kagoshima ken shi* (History of Kagoshima prefecture) has photographs of the original list of the prices and quantities of camphor sold by the Dutch Factory in Surat from 1641 to 1684.[84] Table 28 includes this list together with the profit rates calculated from the Japanese camphor price in the previous year.[85] According to the table, a total of 262,704 pond (210,163 catty) of Japanese camphor were sold in this thirty year period. While annual average sales were 8,757.2 pond (7,005.76 catty), camphor sales in Surat were particularly high from 1647 to 1656 with a total of 143,599.6 pond (114,879.7 catty) and an annual average of 17,950 pond (14,360 catty).

*Table 27: Camphor export destinations recorded in trade books, 1691–1697*

| Year | Ship name | Transit | Quantity (pond) | Export destination |
|------|-----------|---------|-----------------|--------------------|
| 1691 | *Boswijk* | Batavia | 3,505 | Surat (Zouratta) |
|      | *Boswijk* | Batavia | 4,043 | Coromandel (Kormandll) |
|      | *Wijk op Zee* | Batavia | 12,541 | Persia (Persia) |
|      | *Walenburgh* | Batavia | 5,025 | The Netherlands ('t Vaderlant) |
| 1692 | *de Hantboogh* | Malacca | 4,000 | Surat (Suratta) |
|      | *de Hantboogh* | Malacca | 7,000 | Malabar (Mallabaar) |
|      | *Ousthuijsen* | Batavia | 8,000 | The Netherlands ('t Patria) |
|      | *Pampus* | Malacca | 5,989 | Coromandel (Cormandel) |
| 1693 | *Hobree* | Malacca | 2,500 | Ceylon (Ceijlon) |
| 1694 | *de Belois* | Malacca | 5,558 | Surat (Zouratta) |
| 1695 | *Langewijck* | Batavia | 7,506 | Persia (Persia) |
| 1696 | *Schoonderloo* | Malacca | 4,228 | Persia (Persia) |
|      | *Schoonderloo* | Malacca | 5,047 | Surat (Souratta) |
|      | *Jerusalem* | Batavia | 19,998 | The Netherlands ('t Patria) |
|      | *Jerusalem* | Batavia | 3,017 | Batavia (Batavia) |
| 1697 | *t' Huijs te Duijne* | Malacca | 4,026 | Persia (Persia) |
|      | *d' Voetboogh* | Batavia | 19,989 | The Netherlands ('t Patria) |

Source: *Negotie Journalen 1691–1697, Archief Japan*, No.875–881, ARA.

Camphor was also shipped in 1685 and 1686. According to Table 27, 18,110 pond (14,488 catty) of camphor were sent to Surat between 1691 and 1697. In 1699, it was said that camphor and copper bars worth 52,000 gulden would be sent from Malacca to Surat.

## Coromandel

Camphor was sent to Coromandel as well as Surat and Persia in 1636. Sugar, porcelain and camphor were shipped from Tayouan to Coromandel in 1647.[86] Camphor was sent to Masulipatam on the Coromandel coast in 1653[87] and to Coromandel in 1669. 2,000 pond (1,600 catty) were allotted to the region in 1679, 30 picol (3,000 catty) in 1684, and 50 picol from Malacca in 1685.[88] 4,043 pond (3,234 catty) were shipped from Japan in 1691, and 5,989 pond (4,791 catty) in 1692.

## Bengal

2,000 pond (1,600 kin) were allocated to Bengal in 1679 and 20 picol (2,000 kin) in 1684.[89] Camphor was also sent in 1685 and 1686, but the quantities are unknown.

*Table 28: Japanese camphor sales in Surat, 1643-84*

| Year | Quantity (pond) | Unit price (stuiver/pond) | Unit price (tael/picol) | Previous year's unit price in Japan (tael/picol) | Profit rate |
|---|---|---|---|---|---|
| 1643 | 2,626 | 10 86/145 | 22.3 | 12 | 85.8 |
| 1645 | 4,621 | 9 71/145 | 19.99 | 12 | 66.5 |
| 1646 | 9,739 7/8 | 9 71/145 | 19.99 | 12 | 66.5 |
| 1647 | 19,439 5/8 | 9 71/145 | 19.99 | 7 | 185.4 |
| 1648 | 19,660 5/8 | 7 137/145 | 16.7 | 6-7 | 178.3-138.6 |
| 1649 | 17,802 1/4 | 7 137/145 | 16.7 | 7 | 138.6 |
| 1650 | 19,461 | 7 137/145 | 16.7 | 7* | 138.6 |
| 1652 | 13,753 | 7 137/145 | 16.7 | 9 | 85.6 |
| 1653 | 14,731 | 7 137/145 | 16.7 | 9 | 85.6 |
| 1655 | 22,529 3/8 | 9 135/145 | 20.9 | 9 | 132.2 |
| 1656 | 15,922 3/4 | 9 87/145 | 20.2 | 9 | 124.4 |
| 1657 | 661 1/2 | 10 34/145 | 21.5 | 9 | 138.9 |
| 1660 | 4,726 | 39 115/145 | 83.8 | 12.5 | 570.4 |
| 1661 | 6,454 3/4 | 13 35/145 | 27.9 | 11.5 | 142.6 |
| 1662 | 2,944 1/2 | 24 12/145 | 50.7 | 12 | 322.5 |
| 1663 | 5,275 1/2 | 34 62/145 | 72.5 | 13.5 | 437 |
| 1664 | 5,517 | 34 62/145 | 72.5 | 13.5 | 437 |
| 1665 | 4,372 1/2 | 34 90/145 | 72.9 | 13.4 | 444 |
| 1667 | 11,738 1/4 | 32 64/145 | 55.6 | 14 | 304.3 |
| 1669 | 13,309 1/2 | 15 121/145 | 27.1 | 14 | 93.6 |
| 1670 | 5,212 1/8 | 14 98/145 | 25.2 | 13.5 | 86.7 |
| 1671 | 11,285 | 12 52/145 | 21.2 | 13.5 | 57 |
| 1676 | 4,046 1/2 | 56 56/145 | 96.7 | 13.5 | 616.3 |
| 1677 | 3,998 3/4 | 56 64/145 / 46 50/145 | 76.7,79.4 | 13 | 643.8-510.8 |
| 1678 | 5,269 3/4 | 26 38/145 | 45 | 13 | 246.2 |
| 1679 | 5,531 3/4 | 32 64/145 / 29 51/145 | 55.6,50.3 | 13.5 | 311.9-272.6 |
| 1680 | 2,144 1/2 | 30 130/145 | 52.97 | 13.5 | 292.4 |
| 1681 | 1,840 1/8 | 30 130/145 | 52.97 | 13.5 | 292.4 |
| 1683 | 5,377 3/4 | 33 135/145 | 58.2 | 13.5 | 331.1 |
| 1684 | 2,723 3/4 | 29 115/145 | 51.1 | 13.5 | 278.5 |

Source: 'Indo Surato Oranda shōkan hanbai shōnō kagaku sōryō hyō (The price and quantity of camphor sold by the Dutch Factory in Surat, India)' in *Kagoshima ken shi* (History of Kagoshima prefecture), Vol. 2, a photographed list, p. 550-551.

*: This is a unit price from two years earlier as no camphor was exported in the previous year.

*Table 29: Camphor export destinations recorded in trade books, 1743–1746*

| Year | Ship name | Transit | Quantity (pond) | Export destination |
|------|-----------|---------|-----------------|--------------------|
| 1743 | *Benkestein* | Batavia | 4,980 | Coromandel (Cormandel) |
|      | *Benkestein* | Batavia | 516 | Medicinal stores (d' Medicinal) |
| 1744 | *den Heuvel* | Batavia | 960 | Medicinal stores (Medichnal Winkel) |
|      | *den Heuvel* | Batavia | 48,000 | The Netherlands (Nederland) |
| 1745 | *Cleverskerk* | Batavia | 1,078 | Medicinal stores in Batavia (de Medicinall Winkel tot Batavia) |
|      | *Cleverskerk* | Batavia | 48,075 | The Netherlands ('t Patria) |
| 1746 | *Nieuwstad* | Batavia | 1,242 | Medicinal stores in Batavia (de Medicinall Winkel tot Batavia) |
|      | *Nieuwstad* | Batavia | 44,793 | The Netherlands ('t Patria) |

Source: *Negotie Journalen* 1743–1746, *Archief Japan*, No.915–918, ARA.

## Malabar

The shipment of camphor to Malabar was first recorded in 1686; 7,000 pond (5,600 catty) were sent from Japan in 1692.

## The Netherlands

The existence of orders in 1644[90] suggests that the export of camphor to the Netherlands began in around the 1640s. 101 picol (10,100 catty) of Japanese camphor were purchased in Batavia in response to orders for 8,000–10,000 pond from the board of the VOC (*Heren XVII*) in 1681.[91] 16,078 pond (12,862 catty) were sent in 1685 and a total of 25,014 pond (20,011 catty) were sent between 1691 and 1697. According to Table 28, camphor exports to the Netherlands increased in the latter half of the 1690s. The volume of camphor exports to the Netherlands surpassed that to Southwest Asia in the eighteenth century. This is discussed in Chapter Six.

## Other regions

Camphor was often shipped to Batavia first and then allocated to various parts of Asia. For example, the *Generale Missiven* reports in 1654 that copper, camphor and grains worth 110,000 gulden were shipped to Batavia and Tayouan.[92] Table 29 shows records of camphor shipments to medicinal stores in Batavia during the mid-eighteenth century.

Ceylon received 2,000 pond (1,600 catty) in 1679 and 2,500 pond (2,000 catty) in 1693. Ships from Malacca to Persia sometimes stopped over in Ceylon; camphor headed for Persia, Surat, Coromandel or the Netherlands might be stored there temporarily, but only small quantities were consumed there.

Camphor was included in the goods sent from Malacca to Vengulurla in the Konkan region of India in 1665.[93] Camphor and copper bars were sent in 1666 and 20 picol (2,000 catty) were allocated in 1684. Table 27 shows shipments to Malabar in 1692.

## The camphor trade in the eighteenth and nineteenth centuries

### Camphor prices and export conditions in the eighteenth century

The price of camphor rose to its highest level after the turn of the eighteenth century. It more than doubled from 13 tael per picol in 1698 to 30 tael in 1706, according to Table 30.

The export volume dropped considerably; the Dutch were unable to procure as much camphor as they wanted. In 1701, Batavia was very displeased that they had received 8,563 kin from Japan, far less than they had requested.[94] The Dutch were hoping to secure sufficient amounts of camphor in 1702, but the factory in Japan was unable to purchase any camphor as it was bought up by the Chinese.[95] In 1703, Batavia advised the factory in Japan that they could increase the purchase price of Satsuma camphor to 16.5 tael per picol and that orders for camphor had reached 40,000 pond (33,333 kin).[96] Despite the price increase, they were unable to buy camphor in that year.[97] Batavia gave the factory in Japan permission for a further price increase in 1704. This is apparent from a report from Japan on camphor purchasing in that year:

> We were unable to acquire camphor at 24 rixdaalder or 20.6 tael per picol or 120 pond. The Chinese paid 34 tael (per 120 pond). The camphor would be consumed within (China).[98]

In 1705, the Dutch were unable to purchase Satsuma camphor at 24 tael per picol or 120 pond; they were asked by camphor merchants to pay 30 tael.[99] The asking price was too high and the factory in Japan was unable to secure any camphor again. Finally, in 1706, the factory received a directive from Batavia authorizing the purchase of up to 36,000 pond (30,000 kin) of camphor at 30 tael per picol as it was expected to make a profit in the Netherlands.[100] A shipping bill dated 26 October reports that the *Sloten*, carrying 41,099 pond (34,249 kin) of camphor purchased at 30 tael per picol, was scheduled to leave for Batavia.[101] The export of camphor finally got on track from then on.

By the way, no other export prices rose so rapidly as that of camphor from the pre-1697 period to 1706. Copper was a principal export product, but its price rose only by 1.1 tael, from 11.8 tael per picol in 1697 to 12.84 tael in 1702. The price of *koban* remained unchanged at 6.8 tael per *ryō* and the prices of foodstuffs did not rise very much either. It appears extraordinary that the price of camphor jumped and stayed at such a high level without sharp drops even after 1706. There is no doubt that a dramatic decrease in camphor production and substantial growth in demand were behind this huge price rise. Camphor production was suspended frequently in Satsuma prior to the 1660s, but these bans never resulted in a sudden doubling of the camphor price. According to Table 30, the price was relatively stable in the latter half of the seventeenth century. This sudden price change therefore points to the emergence of a new situation in the camphor trade.

The Dutch records of this period often reported that they were unable to procure camphor because the Chinese were buying stocks up at high prices. It appears to have been their view that a buyout of camphor by the Chinese was pushing the price up and causing the scarcity. In 1698, an annual export quota system was introduced for copper, which was an important export commodity for both the Chinese and Dutch fleets, and the copper coinage project was commenced in Japan. Nagasaki began to have a problem with Chinese vessels that were delaying departure because they could not procure all the goods they wanted to export. In this situation, it would be natural for some Chinese vessels to give up on copper and purchase large amounts of camphor instead. Each Chinese ship was an independent business entity, allowing the ship owner to decide the purchase prices of goods in Nagasaki. They were able to react swiftly to changing circumstances such as a sudden rise in the price of camphor. On the other hand, the Dutch Factory in Dejima did not have the authority to decide whether or not to purchase a commodity when there was an extreme price rise that could not have been anticipated in the previous year; it had to seek approval from the governor general and the council in Batavia. Consequently, the Dutch reacted too slowly and continued to miss out on camphor until 1706.

However, camphor was not necessarily an important export for the Chinese fleet. Articles about the unavailability of copper are very conspicuous in the *Tō tsūji kaisho nichiroku* (Diaries of the Chinese interpreters association) in the early eighteenth century, but camphor is rarely mentioned. When the shogunate offered to replace the copper substitution system with

*Table 30: Camphor exports, 1621–1805*

| Year | Quantity (catty)[a] | Unit price (tael/picol)[b] | Net export value (gulden)[c] | Gross export value (gulden)[d] |
|---|---|---|---|---|
| 1621 | 137,000 | 9.5–9.2 | 39,220 | |
| 1622 | 75,800 | 8.5 | 19,329 | |
| 1623 | 0 | | | |
| 1624 | 0 | | | |
| 1625 | 0 | | | |
| 1626 | 0 | | | |
| 1627 | 31,962 | 8 | 7,831 | |
| 1628 | 0 | | | |
| 1629 | - | | | |
| 1630 | - | | | |
| 1631 | - | | | |
| 1632 | - | | | |
| 1633 | 45,690 | 8.5 5.4–7 | 9,892 | |
| 1634 | 35,181 | 6.0–7.2 | 7,185 | |
| 1635 | 58,573 | 6.0–7.0 | 12,438 | |
| 1636 | 20,067 | 7.0–8.5 | 4,566 | |
| 1637 | 1,100 | 10 | 313 | |
| 1638 | 56,678 | 10 | 16,153 | |
| 1639 | 22,576 | 10 | 6,334 | |
| 1640 | 0 | | | |
| 1641 | 35,944 | 11–12 | 11,806 | |
| 1642 | 29,439 | 12 | 10,068 | |
| 1643 | 40,980 | 12 | 14,016 | |
| 1644 | 31,064 | 12 | 10,623 | |
| 1645 | 104,002 | 12 | 35,568 | |
| 1646 | 29,217 | 7 | 5,828 | |
| 1647 | 42,965 | 6–7 | 7,702 | |
| 1648 | 200 | 7 | 39 | |
| 1649 | 0 | | | |
| 1650 | 41,548 | 6.5–7 | 8,073 | |
| 1651 | 22,434 | 9 | 5,754 | |
| 1652 | 31,588 | 9 | 8,102 | |
| 1653 | 0 | | | |
| 1654 | 55,377 | 9 | 14,204 | |
| 1655 | 0 | | | |
| 1656 | 0 | | | |
| 1657 | 11,600 | 10 | 3,306 | |
| 1658 | 9,267 | 10 | 2,641 | |
| 1659 | 25,775 | 12.5 | 9,271 | |
| 1660 | 28,529 | 11.5 | 9,456 | |

| | | | |
|---|---|---|---|
| 1661 | *22,152[e] | 12 | 7,759 | |
| 1662 | *25,337 | 13.5 | 9,748 | |
| 1663 | [37,734] | | | |
| 1664 | [50,000] | [13.4][f] | | |
| 1665[g] | 53,393 | 13.6 | 20,695 | 21,076 |
| 1666 | 45,577 | 14 | 22,332 | 22,647 |
| 1667 | No N. J.[h] | | | |
| 1668 | 34,998 | 14 | 17,144 | 17,317 |
| 1669 | 27,062 | 13.5 | 12,788 | 12,975 |
| 1670 | 0 | | | |
| 1671 | 1,500 | 13.5 | 709 | 747 |
| 1672 | 0 | | | |
| 1673 | 0 | | | |
| 1674 | [0] | | | |
| 1675 | [23,336.2] | [13.5] | | |
| 1676 | <266,132>[i] | [13] | | |
| 1677 | 12,579 | 13 | 5,723 | 5,872 |
| 1678 | [16,643] | [13.5] | | |
| 1679 | 14,972 | 13.5 | 7,074 | 9,749 |
| 1680 | No N. J. | | | |
| 1681 | <18,000> | [13.5] | | |
| 1682 | [24,000] | [13.5] | | |
| 1683 | [20,800] | [13.5] | | |
| 1684 | <30,013.5> | [13.5] | | |
| 1685 | [32,259.2] | [13.5] | | |
| 1686 | 0 | | | |
| 1687 | 15,000 | 13 | 6,825 | 7,858 |
| 1688 | 15,000 | 13 | 6,825 | 7,863 |
| 1689 | 30,610 | 13 | 13,928 | 16,515 |
| 1690 | 20,034 | 13 | 9,115 | 10,690 |
| 1691 | 20,091 | 13 | 9,141 | 10,268 |
| 1692 | 19,991 | 13 | 9,096 | 10,120 |
| 1693 | 18,000 | 13 | 8,190 | 9,112 |
| 1694 | 20,477 | 13 | 9,317 | 10,310 |
| 1695 | 24,041 | 13 | 10,939 | 12,055 |
| 1696 | 25,831 | 13 | 11,753 | 13,002 |
| 1697 | 28,029 | 13 | 12,735 | 14,158 |
| 1698 | No N. J. | | | |
| 1699 | No N. J. | | | |
| 1700 | <13,071.6> | | | |
| 1701 | 8,646[j] | | | |
| 1702 | 0 | | | |
| 1703 | 0 | | | |
| 1704 | 0 | | | |
| 1705 | 0 | | | |

*Table 30: Continued*

| Year | Quantity (catty)[a] | Unit price (tael/picol)[b] | Net export value (gulden)[c] | Gross export value (gulden)[d] |
|---|---|---|---|---|
| 1706 | 34,249 | 30 | 35,961 | 36,380 |
| 1707 | 53,885 | 30 | 56,579 | 58,162 |
| 1708 | 18,903 | 30 | 19,848 | 20,426 |
| 1709 | 35,195 | 30 | 36,955 | 37,839 |
| 1710 | 33,393 | 29.5 | 34,478 | 35,390 |
| 1711 | 35,064 | 29.5 | 36,204 | 37,133 |
| 1712 | 34,748 | 29.5 | 35,877 | 36,940 |
| 1713 | (19,820)[k,] | | | |
| 1714 | 20,973 | 29.5 | 21,655 | 22,350 |
| 1715 | 0 | | | |
| 1716 | 34,982 | 30 | 36,731 | 38,017 |
| 1717 | 34,100 | 30 | 35,805 | 37,065 |
| 1718 | 24,998 | 30 | 26,248 | 27,198 |
| 1719 | No ships | | | |
| 1720 | 0[l] | | | |
| 1721 | 35,000 | 30 | 36,750 | 37,961 |
| 1722 | 20,000 | 30 | 21,000 | 21,687 |
| 1723 | 16,666 | 29 | 16,916 | 17,651 |
| 1724 | 30,000 | 29 | 30,450 | 31,544 |
| 1725 | 30,000 | 30 | 31,500 | 32,464 |
| 1726 | 25,000 | 29 | 25,375 | 26,188 |
| 1727 | 20,000 | 29 | 20,300 | 21,038 |
| 1728 | No N. J. | | | |
| 1729 | No N. J. | | | |
| 1730 | (30,000) | | | |
| 1731 | 10,000 | 29 | 10,150 | 10,494 |
| 1732 | 20,000 | 29 | 20,300 | 20,945 |
| 1733 | 40,000 | 29 | 40,600 | 49,681 |
| 1734 | 34,369 | 29 | 34,885 | 38,909 |
| 1735 | 30,000 | 29 | 30,450 | 35,353 |
| 1736 | No N. J. | | | |
| 1737 | 70,188 | 29 | 71,241 | 73,492 |
| 1738 | No N. J. | | | |
| 1739 | 0 | | | |
| 1740 | 0 | | | |
| 1741 | 0 | | | |
| 1742 | 819 | 29 | 831 | 831 |
| 1743 | 4,580 | 29 | 4,648 | 4,648 |
| 1744 | 40,800 | 25 | 20,400 | 21,152 |
| 1745 | 40,961 | 25 | 20,480 | 21,233 |
| 1746 | 38,363 | 25 | 19,181 | 19,944 |

| | | | | |
|---|---|---|---|---|
| 1747 | 58,344 | 25 | 29,172 | 30,634 |
| 1748 | 40,024 | 25 | 20,012 | 22,012 |
| 1749 | 34,542 | 25 | 17,271 | 18,941 |
| 1750 | 45,766 | 23 | 21,052 | 22,174 |
| 1751 | 25,000 | 23 | 11,500 | 12,559 |
| 1752 | 0 | | | |
| 1753 | 20,787 | 23 | 9,562 | 10,471 |
| 1754 | 20,018 | 23 | 9,208 | 9,599 |
| 1755 | 20,828 | 23 | 9,581 | 10,008 |
| 1756 | 33,399 | 23 | 15,364 | 16,046 |
| 1757 | 49,967 | 23 | 22,985 | 23,965 |
| 1758 | 47,862 | 23 | 22,016 | 22,939 |
| 1759[m] | 10,882 | 23 | 5,006 | 5,215 |
| 1760 | 82,514 | 23 | 37,957 | 39,614 |
| 1761 | 41,878 | 23 | 19,263 | 20,061 |
| 1762 | 41,665 | 23 | 19,166 | 19,961 |
| 1763 | 50,068 | 23 | 23,031 | 24,061 |
| 1764 | 16,777 | 23 | 7,717 | 8,056 |
| 1765 | 16,600 | 23 | 7,636 | 8,276 |
| 1766 | 39,936 | 23 | 18,371 | 19,514 |
| 1767 | 50,349 | 23 | 23,161 | 24,569 |
| 1768 | (45,000) | | | |
| 1769 | No N. J. | | | |
| 1770 | No N. J. | | | |
| 1771 | (58,344) | | | |
| 1772 | (40,675.5) | | | |
| 1773 | No N. J. | | | |
| 1774 | 20,890 | 23 | 7,928 | 8,318 |
| 1775 | 20,849 | 23 | 7,912 | 8,431 |
| 1776 | 66,726 | 23 | 25,322 | 26,639 |
| 1777 | 58,660 | 23 | 22,261 | 23,423 |
| 1778 | 66,723 | 23 | 25,321 | 26,601 |
| 1779 | 75,013 | 23 | 28,467 | 29,917 |
| 1780 | 55.833 | 23 | 21,189 | 22,285 |
| 1781 | 41,719 | 23 | 15,832 | 16,700 |
| 1782 | 0 | | | |
| 1783 | 8,297 | 22 | 3,012 | 3,185 |
| 1784 | 66,679 | 22 | 24,204 | 25,584 |
| 1785 | 41,365 | 22 | 15,016 | 15,900 |
| 1786 | 66,344 | 22 | 24,083 | 25,366 |
| 1787 | 41,350 | 22 | 15,010 | 15,889 |
| 1788 | 41,358 | 22 | 15,013 | 15,892 |
| 1789 | 44,164 | 22 | 16,031 | 16,985 |
| 1790 | 41,383 | 22 | 15,022 | 15,857 |
| 1791 | Incomplete N. J. | | | |

*Table 30: Continued*

| Year | Quantity (catty)[a] | Unit price (tael/picol)[b] | Net export value (gulden)[c] | Gross export value (gulden)[d] |
|------|---------|------------|-----------------|-------------------|
| 1792 | 83,004 | 22 | 30,130 | 31,902 |
| 1793 | 91,003 | 22 | 33,034 | 34,806 |
| 1794 | 49,432 | 22 | 17,944 | 19,614 |
| 1795 | 92,593 | 22 | 33,611 | 36,829 |
| 1796[n] | No N. J. | | | |
| 1797 | 0 | 0 | 0 | |
| 1798 | 50,000 | 22 | 18,150 | 19,709 |
| 1799 | 0 | 0 | 0 | |
| 1800 | 93,280 | 18.4 | 28,320 | 30,037 |
| 1801 | 30,014 | 18.4 | 9,112 | 9667 |
| 1802 | 0 | 0 | 0 | |
| 1803 | 53,312 | 18.4 | 16,186 | 17,154 |
| 1804 | 20,122 | 18.4 | 6,109 | 6,459 |
| 1805 | 90,000 | 18.4,23 | 29,563 | 33,321 |

Source: *Negotie Journalen 1621–1805, Archief Japan*, No.829–971, ARA.

a: The quantity is expressed in catty: 1 catty = 1 kin, 1 picol = 100 kin. The quantity is expressed in pond in trade books from 1666 onward, but the data in pond have been recalculated using catty in the above list for comparison.

     1666–1697: 1 picol = 125 pond

     1698–1781: 1 picol = 120 pond

     From 1783: 1 picol = 120 & 7/8 pond

b: 1 tael = 10 monme of silver, 1 picol = 100 kin = 1 catty.

c: 1 gulden = 20 stuiver, 1 stuiver = 16 penning

     Before 1665: 1 tael = 57 stuiver.

     1666–1743: 1 tael = 70 stuiver.

     1744–1773: 1 tael = 40 stuiver.

     From 1774: 1 tael = 33 stuiver.

d: The gross export value includes packing expenses. Data up to 1662 include packing expenses, therefore the net value and the gross value are not separated.

e: '*' denotes years for which the *Negotie Journalen* are missing but shipping invoices (*facturen*) exist and the figures have been calculated based on them (1661 & 1662).

f: Square brackets [ ] denote figures that have been taken from Nachod's list of camphor exports in *Die beziehungen der Niederländischen Oostindischen Kompagnie zu Japan im siebzehenten jahrhundert*, Beilagen 210, as the *Negotie Journalen* are missing.

g: Six vessels departed with camphor in 1665. The quantity and value of camphor exported on the *Peguw* recorded on 28 October in the *Negotie Journalen* are vastly different. Based on 50 barrels, 3319: 7: 6 tael in the record is likely to be incorrect. 331: 9: 7: 6 tael has been used instead in calculation for this table.

h: 'No N. J.' means that the *Negotie Journalen* is missing and no record is found in other historical materials or documents.

i: Brackets < > denote figures taken from van Dam, p. , '*Beschryvinge van de Oostindische Compagnie* (Description of the East India Company)' in F. W. Stapel (ed.), tweede boek deel. 1 (The Hague: Martinus Nijhoff, 1931). The quantity expressed in pond in van Dam has been converted using catty. The relevant pages are: 1676 459, 1681: 469, 1684: 486, and 1700: 550. The quantity for 1684 on page 486 is 37516.7/8 picol but the use of picol is likely to be a simple error and the conversion to catty has been done on the basis of 37516.7/8 pond.

j:  Although the *Negotie Journalen* are missing, an article dated 22 October in the diary of the Dutch Factory reports that '120 barrels, 10,375 pond of Satsuma camphor were loaded on the *Brandenburg*' (*Kagoshima ken shi*, Vol. 2, 546). A shipment of the same amount of camphor is also reported in Kuiper, J. F. (1927), *Japan en de Buiten wereld in de 18e Eeuw* (Japan and the outside world in the 18th century), The Hague: Martinus Nijhoff, 1927, 303. In the *Generale Missiven*, an article dated 31 December 1701 reports that 'Only 10,275 pond of camphor were acquired' (W. Ph. Coolhaas, (ed.) , *Generale Missiven van Gouverneurs-Generaal en Raden aan Heren XVII der Verenigde Oostindische Compagnie*, Vol. 6, The Hague: Martinus Nijhoff, 1976, 164). There is a discrepancy of 100 pond between these documents. For the purpose of this table, the former figure has been taken as correct and used in conversion into catty.

k:  Brackets ( ) denote figures taken from the list of exports in Kuiper (see Note j above), 303–305.

l:  The *Negotie Journalen* is missing but no camphor was exported in this year. An article dated 15 January 1721 in the *Generale Missiven* reports, 'Camphor could not been obtained due to discord among the governors of Satsuma' (Coolhaas, *op. cit.*, Vol. 7, (1979) 526).

m:  An entry dated 9 November 1759 in the *Negotie Journalen* reads: 'The Leijmuijden, 1358.2/5 pond, 23 tael per 120 pond, 2,502.8.6 tael'. However, the said quantity should come to 260.3.8 tael. Or if the export value is 2,502.8.6 tael, the quantity should be 13,058.2/5 pond. For the table above, 13,058.2/5 pond and 2,502.8.6 tael have been adopted.

n:  While the *Negotie Journalen* for 1796 are missing, no Dutch vessels came to Japan in that year and therefore no camphor was exported (Saitō Agu, *Zūfu to Nihon* [H. Doef and Japan], Tokyo, Kōbunkan 1922, 12).

the camphor substitution system due to a copper shortage, the Chinese ship owners summarily rejected this offer. According to an article in March 1706[102], the Chinese ship owners rejected the proposal because camphor was not profitable in China; it was produced there in abundance and in fact large quantities were exported directly from mainland China to Indochina and further south where it was profitable. There was no subsequent need to ship it from Japan to these regions. If this was the case, the Chinese took camphor to Southeast Asia and sold it to Europeans and, as reported in the *Generale Missiven* in 1704, consumed it in their own country.

The main export goods for the Chinese fleet from 1704 to 1715 were silver, copper, crude copper and *tawaramono* (dried marine products).[103] Camphor was rarely exported from 1716 to the mid-eighteenth century.[104]

Despite the price increase, the volume of Dutch camphor exports increased from 1706, compared with the amount that they were exporting in the 1680s and 1690s. However, the Dutch had great trouble selling Japanese camphor in the Southwestern Asian market due to the high purchase price of 30 tael per picol. For instance, in 1715, the *Generale Missiven* reported that Japanese camphor was not selling.[105] Another article reported, '28,760 pond (23,967 kin) of Japanese camphor are not selling in Persia; they may be sold at cost'.[106] An article in 1720 reported that the Dutch incurred a loss of 12.5 per cent from the sale of Japanese camphor.[107] The Dutch made 200–300 per cent profits selling Japanese camphor in southwest Asia at the end of the seventeenth century, but they could hardly find any buyers at this high price. Camphor did not sell even in Persia in some years.

The VOC also faced greater competition in the export of camphor in the early eighteenth century, making their selling activities more difficult. The British increased their commercial activity in the Indian subcontinent and the French and the Danish began to pursue active trade in Asia as well. An article dated 26 March 1720 in the *Generale Missiven* reported that 'Japanese camphor remains unsold because of the British competitors.'[108] The camphor brought by the British was either produced in mainland China, or else it was produced in Japan, exported by the Chinese fleet and sold in Canton (Guangdong) or Indochina as mentioned above. In this way, the slump in the camphor sale by the Dutch was influenced by the high purchase price of camphor and the slump in the VOC's Asia trade as a whole that was a result of the advancement of European competitors in Asia.

The camphor price rose sharply at the beginning of the eighteenth century, and then tended to fall steadily at intervals of twenty years or so. The volume of export in the first half of the eighteenth century was about 30,000 kin per year on average according to Table 31. The annual average volume of around 47,000 kin in the latter half of the century suggests an upward trend, although it fluctuated from year to year without sharp growth. It was not uncommon in the latter half of the eighteenth century to export 60,000–90,000 kin in one year.

The expansion of the camphor trade in the eighteenth century was deeply linked to export restrictions on copper and *koban*. The importance of camphor among export products increased greatly every time an export restriction was imposed on these products. For the Dutch, camphor was the only product other than copper that sold at a profit overseas. The volume of camphor exports increased as the export of copper became sluggish. The export of *koban* was suspended in the latter half of the century. Table 31 shows that the annual export volume increased from around 30,000 kin in the early eighteenth century to as high as 67,000 kin in the 1790s. Chapter Three showed how a gap appeared between the domestic purchase price of copper and the sale price of copper to the Dutch Factory in the eighteenth century. This gap was compensated by the Shogunate. It should be noted that the same arrangement was put in place for camphor as well.

*Table 31: Camphor exports in the eighteenth century, by decade*

| Decade | Number of years in which camphor was exported | Quantity exported (catty) | Annual average (catty) |
|---|---|---|---|
| 1700–1709 | 5 | 150,878 | 30,176 |
| 1710–1719 | 8 | 238,758 | 29,760 |
| 1720–1729 | 7 | 176,666 | 25,238 |
| 1730–1739 | 7 | 234,577 | 33,508 |
| 1740–1749 | 8 | 258,433 | 32,304 |
| 1750–1759 | 9 | 274,509 | 30,501 |
| 1760–1769 | 9 | 384,787 | 42,754 |
| 1770–1779 | 8 | 407,881 | 50,985 |
| 1780–1789 | 9 | 407,109 | 45,234 |
| 1790–1799 | 6 | 407,415 | 67,903 |

Source: Based on Table 30.

## The camphor trade in the early eighteenth century

The trade restriction decree in 1790 pushed the Japanese–Dutch trade further into a predicament and aggravated the already poor trading conditions. The Asia trade by the Dutch was also being eclipsed by the ascendancy of the British trade in India during the 1750s. The VOC followed a course of decline at an accelerating speed from then on until it was finally wound up in 1799. After that, the business of the VOC was temporarily handed over to the Dutch government. In this chaotic situation, improper accounting practices and corruption were rife among the officers at the Dutch Factory in Japan.

The circumstances surrounding the Japanese–Dutch trade continued to deteriorate. Head Factor W. Wardenaar and Secretary H. Doeff arrived in Japan in 1800 and embarked on the reform of the Japan trade. The Dutch made efforts to normalize their books, enforce discipline among the staff and expand their commercial rights.

But the Dutch Factory had other problems around 1800. One of them was the chartering of ships. The British were gradually extending their dominance in the seas of Asia. The Dutch were therefore unable to dispatch their own ships to Japan and began to charter ships from a third country (mostly the United States) to sail to Japan. The Japanese–Dutch trade by chartered ships continued from 1798 to 1803. The chartering of ships gave rise to a very difficult problem that would not have been experienced had the Dutch been able to use their own ships. Although the quantity of imports to Japan were accurately known and the charterage could be easily determined in Batavia, the charterage for the return voyage had to be set based on the estimated quantity of return cargos from Japan. If the ship returned with less export goods than estimated, the Dutch would suffer a large loss. If the return cargos were different from the initial contract, the Dutch would have to negotiate with the ship's captain and sometimes pay additional freight. For example, the Dutch planned to export 51,700 kin of camphor in 1801.[109] However, they only managed to procure 30,000 kin of camphor and decided to fill the shortfall with copper. This was a variation to the original contract so they had to negotiate with the captain and agreed to pay extra freight in Batavia.[110] Such negotiations continued until 1803.

The Dutch hoped to export between 60,000–80,000 kin of camphor in 1802, but they failed to export any.[111] In 1803 and 1804, the Dutch only managed to export about 53,000 kin and 20,000 kin respectively, although they aimed to export 100,000 kin. Japan requested a price rise in 1806 that took effect in 1807. The Dutch were reluctant to export camphor from that time on. According to an article dated 24 October 1809 in the diary of the Dutch Factory in Nagasaki (*Dagregister*), there was no point in exporting camphor from Japan; the Dutch, who had been a monopolistic seller of camphor in the South China Sea region to a certain degree, were obstructed by the selling activity of the Chinese.[112] Despite these comments, the Chinese had been selling camphor in Canton (Guangdong) before then. The Dutch ships stopped sailing to Java from 1808 as it was under British occupation. Although Doeff does not mention this, the Dutch Factory in Japan must have been fully aware of the situation. He gave the above reasons simply because he wanted to refrain from buying camphor as he was uncertain about when he could export it.

The British occupied Java in 1811. They sent ships disguised as Dutch ships to Japan in 1813 and 1814[113] for the purpose of taking over the Dutch trade in Japan. At that time, Doeff was the head of the factory in Deshima. He succeeded in stopping the British plot and only permitted those ships to trade with the Japanese. For this reason, camphor was exported in these two years, as shown in Table 32. 50,000 kin in 1813 and about 30,000 kin in 1814 were exported at a low price as they were sold to the Dutch Factory for 9.2 tael per picol, whereas the price at the Nagasaki trade association was 28.4 tael.[114] The British occupation of Java ended in 1816; the Dutch regained Java and began to send ships to Japan again from 1818. Table 32 shows that the annual average volume of camphor exported from 1818 to 1820 was about 50,000 kin. After that, the average export volume was 46,777 kin from 1821 to 1830, 70,517 kin from 1831 to 1840, around 70,000 kin from 1841 to 1850, and around 60,000 kin from 1851 to 1857. In this way, camphor was exported in large quantities until the end of the Edo period.

*Table 32: Camphor exports, 1806–1859*

| Year | Quantity (catty) | Year | Quantity (catty) |
|---|---|---|---|
| 1806 | 64,000 | 1833 | 42,772 |
| 1807 | 25,719 | 1834 | 61,356 |
| 1808 | | 1835 | 82,597 |
| 1809 | | 1836 | 94,100 |
| 1810 | | 1837 | 89,088 |
| 1811 | | 1838 | 63,115 |
| 1812 | | 1839 | 67,273 |
| 1813 | 50,000 | 1840 | 59,910 |
| 1814 | 30,003 | 1841 | |
| 1815 | | 1842 | 83,803 |
| 1816 | | 1843 | 50,548 |
| 1817 | 0 | 1844 | 60,987 |
| 1818 | 50,508 | 1845 | 83,012 |
| 1819 | 50,518 | 1846 | 82,449 |
| 1820 | 50,586 | 1847 | 84,886 |
| 1821 | 32,948 | 1848 | |
| 1822 | 50,585 | 1849 | 80,825 |
| 1823 | 37,160 | 1850 | 33,589 |
| 1824 | 51,564 | 1851 | 33,671 |
| 1825 | 49,389 | 1852 | 33,709 |
| 1826 | 38,863 | 1853 | 49,788 |
| 1827 | | 1854 | 101,545 |
| 1828 | 40,431 | 1855 | 155,497 |
| 1829 | 57,808 | 1856 | 33,878 |
| 1830 | 62,206 | 1857 | 12,406 |
| 1831 | 64,609 | 1858 | |
| 1832 | 80,350 | 1859 | |

* The quantity is a net weight (*netto*) based on shipping invoices (*facturen*) and camphor lists (*campfurlijst*) contained in *Japan portefeuille 1800–1842* (Japan portfolio 1800–1842) and *Nederlandsche factorij Japan* 1800–1860 (Dutch Factory Japan 1800–1860).

## Conclusion

Early modern Japan was a resource rich country where the principal export goods were gold, silver and copper. The next important product was camphor, which was extracted from camphor trees found abundantly in the south of the island of Kyūshū, mainly in the Satsuma region (present-day Kagoshima prefecture). In the early part of the seventeenth century, the volume of camphor exports fluctuated from year to year as the lord of the Satsuma domain intermittently banned the production of camphor.

The price of camphor rose sharply in the early eighteenth century. Reasons behind this price hike included the introduction of the annual export quota system for the chief export commodity of copper and the debasement of *koban* from re-coinages. These factors prompted the Dutch to turn their attention to camphor. The demand for camphor increased rapidly and the Chinese and the Dutch competed for supply, pushing up the price. Despite the price rise, the export volume did not fall. The camphor exports continued to grow steadily and gradually became more important in the overall Dutch trade turnover.

Part of the camphor exported from Japan was shipped to Southeast Asia by the Chinese to be sold to the British and other Europeans, who in turn sold it in Southwest Asia in competition with the Japanese camphor exported by the Dutch. This situation was similar to what had happened to the copper trade as discussed in Chapter Three.

After the rapid decline and discontinuation of *koban* exports in the latter half of the eighteenth century, copper and camphor became the only products exported from Japan by the Dutch. Other products had no prospect of making profit abroad. The cargo lists of the Dutch vessels became very simple from the latter half of the eighteenth century, containing these two export products alone. Other goods such as foodstuffs and timber were for the VOC's own consumption rather than for overseas sale.

Changes in the export volume from the seventeenth century to the eighteenth century are demonstrated clearly in Figures 11, 12 and 13. The upward trend continued into the nineteenth century and the period from the 1830s can be regarded as the peak period for camphor exports. The amount of camphor produced in Satsuma around the first year of the Kansei era is said to have been 60,000 kin or so per year.[115] One background factor for this expansion of camphor exports was the improving camphor production technology in the Satsuma domain that enabled more efficient camphor extraction from raw materials. Another factor was the commencement of tree planting to replace felled camphor trees. These efforts allowed camphor to continue to be a valuable export product second only to copper until the end of the Edo period.

The amounts of camphor shipped to the Netherlands increased from the end of the seventeenth century throughout the eighteenth century. This was because the demand for camphor increased rapidly as the advances in medicine and science in the Netherlands expanded the uses of camphor.

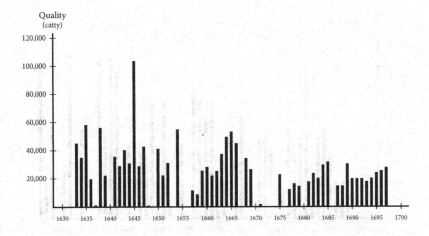

*Figure 11: Camphor exports, 1633–1697*

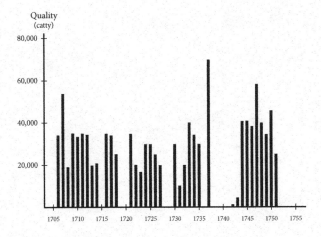

*Figure 12: Camphor exports, 1706–1752*

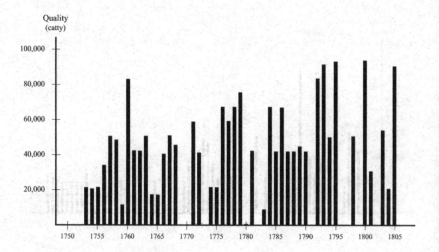

*Figure 13: Camphor exports, 1753–1805*

# Chapter Six

# Japanese Exports in the Early Eighteenth Century

This chapter covers the period from 1701 to 1724. Signs of decline in Dutch trade with Japan became more prominent during this period. In 1726, the VOC prepared a report in order to gain a more concrete understanding of the real benefits of trading with Japan. Using this report as a primary source, this chapter will look at the profitability of the main Japanese export products: copper, *koban* and camphor. It will analyse the significance of Japanese products for the VOC's trade in Asia and Europe at the time.

## The Japan trade report

The report on the VOC trade with Japan dated 5 July 1726 is found among the archives of the VOC that are in the possession of the National Archives of the Netherlands in The Hague.[1] The report was signed by Rogier van Heyningen. He succeeded Piter Colijn as the accountant general (*boekhouder generaal*) in Batavia in 1719[2] and received a promotion to the position of councilor in 1727, a year after writing this report.[3] It reported on the following topics: the profits, losses and expenses made or incurred by the factory in Japan from 1701 to 1724; profits made from Japanese copper and camphor at the factories in Southwest Asia; losses incurred from *koban* in Coromandel; the cargo of seven vessels shipwrecked off Japan; and the volume of copper and camphor shipped to the Netherlands from Batavia and Ceylon over the period. This report is mentioned in the *Generale Missiven* on 5 December 1726[4] and comprises three sections:

1. The annual gross profits, expenses and net profits of the factory in Japan, as seen in Table 33.
2. The annual volume of sales and profits for Japanese copper and camphor in Southwest Asia (Ceylon, Coromandel, Malabar, Bengal, Surat, Persia and Mocha), and the volume of sales and losses from the *koban* trade in Coromandel, as seen in Table 34–1.

*Table 33: Profits and expenses of the Dutch Factory in Japan*

| Year | Gross profit [A] (gulden) | Expense [B] (gulden) | Net profit [A] – [B] (gulden) |
|---|---|---|---|
| 1700/01 | 571,486: 5: 8 | 152,344: 6: 8 | 419,141: 19: - |
| 1701/02 | 558,752: 18: 8 | 144,807: 8: - | 413,945: 10: 8 |
| 1702/03 | 574,578: 12: - | 149,554: 19: 8 | 425,023: 12: 8 |
| 1703/04 | 361,618: 10: 8 | 152,333: 5: - | 209,285: 5: 8 |
| 1704/05 | 527,733: 6: - | 164,378: 12: - | 363,354: 14: - |
| 1705/06 | 451,416: 3: 8 | 156,624: -: 8 | 294,792: 3: - |
| 1706/07 | 609,309: 12: 8 | 151,634: 4: - | 457,675: 8: 8 |
| 1707/08 | 491,718: 14: - | 144,111: 16: 8 | 347,606: 17: 8 |
| 1708/09 | 722,887: 10: - | 136,117: 10: 8 | 586,769: 19: 8 |
| 1709/10 | 792,679: 7: 8 | 141,064: 5: 8 | 651,615: 2: - |
| 1710/11 | 654,993: 8: - | 138,006: 5: - | 516,987: 3: - |
| 1711/12 | 570,301: 3: 8 | 134,671: 6: 8 | 435,629: 17: - |
| 1712/13 | 598,152: 19: 8 | 139,900: 18: - | 458,252: 1: 8 |
| 1713/14 | 632,146: 14: - | 134,960: 14: - | 497,186: -: - |
| 1714/15 | 633,989: 11: - | 126,907: 11: 8 | 507,081: 19: 8 |
| 1715/16 | 558,220: -: - | 140,696: 10: 8 | 417,523: 9: 8 |
| 1716/17 | 544,193: 18: 8 | 136,031: 8: - | 408,162: 10: 8 |
| 1717/18 | 548,802: 7: 8 | 134,052: 18: - | 414,743: 9: 8 |
| 1718/19 | 245,996: 15: 8 | 104,789: 12: 8 | 141,207: 3: - |
| 1719/20 | 524,798: 7: - | 89,541: 12: - | 435,256: 15: - |
| 1720/21 | 521,925: 9: 8 | 158,005: 7: - | 363,920: 2: 8 |
| 1721/22 | 337,798: 14: 8 | 134,982: 18: 8 | 202,815: 16: - |
| 1722/23 | 517,168: 9: - | 142,726: 17: - | 374,441: 12: - |
| 1723/24 | 255,818: 14: 8 | 136,910: 6: 8 | 118,908: 8: - |
| Total | 12,806,487: 12: - | 3,345,160: 13: - | 9,461,326: 19: - |

Notes:
In units of gulden: stuiver: pening.
1 gulden = 20 stuiver, 1 stuiver = 16 pening.
1 tael = 70 stuiver, 1 tael = 10 monme in silver.

3. The value of Dutch–Japanese trade lost on shipwrecked vessels and the total volume of copper and camphor shipments to the Netherlands, as seen in Table 34–2.

The report calculated the amount of profit gained from trade with Japan from 1701 to 1724 as follows: the net profit of the factory in Japan derived from Table 33 (a), plus the difference between the gross profit from the sale of copper and camphor (b) and the loss from *koban* sales (c) derived from Table 34–1, minus the value of shipwrecked cargo (d). This calculation (e) can be numerically expressed as follows:

$$\{f.9461326:19: -(a) + f.8020832: 3: 6(b) - f.1566600:12: -(c)\} -$$
$$f.1725625:18: 8(d) = f.14189932:11:14(e)$$

The merit of this report is that it not only worked out sales revenue and expenditure at the Japan factory alone, but it also investigated sales profits and losses from Japanese products exported and sold by the VOC in other regions of Asia as well. It also anticipated some of the profits that could be made from shipping Japanese products to the Netherlands.

## The performance of the factory in Japan

Table 33 shows profits earned by the factory in Japan from 1701 to 1724. Heyningen collected the amounts of gross profit, expense and net profit for each year and calculated the net profit by subtracting expenses from the gross profit. The net profit figures in this report are mostly consistent with the figures in trade journals of the factory (*Negotie Journalen*) up to 1717, but the figures after that year varied between the two records. Kuiper has a detailed table showing the financial conditions of the factory in the eighteenth century[5]; there are differences of less than several thousand gulden between Kuiper's table and the report and fluctuations are mostly consistent. The net profits in the report are generally smaller than the figures in Kuiper's table.

Looking at the gross profit and expenses in Figure 14, the former fluctuates considerably from year to year while the latter is relatively stable. The gross profit was greatly influenced by shipping accidents and the political situation in India, which was the supplier of many products to Japan. Looking at Table 34–1, it is apparent that falls in the gross profits of 1708, 1719 and 1722 coincided with the wrecking of ships on their way to Japan. The slump from 1704 to 1706 was influenced by a temporary closure of the Dutch Factory in Surat, the imposition of a trade ban on the VOC in Bengal by the Mughal Empire, and political instability in Malabar. These factors had a significant impact on the Indian silk trade and led to a serious slump in trade in Japan and the rest of Asia.[6]

Japan's shogunate government proclaimed a new trade law (*Shōtoku shinrei*) in 1715, but this does not appear to have had a severe adverse impact on Dutch profits. Profits dropped in 1715, but there was a shipwreck in this year and the profit would have increased substantially if not for the sea accident. The new trade law does not appear to have affected the Dutch trade greatly as far as we can see from Table 33. This is evident in the attitude of the governor general of the Dutch East Indies who accepted the order with

Table 34-1: Japanese export sales in Southwest Asia

| Year | Sales region | Copper sales (pond) | Copper profit (A) (gulden) | Camphor sales (pond) | Camphor profit (B) (gulden) | Copper & camphor total profit (gulden) | Koban sales (pieces) | Koban loss (C) (gulden) | (A + B) – C (gulden) |
|---|---|---|---|---|---|---|---|---|---|
| 1701/02 | Ceylon | 164,242.5 | 63,329: 11: 1 | | | | | | |
| | Coromandel | 456,938.5 | 137,432: 19:12 | | | | 22,514. | 71,477: 13: 2 | |
| | Malabar | 126,741. | 46,384: 9: - | | | | | | |
| | Bengal | 291,312. | 96,093:16: - | | | | | | |
| | Surat | 816,904. | 178,308:18: 8 | 3,686.8125 | 1,598: 7: - | | | | |
| | Total | 1,856,138. | 521,549:14: 5 | 3,686.8125 | 1,598: 7: - | 523,148: 1: 5 | | | 45,1670: 8: 3 |
| 1702/03 | Ceylon | 91,562. | 34,039: 11: 8 | 478.5 | 693:10: - | | | | |
| | Coromandel | 406,066. | 125,688: 9: 8 | 23. | 94:17: 9 | | 17,940.3125 | 54,370: 13: 2 | |
| | Malabar | 31,423.5 | 10,768: 1: 8 | | | | | | |
| | Bengal | 516,256. | 147,442: 8: - | | | | | | |
| | Surat | 156,042. | 34,545:18: 8 | | | | | | |
| | Persia | | | 3,150.5 | 3,055: 6: 8 | | | | |
| | Total | 1,201,349.5 | 352,484: 9: - | 3,652. | 3,843:14: 1 | 356,328: 3: 1 | | | 30,1957: 9:15 |
| 1703/04 | Ceylon | 108,159.5 | 40,214: 4:14 | 394. | 457:10: - | | | | |
| | Coromandel | 184,588. | 45,309:12: 4 | 71.5 | 60: 5: 6 | | 11,034. | 34,085: 12:11 | |
| | Malabar | 88,556.25 | 30,704: 5: - | | | | | | |
| | Surat | 158,184.5 | 23,292: 8: 8 | | | | | | |
| | Persia | | | 2,436. | 1,665: 3: - | | | | |
| | Total | 539,488.25 | 139,520:10:10 | 2,901.5 | 2,182:18: 6 | 141,703: 9: - | | | 107,617:16: 5 |
| 1704/05 | Ceylon | 93,773.5 | 35,394:15:14 | 201. | 239: 6:14 | | | 26,764: 17: - | |
| | Coromandel | 158,402.75 | 31,904:16: 4 | 70.5 | 9: 7: 8 | | 8,455. | | |

| Year | Place | | | | | | | | |
|---|---|---|---|---|---|---|---|---|---|
| | Malabar | 90,709.25 | 31,118: 1: 8 | | | | | | |
| | Surat | 101,247.5 | 20,632:12: 8 | | | | 24,864.25 | 81,979:13: 3 | |
| | Persia | | | 1,537. | 874:17: - | | | | |
| | Mocha | 30,000. | 12,340:16: 8 | | | | | | |
| | Total | 474,133. | 13,1391: 2:10 | 1,808.5 | 1,123:11: 6 | 132,514:14: - | | | 105,749: 17: - |
| 1705/06 | Ceylon | 51,331. | 18,658: 6:11 | 317. | 311: 6: 4 | | | | |
| | Coromandel | 269,531.5 | 57,092: 1:14 | 177.625 | 197:17: 2 | | | | |
| | Malabar | 109,859.5 | 39,887:13: 8 | 108. | 79:11: - | | | | |
| | Persia | 75,000. | 15,368: 1: 8 | 4,521. | 2,439: 2: - | | | | |
| | Mocha | 62,500. | 23,115:12: 8 | | | | | | |
| | Bengal | 356,514. | 56,471: 6: 8 | | | | | | |
| | Total | 924,736. | 210,593: 2: 9 | 5,123.625 | 3,027:16: 6 | 213,620:18:15 | | | 131,641: 5:12 |
| 1706/07 | Ceylon | 101,046.75 | 36,478: 3: 8 | 794.5 | 837: 4: - | | | | |
| | Coromandel | 351,747. | 76,917:12: 7 | 3,362.75 | 1,996:15: 8 | | | | |
| | Malabar | 143,414.75 | 50,663: 3: - | 686.0625 | 499: 1: 8 | | | | |
| | Bengal | 297,500. | 50,168: -: - | | | | | | |
| | Surat | 365,000. | 88,635: 3: 8 | | | | 13,500. | *41,319:10: - | |
| | Mocha | 62,500. | 23,541: 7: 8 | | | | | | |
| | Persia | | | 3,046. | 1,716:12: 8 | | | | |
| | Total | 1,321,208.5 | 326,403: 9:15 | 7,889.3125 | 5,049:13: 8 | 331,453: 3: 7 | | | 290,143: 13: 7 |
| 1707/08 | Ceylon | 101,705. | 34,401:12: - | 371. | | | | | |
| | Coromandel | 429,025.5 | 102,888:18:12 | 3,604.125 | 163:16: 8 | | | | |
| | Malabar | 141,042.25 | 49,157: 7: - | 189.25 | 3,535:11: - | | | | |
| | Bengal | 499,664. | 83,862:11: - | 10,269. | 137: 5: - | | | | |
| | Surat | 650,000. | 147,335:19: 8 | 5,971. | 2,148: 3: - | | 5,168.75 | 16,736: 1: 7 | |
| | Persia | | | | 2,956: 5: 8 | | | | |
| | Total | 1,821,436.75 | 417,646: 8: 4 | 20,204.375 | 8,941: 1: - | 426,587: 9: 4 | | | 409,851:7:13 |

Table 34-1: Continued

| Year | Sales region | Copper sales (pond) | Copper profit (A) (gulden) | Camphor sales (pond) | Camphor profit (B) (gulden) | Copper & camphor total profit (gulden) | Koban sales (pieces) | Koban loss (C) (gulden) | (A + B) – C (gulden) |
|---|---|---|---|---|---|---|---|---|---|
| 1708/09 | Ceylon | 125900. | 42,519:12: - | 1,033.5 | 1,040:14: - | | | | |
| | Coromandel | 414,566.5 | 105,862: 2:14 | 6,707.875 | 6,090:11: 7 | | 22,121.75 | 72,311: 8:13 | |
| | Malabar | 124,814.875 | 40,859:11: - | 177.625 | 146:16: 8 | | | | |
| | Surat | 473,062.5 | 114,950:10: - | | | | | | |
| | Mocha | 75,000. | 26,571:13: 8 | 808. | 280:15: 8 | | | | |
| | Persia | 37,500. | 5,913: 9: - | 7,457.4 | 2,437: 5: - | | | | |
| | Bengal | 561,000. | 99,988:11: 8 | | | | | | |
| | Total | 1,811,843.875 | 436,665: 9:14 | 16,184.4 | 10,002: 2: 7 | 446,667:12: 5 | | | 374,356: 3: 8 |
| 1709/10 | Ceylon | 59,846.5 | 20,584: 5: - | 919. | 865:12: - | | | | |
| | Coromandel | 414,133.75 | 118,801: 7: 7 | 753.25 | 698: 4: - | | 12,468.25 | 41,296:12:11 | |
| | Malabar | 123,261. | 45,256:19: - | 1,606.625 | 790:17: 8 | | | | |
| | Bengal | 635,868. | 169,853:16: - | | | | | | |
| | Surat | 525,000. | 125,542: -: - | 6,260.25 | 765:15: 8 | | | | |
| | Persia | 62,500. | 7,906:12: - | 7,804. | 1,900: 9: - | | | | |
| | Mocha | 124,368.75 | 34,263: 3: - | 953. | 364:13: - | | | | |
| | Total | 1,944,978. | 522,208: 2: 7 | 18,296.125 | 5,385:11: - | 27,593:13: 7 | | | 486,297: -:12 |
| 1710/11 | Ceylon | 40,965. | 14,183: 8: 8 | 402. | 361:15: 8 | | 16,228. | 52,451:15: 9 | |
| | Coromandel | 378,312. | 106,610: 5: 4 | 61.25 | 71: 2: - | | | | |
| | Malabar | 89,927. | 31,692: -: 8 | 566.2 | 481: 7: - | | | | |
| | Bengal | 676,098. | 177,689: 6: - | | | | | | |
| | Surat | 520,239.25 | 111,751: 4: - | | | | | | |

| | | | | | | | | |
|---|---|---|---|---|---|---|---|---|
| Mocha | 49,945. | 15,661: 8: 8 | 1,029.45 | 914: 4: 8 | | | | |
| Total | 1,755,486.25 | 457,587:12:12 | | | 458,501: 17: 4 | | | 406,050:1:11 |
| 1711/12 Ceylon | 67,590. | 23,053:13: - | 713. | 669: 18: 8 | | | | |
| Coromandel | 406,202.75 | 97,626:11:14 | | | | | | |
| Malabar | 105,800. | 37,913: 6: 8 | 36. | 41: 18: 6 | | 21,996. | 73,168:13:15 | |
| Bengal | 143. | 37:11: - | | | | | | |
| Surat | 400,000. | 98,464:14: 8 | | | | | | |
| Mocha | | | 1,198.8 | 516: 6: 8 | | | | |
| Total | 979,735.75 | 257,095:16:14 | 1,947.8 | 1,228: 3: 6 | 258,324: -: 4 | | | 185,155: 6: 5 |
| 1712/13 Ceylon | 106,031.875 | 35,730:15: 8 | 302.25 | 339: 15: - | | | | |
| Coromandel | 499,165.75 | 126,466:12: 2 | | | | 3,920. | 10,907:15:14 | |
| Malabar | 50,974. | 18,450: 4: 8 | 352.25 | 297:18: - | | | | |
| Bengal | 335,920. | 81,874:12: 8 | | | | | | |
| Surat | 325,000. | 81,124: 6: 8 | | | | | | |
| Mocha | 79,431.3 | 19,544: 5: - | | | | | | |
| Total | 1,396,523.925 | 363,190:16: 2 | 654.5 | 637: 13: - | 363,828: 9: 2 | | | 352,920: 13: 4 |
| 1713/14 Ceylon | 278,602.5 | 92,690:13: - | | | | | | |
| Coromandel | 99,994.5 | 29,982:17: 4 | | | | 29,538.25 | 205,701:12:12 | |
| Malabar | 94,702. | 34,002:19: - | | | | | | |
| Bengal | 387,783.5 | 92,996:19: - | | | | | | |
| Surat | 293,750. | 75,959:16: 8 | | | | | | |
| Persia | | | 5,944. | 1,696:10: 8 | | | | |
| Mocha | 69,575. | 16,995:19: - | 1,988.05 | 294:16: 8 | | | | |
| Total | 1,224,407.5 | 342,629: 3:12 | 7,932.05 | 1,991: 7: - | 344,620: 10:12 | | | 138,918: 18: - |

Table 34-1: Continued

| Year | Sales region | Copper sales (pond) | Copper profit (A) (gulden) | Camphor sales (pond) | Camphor profit (B) (gulden) | Copper & camphor total profit (gulden) | Koban sales (pieces) | Koban loss (C) (gulden) | (A + B) – C (gulden) |
|---|---|---|---|---|---|---|---|---|---|
| 1714/15 | Ceylon | 145616.25 | 49,807: 4: 8 | 274.25 | 324: 4: - | | | | |
| | Coromandel | 346,155.5 | 120,293: -: 4 | | | | 15,200. | 98,392: 4: 9 | |
| | Malabar | 76,378.5 | 25,849:13: 8 | 279.375 | 236:19: 8 | | | | |
| | Bengal | 547,536. | 150,519: -: - | | | | | | |
| | Surat | 34,375. | 9,088: 4: - | | | | | | |
| | Persia | | | 4,714.4 | 1,019:10: 8 | | | | |
| | Mocha | 62,291.67 | 13,254:15: 8 | 1,434. | *657: 4: 8 | | | | |
| | Total | 1,212,352.92 | 368,811:17:12 | 6,702.025 | 2,237:18: 8 | 371,049:16: 4 | | | 272,657: 11:11 |
| 1715/16 | Ceylon | 136,476.25 | 46,340:12: 8 | 449.75 | 505:19: 8 | | | | |
| | Coromandel | 158,396.75 | 56,170:12: 9 | 2,320.75 | 1,092: 8: - | | 2,000. | 6,152: 1: 4 | |
| | Malabar | 70,598. | 23,464: 6: - | 489.25 | 413: 8: 8 | | | | |
| | Bengal | 650,934. | 197,151:16: 8 | | | | | | |
| | Surat | 187,500. | 52,490:13: - | | | | | | |
| | Persia | 25,000. | 6,314:16: - | 7,351. | 2,524: 5: - | | | | |
| | Mocha | 70,000. | 16,382: 1: 8 | | | | | | |
| | Total | 1,298,905. | 398,314:18: 1 | 10,610.75 | 4,536: 1: - | 402,850:19: 1 | | | 396,698: 17:13 |
| 1716/17 | Ceylon | 180,254. | 62,356: 17: - | 483.25 | 543:13: - | | | | |
| | Coromandel | 364,553.5 | 136,139: 2: 1 | 9,491.75 | 1,943: 2: 7 | | 17,556. | 143,853: 5:12 | |
| | Malabar | 96,210. | 32,039:14: 8 | 941.125 | 796: 7: - | | | | |
| | Bengal | 148,512. | 43,781:10: 8 | | | | | | |
| | Surat | 125,000. | 34,644:10: 8 | | | | | | |

| Year | Place | | | | | | | |
|---|---|---|---|---|---|---|---|---|
| | Persia | 25,000. | 5,446:16:- | 11,672. | 9,543:19:- | | | |
| | Mocha | 50,000. | 8,518:2:- | 3,028. | 1,009:5:8 | | | |
| | Total | 989,529.5 | 322,926:12:9 | 25,616.125 | 13,836:6:15 | 336,762:19:8 | | 192,909:13:12 |
| 1717/18 | Ceylon | 208,403.25 | 67,462:12:8 | | | | | |
| | Coromandel | 245,594.25 | 95,529:10:12 | 720. | 214:13:9 | | | |
| | Malabar | 129,309.5 | 37,029:14:8 | 477. | 407:13:- | | | |
| | Bengal | 433,160. | 130,190:-:8 | | | | | |
| | Surat | 187,500. | 52,615:16:- | | | | | |
| | Persia | 31,250. | 5,324:9:8 | 7,739. | 2,495:-:- | | | |
| | Mocha | 40,000. | 5,073:17:8 | 2,000.4 | 427:2:- | | | |
| | Total | 1,275,217. | 393,226:1:4 | 10,936.4 | 3,544:8:9 | 396,770:9:13 | 5,312. | 46,166:19:4 · 350,603:10:9 |
| 1718/19 | Ceylon | 159,846.375 | 58,636:16:- | 427.25 | 480:13:8 | | | |
| | Coromandel | 132,740.25 | 46,355:10:7 | 592.875 | 248:19:15 | | | |
| | Malabar | 135,622.5 | 36,991:2:- | 764. | 625:16:8 | | | |
| | Bengal | 340,000. | 77,361:19:- | | | | | |
| | Surat | 165,625. | 46,711:10:- | | | | | |
| | Persia | 31,250. | 4,365:7:8 | 7,666. | 3,764:6:- | | | |
| | Mocha | 50,000. | 6,606:11:8 | | | | | |
| | Total | 1,015,084.125 | 277,028:16:7 | 9,450.125 | 5,119:15:15 | 282,148:12:6 | 3,714. | 32,274:12:2 · 249,874:-:4 |
| 1719/20 | Ceylon | 227,353.375 | 87,567:17:8 | | 4,604:15:8 | | | |
| | Coromandel | 148,272.5 | 51,311:16:8 | 3,868.25 | | | | |
| | Malabar | 128,126. | 34,625:12:- | 502.1 | 403:16:8 | | | |
| | Bengal | 176,800. | 36,148:2:- | | | | | |
| | Surat | 606,516. | 130,148:2:8 | | | | | |
| | Persia | | | 2,887. | 1,330:15:- | | | |
| | Mocha | 50,000. | 6,920:11:- | 2,392. | 529:4:8 | | | |
| | Total | 1,337,067.875 | 346,722:1:8 | 9,649.35 | 6,868:11:8 | 353,590:13:- | 4,660. | 39,677:8:2 · 313,913:4:14 |

Table 34-1: Continued

| Year | Sales region | Copper sales (pond) | Copper profit (A) (gulden) | Camphor sales (pond) | Camphor profit (B) (gulden) | Copper & camphor total profit (gulden) | Koban sales (pieces) | Koban loss (C) (gulden) | (A + B) – C (gulden) |
|---|---|---|---|---|---|---|---|---|---|
| 1720/21 | Ceylon | 176,858.25 | 69,468: 7: 8 | | | | | | |
| | Coromandel | 212,263. | 74,863:5:10 | | | | 8,400. | 30,003:19: 9 | |
| | Malabar | 105,530. | 29,737:15: - | 70. | 55:19: 8 | | | | |
| | Bengal | 234,600. | 52,353: 5: 8 | | | | | | |
| | Surat | 73,166. | 15,543: 2: - | | | | | | |
| | Total | 802,417.25 | 241,965:15:10 | 70. | 55:19: 8 | 242,021:15: 2 | | | 212,017:15: 9 |
| 1721/22 | Ceylon | 262,355.125 | 102,512:19: - | | | | | | |
| | Coromandel | 427,553.25 | 145,203: 6: 4 | 75.75 | 37: 7:12 | | 5,406. | 46,998:16: 4 | |
| | Bengal | 182,454.5 | 40,526:18: - | | | | | | |
| | Surat | 328,661.5 | 62,918: 2: - | | | | | | |
| | Mocha | 59,562. | 11,378:15; 8 | | | | | | |
| | Total | 1,260,586.375 | 362,540: -:12 | 75.75 | 37: 7:12 | 362,577: 8: 8 | | | 315,578:12: 4 |
| 1722/23 | Ceylon | 265,743.75 | 105,225: 1: - | | | | | | |
| | Coromandel | 366,305.75 | 121,244:16: 6 | | | | 8,828. | 157,225: -: 6 | |
| | Malabar | 155,812. | 44,303:12: 8 | 1,299. | 1,059:10: - | | | | |
| | Bengal | 399,221. | 87,936: 9: 8 | | | | | | |
| | Surat | 292,393. | 52,590:19: - | | | | | | |
| | Mocha | 69,795. | 8,705:19: 8 | | | | | | |
| | Total | 1,549,270.5 | 420,006:17:14 | 1,299. | 1,059:10: - | 421,066: 7:14 | | | 263,841: 7: 8 |
| 1723/24 | Ceylon | 215,666.75 | 84,181: -: 8 | 964. | 1,145: 5: - | | | | |
| | Coromandel | 265,367.875 | 98,368: 8:15 | 1,084. | 466: 4: 5 | | 10,760. | 183,284: 4: 9 | |

| Region | | | | | | | |
|---|---|---|---|---|---|---|---|
| Malabar | 213,408.5 | 60,173: 1: 8 | 520.5 | 425: 3: 8 | | | 143,816: 15: 3 |
| Bengal | 179,157.25 | 40,078: -: - | | | | | |
| Surat | 182,749. | 39,545: 11: 8 | 4,724. | 332:15: 8 | | | |
| Persia | | | 1,355.9 | 2,385: 9: - | | | |
| Total | 1,056,349.375 | 322,346: 2: 7 | *8,648.4 | 4,754: 17: 5 | 327,100: 19:12 | | |
| Grand total | 29,048,245.095 | 7,932,855: 3: 6 | *174,368.375 | 87,977: -: : - | 8,020,832: 3: 6 | 291,584.5625 | 1,566,660: 12: - 6,454,231: 11: 6 |

Profit balance after subtracting the loss on *koban* from the total copper and camphor profit    f.6,454,231: 11: 6

The above profit plus profits of the Dutch Factory in Japan (See Table 33)    f.15,915,558:10: 6

Notes:

The items are listed in the source document in the following order: year, sales region, copper sales volume by region, copper sales profit by region, total copper sales volume, total copper sales profit, camphor sales volume by region, camphor sales profit by region, total camphor sales volume, total camphor sales profit, *koban* sales quantity, *koban* sales loss, and the balance after subtracting the loss on *koban* from the total copper and camphor profit. The order has been partly modified for the purposes of the above table for convenience.

'*' denotes numbers that have been corrected as the original numbers were miscalculated.

Quantity is expressed in pond: 120 pond = 1 picol, 1 picol = 100 kin = 100 catty.

Price is expressed in gulden: stuiver: pening; 1 gulden = 20 stuiver, 1 stuiver = 16 pening, 1 tael = 70 stuiver, 1 tael = 10 monme in silver.

*Table 34-2: The value of shipwrecked cargo and the volume of homeward shipments of copper and camphor (f means gulden)*

**1. The value of cargo on board the vessels shipwrecked in their way to/from Japan**

| | | |
|---|---|---|
| 1707/08 | *Monster* | f.194,139: 12: - |
| 1714/15 | *Arion* | f.419,804: 19: 8 |
| 1719/20 | *Meeroog, Catharina, Slot van Capelle* | f.541,303: 7: - |
| 1721/22 | *Valkenbos* | f.272,635: 15: - |
| 1723/24 | *Appollonia* | f.297,742: 5: - |
| Total | | f.1,725,625: 18: 8 |

The balance after the total loss above is subtracted from
the total profit (f.15,915,558: 10: 6, see Table 34-1)        f.14,189,942: 11: 14

**2. The estimated amounts of copper and camphor shipped to the Netherlands during the same period**

| | | | |
|---|---|---|---|
| 1. Copper | 5,841,368 pond (made up as follows): | | |
| | 4,711,922 pond | 173 vessels from Batavia | f.1,984,550: 15: 8 |
| | 1,129,446 pond | 29 vessels from Ceylon | f. 448,796: 9: 8 |
| Sub-total | 5,841,368 pond | 202 vessels in total | f.2,433,347: 5: - |
| 2. Camphor | 488,891.5 pond | 201 vessels from Batavia only | f. 426,371: 6: - |
| Total | | | f.2,859,718: 11: - |

equanimity and never petitioned the shogunate for trade improvements after that.[7]

## The sale of Japanese exports

The report examines the sales performances of just copper, *koban* and camphor from Japan. *Koban* and copper were principal export products as the export of silver was banned in 1668. *Koban* was only exported in large quantities from 1666 to 1675, with about 30,000–100,000 pieces exported yearly[8]; the quantity tended to decrease from then on. Still, *koban* was as important a product as copper and continued to make substantial profits in Coromandel until its debasement in 1695.[9] It was an attractive product for the VOC as the market price in Batavia was 10 rixdaalder, or about 30 gulden per *ryō*, about 20 per cent higher than the price in Japan.[10] Camphor was also an important export product in Japanese–Dutch trade during the Edo

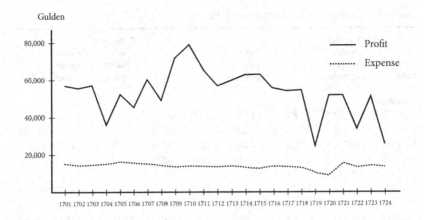

Figure 14: Total profits and expenses of the Dutch Factory in Japan (gulden)

period, after gold, silver and copper. Since most of the camphor was produced in Satsuma, the product was often described as 'Satsuma camphor'.[11]
There was an extensive demand for camphor as a substitute for borneol, a
highly prized precious medicine, in Southwest Asia and Europe.[12]

Copper, *koban* and camphor accounted for the bulk of the total export
during the period covered by the report. For example, the *Kasteel van
Woerden* was the only ship to arrive in Japan in 1724; its export cargo
consisted of 62.4 per cent copper, 29.2 per cent *koban* and 6.1 per cent
camphor. These three products accounted for 97.7 per cent of the total
shipment.[13] A survey of the sales records of these three export products
would subsequently represent the trade conditions of the Japanese export
products as a whole.

Heyningen's report summarizes the annual sales conditions in each
region under the control of the VOC. The regional summaries are arranged
in the predetermined order of relative importance within Southwest Asia
(hereafter called Asia for simplicity).[14]

Table 35 shows the annual sales of the aforementioned Japanese products
in each Asian region. The market conditions for Japanese trade goods in
each region, based on the table, are explained below.

## Ceylon
Ceylon is the general name for a region including Ceylon Island, Mannar
Island and part of the Indian subcontinent. Total copper sales for the
report period were 3,369,329.5 pond, which means that 11.6 per cent of

*Table 35: Copper and camphor sales by region*

| Year | Copper sales volume (pond) | A | Copper profit (gulden) | B | C | Camphor sales volume (pond) | Camphor profit (gulden) | D |
|------|------|------|------|------|------|------|------|------|
| *1. Ceylon* | | | | | | | | |
| 1701/02 | 164,242.5 | 8.8 | 63,329. | 12.1 | 38.6 | | | |
| 1702/03 | 91,562. | 7.6 | 34,039. | 9.7 | 37.18 | 478.5 | 693. | 144.83 |
| 1703/04 | 108,159.5 | 20.1 | 40,214. | 28.9 | 37.18 | 394. | 457. | 116. |
| 1704/05 | 93,773.5 | 19.8 | 35,394. | 27.0 | 37.34 | 201 | 239. | 118.91 |
| 1705/06 | 51,331. | 5.6 | 18,658. | 8.9 | 36.35 | 317. | 311. | 98.11 |
| 1706/07 | 101,046.75 | 7.6 | 36,478. | 11.2 | 36.1 | 794.5 | 837. | 105.35 |
| 1707/08 | 101,705. | 5.6 | 34,401. | 8.2 | 33.82 | 371. | 163. | 43.94 |
| 1708/09 | 125,900. | 6.9 | 42,519. | 9.7 | 41.71 | 1,033.5 | 1,040. | 100.63 |
| 1709/10 | 59,846.5 | 3.1 | 20,584. | 3.9 | 34.39 | 919. | 865. | 94.12 |
| 1710/11 | 40,965. | 2.3 | 14,183. | 3.1 | 34.62 | 402. | 361. | 89.8 |
| 1711/12 | 67,590. | 6.9 | 23,053. | 9. | 34.26 | 713. | 669. | 93.83 |
| 1712/13 | 106,031.875 | 7.6 | 35,730. | 9.8 | 33.7 | 302.25 | 339. | 112.16 |
| 1713/14 | 278,602.5 | 22.8 | 92,690. | 27.1 | 33.27 | | | |
| 1714/15 | 145,616.25 | 12. | 49,807. | 13.5 | 34.27 | 274.25 | 324. | 118.14 |
| 1715/16 | 136,476.25 | 10.5 | 46,340. | 11.6 | 33.95 | 449.75 | 505. | 112.28 |
| 1716/17 | 180,254. | 18.2 | 62,356. | 19.3 | 34.59 | 483.25 | 543. | 112.36 |
| 1717/18 | 208,403.25 | 16.3 | 67,462. | 17.2 | 32.37 | | | |
| 1718/19 | 159,846.375 | 15.7 | 58,636. | 21.2 | 36.75 | 427.25 | 480. | 118.35 |
| 1719/20 | 227,353.375 | 17. | 87,567. | 25.3 | 38.52 | 3,868.25 | 4,604. | 119.02 |
| 1720/21 | 176,858.25 | 22. | 69,468. | 28.7 | 39.34 | | | |
| 1721/22 | 262,355.125 | 20.8 | 102,512. | 28.3 | 39.07 | | | |
| 1722/23 | 265,743.75 | 17.2 | 105,225. | 25.1 | 39.6 | | | |
| 1723/24 | 215,666.75 | 20.4 | 84,181. | 26.1 | 39.03 | 964. | 1,145. | 118.78 |
| *2. Coromandel* | | | | | | | | |
| 1701/02 | 456,938.5 | 24.6 | 137,432. | 26.4 | 30.1 | | | |
| 1702/03 | 406,066. | 33.8 | 125,688. | 35.7 | 30.95 | 23. | 94. | 408.7 |
| 1703/04 | 184,588. | 34.2 | 45,309. | 32.5 | 24.55 | 71.5 | 60. | 83.92 |
| 1704/05 | 158,402.75 | 33.4 | 31,904. | 24.3 | 20.14 | 70.5 | 9. | 1.28 |
| 1705/06 | 269,531.5 | 29.1 | 57,092. | 27.1 | 21.18 | 177.625 | 197. | 110.91 |
| 1706/07 | 351,747. | 26.6 | 76,917. | 23.6 | 21.87 | 3,362.75 | 1,996. | 59.36 |
| 1707/08 | 429,025.5 | 23.6 | 102,888. | 24.6 | 23.98 | 3,604.125 | 3,535. | 98.08 |
| 1708/09 | 414,566.5 | 22.9 | 105,862. | 24.2 | 25.54 | 6,707.875 | 6,090. | 90.79 |
| 1709/10 | 414,133.75 | 21.3 | 118,801. | 22.7 | 28.69 | 753.25 | 698. | 92.67 |
| 1710/11 | 378,312. | 21.6 | 106,610. | 23.3 | 28.18 | 61.25 | 71. | 115.92 |
| 1711/12 | 406,202.75 | 41.5 | 97,626. | 38. | 24.03 | 36. | 41. | 113.89 |
| 1712/13 | 499,165.75 | 35.7 | 126,466. | 34.8 | 25.34 | | | |
| 1713/14 | 99,994.5 | 8.2 | 29,982. | 8.8 | 29.98 | | | |
| 1714/15 | 346,155.5 | 28.6 | 120,293. | 32.6 | 34.75 | | | |
| 1715/16 | 158,396.75 | 12.2 | 56,170. | 14.1 | 35.46 | 2,320.75 | 1,092. | 47.05 |

| 1716/17 | 364,553.5 | 36.8 | 136,139. | 42.2 | 37.34 | 9,491.75 | 1,943. | 20.47 |
| 1717/18 | 245,594.25 | 19.3 | 95,529. | 24.3 | 38.9 | 720. | 214. | 29.72 |
| 1718/19 | 132,740.25 | 13.1 | 46,355. | 16.7 | 34.92 | 592.875 | 248. | 41.83 |
| 1719/20 | 148,272.5 | 11.1 | 51,311. | 14.8 | 34.61 | | | |
| 1720/21 | 212,263. | 26.5 | 74,863. | 30.9 | 35.27 | | | |
| 1721/22 | 427,553.25 | 33.9 | 145,203. | 40. | 33.96 | 75.75 | 37. | 48.48 |
| 1722/23 | 366,305.75 | 23.6 | 121,244. | 28.9 | 33.1 | | | |
| 1723/24 | 265,367.875 | 25.1 | 98,368. | 30.5 | 39.03 | 1,084. | 466. | 42.99 |

3. Malabar

| 1701/02 | 126,741. | 6.8 | 46,384. | 8.9 | 36.6 | | | |
| 1702/03 | 31,423.5 | 2.6 | 10,768. | 3.1 | 34.27 | | | |
| 1703/04 | 88,556.25 | 16.4 | 30,704. | 22.0 | 34.67 | | | |
| 1704/05 | 90,709.25 | 19.1 | 31,118. | 23.7 | 34.31 | | | |
| 1705/06 | 109,859.5 | 11.9 | 39,887. | 18.9 | 36.31 | 108. | 79. | 73.15 |
| 1706/07 | 143,414.75 | 10.9 | 50,663. | 15.5 | 35.33 | 686.0625 | 499. | 72.73 |
| 1707/08 | 141,042.25 | 7.7 | 49,157. | 11.8 | 34.85 | 189.25 | 137. | 72.39 |
| 1708/09 | 124,814.875 | 6.9 | 40,859. | 9.4 | 32.74 | 177.625 | 146. | 82.2 |
| 1709/10 | 123,261. | 6.3 | 45,256. | 8.7 | 36.72 | 1,606.625 | 790. | 49.17 |
| 1710/11 | 89,927. | 5.1 | 31,692. | 6.9 | 35.24 | 566.2 | 481. | 84.95 |
| 1711/12 | 105,800. | 10.8 | 37,913. | 14.7 | 35.83 | | | |
| 1712/13 | 50,974. | 3.7 | 18,450. | 5.1 | 36.19 | 352.25 | 297. | 84.32 |
| 1713/14 | 94,702. | 7.7 | 34,002. | 9.9 | 35.9 | | | |
| 1714/15 | 76,378.5 | 6.3 | 25,849. | 7. | 33.84 | 279.375 | 236. | 84.47 |
| 1715/16 | 70,598. | 5.4 | 23,464. | 5.9 | 33.24 | 489.25 | 413. | 84.41 |
| 1716/17 | 96,210. | 9.7 | 32,039. | 9.9 | 33.3 | 941.125 | 796. | 84.58 |
| 1717/18 | 129,309.5 | 10.1 | 37,029. | 9.4 | 28.64 | 477. | 407. | 85.32 |
| 1718/19 | 135,622.5 | 13.4 | 36,991. | 13.4 | 27.27 | 764. | 625. | 81.81 |
| 1719/20 | 128,126. | 9.6 | 34,625. | 10. | 27.02 | 502.1 | 403.. | 80.26 |
| 1720/21 | 105,530. | 13.2 | 29,737. | 12.3 | 28.18 | 70. | 55. | 78.57 |
| 1721/22 | | | | | | | | |
| 1722/23 | 155,812. | 10.1 | 44,303. | 10.5 | 28.43 | 1,299. | 1,059. | 81.52 |
| 1723/24 | 213,408.5 | 20.2 | 60,173. | 18.7 | 28.2 | 520.5 | 425. | 81.65 |

4. Bengal

| 1701/02 | 291,312. | 15.7 | 96,093. | 18.4 | 33. | | | |
| 1702/03 | 516,256. | 43. | 147,442. | 41.8 | 28.56 | | | |
| 1703/04 | | | | | | | | |
| 1704/05 | | | | | | | | |
| 1705/06 | 356,514. | 38.6 | 56,471. | 26.8 | 15.84 | | | |
| 1706/07 | 297,500. | 22.5 | 50,168. | 15.4 | 16.86 | | | |
| 1707/08 | 499,664. | 27.4 | 83,862. | 20.1 | 16.78 | | | |
| 1708/09 | 561,000. | 31. | 99,988. | 22.9 | 17.82 | | | |
| 1709/10 | 635,868. | 32.7 | 169,853. | 32.5 | 26.71 | | | |
| 1710/11 | 676,098. | 38.5 | 177,689. | 38.8 | 26.28 | | | |
| 1711/12 | 143. | 0. | 37. | 0. | 25.87 | | | |
| 1712/13 | 335,920. | 24.1 | 81,874. | 22.5 | 24.37 | | | |
| 1713/14 | 387,783.5 | 31.7 | 92,996. | 27.1 | 23.98 | | | |

*Table 35: Continued*

| Year | Copper sales volume (pond) | A | Copper profit (gulden) | B | C | Camphor sales volume (pond) | Camphor profit (gulden) | D |
|------|------|------|------|------|------|------|------|------|
| 1714/15 | 547,536. | 45.2 | 150,519. | 40.8 | 27.49 | | | |
| 1715/16 | 650,934. | 50.1 | 197,151. | 49.5 | 30.29 | | | |
| 1716/17 | 148,512. | 15. | 43,781. | 13.6 | 29.48 | | | |
| 1717/18 | 433,160. | 34. | 130,190. | 33.1 | 30.06 | | | |
| 1718/19 | 340,000. | 33.5 | 77,361. | 27.9 | 22.75 | | | |
| 1719/20 | 176,800. | 13.2 | 36,148. | 10.4 | 20.45 | | | |
| 1720/21 | 234,600. | 29.2 | 52,353. | 21.6 | 22.32 | | | |
| 1721/22 | 182,454.5 | 14.5 | 40,526. | 11.2 | 22.21 | | | |
| 1722/23 | 399,221. | 25.8 | 87,936. | 20.9 | 22.03 | | | |
| 1723/24 | 179,157.25 | 17. | 40,078. | 12.4 | 22.37 | | | |
| **5. Surat** | | | | | | | | |
| 1701/02 | 816,904. | 44. | 178,308. | 34.2 | 21.8 | 3,686.8125 | 1,598. | 43.35 |
| 1702/03 | 156,042. | 13. | 34,545. | 9.8 | 22.19 | | | |
| 1703/04 | 158,184.5 | 29.3 | 23,292. | 16.7 | 14.72 | | | |
| 1704/05 | 101,247.5 | 21.4 | 20,632. | 15.7 | 20.38 | | | |
| 1705/06 | | | | | | | | |
| 1706/07 | 365,000. | 27.6 | 88,635. | 27.2 | 24.28 | | | |
| 1707/08 | 650,000. | 35.7 | 147,335. | 35.3 | 22.67 | 10,269. | 2,148. | 20.92 |
| 1708/09 | 473,062.5 | 26.1 | 114,950. | 26.3 | 24.3 | | | |
| 1709/10 | 525,000. | 27. | 125,542. | 24. | 23.91 | 6,260.25 | 765. | 12.22 |
| 1710/11 | 520,239.25 | 29.6 | 111,751. | 24.4 | 21.48 | | | |
| 1711/12 | 400,000. | 40.8 | 98,464. | 38.3 | 24.62 | | | |
| 1712/13 | 325,000. | 23.3 | 81,124. | 22.3 | 24.96 | | | |
| 1713/14 | 293,750. | 24. | 75,959. | 22.2 | 25.86 | | | |
| 1714/15 | 34,375. | 2.8 | 9,088. | 2.5 | 26.44 | | | |
| 1715/16 | 187,500. | 14.4 | 52,490. | 13.2 | 27.99 | | | |
| 1716/17 | 125,000. | 12.6 | 34,644. | 10.7 | 27.72 | | | |
| 1717/18 | 187,500. | 14.7 | 52,615. | 13.4 | 28.06 | | | |
| 1718/19 | 165,625. | 16.3 | 46,711. | 16.9 | 28.2 | | | |
| 1719/20 | 606,516. | 45.4 | 130,148. | 37.5 | 21.46 | | | |
| 1720/21 | 73,166. | 9.1 | 15,543. | 6.4 | 21.24 | | | |
| 1721/22 | 328,661.5 | 26.1 | 62,918. | 17.4 | 19.14 | | | |
| 1722/23 | 292,393. | 18.9 | 52,590. | 12.5 | 17.99 | | | |
| 1723/24 | 182,749. | 17.3 | 39,545. | 12.3 | 21.64 | 4,724. | 332. | 7.03 |
| **6. Persia** | | | | | | | | |
| 1701/02 | | | | | | | | |
| 1702/03 | | | | | | 3,150.5 | 3,055. | 96.97 |
| 1703/04 | | | | | | 2,436. | 1,665. | 68.35 |
| 1704/05 | | | | | | 1,537. | 874. | 56.86 |
| 1705/06 | 75,000. | 8.1 | 15,368. | 7.3 | 20.49 | 4,521. | 2,439. | 53.95 |

| Year | | A | | B | C | | | D |
|---|---|---|---|---|---|---|---|---|
| 1706/07 | | | | | | 3,046. | 1,716. | 56.34 |
| 1707/08 | | | | | | 5,971. | 2,956. | 49.51 |
| 1708/09 | 37,500. | 2.1 | 5,913. | 1.4 | 15.77 | 7,457.4 | 2,437. | 32.68 |
| 1709/10 | 62,500. | 3.2 | 7,906. | 1.5 | 12.65 | 7,804. | 1,900. | 24.35 |
| 1710/11 | | | | | | | | |
| 1711/12 | | | | | | | | |
| 1712/13 | | | | | | | | |
| 1713/14 | | | | | | 5,944. | 1,696. | 28.53 |
| 1714/15 | | | | | | 4,714. | 1,019. | 21.61 |
| 1715/16 | 25,000. | 1.9 | 6,314. | 1.6 | 25.26 | 7,351. | 2,524. | 34.34 |
| 1716/17 | 25,000. | 2.5 | 5,446. | 1.7 | 21.78 | 11,672. | 9,543. | 81.76 |
| 1717/18 | 31,250. | 2.5 | 5,324. | 1.4 | 17.04 | 7,739. | 2,495. | 32.24 |
| 1718/19 | 312,50. | 3.1 | 4,365. | 1.6 | 13.97 | 7,666. | 3,764. | 49.1 |
| 1719/20 | | | | | | 2,887. | 1,330. | 46.07 |
| 1720/21 | | | | | | | | |
| 1721/22 | | | | | | | | |
| 1722/23 | | | | | | | | |
| 1723/24 | | | | | | 1,355.9 | 2,385. | 175.9 |

7. Mocha

| Year | | A | | B | C | | | D |
|---|---|---|---|---|---|---|---|---|
| 1701/02 | | | | | | | | |
| 1702/03 | | | | | | | | |
| 1703/04 | | | | | | | | |
| 1704/05 | 30,000. | 6.3 | 12,340. | 9.4 | 41.13 | | | |
| 1705/06 | 62,500. | 6.6 | 23,115. | 11. | 36.98 | | | |
| 1706/07 | 62,500. | 4.7 | 23,541. | 7.2 | 37.67 | | | |
| 1707/08 | | | | | | | | |
| 1708/09 | 75,000. | 4.1 | 26,571. | 6.1 | 35.43 | 808. | 280. | 34.65 |
| 1709/10 | 124,368.75 | 6.4 | 34,263. | 6.6 | 27.55 | 953. | 364. | 38.2 |
| 1710/11 | 49,945. | 2.8 | 15,661. | 3.4 | 31.36 | | | |
| 1711/12 | | | | | | 1,198.8 | 516. | 43.04 |
| 1712/13 | 79,431.3 | 5.7 | 19,544. | 5.4 | 24.6 | | | |
| 1713/14 | 69,575. | 5.7 | 16,995. | 5. | 24.43 | 1,988.05 | 294. | 14.79 |
| 1714/15 | 62,291.67 | 5.1 | 13,254. | 3.6 | 21.28 | 1,434. | 675. | 45.82 |
| 1715/16 | 70,000. | 5.4 | 16,382. | 4.1 | 23.4 | | | |
| 1716/17 | 50,000. | 5.1 | 8,518. | 2.6 | 17.04 | 3,028. | 1,009. | 33.32 |
| 1717/18 | 40,000. | 3.1 | 5,073. | 1.3 | 12.68 | 2,000.4 | 427. | 21.35 |
| 1718/19 | 50,000. | 4.9 | 6,606. | 2.4 | 13.21 | | | |
| 1719/20 | 50,000. | 3.7 | 6,920. | 2. | 13.84 | 2,392. | 529. | 22.12 |
| 1720/21 | | | | | | | | |
| 1721/22 | 59,562. | 4.7 | 11,378. | 3.1 | 19.1 | | | |
| 1722/23 | 69,795. | 4.5 | 8,705. | 2.1 | 12.47 | | | |

A: Percentage (%) of the total copper sales
B: Percentage (%) of the total copper sales profit
C: Sales profit per 100 pond of copper in gulden, disregarding fractions below gulden
D: Sales profit per 100 pond of camphor in gulden, disregarding fractions below gulden

Asia's total copper sales were made in the Ceylon region. While it recorded annual average sales of 92,680 pond from 1702 to 1713, the sales quantity rose to 205,198 pond from 1714 to 1724. The average profit per 100 pond was more stable, and considerably higher at 36.36 gulden compared with other regions. It recorded the highest profit of 41.71 gulden in Asia for this period in 1709. Consequently, Ceylon had the largest share of the profits of all the regions.

Camphor was sold in Ceylon over a period of seventeen years, which was longer than in the other regions, but the total sales volume was only 12,392.5 pond, about 500 pond per year. Nevertheless, the profit rate was high at 99.52 gulden per 100 pond.

## Coromandel

The region of Coromandel extended from the Godavari River to Cape Calimere, although the exact boundaries varied at different times.[15] Copper coins were used as low-denomination currency in this region; coins included the kasu, dubbu and nevel. The region had been procuring copper for coinage from throughout Southeast Asia even before the Europeans brought copper. The copper traded in those days came from China or Japan.[16] After the turn of the seventeenth century, the VOC made huge profits by exporting large quantities of Japanese copper to this region. However, the company was hampered by competition from Indian and British merchants[17]; they became even more active in the eighteenth century further weakening the VOC's monopoly over copper export to India.[18]

According to the *Generale Missiven*, the selling price of copper fell from 66.5 pagoda to 61.5 pagoda per bale (480 pond) in 1703[19] and 58 pagoda in 1705.[20] It was reported in 1706 that the copper sales had been poor because of British competition, causing the price to drop to 48 pagoda.[21] The price recovered from 1714. It was reported in 1715 that 'Japanese copper bars sold for 60–64 pagoda per bale in Coromandel; they made more profits than other products of the company'.[22] However, the company was still troubled by competition with the British, reporting in 1720, 'Although the copper price dropped to 66 pagoda per bale, the sales were still sluggish because the British brought [copper] from China and Tonkin'.[23]

A total of 7,315,857 pond of copper were sold in Coromandel from 1701 to 1724, accounting for 24.6 per cent of total copper sales in Asia. The profit in Coromandel was 30.08 gulden per 100 pond, which was the third highest after Ceylon and Malabar. While Bengal sold the highest quantity of copper, Coromandel made the largest amount of profit from copper sales, surpassing Bengal.

29,153 pond of camphor were sold during this period. The average profit was about 90–110 gulden per 100 pond from 1701 to 1712. Camphor was not sold for three years from 1713, after which the profit fell to 20–50 gulden, less than one half of the previous level. The sale of *koban* will be discussed later.

## Malabar

The Malabar region extends from Goa on the west coast of India to Cape Comorin. A total of 2,432,220 pond of copper were sold here, 8.4 per cent of the total copper sales volume in Asia. The annual average volume was 105,749 pond. The profit was high at 33–36 gulden per 100 pond until 1718 when it dropped to 27–28 gulden. Overall, yearly sales volumes and profits were relatively stable in Malabar. The average profit in Malabar was 33.05 gulden per 100 pond. The selling price of copper in Malabar was second only to Ceylon.

Like Ceylon, only small quantities of camphor were sold in Malabar; the total volume for this period was even smaller than that of Ceylon at 9,028 pond. Camphor sales were recorded over sixteen years during the report period; while the yearly sales volume was small, the profit was stable at 70–85 gulden per 100 pond.

## Bengal

Bengal refers to the region along the lower Ganges River. 7,850,433 pond of copper were sold during this period, accounting for 27 per cent of the total copper sales in Asia. Bengal was the largest market for copper in Asia for this period. The annual average volume was 341,323 pond, but the actual volume was unstable and fluctuated greatly from year to year. The profit, which was low at 15–17 gulden per 100 pond from 1706 to 1709, gradually rose to 30 gulden in 1716, then fell to around 22 gulden in 1719. The average profit was 24.07 gulden per 100 pond.

As in Coromandel, the Dutch were obstructed by the activity of the British. The *Generale Missiven* reported in 1704 that the British relied on copper from China, thus presenting the VOC with an obstacle.[24] There were no copper sales in 1704 and 1705. Only 143 pond was sold in 1712 and, according to the report, 'The British brought large quantities of Japanese copper from China to Bengal. The VOC sold (copper) for 32 ropia per man = 68 pond'.[25] This activity of the British caused the copper price in Bengal to drop.[26] The VOC were unable to sell their copper at their desired price. It appears that much of the copper was used in copper coin minting, although local copper coins such as dam and paisa were reportedly not used very much in Bengal.[27]

## Surat

The Surat region is on the northwestern coast of India facing the Gulf of Cambay. In a narrow sense it is also the name of a trade port near the mouth of the Tapti River. Total copper sales in Surat were 6,967,915 pond, with an annual average of 302,953 pond, accounting for 24 per cent of the total sales in Asia. The region recorded poor sales from 1703 to 1706, from 1715 to 1719, and in 1721. The selling price of copper had been on a downward trend even before the reporting period, falling from 18 ropia to 16 ropia per man (34 pond) in 1700[28] and down to 15.3/8 ropia per man in 1703.[29] It was reported in 1704 that 'Japanese copper bars sold for [a price that could earn] a profit of only 21 per cent'.[30] The profit began to increase from 1707 and reached 28 gulden in 1718 before falling again from 1720. The profit in Surat was small, averaging at 23.23 gulden per 100 pond.

Although camphor was only sold for four years during the period, the total sales volume reached 24,940 pond, surpassing the amounts sold in Ceylon or Malabar.

## Persia

Copper did not sell well in Persia during this period. Total copper sales were 287,500 pond, less than 1 per cent of the total volume sold in Asia. The average profit was 18.14 gulden per 100 pond, the lowest in Asia. There was little demand for copper in the Persian region.

Persia was Asia's largest market for camphor. Total camphor sales were 85,252 pond, almost one half (48.9 per cent) of camphor sales in Asia. However, the profit was not very high; it gradually fell after rising to 96.97 gulden per 100 pond in 1702, dropping to 24.35 gulden by 1710. Perhaps for this reason, camphor was not sold for the next three years; the profit fluctuated greatly after the resumption of sales in 1714.

## Mocha

Mocha was a trading port city at the southern tip of the Arabian Peninsula on the Red Sea. Total copper sales were 1,004,969 pond, 3.5 per cent of the total copper sales in Asia. The volume is quite high considering there was only one factory in this region, unlike the other larger regions with multiple factories. The profit from copper sales was high at an average of 35.02 gulden per 100 pond up to 1712, but it began to decline in 1713, reaching 12.47 gulden in 1723, only about one third of the previous level.

Camphor was sold for eight years during the period, a total volume of 13,802 pond. The average profit was 31.66 gulden per 100 pond, varying greatly from year to year.

## Exports and sales by product

Table 36 shows the volume of copper, camphor and *koban* exported from Japan on individual ships during the early eighteenth century. The shogunate limited the number of Dutch vessels arriving in Japan to four a year from 1700.[31] The number was reduced to two a year from 1716 by the new trade law of *Shōtoku shinrei*, which was proclaimed in the previous year. When there was an allowance of four ships, the quantity of copper carried on each ship was between 200,000 and 500,000 pond, but this was increased to 780,000 pond (650,000 kin) per vessel once the allowance was limited to two.

In 1706, the board of directors of the VOC (*Heren XVII*) proposed to send two or three large ships instead of five small ships to Japan, but the proposal was not considered feasible by the governor general of the Dutch East Indies in Batavia because large ships would be too hard to manage. Large ships were also needed as warships or homebound ships in Asia.[32] The majority of arrivals from 1706 were small ships with the carrying capacity of around 600 tons. The board's proposal was only implemented when the annual limit was reduced to two under the *Shōtoku sinrei*. All arrivals from 1716 onward were large ships with the carrying capacity of between 800 and 900 tons.[33] The maximum load of copper on the large ships was 780,000 pond (650,000 kin).[34] The destination for ships returning from Japan had been either Malacca or Batavia, but after 1716 all returning ships headed for Batavia.

### Copper
It was the policy of the VOC board to acquire Japanese copper for its factories in Asia; shipment to the European market was secondary.[35] A total of 34,889,613 pond (29,074,678 kin) of copper were marketed during this period, 29,048,245 pond (24,206,871 kin) of which were sold in Asia and 5,841,368 pond (4,867,807 kin) were shipped to the Netherlands. The Asian sales accounted for 83.3 per cent and the homeward shipments accounted for 16.7 per cent. It is clear that the majority of copper was consumed within Asia in accordance with the board's policy for this period.

A larger amount of copper than normal was shipped to the Netherlands from 1704 to 1708[36], even though the copper price there was not high during this period.[37] This was due to the sluggish copper sales at various factories caused by political instability in India from around 1703 to 1706. Only small amounts of copper were shipped to India for a few years after that as there was enough old stock within the country.[38]

Following a report in 1709 that 'Japanese copper is needed in Asia more than in Europe'[39], the amount of homeward copper shipment decreased, as shown

*Table 36: The volume of Japanese export goods, 1702–1724*

| Year | Ship name | Destination | Copper (pond) | Camphor (pond) | Koban (pieces) |
|------|-----------|-------------|---------------|----------------|----------------|
| 1702 | Diemen | Malacca | 360,000 | | |
| | Westhoven | Malacca | 600,000 | | |
| | Concordia | Malacca | 581,160 | | |
| | Berkenrode | Batavia | 312,000 | | 21,111.5 |
| | Total | | 1853,160 | – | 21,111.5 |
| 1703 | Taxisboom | Malacca | 300,000 | | |
| | Kiefhoek | Malacca | 587,943.6 | | |
| | Brandenburg | Batavia | 480,000 | | 19,245.5 |
| | Elemeet | Malacca | 588,000 | | |
| | Total | | 1,955,943.6 | – | 19,245.5 |
| 1704 | Lokhorst | Malacca | 390,000 | | |
| | Popkensburg | Malacca | 660,000 | | |
| | Waarde | Malacca | 660,000 | | |
| | Kattendijk | Batavia | 485,306.4 | | 2,427 |
| | Total | | 2,195,306.4 | – | 2,427 |
| 1705 | Bon | Batavia | 528,000 | | |
| | Bredenhof | Batavia | 528,000 | | |
| | Nieuwburg | Batavia | 480,000 | | 5,000 |
| | Prins | Batavia | 660,000 | | 4,290.25 |
| | Total | | 2,196,000 | – | 9,290.25 |
| 1706 | Abbekerk | Malacca | 360,000 | | |
| | Bredenhof | Malacca | 360,000 | | |
| | Lokhorst | Malacca | 360,000 | | |
| | Belvliet | Batavia | 360,000 | | 3,000 |
| | Sloten | Batavia | 360,000 | 41,098.6 | 1,978.5 |
| | Total | | 1,800,000 | 41,098.6 | 4,978.5 |
| 1707 | Zoelen | Malacca | 480,000 | 8,032.8 | 2,110 |
| | Veenhuien | Malacca | 480,000 | 7,954.8 | 2,110 |
| | Haring | Malacca | 480,000 | 8,167.2 | 2,100 |
| | Zuidenburg | Batavia | 360,000 | 40,507 | 13,296.25 |
| | Total | | 1,800,000 | 64,661.8 | 19,626.25 |
| 1708 | Haak | Malacca | 288,000 | | 4,500 |
| | Zoelen | Batavia | 348,000 | 11,177.4 | 4,500 |
| | Baarzande | Batavia | 356,640 | 11,505.6 | 11,968.25 |
| | Total | | 992,640 | 22,683 | 20,968.25 |
| 1709 | Korssloot | Malacca | 420,000 | 7,419.6 | |

|      |                   |         |           |          |          |
|------|-------------------|---------|-----------|----------|----------|
|      | *Standvastigheid* | Malacca | 480,000   | 7,465.2  |          |
|      | *Berg*            | Batavia | 480,000   | 27,349.2 | 5,000    |
|      | *Arion*           | Batavia | 420,000   |          | 15,228   |
|      | Total             |         | 1,800,000 | 42,234   | 20,228   |
| 1710 | *Lokhorst*        | Batavia | 420,000   | 15,285.6 | 4,000    |
|      | *Nederhoven*      | Malacca | 420,000   |          | 4,000    |
|      | *Bon*             | Batavia | 420,000   | 14,743.8 | 7,596    |
|      | *Samson*          | Malacca | 540,000   | 10,042.5 | 4,500    |
|      | Total             |         | 1,800,000 | 40,071.9 | 20,096   |
| 1711 | *Lokhorst*        | Batavia | 300,000   |          |          |
|      | *Bredenhof*       | Batavia | 300,000   | 22,450.8 |          |
|      | *Raadhuis*        | Batavia | 300,000   | 19,626   |          |
|      | *Rijnestein*      | Batavia | 300,000   |          |          |
|      | Total             |         | 1,200,000 | 42,076.8 | –        |
| 1712 | *Nederhoven*      | Malacca | 240,000   |          | 10,400   |
|      | *Abbekerk*        | Malacca | 240,000   |          | 10,400   |
|      | *Ouwerkerk*       | Malacca | 238,320   |          |          |
|      | *Charlois*        | Batavia | 177,960   | 41,697.6 | 13,616.5 |
|      | Total             |         | 896,280   | 41,697.6 | 34,416.5 |
| 1713 | *Negotie Journalen* missing |  |        |          |          |
| 1714 | *Strijkebolle*    | Malacca | 324,000   |          | 5,000    |
|      | *Zanderhoeff*     | Batavia | 468,000   | 25,167.6 | 5,000    |
|      | *Arion*           | Batavia | 468,000   |          | 9,236    |
|      | Total             |         | 1,260,000 | 25,167.6 | 19,236   |
| 1715 | *Risdam*          | Malacca | 462,000   |          | 6,000    |
|      | *Sleewijk*        | Batavia | 462,000   |          | 6,000    |
|      | *Zanderhoeff*     | Batavia | 456,000   |          | 5,556    |
|      | Total             |         | 1,380,000 | 0        | 17,556   |
| 1716 | *Rijksdorf*       | Batavia | 780,000   | 41,978.4 | 2,700    |
|      | *Ternisse*        | Batavia | 780,000   |          | 2,612    |
|      | Total             |         | 1,560,000 | 41,978.4 | 5,312    |
| 1717 | *Noordbeek*       | Batavia | 780,000   | 40,920   | 2,000    |
|      | *Luchtenburg*     | Batavia | 780,000   |          | 1,736    |
|      | Total             |         | 1,560,000 | 40,920   | 3,736    |
| 1718 | *Meeroog*         | Batavia | 780,000   | 29,997.6 | 2,000    |
|      | *Ternisse*        | Batavia | 780,000   |          | 2,660    |
|      | Total             |         | 1560,000  | 29,997.6 | 4,660    |
| 1719 | No Ships          |         |           |          |          |

*Table 36: Continued*

| Year | Ship name | Destination | Copper (pond) | Camphor (pond) | Koban (pieces) |
|------|-----------|-------------|---------------|----------------|----------------|
| 1720 | *Negotie Journalen* missing | | | | |
| 1721 | *Bentveld* | Batavia | 780,000 | 42,000 | 2,400 |
|      | *Boekenrode* | Batavia | 780,000 | | 2,400 |
|      | *Valkenbos* | Batavia | 780,000 | | 2,422 |
|      | Total | | 2,340,000 | 42,000 | 7,222 |
| 1722 | *Hillegonda* | Batavia | 780,000 | 24,000 | 3,538 |
|      | Total | | 780,000 | 24,000 | 3,538 |
| 1723 | *Cornelia* | Batavia | 624,000 | 19,999.2 | 6,400 |
|      | *Appollonia* | Batavia | 622,080 | | 6,422 |
|      | Total | | 1246,080 | 19,999.2 | 12,822 |
| 1724 | *Kasteel van Woerden* | Batavia | 720,240 | 36,000 | 3,187 |
|      | Total | | 720,240 | 36,000 | 3,187 |

This table has been compiled based on shipping invoices contained in *Negotie Journalen* No. 882–901 among the documents of the Dutch factory in Japan. They are in the possession of the National Archives (Algemeen Rijksarchief) in The Hague.

in Table 37, increasing again only between 1718 and 1822.[40] Perhaps this copper was sent to the Netherlands because the copper price fell in Asia around 1718 and 1720, judging from the decline in profit per 100 pond shown in Table 35.

Although the VOC hoped to export 22,000 kisten (2,640,000 pond) of copper per year from Japan[41], the actual volume was only around 1,460,000 pond per year on average. This volume was far short of its requirement. According to Figure 15, the difference between the sales volume in Asia and the export volume from Japan was not very large, with the following exceptions: in 1719, when no copper was exported as three ships were wrecked on their way to Japan; in 1721, when large quantities of copper were exported as the shogunate gave special permission to allow three ships[42]; and during the aforementioned period of sluggish trade in Asia. The rate of profit from Japanese copper sales shown in Table 37 was calculated from the copper price in Japan and the sales profit in Asia. It ranged from 50 to 70 per cent during the report period. However, the actual profit rate would have been several per cent lower than that because expenses incurred from the procurement of copper in Japan to its sale in Asia have not been taken into account in the calculation.

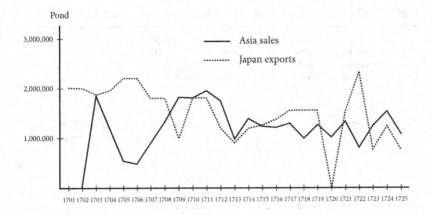

*Figure 15: Volumes of copper exports from Japan and copper sales in Asia (pond)*

Copper was sold throughout Asia, but Bengal, Coromandel and Surat in particular were large markets. The price was consistently high in the southern regions of Ceylon and Malabar (followed by Coromandel) and tended to be lower in northern regions. The total sales volume was high in Bengal and Surat in the north, but the volume and the profit fluctuated from year to year and the price was generally low. Both the sales volume and profit were low in Persia and Mocha.

## Camphor[43]
The total camphor sales volume in Asia were 174,368 pond (145,307 kin), 48.9 per cent of which were sold in Persia, 16.7 per cent in Coromandel, 14.3 per cent in Surat, 7.9 per cent in Mocha, 7.1 per cent in Ceylon, 5.1 per cent in Malabar, and nil in Bengal. Persia was Asia's largest camphor consuming region at the time. Nevertheless, camphor was not sold regularly even in Persia; it was not in consistent demand throughout Asia in general. In some regions, such as Ceylon, camphor was sold almost every year, but the sales volume tended to be very small. While the sales profit was high and stable in Ceylon and Malabar, the price varied considerably from year to year in the other regions. The demand for camphor was stronger in Europe than Asia; a total of 488,891.5 pond (407,410 kin) were shipped to the Netherlands during this period. The homeward shipments of camphor accounted for 73.7 per cent, while the sales in Asia accounted for 26.3 per cent. Unlike copper, the majority were sent to the Netherlands. An annual average of 21,000 pond were shipped to the Netherlands[44], more than satisfying the amount required there, which was around 20,000 pond per year.

*Table 37: The volume and sales of Japanese exports by product*

| Year | Sales volume in Asia (pond) | Sales profit* (gulden) | A | Profit rate (B) | Japanese export volume (pond) | (catty) | C | D | E |
|---|---|---|---|---|---|---|---|---|---|
| *1. Copper* | | | | | | | | | |
| 1701/02 | 1,856,138. | 52,1549. | 28.1 | 75. | 1,853,160. | 1,544,300. | 12.84 | 37.45 | 46,875. |
| 1702/03 | 1,201,349.5 | 35,2484. | 29.34 | 78.3 | 1,955,944. | 1,629,953. | 12.84 | 37.45 | 30,250. |
| 1703/04 | 539,488.25 | 139,520. | 25.86 | 69. | 2,195,306. | 1,829,422. | 12.84 | 37.45 | 75,000. |
| 1704/05 | 474,133. | 131,391. | 27.71 | 74.2 | 2,196,000. | 1,830,000. | 12.8 | 37.35 | 523,120. |
| 1705/06 | 924,736. | 210,593. | 22.77 | 61. | 1,800,000. | 1,500,000. | 12.8 | 37.35 | 968,625. |
| 1706/07 | 1,321,208.5 | 326,403. | 24.7 | 66.1 | 1,800,000. | 1,500,000. | 12.8 | 37.35 | 532,250. |
| 1707/08 | 1,821,436.75 | 417,646. | 22.9 | 61.3 | 99,2640. | 827,200. | 12.8 | 37.35 | 306,250. |
| 1708/09 | 1,811,843.875 | 436,665. | 24.1 | 64.5 | 1,800,000. | 1,500,000. | 12.8 | 37.35 | 698,000. |
| 1709/10 | 1,944,978. | 522,208. | 26.85 | 71.9 | 1,800,000. | 1,500,000. | 12.8 | 37.35 | 231,026. |
| 1710/11 | 1,755,486.25 | 457,587. | 26.07 | 69.8 | 1,200,000. | 1,000,000. | 12.8 | 37.35 | 118,750. |
| 1711/12 | 979,735.75 | 257,095. | 26.24 | 70. | 896,280. | 746,900. | 12.85 | 37.48 | 0. |
| 1712/13 | 1,396,523.925 | 363,190. | 26. | | 1,200,000. | 1,000,000. | | | 93,750. |
| 1713/14 | 1,224,407.5 | 342,629. | 27.98 | 72.4 | 1,260,000. | 1,050,000. | 13.25 | 38.65 | 127,277. |
| 1714/15 | 1,212,352.92 | 368,811. | 30.42 | 79.4 | 1,380,000. | 1,150,000. | 13.25 | 38.65 | 95,949. |
| 1715/16 | 1,298,905. | 398,314. | 30.67 | 70.9 | 1,560,000. | 1,300,000. | 14.84 | 43.28 | 41,853. |
| 1716/17 | 989,529.5 | 322,926. | 32.63 | 75.4 | 1,560,000. | 1,300,000. | 14.84 | 43.28 | 41,512. |
| 1717/18 | 127,5217. | 393,226. | 30.84 | 71.3 | 1,560,000. | 1,300,000. | 14.84 | 43.28 | 0. |
| 1718/19 | 1,015,084. | 277,028. | 27.37 | | 0. | 0. | | | 219,918. |
| 1719/20 | 1,337,067.875 | 346,722. | 25.93 | 59.9 | 1,560,000. | 1,300,000. | 14.84 | 43.28 | 396,922. |
| 1720/21 | 802,417.25 | 241,965. | 30.15 | 69.7 | 2,340,000. | 1,950,000. | 14.84 | 43.28 | 396,212. |
| 1721/22 | 1,260,586.375 | 362,540. | 28.76 | 66.5 | 780,000. | 650,000. | 14.84 | 43.28 | 93,249. |
| 1722/23 | 1,549,270.5 | 420,006. | 27.11 | 62.6 | 1,246,240. | 1,038,400. | 14.84 | 43.28 | 561,094. |
| 1723/24 | 1,056,349.375 | 322,346. | 30.52 | 70.5 | 720,240. | 600,200. | 14.84 | 43.28 | 574. |
| *2. Camphor* | | | | | | | | | |
| 1701/02 | 3,686.8125 | 1,598. | 43.35 | | 0. | 0. | | | |
| 1702/03 | 3,652. | 3,843. | 105.23 | | 0. | 0. | | | |
| 1703/04 | 2,901.5 | 2,182. | 75.2 | | 0. | 0. | | | |
| 1704/05 | 1,808.5 | 1,123. | 62.1 | | 0. | 0. | | | |
| 1705/06 | 5,123.625 | 3,027. | 59.8 | 68.3 | 41,098.6 | 34,249. | 30. | 87.5 | |
| 1706/07 | 7,889.3125 | 5,049. | 64. | 73.1 | 64,661.8 | 53,885. | 30. | 87.5 | |
| 1707/08 | 20,204.375 | 8,941. | 44.5 | 50.9 | 22,683. | 18,903. | 30. | 87.5 | |
| 1708/09 | 16,184.4 | 10,002. | 61.76 | 70.6 | 42,234. | 35,195. | 30. | 87.5 | |
| 1709/10 | 18,296.125 | 5,385. | 29.43 | 34.2 | 40,071.6 | 33,393. | 29.5 | 86.04 | |
| 1710/11 | 1,029.45 | 914. | 88.79 | 103.2 | 42,076.8 | 35,064. | 29.5 | 86.04 | |
| 1711/12 | 1,947.8 | 1,228. | 63.05 | 73.3 | 41,697.6 | 34,748. | 29.5 | 86.04 | |
| 1712/13 | 654.5 | 637. | 97.33 | | (23,784.) | (19,820.) | | | |
| 1713/14 | 7,932.05 | 1,991. | 25.1 | 28.7 | 25,167.6 | 20,973. | 30. | 87.5 | |
| 1714/15 | 6,702.025 | 2,237. | 33.38 | | 0. | 0. | | | |
| 1715/16 | 10,610.75 | 4,536. | 42.75 | 48.9 | 41,978.4 | 34,982. | 30. | 87.5 | |
| 1716/17 | 25,616.125 | 13,836. | 54.01 | 61.7 | 40,920. | 34,100. | 30. | 87.5 | |
| 1717/18 | 10,936.4 | 3,544. | 32.41 | 37. | 29,997.6 | 24,998. | 30. | 87.5 | |
| 1718/19 | 9,450.125 | 5,119. | 54.17 | | (0.) | (0.) | | | |

| Year | Sales in Coromandel (pieces) | Loss* (gulden) | Loss per piece (gulden) | | Exports from Japan (pieces) | Price per piece in Japan (tael) | | |
|------|------|------|------|------|------|------|------|------|
| 1719/20 | 9,649.35 | 6,868. | 71.18 | | (0.) | (0.) | | |
| 1720/21 | 70. | 55. | 78.57 | 89.8 | 42,000. | 35000. | 30. | 87.5 |
| 1721/22 | 75.75 | 37. | 48.48 | 55.4 | 24,000. | 20000. | 30. | 87.5 |
| 1722/23 | 1,299. | 1,059. | 81.52 | 96.4 | 19,199.2 | 16000. | 29. | 84.58 |
| 1723/24 | 8,648.4 | 4,754. | 54.97 | 65. | 36,000. | 30000. | 29. | 84.58 |

3. Koban

| Year | Sales in Coromandel (pieces) | Loss* (gulden) | Loss per piece (gulden) | Exports from Japan (pieces) | Price per piece in Japan (tael) |
|------|------|------|------|------|------|
| 1701/02 | 22,514. | 71,477. | 3.17 | 21,111.5 | 6.8 |
| 1702/03 | 17,940.3125 | 54,370. | 3.03 | 19,245.5 | 6.8 |
| 1703/04 | 11,034. | 34,085. | 3.1 | 2,427. | 6.8 |
| 1704/05 | 8,455. | 26,764. | 3.17 | 9,290.25 | 6.8 |
| 1705/06 | 24,864.25 | 81,979. | 3.7 | 4,978. | 6.8 |
| 1706/07 | 135,00. | 41,319. | 3.06 | 19,626.75 | 6.8 |
| 1707/08 | 5,168.75 | 16,736. | 3.24 | 30,968. | 6.8 |
| 1708/09 | 22,121.75 | 72,311. | 3.27 | 20,228. | 6.8 |
| 1709/10 | 12,468.25 | 41,296. | 3.31 | 20,096. | 6.8 |
| 1710/11 | 16,228. | 52,451. | 3.23 | 0. | 6.8 |
| 1711/12 | 21,996. | 73,168. | 3.33 | 44,816.5 | 6.8 |
| 1712/13 | 3,920. | 10,907. | 2.78 | 19,845. | 6.8 |
| 1713/14 | 29,538.25 | 205,701. | 6.96 | 19,236. | 6.8 |
| 1714/15 | 15,200. | 98,392. | 6.47 | 17,556. | 6.8 |
| 1715/16 | 2,000. | 6,152. | 3.08 | 5,312. | 6.8 |
| 1716/17 | 17,556. | 143,853. | 8.19 | 3,736. | 6.8 |
| 1717/18 | 5,312. | 46,166. | 8.69 | 4,660. | 6.8 |
| 1718/19 | 3,714. | 32,274. | 8.69 | 0. | 6.8 |
| 1719/20 | 4,660. | 39,677. | 8.51 | 5,406. | 6.8 |
| 1720/21 | 8,400. | 30,003. | 3.57 | 7,222. | 6.8 |
| 1721/22 | 5,406. | 46,998. | 8.69 | 3,538. | 13.6 |
| 1722/23 | 8,828. | 157,225. | 17.81 | 12,822. | 13.6 |
| 1723/24 | 10,760. | 183,284. | 17.03 | 3,187. | 13.6 |

* = Fractions below gulden are discarded.

A = Sales profit per 100 pond (gulden): 1 gulden = 20 stuiver, 1 tael = 70 stuiver, 1 tael = 10 monme in silver.

B = Based on the copper price in Japan and the sales profit in Asia (%).

C = The price per 100 kin (= 100 catty = 120 pond) of copper in Japan (tael): 1 tael = 10 monme in silver.

D = The copper price per 100 pond in Japan (gulden).

E = The exports/sales to Europe (pond) are quoted from K. Glamann, 'The Dutch East India Company's trade in Japanese copper 1645–1736', *Scandinavian Economic History Review*, Vol. 1, No. 1, 1953, 52–53.

Notes:

The export volume and price of copper are quoted from the table of copper exports in Table 11.

The volume and price of camphor are quoted from Table 30.

The volume and price of *koban* are quoted from Table 20 of Chapter 4.

## Koban

In addition to the three types of *koban* exported during this period, the
Keichō *koban*, which was exported prior to this period, is included in this
discussion for reasons of expediency. The Dutch used simple descriptions to
distinguish between different types of *koban*. The Keichō *koban* was called
'old fine *koban*' or simply 'old *koban*', the Genroku *koban* was 'new crude
*koban*', the Kenji *koban* was 'small *koban*'[45] or 'light-weight *koban*', and the
Kyōhō *koban* was 'new large *koban*' or 'double *koban*'. The Keichō *koban*
was of fine quality, with a purity of 20 carat 8.5–10 grain (86.3–86.9 per cent
gold content).[46] It was exported from Japan in the seventeenth century and
made great profits in Coromandel.

The Genroku *koban* was minted in 1695. The purity of this *koban* was
13 carat 6–7 grain (56.25–56.58 per cent gold content)[47], about 35 per cent
lower than that of the Keichō *koban*. Although the Dutch disliked this
crude *koban*, they began to export it at the same price as the Keichō *koban*
when the export of the Keichō *koban* was banned by the shogunate in 1697.[48]
Consequently, the Dutch incurred a loss of 15–16 per cent from every re-
mintage in Coromandel from then on, whereas they used to enjoy a profit
of 25 per cent from the Keichō *koban*.[49]

The export of the Genroku *koban* continued to the end of 1712. While the
Dutch were ordered to export the Kenji *koban*, the minting of which started
in 1710, instead of the Genroku *koban* in 1712, the export of Kenji *koban*
actually began in 1713.[50] As suggested by its description of 'small *koban*',
the Kenji *koban* was light and weighed only 25 condrijn. In comparison,
the Keichō and Genroku *koban* weighed 47 condrijn.

The VOC suffered a loss of 34–36 per cent by paying the same price for
a half-weight coin.[51] However, its purity was similar to that of the Keichō
*koban*: 19 carat 11.7/8 grain according to Adriaan van Houten's analysis.[52]
The Kenji *koban* was exported to Coromandel from 1714 and, according
to Table 37, the loss per piece of *koban* increased from about 3 gulden to
6–8 gulden. By a simple calculation based on its price in Japan (6.8 tael or
23.8 gulden), the loss rate was 13.4 per cent, which jumped to 29.3 per cent
between 1714 and 1722. When expenses were added, the figures would be
close to 15–16 per cent and 34–36 per cent respectively, as estimated by G.
W. van Imhoff, the governor general of the Dutch East Indies.

The Dutch exported the 'double, or large' Kyōhō *koban* from 1722.[53] It is
said that the Kyōhō *koban* was called the 'double *koban*' to distinguish it
from the Keichō *koban*, which was almost identical in weight and purity[54]
and described as the 'large *koban*' in the *Generale Missiven*.[55] It was called so
perhaps in contrast to the 'small' Kenji *koban*; the Kyōhō *koban* was not only

twice the weight but also twice the price of the Kenji *koban*. According to a report, 'The shogun set the price of the large new *koban* at 11.6 tael and the price of the small *koban* at 5.8 tael. However, foreigners must receive them at 13.6 tael and 6.8 tael respectively from the Nagasaki trade association (*Nagasaki Kaisho*)'.[56] Although the Kyōhō *koban* was of fine quality with the same weight and purity as the Keichō *koban*, it cost twice as much as the Keichō *koban*. For this reason, the export of Kyōhō *koban* did not alleviate the VOC's losses. The loss on *koban* in Coromandel increased from about 8 gulden per piece to 17 gulden per piece after the export of the Kyōhō *koban* began. This does not mean that the loss rate suddenly doubled; since the Kyōhō *koban* was twice the weight and price of the Kenji *koban*, the amount of loss per piece also doubled. The actual loss rate was only marginally higher than that on the Kenji *koban*.

## Conclusion

Japanese trade goods were first shipped to either Batavia or Malacca before being allotted to other regions in Asia. Copper was exported variously, *koban* was mainly shipped to Coromandel, and a large volume of camphor was sent to the Netherlands. It is clear from Heyningen's report that, while the destinations for each product varied according to demand and price, Japanese trade goods were distributed to every corner of the VOC's Asian territory through its sales network and some were shipped to the home country as well.

The report suggests a sense of impending crisis for the VOC in its attempt to get an accurate grasp of its situation. The Dutch had been troubled by a number of impediments to their trade with Japan prior to the preparation of Heyningen's report. In Japan, the copper price was rising and copper export restrictions had been imposed. In Asia, interference by the British and other competitors sometimes led to drops in the copper price, even though the demand for copper was on the rise. The purchase price of camphor in Japan soared rapidly at the beginning of the eighteenth century and stayed at that high level.[57] The highly profitable export of the Keichō *koban* was banned at the end of the seventeenth century and the export of subsequent series of *koban* proved unprofitable. 'Re-coinage is a hobby of the Japanese', as Jacob van der Vaeijen, the head of the Dutch Factory in Japan in later years, sardonically put. Re-coinage was carried out frequently[58] and the losses suffered by the Dutch worsened every time. The shogunate also imposed strict quotas on the amount of turnovers and the number of ships that the Dutch were allowed each year.

During the seventeenth century, Dutch trade with Japan was still flour-
ishing and quite profitable; no one prepared a report like Heyningen's
examining profits from trade with Japan over a period of a few decades as far
as my research shows. In the seventeenth century, the Dutch must have been
so certain of great profits that they did not feel the need for such a report.
This report therefore is a sign that the VOC was aware of the deterioration
of its trade with Japan from its 'quite profitable' level of the seventeenth
century. The company might have felt somewhat relieved by the report's
conformation that their trade with Japan was 'still profitable'. However, this
optimistic view would gradually be overturned as the eighteenth century
rolled by. The grim conditions of the Dutch trade with Japan were revealed by
later reports prepared by Governor General van Imhoff (1743) and Councilor
van der Waeijen of the Dutch East Indies (1756).

# Conclusion

The first five chapters of this book examined the conditions of principal export products in the early modern period. Chapter Six analysed the conditions of Japanese exports as a whole at the beginning of the eighteenth century. Let us discuss the significance of Japanese–Dutch trade in general based on the above analysis.

Firstly, the domestic factors that most affected Japanese–Dutch trade in the early modern period were the demand for coinage and fluctuating mining production in Japan.

Mineral resources such as silver, copper and gold (*koban*) made up the bulk of Japan's principal export products. While in the middle ages the Muromachi government relied on the use of Chinese coins instead of creating a currency for Japan, the Edo shogunate actively pursued currency unification by establishing a three-layered monetary standard using gold, silver and copper coins. Coinage projects meant that it could not afford to export all mineral resources to foreign countries; export bans and restrictions adversely affected foreign trade. The first of such cases occurred in a period from the second half of the 1630s to the first half of the 1640s. The shogunate conducted a large-scale copper coin (*Kanei tsūho*) minting project. The export of copper was banned and the export of gold (*koban*) was not readily permitted because it was yet to achieve wide circulation in the domestic market. Silver therefore accounted for the bulk of exports at the time. Japanese silver played an important role in providing capital to the Dutch for their trade with China, which ran smoothly until the middle of the 1640s. As Japan produced silver in abundance at that time, the Japanese and Dutch had no problem filling Dutch ships with silver alone.

After silver production in Japanese mines peaked in the 1650s, it started a decline that adversely affected trade conditions from then on. The problem was made worse by mass outflows of silver from Japan, mainly on the Chinese fleet, after the shogunate removed trade regulations in 1655. The shogunate adopted policy measures to curtail the outflow of silver in the 1660s and issued a ban on silver exports in 1668. While the Chinese resumed silver exports in 1672, the Dutch no longer desired silver and did not export it again until the end of the Edo period. In those days, the Dutch needed gold (*koban*) from Japan, not silver. They petitioned the shogunate for the lifting of *koban* embargo in 1664. Their wish was readily granted and the export of *koban* commenced as it complied with the shogunate policy of silver export restriction.

When a copper coin minting project began in 1668, the export of copper was also banned for a brief period, but the situation then was very different from that of the latter half of the 1630s. If the export of both silver and copper was banned, Japan's foreign trade would collapse in this period. The copper export ban was soon withdrawn. The shogunate changed its policy direction by strengthening control over foreign trade in Nagasaki through the *shishō kamotsu shishō* (appraisal trade) system in 1672.

A series of re-coinages struck Dutch trade in waves from the end of the seventeenth century. The shogunate produced the Genroku *koban*, which had a low gold content, and tried to circulate it at the same value as the fine quality Keichō *koban*. This pricing was applied to the purchase price of *koban* by the Dutch and the *koban* trade came under serious threat. The currency debasement by the shogunate (more specifically, the policy devised by later Kanjo governor Ogiwara Shigehide) had two purposes. One was to resolve currency shortages resulting from economic development and material shortages due to a decline in gold production. It was considered, at least by Ogiwara, that the Tokugawa administration had entered a period that was stable enough to transition from real money, which had the same value as the coin itself, to nominal money, such as paper money.

The second purpose of Ogiwara's currency debasement policy was financial reconstruction during a time of crisis. The shogunate would earn a huge profit by circulating the lower quality Genroku *koban* at the same value as the Keichō *koban*. In addition, the shogunate was aware of the prosperity of the Nagasaki-based trade. *Nagasaki Kaisho* (the Nagasaki trade association) was established in 1698 to regulate trade in Nagasaki under the auspices of the treasury of the shogunate. It collected taxes from Nagasaki.

The fortune of copper mines also peaked at the end of the seventeenth century and gradually waned in the eighteenth century. The conditions in the eighteenth century worsened when a copper coinage project commenced at the same time that copper production began to decrease. In 1701, the *dōza* agency was established for the purpose of coordinating copper supply for both coinage and Nagasaki export.

More gold and silver re-coinages ensued; a sense of crisis grew within the shogunate about allowing the export of large quantities of copper and *koban* to foreign countries. In the famous words of Arai Hakuseki, who had a great influence on the shogunate government in the first half of the 1710s, 'Cereal crops are like human hair in that they grow back but metals are like human bone in that once harvested they are gone; it is hardly a good policy to allow these important metals to drain out of the country in payment for foreign imports of no value'. The shogun instigated the minting of the Shōtoku *koban*, which had with the same weight and purity as the Keichō *koban*. This policy was inherited by shogun Yoshimune. However, Yoshimune began minting low-purity *koban* (Genbun *koban*) in the latter half of the 1730s. At this time the *koban* trade lost its appeal to the Dutch.

Copper production had declined markedly by then and the *dōza* was revived to coordinate copper supply for export and coinage. The difficult situation persisted and a copper shortage in the first half of the 1740s forced the shogunate to order the halving of trade turnovers. Japanese–Dutch trade subsequently fell into disorder and finally reached a crisis point in 1751. In this way, every time the shogunate embarked on a coinage project and every time production at gold, silver and copper mines decreased, Japanese–Dutch trade was shaken, causing damage that snowballed over the years and exacerbating its decline.

Raw silk and silk fabric were principal products that accounted for a large part of Japanese imports in the seventeenth century, although a close analysis of these items is outside the scope of this study. Raw silk was essential for high-quality clothing at the time; it was customary for shogun and feudal lords to reward distinguished subordinates with either money or a kimono. Shogun Yoshimune actively promoted import substitution from the first half of the eighteenth century; the production of raw silk began in all parts of the country at the end of the century. Sugar and medicines became principal imports from then on.

The shogunate scaled down further its trade with the Dutch in 1790 by limiting the number of Dutch ships permitted to export goods to just one a year. This suggests that the shogunate did not necessarily consider Dutch trade as important. In fact, sugar and medicines were available from the Chinese as well. The shogunate continued to trade with the Netherlands partly because it had to carry on traditions established in the founding shogun Ieyasu's times and partly because it was compelled by the need to gather foreign intelligence and import European scientific knowledge and technology.

The study of Western sciences in the Dutch language flourished in Japan in the latter half of the eighteenth century. Those who aspired to study the latest developments in medicine, astronomy, natural history and other sciences learned the Dutch language first and went on to gain

new knowledge from Dutch books. Japanese interest in foreign countries
increased during the eighteenth century. Although relations between Japan
and the Netherlands appeared to centre on trade, Western books, stationery,
and scientific and medical devices were also increasingly important.

Nagazumi Yōko aptly described this transition as one 'from a trading
nation to an information nation'. In other words, the Netherlands transformed its role in relation to Japan from a trade partner to a transmitter
of information about foreign affairs. By the nineteenth century, the
relative importance of trade in Japanese–Dutch relations had decreased
considerably. In fact, transactions conducted by the factory in Japan were
not recorded properly after the bankruptcy of the VOC in 1799 and no trade
books exist after 1805.

The centre of the European precious metal market shifted from Antwerp
to Amsterdam in the early seventeenth century. Silver real coins minted in
large quantities in Spain and America flowed into the Amsterdam market
via Germany, France and England. After Portugal gained independence
from Spain in the 1640s, silver real coins became readily available in the
Netherlands via Portugal. At that time, the independence of the Netherlands
from Spain was also formally approved, and even larger amounts of silver
real flowed into the Amsterdam market. Only some of the reales were used
for trading in Asia; the rest were used for trade in the Baltic Sea, Levant and
continental Europe. The outflow of imported silver from the Netherlands
was seen as a problem by the Dutch minting authority, who attempted to
issue a ban on the export of currency and precious metal bars. However, the
urban merchant class was powerful in the Netherlands, so there was never
a total ban on silver exports.

In Asia, the Dutch had taken over the transit trade in Chinese silk and
Japanese silver, which had been carried out by the Portuguese since the
latter half of the sixteenth century. Japanese silver was preferred in China
and the Dutch were able to acquire large amounts as capital for their trade
there, helped by the close geographical proximity of China and Japan. But
in the 1640s the Dutch trade between Japan and China trade was thrown
into disorder by the civil war that marked the transition from the Ming
dynasty to the Qing dynasty.

As the Dutch trade in China trade gradually declined from the 1640s,
Japanese silver exports were diverted from China to Tonkin and Southwest
Asia. Japanese silver (chōgin) was not highly valued in those regions as it had
a lower purity than the the silver real, then the international currency. At the
same time, the value of silver began to fall in Asian and European markets
due to the oversupply of silver reales. For these reasons, the export of silver

from Nagasaki stagnated from the 1640s to the latter half of the 1660s. The Dutch therefore decided not to resume their export of silver when asked to by the shogunate in 1672 following the 1668 ban on silver exports.

In the 1650s, the English East India Company was transformed from a makeshift entity into a strong organization by Oliver Cromwell's reforms. At the beginning of the eighteenth century a new English East India Company was merged with the old company to form a powerful organization. With plentiful capital and strong trade organization, the British extended their influence eastward from the west of India and from the 1650s began to operate in Coromandel on the east coast and Bengal in the north. They began trading with the Chinese on the Malay Peninsula and opened a trading factory in Canton in the 1710s.

After the War of Spanish Succession at the beginning of the eighteenth century, Amsterdam went from being the centre of the European precious metals market in the seventeenth century to third place after England and France in the acquisition of the silver real. The European centre for silver distribution shifted from Amsterdam to London. Since silver coins were the basic currency of the Mughal Empire in India, it goes without saying that the Dutch needed silver as capital. The Netherlands considered resuming silver exports from Japan at the end of the seventeenth century, but, as silver coins had been debased considerably in re-coinages during the 1690s, it did not implement any policies. With abundant capital, the British came to threaten Dutch trade in Asia.

The decline of Dutch trade in Japan trade in the eighteenth century was characterized by restrictive shogunate trade laws, falling import prices, falling copper exports, losses from the *koban* trade, mounting expenses and increasingly frequent incidences of shipwrecking to and from Japan. The Dutch investigated measures to improve their trade in Japan during the 1720s, but they saw little prospect of improvement or good future returns. They seriously considered closing down the Japan factory during the 1730s. However, there was strong demand for copper in India as a material for weapons and coin production; cutting off supplies of copper and camphor from Japan would put the VOC's trade in India in an even more difficult position.

The Netherlands could have maintained its predominance over the India trade if it had been able to supply large quantities of copper to India. The Mughal Empire was perpetually at war inside and outside the country and was in constant need of copper for military purposes. Further, the entry of more Europeans into the India trade promoted a rapid expansion of the monetary economy in Indian society, strengthening the demand for copper coins as the low-denomination currency in particular. However, the Dutch could not expect to acquire as much copper as it desired from Japan as restrictions on copper exports were gradually tightened in the eighteenth century due to declining production at Japanese copper mines and frequent re-coinages. The Dutch copper trade in India was also threatened by the British, who shipped not only silver but also copper from Europe to India in large quantities. Britain also acquired Japanese copper and camphor from the Chinese.

The first trade agreement between Japan and the Netherlands was signed in 1752. It culminated from the trade improvement policies of van Imhoff, who became the governor general of the Dutch East Indies in Batavia in 1743. Although the agreement prevented further reductions in copper exports, it only maintained the status quo; the Dutch were forced to accept that their need for more copper exports could not be satisfied. It was clearly a setback for the VOC's Japan trade policy. The Dutch ended active measures to improve the Japan trade from then on. At the time, the Netherlands were experiencing bitter experiences at home, the French Revolution, the bankruptcy of the VOC and the British occupation of Java from the end of the eighteenth century. The meaning of the Japan factory to the Dutch also changed. No longer regarded as a 'hugely profitable factory', it came to be thought of as 'a Dutch stronghold in Far East'.

The vicissitudes of the Japan trade vividly reflect the fortunes of the VOC. It might appear to be a strange coincidence that Japan's expectations for trade with the Dutch had mostly expired by the time the VOC went bankrupt. The first encounter between the two countries came about by a curious turn of fate and over the long period of their relations each unwittingly left their mark on the other's fortunes. The interchange between these two far removed countries, Japan in the Far East and the Netherlands in Europe, played a spectacular role in the Asia trade during the seventeenth and eighteenth centuries.

# Appendix

## Japanese–Dutch trade research in Japan

Let us put studies of early modern Japanese–Dutch relations, especially trade relations, in order. The historical study of early modern Japanese–Dutch relations was greatly advanced by a series of translations and studies undertaken by Naojirō Murakami. It is no exaggeration to say that it was the starting point of the post-Meiji study of the Japanese–Dutch relations. Murakami's major translation works include the *Dejima rankan nisshi* (Diary of the Dutch Factory in Dejima) (1938–1939), *Nagasaki Oranda shōkan no nikki* (Diaries of the Dutch Factory in Nagasaki) (1956–1958) and the *Batavia jō nisshi* (Diary of the Castle of Batavia) (1970–1975). He also published many studies that paved the way for the study of not only early modern Japan–Netherlands relations, but also a broader history of international relations in the early modern period, such as *Nihon to Oranda* (Japan and the Netherlands) (1915) and *Bōeki shihjō no Hirado* (Hirado in the history of trade) (1917). He was followed by Okamoto Yoshitomo, who wrote *Nagasaki kaikō izen ōhaku raiō kō* (A study of visiting European ships before the opening of Nagasaki port) (1932) and *Jūroku seiki nichiō kōtsū shi no kenkyū* (A study of the history of traffic between Japan and Europe in the sixteenth century) (1936), and Zennosuke Tsuji, who wrote *Kaigai kōtsū shi wa* (A history of international traffic) (1930). Kōda Shigetomo advanced the historical study of foreign relations by publishing *Shiwa higashi to nishi* (Historical considerations of east and west) (1940) and *Nichiō tsūkō shi* (History of Japan–European relations) (1942), which was reprinted in *Kōda Shigetomo chosakushū* (Collective works of Shigetomo Kōda), (1971–1974). The primary aim of research at this time was to elucidate the overall flow of the history of foreign relations.

The study of Japan–Netherlands relations was later deepened by Itazawa Takeo, Iwao Seiichi and Okada Akio. Itazawa wrote a study entitled *Nichiran bōeki shi* (History of the Japanese–Dutch trade) (Heibonsha, Tokyo, 1949). It is composed of three chapters: Chapter 1 'An overview of the history of the Japanese–Dutch relations'; Chapter 2 'Changes in the system of the Japanese–Dutch trade'; and Chapter 3 'The contents of the Japanese–Dutch trade'. Chapter 1 summarizes the history from the Netherlands' foray into Asia and the beginning of trade with Japan to the end of the Edo period. Chapter 2 addresses changes in the Nagasaki-based foreign trade laws. Chapter 3 describes import and export goods in Japanese–Dutch trade. This work is a general overview of the Japanese–Dutch trade that is indicative of the standard of research on the Japanese–Dutch trade and the Nagasaki trade at the time. Itazawa also examined early modern Japanese–Dutch relations from various angles in his other works, such as *Nichiran kōtsū shi wa* (History of traffic between Japan and the Netherlands) (1940), *Nichiran bunka kōshō shi no kenkyū* (A study of the history of the Japanese–Dutch cultural relations) (1959) and *Nihon to Oranda* (Japan and the Netherlands) (1966).

Okada focused on and analysed imported goods in the beginning of the early modern period. The subjects of his study included gold, iron, mercury, lead, buckskin and woolen textiles. His papers, 'Kensetsu ki no edo bakufu ni yoru gunjuhin no yunyū ni tsuite (The import of military supplies by the construction-era shogunate government)' (1936), 'Kinsei ni okeru shikagawa no yunyū ni kansuru kenkyū (A study of buckskin imports in the early modern period)' (1937), and 'Kinsei ni okeru shuyō na yunyū busshi ni tsuite (Major imported goods in the early modern period)' (1939) are contained in *Okada Akio chosakushū* (Collective works of Okada Akio) III (1983).

Iwao Seiichi presents clear and concise accounts of internal and external circumstances from the time of the Netherlands' arrival in Japan to the monopolization of the Japan trade ahead of other European nations in 'Kinsei Nihon no kaigai bōeki (Foreign trade by early modern Japan)' (1962). He explains the types and destinations of export goods from Japan in 'Sakoku jidai ni okeru Nihon bōekihin no hanro (Sales channels of Japanese trade goods in the seclusion era)' (1947). In 'Edo jidai no satō bōeki ni tsuite (Sugar trading in the Edo period)' (1973), he discusses the trade in sugar, which became a major import product of the Japanese–Dutch trade in the late early modern period. Iwao describes the type of Persian horses which Shogun Yoshimune ordered the Dutch to import to Japan from the 1720s and the process of importation in *Edo jidai nichiran bunka kōshō shiryōshū 1 Meiji izen no yōba no yunyū to zōshoku* (Collection of materials on the Japanese–Dutch cultural relations in the Edo period 1: Importation and propagation of foreign horses before the Meiji period) (1980). His *Sakoku* (National seclusion) (1974) presents a comprehensive view of foreign relations in the beginning of the early modern period and is regarded as a seminal work that promoted the advancement of historical research on early modern foreign relations.

It is reasonable to say that the study of the history of Japanese–Dutch trade is founded on the achievements of these scholars. In addition, Saitō Agu shed light on Japan–Netherlands relations in the early nineteenth century in *Zūfu to Nihon* (H. Doef and Japan) (1922). Numata Jirō studied changes in the Nagasaki trade laws in 'Edo jidai no bōeki to taigai kankei (Trade and foreign relations in the Edo period)' (1964). In *Dejima* (1947), he described the lifestyle of the Dutch in Dejima and the trade that was conducted there.

The study of the Japanese–Dutch trade gained momentum from the 1970s through the efforts of leading scholars like Yamawaki Teijirō, Nagazumi Yōko and Katō Ēichi. Yamawaki began with the study of trade books ('Nagasaki Oranda shōkan no kaikei chōbo [Accounting books of the Dutch Factory in Nagasaki]' (1971) and moved on to examine the conditions of import and export by the Dutch Factory and the sales channels of Japanese goods in overseas markets based on these trade books. He wrote papers on raw silk, *koban*, textiles and sugar in particular: 'Nagasaki bōeki ron—Oranda shōkan no satō bōeki wo megutte—(A study of Nagasaki trade—sugar trading by the Dutch Factory—(1976a), 'Oranda Higashi Indo Gaisha no tainichi kiito bōeki (Raw silk trade with Japan by the Dutch East India Company)' (1975), and 'Oranda sen no yunyū orimono (Textiles imported by the Dutch fleet)' (1976b). His *Kaigai kōshō shi* (History of foreign relations) (1978) and *Nagasaki no Oranda shōkan* (The Dutch Factory in Nagasaki) (1980) are the culminations of these earlier works. Yamawaki mainly undertook quantitative research on the selling channels of Japanese trade goods in Asia and export quantities. The details of imports and exports in the Japanese–Dutch trade became much clearer through his research.

In recent years, Yamawaki has been studying some export and import goods individually in *Kinsei Nihon no iyaku bunka* (The medical and pharmaceutical culture of early modern Japan) (1995) and *Kinu to momen no edo jidai* (Silk and cotton in the Edo period) (2002), discussing issues such as distribution of foreign goods in Japan and import substitution.

Nagazumi translated *Hirado Oranda shōkan no nikki* (Diary of the Dutch Factory in Hirado) (1969–1970), which helped the advancement of the study of Japanese–Dutch trade. She shed light on the actual conditions of the Japanese–Dutch trade when the Dutch Factory was located in Hirado, relationships between the Dutch, the feudal lord of Hirado and the leading figures of the shogunate government, and channels of command and information in a series of works, including 'Hirado Oranda shōkan nikki wo tōshite mita Pancado (Pancado through the diary of the Dutch Factory in Hirado)' (1970), 'Hirado han to Oranda bōeki (The Hirado domain and the

Dutch trade)' (1972), 'Oranda bōeki no tōgin to shakunyūkin (Investments and borrowings in the Dutch trade)' (1977), *Hirado Oranda shōkan Igirisu shōkan nikki* (Diaries of the Dutch Factory and the English Factory in Hirado) (co-authored by Takeda Mariko, 1981), and *Kinsei shoki no gaikō* (Diplomacy in the beginning of the early modern period) (1990). Nagazumi has also discussed the trade of other periods in 'Oranda shōkan no wakini bōeki ni tsuite (Unofficial trading by the Dutch Factory)' (1979), 'Shōtoku shinrei to Oranda bōeki (The new law of Shōtoku and the Dutch trade)' (1985), 'Tsūshō no kuni kara tsūshin no kuni e (From a trading nation to an information nation)' (1986), 'Kaisha no bōeki kara kojin no bōeki e (From company trade to private trade)' (1994), and 'Jūhachi seiki no bōeki suitai to Roshia sekkin (Declining trade and closer ties with Russia in the eighteenth century)' (2000). Her studies on issues relating to the trade network between Japan and Southeast Asia are also notable. She has raised and ambitiously investigated new issues in relation to Japanese–Dutch trade in papers such as 'Jūshichi seiki no Higashi Ajia bōeki (The East Asian trade in the seventeenth century)' (1991), 'Tōzai kōeki no chūkeichi Taiwan no seisui (The rise and fall of Taiwan, the hub of the entrepot trade between east and west)' (1999), 'Jūshichi seiki chūki no Nihon Tonkin bōeki ni tsuite (The trade between Japan and Tonkin in the mid seventeenth century)' (1992), and *Shuin sen* (Red-seal ships) (2002).

Katō Ēichi advanced this research on the trade books of the Dutch Factory. His studies of the trade books from the Hirado era in particular provided a strong impetus to subsequent studies. He published '1636 nen Hirado Oranda shōkan no yushutsunyū shōhin (The goods imported and exported by the Dutch Factory in Hirado in 1636)' (1969), '1637 nen Hirado Oranda shōkan bōeki hyō (1 & 2) (Statistical tables for trade by the Dutch Factory in Hirado in 1637, 1 & 2)' (1970 & 1971), and 'Hirado Oranda shōkan no shōgyō chōbo ni mirareru Nichiran bōeki no ichi danmen (A cross-section of the Japanese–Dutch trade revealed by the trade books of the Dutch Factory in Hirado) (1968). Later on, Katō examined the importance of foreign relations under the shogunate and domain system and the significance of the Japan trade in the context of the Asia trade by the VOC in 'Genna/Kanei ki ni okeru Nichiran bōeki (The Japanese–Dutch trade in the Genna and Kanei eras)' (1978), 'Rengō Higashi Indo Gaisha no shoki kaikei kiroku to Hirado shōkan (The early accounting records of the United East India Company and the Dutch Factory in Hirado)' (1980), 'Sakoku to bakuhansei kokka (National seclusion and the shogunate and domain system state)' (1981), 'Rengō Higashi Indo Gaisha no senryaku kyoten to shite no Hirado shōkan (The Dutch Factory in Hirado as a strategic

stronghold of the United East India Company) (1987), '"Kōgi" to Oranda
(The "shogunate" and the Netherlands)' (1989), and *Bakuhansei kokka no
seiritsu to taigai kankei* (The formation of the shogunate and domain system
state and foreign relations) (1998).

Research on the trade books of the Dutch Factory was also advanced in
the field of the study of Western economic history. One example is 'Jūshichi
seiki shotō Oranda ni okeru kaikei jijō (Accounting practice in the early
seventeenth century Netherlands)' (1976) by Moteki Torao. In addition to
Katō, Kōzō Shinano conducted his own analysis of accounting books in the
field of Japanese history. Analysis of the trade books of the Dutch Factory
was the focus of his three studies: *Kinsei Nichiran bōeki kō* (A study of the
history of the early modern Japanese–Dutch trade) (1984a), *Oranda Higashi
Indo Gaisha* (The Dutch East India Company) (1984b) and *Oranda Higashi
Indo Gaisha no rekishi* (History of the Dutch East India Company) (1988).
Yukutake Kazuhiro developed this field further in '1641 nen no Nichiran
bōeki ni okeru "torihiki" ni tsuite ("Transactions" in the Japanese–Dutch
trade in 1641)' (1986), 'Dejima Oranda shōkan no kaikei chōbo (The
accounting books of the Dutch Factory in Dejima)' (1988–1990), 'Oranda
Higashi Indo Gaisha no Nihon muke shōhin sentei ni tsuite (Selection of
trade goods for Japan by the Dutch East India Company)' (1990a), 'Sakoku
taiseino kansei to Nichiran bōeki (The completion of the seclusion regime
and the Japanese–Dutch trade)' (1990b), and 'Dejima Oranda shōkan no
kaikei chōbo (The accounting books of the Dutch Factory in Dejima)'
(1992). Yukutake attempted a thorough analysis and examination of the
trade books of the Dutch Factory from the 1630s and the 1640s in order to
promote a more accurate understanding of the accounting practice at the
factory and thereby to elucidate the actual conditions of trade dealings and
management of the factory in those days.

From the 1980s, further research and analysis of the individual products
of the Japanese–Dutch trade was undertaken by Suzuki Yasuko, Yao
Keisuke and Ishida Chihiro. Suzuki mainly investigated export products.
Yao discussed the export of copper and rice in limited periods. His study of
sugar, which became increasingly important as an imported product from
the eighteenth century, is notable. Yao's *Kinsei Oranda bōeki to sakoku* (The
early modern Dutch trade and Japanese seclusion) (1998) is a compilation
of these earlier studies. Ishida analysed the cargos of Dutch ships and
imported textiles in 'Kinsei Nichiran bōeki no kisoteki kenkyū (A study
of the early modern Japanese–Dutch trade)' (1984), 'Dejima bōeki hin no
kisoteki kenkyū (A study of trade goods in Dejima)' (1985a), 'Kinsei chūki
Oranda funazumi nimotsu no kisoteki kenkyū (A study of merchandise

on Dutch vessels that arrived in the middle of Edo period)' (1985b), 'Kinsei kōki ni okeru Dejima bōeki hin to sono torihiki katei (Trade goods and the process of transaction in Dejima in the late early modern period)' (1988), 'Oranda sen no yunyū keorimono (Woolen textiles imported by Dutch vessels)' (1989), 'Edo jidai kōki no Oranda funazumi nimotsu ni tsuite (Merchandise on Dutch vessels in the late Edo period)' (1991), 'Edo kōki ni okeru Ran funazumi nimotsu to sono hanbai (Merchandise on Dutch vessels and their sale in the late Edo period)' (1992), and 'Edo jidai no sarasa yunyū (The import of cotton in the Edo period)' (1993). These works are included in *Nichiran bōeki no shiteki kenkyū* (A historical study of Japanese–Dutch trade) (2004) and *Nichiran bōeki no kōzō to tenkai* (The structure and development of Japanese–Dutch trade) (2009). Kayoko Fujita's 'Oranda shiryō kara mita yushutsu gin (Export silver in the Dutch historical resources)' (1999) covers the flow of export silver from the latter half of the 1630s to the latter half of the 1660s, examining the issue of Japanese silver from the viewpoint of Asian trade. In this way, the real picture of the trade sector of early modern Japan–Netherlands relations has been slowly unveiled from various angles in recent years. Matsui Yōko's '1622 nen ni okeru Nichiran bōeki no tenbō (An outlook of the Japanese–Dutch trade in 1622)' (2003) describes the state of trade in around 1622, based on reports written by the head of the Dutch Factory.

As for the history of early modern Nagasaki trade, *Bakufu jidai no Nagasaki* (Nagasaki in the Edo period) (1913) gives an overview of the city's early modern trade, politics, economy and culture. *Nagasaki shi shi tsūkō bōeki hen seiyō shokoku bu* (The history of Nagasaki city foreign relations/ trade section: Western countries) (1935), by Murakami Naojirō, describes the important matters of Japan–European relations in the seventeenth century, such as Japan's relationship with Portugal, the opening of the port of Nagasaki, the Dutch and English factories in Hirado, the Tayouan incident, the prohibition of arrivals of the Portuguese vessels, the relocation of the Dutch Factory to Nagasaki, and the arrival of the Portuguese envoy and the English trade ship *The Return* during the period of seclusion.

*Nagasaki ken shi taigai koshō hen* (History of Nagasaki prefecture foreign relations edition) (1986) is a compilation of earlier study findings. It is composed of the following chapters: Chapter 1 'The arrival of the Europeans and Christian missionaries in Japan'; Chapter 2 'The opening of the port of Nagasaki and trade'; Chapter 3 'The establishment of national seclusion'; Chapter 4 'International relations immediately after seclusion and early Nagasaki-based trade'; Chapter 5 'Politics and people's lives in Nagasaki';

Chapter 6 'The development of controlled trade'; Chapter 7 'Influences of foreign cultures'; Chapter 8 'The opening of Japan and Nagasaki'. The book discusses changes in the Nagasaki foreign trade laws such as the *itowappu* system from the opening of Nagasaki Port to the end of the Edo period, the government structure in Nagasaki, the actual conditions of foreigner control and trade goods, and the introduction of foreign cultures. Contributing authors include Yanai Kenji, Okada Akio, Nakada Yasunao, Takeno Yōko, Nakamura Tadashi, Morioka Yoshiko, Yamawaki Teijirō and Numata Jirō.

Yanai Kenji's *Nagasaki* (1959) presents a general view of early modern Nagasaki and provides systematic descriptions of the situation in Nagasaki, including trade. Harada Tomohiko's *Nagasaki* (1974) addresses some noteworthy topics such as trade, culture, urban development and scientific progress over a period from the opening of Nagasaki Port to modern times. Morioka Yoshiko mainly studied institutional changes in the Nagasaki trade in 'Nagasaki bōeki ni okeru kanzei (Tariffs in Nagasaki trade)' (1954), 'Kinsei shotō ni okeru kiito bōeki (Trade in raw silk in the beginning of the early modern period)' (1962) and 'Kinsei kōhan ki ni okeru Nagasaki bōeki no henshitsu (Changes in Nagasaki trade in the late early modern period)' (1966). Yōko Takeno mainly examined the conditions of Nagasaki trade and various domains in the Kyūshu region in *Han bōeki shi no kenkyū* (A study of the history of trade by feudal domains) (1979).

Nakada Yasunao elucidated the structure of Nagasaki trade based mainly on the establishment of the *itowappu* system in *Kinsei taigai kankei shi no kenkyū* (A study of the history of foreign relations in the early modern period) (1984). Kōichirō Takase shed light on trade in the beginning of the early modern period, mainly based on the Portuguese and Spanish historical materials, in *Kirishitan jidai no kenkyū* (A study of Christianity in feudal Japan) (1977). He addresses the issue of the *itowappu* system in *Kirishitan jidai no bōeki to gaikō* (Trade and diplomacy at the time of Christianity in feudal Japan) (2002), about which he had a heated debate with Nakada.

In *Kinsei Nagasaki bōeki shi no kenkyū* (A study of the history of the Nagasaki trade in the early modern period) (1989), Nakamura Tadashi introduced and analysed the Japanese folding screen document in Lisbon, which is a Christian-related historical material from the age of Toyotomi Hideyoshi. Nakamura highlights Hideyoshi's Korean campaign, the *itowappu* system and the problems with the establishment of national seclusion. He described changes in the Nagasaki trade laws after the abolishment of the *itowappu* system to *Shōtoku shinrei* and analysed the establishment of the accounting system of the Nagasaki trade association up to the nineteenth century. He also touched on import products of the Chinese trade and their sales channels. *Kinsei taigai kōshō shi ron* (Studies of the early modern history of foreign relations) (2000) is a posthumous collection of Nakamura's writings on subjects such as the prisoners of the invasions of Korea during the Bunroku and Keichō eras, rules for the forwarding of drifting vessels, and illicit marketing of imported goods.

Ōta Katsuya introduced many historical resources and empirically analysed changes in and the actual condition of the Nagasaki trade laws from the seventeenth century to *Shōtoku shinrei* in *Nihon bōeki shi no kenkyū (kinsei)* (A study of the history of Japanese trade (early modern times)) (1980), *Sakoku jidai Nagasaki bōeki shi no kenkyū* (A study of the history of trade in seclusion-era Nagasaki) (1992), and *Nagasaki bōeki* (Nagasaki trade) (2000). Shimizu Hirokazu discussed the shogunate's seclusion policy and diplomacy in the early modern period in 'Sakoku jidai no bōeki sen ni tsuite (Trade ships during the seclusion period)' (1976), 'Nukeni kō (A study of smuggling)' (1979), 'Nichiō kōshō no kigen (The origin of the Japan–Europe relations)' (1985), and 'Kanei sakoku rei wo megutte (The Kankei edicts of seclusion)' (1990). Masashi Wakamatsu initially concentrated on studying trade-related problems in the trading city of Nagasaki, but many of his recent works are on Nagasaki from the viewpoint of urban history. They include 'Nagasaki kaisho no setsuritsu ni tsuite (The founding of the Nagasaki trade association)' (1990a), 'Nagasaki tōjin bōeki ni kansuru bōeki rigin no kisoteki kōsatsu (A study of trade profits relating to the Chinese trade in Nagasaki)' (1990b), and 'Kinsei zenki ni okeru Nagasaki chōnin to bōeki (Townspeople of Nagasaki and trade in the first half of the early modern period)' (1992).

Further, Kobata Atsushi examined various issues relating to silver export at the start of the early modern period in *Kingin bōeki shi no kenkyū* (A study of the history of trade in gold and silver) (1976). Arano Yasunori described the Nagasaki trade system and smuggling in the middle of early modern times in *Kinsei Nihon to Higashi Ajia* (Early modern Japan and East Asia) (1988). Miyashita Saburō studied imported medicines in *Nagasaki bōeki to Osaka* (Nagasaki trade and Osaka) (1997).

There have been studies on the VOC from a Japanese point of view, such as Ōtsuka Hisao's *Kabushiki gaisha hassei shi ron* (A study of the history of the joint stock company) ([1947] 1969), which described the VOC's formation process, organizational structure and powers. Nagazumi Akira's *Oranda Higashi Indo Gaisha* (The Dutch East India Company) (1971) presented the picture of the rise and fall of the VOC in Asia in the context of the history of Indonesia.

Collected papers in relation to the early modern Japanese–Dutch trade include Nakada Yasunao (ed.), *Kinsei taigai kankei shi ron* (Studies of the early modern history of foreign relations) (1977), Yanai Kenji (ed.), *Sakoku Nihon to kokusai kōryū* (Japan in seclusion and international relations) (1988), Hamashita Takeshi and Kawakatsu Heita, *Ajia kōekiken to Nihon kōgyōka 1500–1900* (The Asian trading sphere and the industrialization of Japan 1500–1900) (1991), Nakamura Tadashi (ed.), *Sakoku to kokusai kankei* (National seclusion and international relations) (1997), Yanai Kenji (ed.), *Kokusai shakai no keisei to kinsei Nihon* (The formation of international society and early modern Japan) (1998), Nichiran Gakkai (ed.), *Nichiran kōryū yonhyakunen* (400 years of Japan–Netherlands relations) (2001), and Katagiri Kazuo (ed.), *Nichiran kōryū jinbutsu jōhō* (Japan–Netherlands relations: people and information) (2002).

Monographs and documents on the subject of the early modern Japan–Netherlands relationship for research purposes can be found in Matsuda Kiichi (ed.), *Nichiō kōshō shi bunken mokuroku* (Catalogue of literature on the history of Japan–Europe relations) (1965), Nichiran Gakkai (ed.), *Yōgaku kankei kenkyū bunken yōran* (A general survey of research papers on Western learning) (1984), a series of 'Nichiran kankei bunken (Literature on Japan–Netherlands relations)' in *Nichiran gakkai shi* (Bulletin of the Japan–Netherlands Institute), and Nakada Yasunao (ed.), *Kinsei Nihon taigai kankei bunken mokuroku* (Catalogue of documents on foreign relations of early modern Japan) (1999).

## International studies of Japanese–Dutch trade

For international research on the Japanese–Dutch trade, one of the early catalogues of Japan-related publications and historical resources is found in Roessingh, M. p. H. (ed.) (1982–1983), *Sources of the History of Asia and Oceania in the Netherlands. A Critical Survey of Studies on Dutch Colonial History*, by Coolhaas, W. Ph. (1980) classifies and reviews many documents relating to the VOC. Published historical resources and documents in the field are also listed in *Oranda ni okeru Ajia Oseania kankei shiryō shozai mokuroku* (The catalogue of locations of historical resources relating to Asia and Oceania in the Netherlands) (1982).

Some of the important later documents have been reviewed in *Itinerario: European Journal of Overseas History*, Leiden University (currently published by Cambridge University Press). *VOC: A Bibliography of Publications Relating to the Dutch East India Company 1602–1800* by J. Landwehr, edited by p. van der Krogt (1991), also reviews later documents, but it has only a

small number of records relating to Japanese–Dutch trade. Another relevant
publication is Buck, H. de (ed.) (1979), *Bibbliografie der geschiedenis van
Nederland* (Bibliography of the history of the Netherlands).

Early modern Japanese–Dutch trade is mentioned in the writings of
European scholars who visited Japan as physicians attached to the Dutch
Factory during the Edo period. They include E. Kaempfer (1727), *The His-
tory of Japan*, translated by J. G. Scheuchzer (the Japanese version is *Nihon
shi* (Japanese history), translated by Tadashi Imai) (1973), Thunberg, C. p.
(1788–1793), *Resa uti Europa Africa, Asia, förratta åren 1770–79* (Travels to
Europa, Africa, Asia etc. 1770–1779). The Japanese version of this book is
Yamada Tamaki (tr.) (1928), *Tsunberuku Nihon kikō* (Thunberg's travel in
Japan). Von Siebold's *Nippon: Archivzur Beschreibung von Japan und dessen
Neben- und Schutzländern Jezo mit den Süldichen Kurilen, Sachalin, Korea
und den Liu-Kiu Inseln* (1832–1852) is also important. The Japanese version
of this book is *Nihon kōtsū bōeki shi* (The history of foreign relations and
trade of Japan) (1929).

G. F. Meijlan, who was the head of the factory in Japan in the latter
half of the 1820s, later wrote 'Geschiedkundig overzigt van den handel
der Europezen op Japan (Historical Overview of the Trade of Europeans
in Japan)' (1833). This is a valuable reference describing the history of the
Japanese–Dutch trade from its inception.

O. Münsterberg provided an overview of the Japanese–Dutch in *Japans
Answärtiger Handel von 1542 bis 1854* (Japanese trade from 1542 to 1854)
(1896). O. Nachod presented detailed accounts of Japanese–Dutch relations
centering on trade during the seventeenth century in *Die Beziehungen
der Niederländischen Ostindischen Kompagnie zu japan im Siebzehnten
Jahrhundert* (The relations between the Dutch East India Company and
Japan in the seventeenth century) (1897). The Japanese version of this
book is *Jūshichi seiki Nichiran kōshō shi* (Japan–Netherlands relations in
the seventeenth century), translated by Makita Tominaga (1956). Detailed
descriptions of Japanese–Dutch relations in the eighteenth century can
be found in Kuiper, J. F. (1921), *Japan en de Buitenwereld in de 18e Eeuw*
(Japan and the outside world in the eighteenth century). Glamann, K.
(1921) presented a comprehensive survey of the VOC's trading activity
in Asia in *Dutch–Asiatic Trade 1620–1740*. His papers, 'The Dutch East
India Company's Trade in Japanese Copper, 1635–1736' (1953), 'Kinsei no
kokusai bōeki to kikinzoku no ryūtsū ni kansuru ichi kōsatsu (A study of
international trade and distribution of precious metals in the early modern
period)' and 'Nihon dō to jūshichi seiki Yōroppa no pawā poritikkusu
(Japanese copper and European power politics in the sixteenth century)',

(translated by Yoneo Ishii (1978)), consider the role of Japanese copper in the VOC's India trade. H. Doeff, who was the head of the Dutch Factory in Japan during the eighteenth century, described the state of Japanese–Dutch relations in the early nineteenth century in *Herinneringen uit Japan* (Memories from Japan) (1933). The Japanese version of this book is *Nihon kaisō roku* (Memories from Japan); it was translated by Agu Saitō (1941) and Nagazumi Yōko (2003).

J. A. van der Chijs explained how the Netherlands contributed to the opening of Japan to the world market at the end of the seclusion era in *Neêrlands Streven tot de Openstelling van Japan voor de Wereldhandel* (The Netherlands' commitment to the opening of Japan to the world trade) (1867). J. S. Furnivall's *Netherlands India, A Study of Plural Economy* (1939) describes the state of affairs in Indonesia under Dutch rule, including during the time of the VOC's operation. The Japanese version of this book is titled *Ranin keizai shi* (An economic history of the Dutch India); it was translated by Minami Taiheiyō Kenkyū Kai (1942).

P. van Dam surveyed the history of the VOC in Asia, its organizational structure and activities, in *Beschrijvinge van de Oost-Indische Compagine* (Description of the East India Company) (1927–1954), at the request of the VOC at the end of the seventeenth century. D. W. Davis' *A Primer of Dutch Seventeenth Century Overseas Trade* (1961) concisely accounts the VOC's trading activity. C. R. Boxer's *The Dutch Seaborne Empire, 1600–1800* (1965) reveals the course of history from the independence of the Netherlands to its prosperity as a seaborne empire. In *Dutch Merchants and Mariners in Asia 1602–1965* (1988), Boxer depicts the activity of crewmen and officers in Asia as well as various problems leading to the demise of the VOC. In *De Geschiedenis van de VOC* (The history of the VOC), Gaastra (1982) presents independent research on the VOC, based on the achievements of the company investigated in preceding studies.

Regarding the VOC's trading activity in regional India, *The East India Company and the Economy of Bengal*, by Bhattacharyya (1969), describes the trade activity of the British and the VOC in Bengal. Meilink-Roelofsz (1962) examined the commercial activities of Europeans in Malacca, the Malay Peninsula and the Indonesian Archipelagoes from the sixteenth century. *The Trading World of Asia and the English India Company 1660–1760*, by K. N. Chaudhuri (1978), is a study of structural changes in the VOC's India trade in particular; it is highly acclaimed for its analysis of the conditions of the VOC's trade in India. Prakash (1984) introduced some correspondences between the government general in Batavia and its regional factories in India in *The Dutch Factories in India 1617–1623*. Prakash (1985) described the VOC's economic activity in Bengal and the types and profits of its trade goods in *The Dutch East India Company and the Economy of Bengal 1630–1720*. He examined trade in Bengal in the seventeenth and eighteenth centuries and the conditions of precious metal imports in India in *Precious Metals and Commerce* (1994).

In *Strange Company*, J. L. Blussé (1986) sheds light on the state of affairs of the VOC mainly in Batavia in the seventeenth and eighteenth centuries. Chapter 8 of book follows the life of Cornelia, the daughter of the head of the Dutch Factory and his Japanese wife; it has been translated and published in Japanese as *Otenba Koruneria no tatakai* (Skittish Cornelia's battles) (1988). H. Furber (1948) describes the activity of the English East India Company in India and the movement of the VOC in *John Company at work*. Furber's *Rival Empire of Trade in the Orient, 1600–1800* (1976) discusses keen trade competition of the Dutch, English and French East India Companies in India. He highlights the various problems of the VOC in India in *Private Fortunes and Company Profits in the India Trade in the 18th Century* (1997).

*De V.O.C. in Azië* (The VOC in Asia), edited by Meilink-Roelofsz (1976), shows the changes in the VOC's activity in Asia by regions. Innes' *The Door Ajar* (1980) presents an overview of trade between Japan and foreign countries, mainly in the first half of the seventeenth century. 'The exports of precious metal from Europe to Asia by the Dutch East India Company', by Gaastra (1973), demonstrates that large quantities of gold and silver were brought from the Netherlands to Asia by the VOC, mainly in the seventeenth century. J. L. Blussé and F. Gaastra's edited volume, *Companies and Trade* (1981) and J. van Goor's edited volume, *Trading Companies in Asia 1600–1830* (1986), are both about the VOC's activity in Asia.

Arasaratnam's (1986) *Merchants, Companies and Commerce on the Coromandel Coast 1650–1740* and Reid's (1988) *Southeast Asia in the Age of Commerce 1450–1680* describe the societies and cultures of Southeast Asia during the period of active trading by Europeans. Israel's (1989) *Dutch Primacy in World Trade 1585–1740* describes the ups and downs of the Dutch economy in the seventeenth century. Massarella's (1990) *A World Elsewhere: Europe's Encounter with Japan in the 16th and 17th Centuries* offers an overview of Japan–Europe relations, particularly in regard to England, from the latter half of the sixteenth century to the mid-seventeenth century. Arasaratnam's (1995) *Maritime Trade, Society and European Influence in Southern Asia, 1600–1800* discusses the economic relationships between the economic sphere around India's Coromandel region and European East India Companies.

Ryūto Shimada (2006) presents a detailed analysis of Japanese copper sales in the context of the VOC's intra-Asian trade in the eighteenth century in *The Intra-Asian Trade in Japanese Copper by the Dutch East India Company during the Eighteenth Century.*

## Locations and publication details of Japanese resources

### Locations of Japanese archives
The first step in studying early modern Japanese–Dutch trade is to analyse Nagasaki-based trade by examining local historical documents in relation to Nagasaki. The following are some noteworthy institutions in possession of Nagasaki-related historical resources.

**Kyū Nagasaki Kenritsu Nagasaki Toshokan (Former Nagasaki Prefectural Nagasaki Library)**
The prefectural library is a rich source of local historical documents dating from early modern Nagasaki. *Kenritsu Nagasaki toshokan kyōdo shiryō mokuroku (jō)* (The prefectural Nagasaki library catalogue of local resources [Vol. 1]) (1965) has many historical materials relating to early modern Nagasaki in the fields of history, politics (government/diplomacy) and commerce (trade) under the standard system of library classification. Vol. 2 of this catalogue (1966) lists documents by individual collections/archives. Among them, the Fuji Collection, the Koga Collection (resources collected by the local historian Koga Jūjirō) and the Watanabe Collection (resources collected by the local historian Watanabe Kurasuke) carry other important materials. Historical materials and documents that were deposited after the compilation of the above catalogue are contained in *Kenritsu Nagasaki toshokan kyōdo shiryō mokuroku zōka hoi no bu* (The additional and supplementary edition of the prefectural Nagasaki library catalogue of local resources), Vol. 1 (1973) & Vol. 2 (1984).

**Kyū Nagasaki Shiritsu Hakubutsukan (Former Nagasaki City Museum)**
Like the prefectural library, the city museum is in possession of many local resources. Historical materials are split between the prefectural library and the city museum; the museum is as much a treasure trove of historical resources relating to the Nagasaki trade as the prefectural library. Materials and documents in the museum's possession are found in *Nagasaki shiritsu hakubutsukan shiryō mokuroku bunsho shiryō hen* (The Nagasaki city museum resources catalogue documents edition) (1989).

The local history division of the prefectural library and the city museum have merged into Nagasaki Rekishi Bunka Hakubutsukan (Nagasaki Museum of History and Culture); all the resources previously held in these two institutions are now stored in this new museum. However, at the time of the publication of this book, those who wished to check the availability of historical resources still had to use the abovementioned catalogues as the new museum did not yet have its own catalogue.

### Kyūshū Daigaku Kyūshū Bunkashi Kenkyūjo (The Research Institute of Kyūshū Cultural History, Kyūshū University)

Kyūshū Daigaku Kyūshū Bunkashi Kenkyū Shisetsu holds the *Kyūshū Bunkashi Kenkyūjo shozō komonjo mokuroku 6* (Catalogue of ancient documents in the possession of the Research Institute of Kyūshū Cultural History, Vol. 6). This catalogue includes the Matsuki Collection (resources collected by Matsuki Chōbei) and the Koga Collection (resources collected by Koga Jūjirō that are split between here and the prefectural library). Vol. 3 of the same catalogue has documents grouped according to the domains of the early modern Kyūshū region; there are some Nagasaki-related materials in the 'shogunal demesne Nagasaki' group.

### Tokyo Daigaku Shiryō Hensanjo (Historiographical Institute, The University of Tokyo)

This institute is in possession of documents such as 'Oranda sen Hirado nyūshin shimatsu (Records of arriving Dutch ships at Hirado)' and 'Nagasaki shū (Records of Nagasaki)' (*Tokyo Daigaku Shiryō Hensanjo tosho mokuroku dainibu wakansho shahon* (The Historiographical Institute, The University of Tokyo catalogue Vol. 2, Japanese and Chinese manuscripts). It also maintains the photographed copies of valuable materials that are in the possession of other archives in various parts of Japan in *Tokyo Daigaku Shiryō Hensanjo shashin chō mokuroku* (The Historiographical Institute, The University of Tokyo photographic archive catalogue).

### Kokuritsu Kōbunsho Kan (National Archives of Japan)

Among its holdings, the Naikaku Bunko (Cabinet Library) contains the documents of the Edo shogunate. The Japanese local records for the southern sea region and the Hizen province section of *Naikaku bunko kokusho bunrui mokuroku (jō ge)* (A classified catalogue of books in the cabinet library 2 vols.) has local records of Nagasaki that are not found in historical sections, such as 'Nagasaki jitsuroku taisei (Compendium of authentic records of Nagasaki)' and 'Kiyō gundan (A collection of records of the Nagasaki region)'.

The commerce section has 'Tōban kamotsu chō (Registers of Chinese and European cargos)', 'Oranda kata shōbai oboe chō (Records of business with the Dutch)', 'Nagasaki goyō tome (Records of official business of Nagasaki)', 'Tō Oranda shōhō (Rules of trading with the Chinese and the Dutch)' and 'Tōran tsūshō toriatsukai (The manner of trading with the Chinese and the Dutch)'. Dutch books previously in the possession of the shogunate during the Edo period are now held at the National Diet Library (Nichiran Gakkai, 1980).

Other historical resources relating to Nagasaki trade can be found in many establishments, such as Kokuritsu Kokkai Toshokan (National Diet Library), Nagasaki Daigaku Keizai Gakubu Mutō Bunko (the Mutō Library at the Faculty of Economics, Nagasaki University), Ōmura Shiritsu Shiryōkan (Ōmura City Archive), Saga Kenritsu Toshokan Shozō Nabeshima Bunko (the Nabeshima Collection at Saga Prefectural Library), Hirado Rekishi Shiryōkan (Hirado Museum of History), Shizuoka Kenritsu Toshokan Shozō Nanki Bunko (Nanki Collection at Shizuoka Prefectural Library), Sonkeikaku Bunko (Sonkeikaku Library), Kanazawa Shiritsu Tamagawa Toshokan Shozō Kaetsunō Bunko (the Kaetsunō Collection at Kanazawa City Tamagawa Library), Kagoshima Daigaku Toshokan Shozō Tamazato Bunko (the Tamazato Collection at Kagoshima University Library), and Tōhoku Daigaku Fuzoku Toshokan Shozō Kanō Bunko (the Kanō Collection at Tōhoku University Library).

## Japanese published resources

One important resource relating to the Nagasaki trade is *Tsūkō ichiran* (Records of dealings with foreign countries) (1913), which is a collection of historical materials on early modern diplomacy. It contains various historical materials concerning trade in Nagasaki, including Japanese–Dutch trade. There is a series of publications under the name of Nagasaki Bunken Sōsho (Nagasaki document series) (Nagasaki Bunkensha, Nagasaki, 1973–1977), including *Nagasaki jitsuroku taisei* (Compendium of authentic records of Nagasaki) (1973), *Zoku Nagasaki jitsuroku taisei* (Compendium of authentic records of Nagasaki, second series) (1974), *Nagasaki minatogusa* (Records of Nagasaki port) (1973), *Nagasaki kokon shūran jōgekan* (Collection of stories of Nagasaki past and present) (1976), and *Kanpō nikki to hankachō* (Kanpō diaries and crime records) (1977). *Nagasaki ken shi shiryō-hen 4* (History of Nagasaki prefecture, historical resources edition Vol. 4) (1974) contains

'Nagasaki kaisho gosatsumono (Five-volume books of Nagasaki trade association)' and 'Kaban kōeki meisai ki (Detailed records of the trade with the
Chinese and the Dutch)'. *Nagasaki jikki nendairoku* (The true chronicles of
Nagasaki) (1999), written by interpreters working for the Dutch Factory, contains detailed records of annual trade quantities. Other publications include
*Nagasaki kongen ki* (A history of Nagasaki) (1928), *Nagasaki ikyō* (Local history of Nagasaki) (1943), *Kiyō gundan* (A collection of records of the Nagasaki
region) (1974), *Tō tsūji kaisho nichiroku* (Diaries of the Chinese interpreters
association) 7 vols. (1944–1968), *Nagasaki shū* (Nagasaki collection) (1993),
*Nagasaki jūkai Kaban yōgen* (1988), 'Tō ran sen kōeki oboegaki (Records of
the Chinese and Dutch sea trade in Nagasaki)', *Tōban kamotsu chō* (Registers
of Chinese and European cargos) (1970), and *Shōhō jiroku* (Official notices
and decrees in the Shōho and Hōreki eras) (1964–1966). *Nagasaki ryakushi*
(An abridged history of Nagasaki) (1926) is a later compilation.

Nihon Kobunka Kenkyūjo's *Oranda fūsetsusho no kenkyū* (A study of
Dutch reports) (1974) is an edited volume about the foreign information
that the Japanese derived from the Dutch. *Senoku sōkō* (Collected records
of Izumiya) (20 vols., 1951–1983) and *Sumitomo shiryō sōsho* (Sumitomo
historical resource series) (1985) contain historical information about the
export of copper. Publications in other disciplines that contain historical
materials related to trade in Nagasaki include *Nihon zaisei keizai shiryō*
(Japan's financial and economic archival materials) (1922–1925), *Tokyo
shi shi kō sangyō-hem* (Historical materials for the city of Tokyo, industry
edition) (1935–1989), *Tokugawa jikki* (Official chronicles of the Tokugawa
house), (1940–1976), *Kinsei shakai keizai sōsho* (Early modern society
and economy series) (1925–1927), *Taisei rei* (A large compilation of laws)
(1982), *Kenkyō ruiten* (Classified collection of laws) (1984), *Ofuregaki
shūsei* (Collection of official announcements) (1934–1941), *Tokugawa
kinrei kō* (A study of Tokugawa interdicts) (1959–1960), *Nihon keizai taiten*
(Compendium of the Japanese economy) (1928–1929), and *Nihon keizai
sōsho* (Japanese economy series) (1914–1917).

## Locations and publication details of Dutch resources

### Locations of Dutch archives
Roessingh's *Sources of the History of Asia and Oceania in the Netherlands*
(1982–1983) contains bibliographies for Asia-related historical materials
held at various archives in the Netherlands. The National Archives of the
Netherlands in The Hague are the important source of materials for the
study of early modern Japanese–Dutch trade in particular.

**The National Archives of the Netherlands, The Hague (Het Algemeen Rijksarchief)**

The most noteworthy archive at the national archives (ARA) is Het Archief van de Nederlandse Factrij in Japan 1609–1860, which contains documents relating to the Dutch Factory in Japan. The catalogue for this archive was edited by Roessingh (1964). The archive contains the documents of the Dutch Factory from its beginning in 1609 to the end of the Edo period, including trade journals (*Negotie Journalen*), which were recorded every year except in the early years, ledgers (*negotie boeken*) and shipping bills (*facturen*). It also includes interesting historical materials such as the diaries of the head factor (*dagregisters*), resolutions (*resolutien*), correspondences (*afgaande en ontwangen brieven*), secret letters received in Japan (*secrete brieven ontvangen in Japan*), order books (*eijschboeken*), and the governor general's letters to the shogun.

These documents can be viewed on microfiche at the Historiographical Institute of the University of Tokyo. The catalogue is called *Nihon kankei kaigai shiryō mokuroku 1–4: Oranda koku shozai bunsyo (1–4)* (The catalogue of Japan-related overseas historical resources 1–4: documents in the Netherlands (1–4). It should be noted that the resource numbers used at the Historiographical Institute are old numbers; numbers starting with 'KA' denote colonial documents. Monographs relating to the VOC up to the 1960s are classified using this prefix. The comparative table for old and new numbers is available at the ARA.

Documents relating to the Japanese–Dutch trade are found among De Archieven van de Verenigde Oost Indische Compagnie 1602–1796. The titles, contents and composition of these documents are listed according to their document numbers in Raben and Spijkerman (1992), *The Archives of the Dutch East India Company 1602–1795*. The archives contain enormous amounts of historical resources relating to the VOC. Year after year, the VOC dispatched reports from factories in Asia to the Netherlands; various minutes of resolutions and proposals were also sent there from the government general in Batavia. Many documents about policy decisions for the Asia trade were sent from the Netherlands to Batavia. It is important for researchers to have a clear idea about the objectives of their research as there are vast amounts of resources for each year.

Het Archief van de Hoge Regering van Batavia is an archive of documents relating to non-Dutch territories that were in the possession of the government general in Batavia; they were shipped to the Netherlands in around 1862–1863. The archive contains Japan-related documents dating from 1611 to 1793. Historical materials in the Japanese and Chinese languages previously held by the Dutch Factory in Nagasaki are listed in Arano Yasunori and Fujita Kayoko (1996), 'ARA (Het Algemeen Rijksarchief) shozai no Nagasaki shōkan kyūzō no nihongo oyobi chūgokugo bunsho no genjō (The present state of the Japanese and Chinese language documents previously held by the Dutch Factory in Nagasaki presently held by ARA [Hague National Archive])'.

It is likely that more Japan-related historical materials are held at archives in the member cities of the VOC in which its *kamers* (chambers) were situated (Amsterdam, Middelburg, Hoorn, Delft, Utrecht, etc.), but at the time of publication even the above three archives had not yet been fully studied.

### Arsip Nasional Republik Indonesia (National Archives of the Republic of Indonesia)

The national archives are situated in Jakarta, which used to be the stronghold of the VOC in the East Indies and therefore possesses many VOC-related documents. Archives relating to the Japanese–Dutch trade relations include 'Generaal Resolutiën van het Kasteel Batavia (General resolutions of the castle of Batavia) 1633–1803', 'Naskah-naskah Djepang jang bernomor (Numbered Japanese documents) 1744–1868' and 'Bundel-bundel Djepang jang terlepas dan tidak bernomor (Loose and unnumbered Japanese documents) 1762–1846'. They are available on microfiche at the Historiographical Institute in Tokyo (*Nihon kankei kaigai shiryō mokuroku* (The catalogue of Japan-related overseas historical resources) (1969).

In addition to the Netherlands and Indonesia, documents relating to the purchase of merchandise for Japan and the sale of goods exported from Japan would be held in archives in Asia, especially in Indian cities where major factories were once situated, but little information on these resources is available at this stage.

### Dutch published resources

The most notable of the historical texts that have already appeared in print is *Generale Missiven van Gouverurs-Generaal en Raden aan Heren XVII der Verenigde Oostindische Compagnie* (Official letters from the governors-general and the committees to the gentlemen XVII of the United East India Company), edited by Coolhaas (1950–1985). A ninth volume is edited by van Goor (1988); Volume 10 is yet to be published, while Volume 11 was edited by Schooneveld-Oosterlin (2000). The *Generale Missiven* are reports submitted by Batavia to the VOC's board of directors every year and are contained in the aforementioned De Archieven van de Verenigde

Oost Indische Compagnie 1602–1796, which is held by the National Archives, The Hague.

The *Genrale Missiven* describe the activities of the VOC's factories in various parts of Asia. They present an overview of the actual state of Asian trade by the VOC from the 1610s to the 1750s. Van der Chijs' *Dagregisters, gehouden op het Kasteel Batavia 1624–1682* (Diary of the castle of Batavia 1624–1682) (1887–1931) shed light on VOC activities over 31 volumes, as do the 17 volumes of van der Chijs' *Nederlandsch-Indisch Plakaatboek 1602–1811* (Proclamations in the Dutch East Indies 1602–1811).

*The Deshima Diaries Marginalia 1700–1740* (Blussé and Remmelink, 1992) is comprised of the English translation of notes written in the margins of the head factors' diaries, mostly in the eighteenth century. Blussé edited *The Deshima Dagregisters their original tables of contents, 1740–1760* (1993), while van der Velde and Vialle edited *The Deshima Dagregisters their original tables of contents 1760—1780* (1995).

Dunlop's *Bronnen tot de Geschiedenis der VOC in Perzie 1611–1638* (1930) presents sales details of Japanese exports in Asia, especially through to the 1630s. Blussé, van Opstall and Ts'ao Yung-Ho edited volume 1 of *De Dagregisters van Het Kasteel Zeelandia* (1986), which details the VOC's trading activity in Taiwan from 1629 to 1641. Blussé, Milde and Ts'ao Yung-Ho edited volumes 2–4 (1995–2000), which detail the VOC's trading activity in Taiwan from 1641 to 1662. This publication will benefit the study of the Japanese–Dutch trade in the seventeenth century greatly. Bruijn, Gaastra and Schöffer edited three volumes of *Dutch–Asiatic Shipping in the 17th and 18th centuries* (1979–1987); it is a handy reference in finding out the activity of the VOC ships in Asia.

The original and translated versions of historical materials in Japan include the following: Murakami Naojirō (tr.) (1956–1958), *Nagasaki Oranda shōkan no nikki* (Diaries of the Dutch Factory in Nagasaki), 3 vols.; Nagazumi Yōko (tr.) (1969–1970), *Hirado Oranda shōkan no nikki* (Diary of the Dutch factory in Hirado), 4 vols.; and Tokyo Daigaku Shiryō Hensanjo (ed.) (1974–2003), *Oranda shōkanchō nikki* (Diaries of the head of the Dutch Factory) original text edition 10 vols.; (1976–2001), translation edition 9 vols. They are the Japanese-translation versions of the *Dagregisters* in Het Archief van de Nederlandse Factrij in Japan, which are held by the ARA. Murakami's *Batavia jō nisshi* (Diary of the castle of Batavia) (1974–1975) is the translation of Japan-related sections of *Dagregisters, gehouden op het Kasteel Batavia*.

Other publications providing the details of the conditions of the Japanese–Dutch trade in the early nineteenth century include François

Caron (1967), *Nihon dai ōkoku shi* (A true description of the mighty kingdoms of Japan), translated by Shigetomo Kōda; Nagazumi Yōko (tr.) (1985), *Konrāto Kurāmeru no Kyoto sanpu nikki* (Coenraad's diary of a visit to Kyoto); and Nichiran Gakkai (ed.) (1989–1999), *Nagasaki Oranda shōkan nikki* (The diary of the Dutch factory in Nagasaki) 1801–1823. *Hirado shi shi* (The history of Hirado city), overseas resources edition II & III (1998, 2000), has the translation of the trade journals of the Dutch Factory in Hirado from 1638 to 1641.

I would like to add that the above particulars on research trends, bibliographical and historical resources, and the locations of these resources in the study of early modern Japanese–Dutch trade and related fields, were current around 2000.

# Notes

## Chapter 1

1 Taya Hirokichi (1956), 'Kinsei shoki nichiran bōeki ni yoru kingin ryūshutsu jijō (The state of the outflow of gold and silver through Japanese–Dutch trade in the beginning of the early modern period)', *Osaka Furitsu Daigaku kiyō: jinbun shakai kagaku* (Bulletin of the University of Osaka Prefecture: humanities and social sciences), Vol. 4; Taya (1963), *Kinsei ginza no kenkyū* (A study of the silver mint in the early modern period), Tokyo: Yoshikawa Kōbunkan.

2 Kobata Atsushi (1962), 'Nihon kingin gaikoku bōeki ni kansuru kenkyū (A study of foreign trade in Japanese gold and silver)', *Shigaku zasshi* (Journal of the Historical Society), Vol. 44, No. 10–11; Kobata (1962), 'Kinsei shotō ni okeru gin yushutsu no mondai (The problem of silver export in the beginning of the early modern period)', *Rekishi kyōiku* (History education), 1019; Kobata (1970), '16, 17-seiki ni okeru kyokutō no gin ryūtsū (The circulation of silver in the Far East in the 16th and 17th centuries)', *Kobata Atsushi kyōju taikan kinen kokushi ronshū* (A collection of papers on Japanese history commemorating the retirement of Professor Kobata Atsushi), Kyoto; Kobata (1976), *Kingin bōeki shi no kenkyū* (A study of the history of trade in gold and silver), Tokyo: Hōsei Daigaku Shuppan.

3 Katō Eichi (1993), *Bakuhansei kokka no keisei to gaikoku bōeki* (The formation of the shogunate and domain system state and foreign trade), Tokyo: Azekura Shobō; Katō (1978), 'Genna, kanei ki ni okeru nichiran bōeki—Sakoku keisei ki ni okeru bōeki gin wo megutte—(Japanese–Dutch trade in the Genna and Kanei eras—The silver trade in the formative period of a seclusionist state—)' in Kitajima Masamoto (ed.), *Bakuhansei kokka seiritsu katei no kenkyū* (A study of the formation process of the shogunate and domain system state), Tokyo: Yoshikawa Kōbunkan.

4 Yamawaki Teijirō (1980), *Nagasaki no Oranda shōkan* (The Dutch factory in Nagasaki), Tokyo: Chūōkōronsha.

5 Nagazumi Yōko (1999), 'Oranda shiryō kara mita yushutsu gin (Export silver in Dutch historical records)' in Rekishi Bunken Kenkyūkai (ed.), *Iwami ginzan iseki sōgō chōsa hōkokusho* (A comprehensive report on the former Iwami silver mine), Vol. 4, Shimane; Iwami Ginzan Reki-

shi Bunken Chōsadan (ed.) (2003), *Iwami ginzan* (Iwami silver mine), research paper, Kyoto: Shibunkaku Shuppan.

6  Fujita Kayoko (1999), 'Oranda Higashi Indo Gaisha shiryō ni yoru nihon gin yushutsu no sūryōteki kōsatsu (A quantitative study of Japanese silver exports according to the archival records of the VOC)' in Rekishi Bunken Kenkyūkai (ed.), *Iwami ginzan iseki sōgō chōsa hōkokusho* (A comprehensive report on the former Iwami silver mine), Vol. 4, Shimane.

7  Nagazumi Yōko and Takeda Mariko (1981), *Hirado Oranda shōkan Igirisu shōkan nikki* (Diaries of the Dutch and English factories in Hirado), Tokyo: Soshietesha, pp. 18–19.

8  W. Ph. Coolhaas (ed.) (1960–1985), *Generale Missiven van Gouverneurs-Generaal en Raden aan Heren XVII der Oost-indische Compagnie* (The general missives from the governor general and council to the directors of the Dutch East India Company), Vol. 1, 47, The Hague.

9  Tokyo Daigaku Shiryō Hensanjo (ed.) (1980), *Igirisu shōkanchō nikki* (Diary kept by the head of the English factory in Japan: Diary of Richard Cocks), Vol. 2 of the Japanese translation, Tokyo: Tokyo Daigaku Shuppankai, p. 621.

10  *Ibid.*, pp, 553, 595, 736, 717. Both the Japanese and foreign tradesmen were paid in silver reales rather than the *chōgin*.

11  *Ibid.*, p. 548.

12  Nagazumi Yōko and Takeda Mariko, *op. cit.*, p. 320.

13  *Negotie Journalen 1620/24, Het Archief van de Nederlandse Factorij in Japan 1609–1860* (Trade Journal 1620/24, the archive of the Dutch Factory in Japan 1609–1860), No.829, ARA (hereinafter referred to as '*Archief Japan*'). It contains four entries about exchanging silver reales for schuit silver: 16 January, 28, 22 September and 23 September 1621.

14  Katō Êichi (1993), *op. cit.*, pp. 198–199; or (1978) *op. cit.*, p. 586.

15  Nagazumi Yōko and Takeda Mariko, *op. cit.*, pp. 20–21, 23.

16  Nagazumi Yōko and Takeda Mariko, *op. cit.*, p. 31.

17  Nagazumi Yōko (tr.) (1969), *Hirado Oranda shōkan no nikki* (Diary of the Dutch factory in Hirado), Vol. 1, Tokyo: Iwanami Shoten, Note 57, p. 473. *Batavia jō nisshi* (Diary of the castle of Batavia), Vol. 1, translated and annotated by Murakami Naojirō and edited and annotated by Nakamura Takashi (1974), Tokyo: Heibonsha, p. 149.

18  Nihon Ginkō Chōsa Kyoku (ed.) (1973), *Zuroku Nihon no kahei* (A pictorial record of Japanese money), Vol. 2, Tokyo: Tōyō Keizai Shimpōsha, pp. 283–286. It contains the 'list of types of silver produced in Japan'. The section under 'cupellated grade' shows that a type of silver called

*yamagin* was produced at silver mines in Mino, Shinano, Mutsu, Kaga, Ecchū and Sado.

19 *Negotie Journalen 1628/33, Archief Japan*, No.832, 833, ARA. Soma silver was transacted on 8 January and 9 March 1628, 18 July, 3 August, 29 August, 5 September and 25 October 1630, 7 January, 25 March, 11 April, 29 May, 20 November and 10 December 1631, and 5 January (2 transactions in one day), 4 February, 12 February, 22 February and 8 November 1633.

20 The total silver export from 1622 to 1628 was about 578,524 tael; it consisted of 461,598 tael (79.8 per cent) of soma silver, 78,895 tael (13.6 per cent) of berg silver, 1,600 tael (0.3 per cent) of schuit silver, 1,460 tael (0.3 per cent) of refined silver and 34,971 tael (6 per cent) of the silver real.

21 Kobata Atsushi (1968), *Nihon kōzan shi no kenkyū* (A study of the history of mining in Japan), Tokyo, pp. 123, 150–152.

22 Taya Hirokichi, *op. cit.*, p. 69.

23 *Ibid.*, pp. 71–73.

24 *Ibid.*, pp. 73–74.

25 Enomoto Sōji (1977), *Kinsei ryōgoku kahei kenkyū josetsu* (An introductory study of domain coins in the early modern period), Tokyo: Tōyō Shoin, pp. 113–115.

26 See Note 25 (p. 215) in Katō (1993), *op. cit.* or Note 27 (p. 611) in Katō (1978), *op. cit.*

27 Note 20 (p. 467) in Vol. 1 of the Japanese version of *Diary of the Dutch Factory in Hirado* translated by Nagazumi Yōko states: 'The then Japanese currency of *chōgin* was not yet circulating throughout the country and its purity was 80 percent, which meant that foreigners had to have it refined before taking it away. The refined silver was called by such names as the cupellated silver, the Soma silver, the Nagito silver and the Seda silver'. And Note 32 (p. 562) of Vol. 3 explains: 'The Dutch often had the current Schuit silver (*chōgin*) recast into the higher-purity Soma silver (cupellated silver) before exporting at the time'.

28 Taya, *op. cit.*, p. 4.

29 *Ibid.*, pp. 61–62.

30 The Historiographical Institute, The University of Tokyo (ed.) (1979), *Diary Kept by the Head of the English Factory in Japan*, Vol. 2, Tokyo: University of Tokyo Press, p. 224. Tokyo Daigaku Shiryō Hensanjo, *op. cit.*, p. 194.

31 Kobata (1976), *op. cit.*, pp. 33–44.

32 Tokyo Daigaku Shiryō Hensanjo (ed.) (1982), *Igirisu shōkanchō nikki*
   (Diary kept by the head of the English factory in Japan: Diary of
   Richard Cocks), Vol. 2 of the appendix to the Japanese translation,
   Tokyo: Tokyo Daigaku Shuppankai, p. 389. The general index instructs
   the reader to refer to '*nagaitagin*' for '*nagita*', '*nagite*' and '*nagitegin*'.
   The '*nagites*' in the entry for the *Sea Adventur* also comes under
   '*nagaitagin*'.
33 Coolhaas, *op. cit.*, Vol. 1, p. 369.
34 An article dated 20 December 1631 on p. 115 of Vol. 1 in the Japanese
   translation by Murakami Naojirō of *Diary of the Castle of Batavia* states
   that 'there was a reserve of the *somma* silver [refined silver, cupellated
   silver] worth 150,000 real in Japan (meaning the Hirado Factory)' and
   an article dated 31 January 1636 states that 'the above cargos were all
   Japanese Schuit silver [*chōgin*, a semi-cylindrical silver coin], *somma*
   [cupellated silver]'.
35 See the types of export copper in Chapter 2 of this book.
36 Kobata (1968), *op. cit.*, p. 108.
37 The Historiographical Institute, The University of Tokyo, *op. cit.*, Vol.
   1, p. 54. Tokyo Daigaku Shiryō Hensanjo (1979), *op. cit.*, Vol. 1, p. 80.
38 The Historiographical Institute, The University of Tokyo, *op. cit.*, Vol.
   2, p. 212. Tokyo Daigaku Shiryō Hensanjo, *op. cit.*, Vol. 2, p. 174.
39 The *sampan* is a small boat widely used in Southeast Asia and China. It
   was originally called '*sanpan*' in the Chinese language. It is one of the
   most common words meaning 'ship' in China (Murray, J. (ed.) (1903),
   *Hobson-Jobson*, London).
40 *Hirado Oranda shōkan no nikki*, Vol. 3, p. 254.
41 Zokugunshoruijū Kanseikai (1996), *Tōdai ki, Sunpu ki* (Records of the
   present generation, Records of Sunpu) (shiryō zatsusan [collection
   of miscellaneous articles]), Tokyo: p. 155. 'Kanpon tōdai ki (Official
   records of the present generation)' in Kokusho Kankōkai (1913), *Tsūkō
   ichiran* (Records of dealings with foreign countries), Vol. 4, p. 272
   has a different date (29 September in the fourteenth year of Keichō).
   It has a slightly different description too: 'The Chinese used to have
   silver ingots minted into the Nanryō before receiving them. An order
   came from Sunpu that they should receive silver in the form of the
   *chōgin* from now on. The Chinese were annoyed but they followed the
   order'.
42 'Nagasaki oboegaki (Nagasaki memoranda)' in *Tsūkō ichiran*, Vol. 4, p.
   272 states: 'Received an order to set up a silver coin mint here and not
   to hand over cupellated silver coins to foreign countries. In particular,

ships returning to China must be checked thoroughly for converted silver'. And Nakada Yasunao and Nakamura Tadashi (eds) (1974), *Kiyō gundan* (A collection of records of the Nagasaki region), Tokyo: Kondō Shuppansha, p. 139 states: 'The decision has been in place since around 1616 which stipulated that two people from Kyoto silver coin mint were to be sent to Nagasaki and stay there to look out for counterfeit silver and prevent Chinese ships from taking cupellated silver'.

43  Nagazumi and Takeda, *op. cit.*, p. 145.

44  Coolhaas, *op. cit.*, Vol. 1, p. 642 (9 December 1937).

45  The development of the currency system by the government made rapid progress from 1634. For example, the minting of *Kanei-tsūhō* copper coins officially commenced nationally in 1636 and the export of copper was banned in the following year. However, the minting of the *Kanei-tsūhō* appears to have actually started in some places before 1634 (see Chapter 2). The Japanese government became aware in 1640 that the Dutch were exporting the *koban* and issued a strict ban on the export of the *koban* to the Netherlands (see Chapter 4).

46  Nagazumi Yōko (1990), *Kinsei shoki no gaikō* (Diplomacy in the beginning of the early modern period), Tokyo: Tokyo Daigaku Shuppankai, p. 169.

47  Coolhaas, *op. cit.*, Vol. 2, p. 99.

48  *Ibid.*, pp. 46, 94.

49  *Ibid.*, p. 83.

50  Tominaga Makita (tr.) (1956), *17-seiki nichiran kōshō shi* (A history of the Japanese-Dutch relations in the seventeenth century), Nara: Yōtokusha, pp. 201–211 which is a translation of Oskar Nachod (1897), *Die Beziehungen der Niederländischen Ostindischen Kompagnie zu Japan im siebzehnten Jahrhundert*.

51  *Tokugawa jikki* (Official chronicles of the Tokugawa house), Vol. 3, Tokyo: Yoshikawa Kōbunkan, 1939, p. 226.

52  It reports the amount of profit for each factory in Asia (fractions below gulden are discarded): Maccassar, 19,517 gulden; Solor, 10,222 gulden; Wingurla, 3,443 gulden; Malabar coast, 9,151 gulden; Guseratte and Hindustan combined, 38,129 gulden; Coromandel coast combined, 120,069; Atchin, 1,008 gulden; Tayouan, 96,003 gulden; and Nagasaki, 659,583 gulden (Coolhaas, *op. cit.*, Vol. 2, p. 225).

53  K. N. Chaudhuri (1987), *The Trading World of Asia and the English East India Company 1660–1760*, London, p. 155.

54  Attman, A. (1983), *Dutch Enterprise in the World Bullion Trade 1550–1800*, Goteborg: Kungl. Vetenskaps-och Vitterhets-Samhället, p. 155.

55 *Ibid.*, p. 30.
56 K. Glamann (1958), *Dutch–Asiatic Trade 1620–1740,* The Hague: Martinus Nijhoff, pp. 51–52. Gaastra, F.S. (1983), 'The export of precious metal from Europe to Asia by the Dutch East India Company, 1602–1795' in J. F. Richards, (ed.), *Precious Metals in the Later Medieval and Early Modern World,* Durham: Carolina Academic Press, p. 452.
57 *Ibid.*
58 Glamann, *op. cit.*, p. 52; Gaastra, *op. cit.*, p. 449.
59 Gaastra, *op. cit.*, p. 470.
60 Coolhaas, *op. cit.*, Vol. 3, p. 30.
61 *Ibid.*, p. 263.
62 Murakami and Nakamura, *op. cit.*, p. 252.
63 Nagazumi (1990), *op. cit.*, pp. 183–184.
64 Nagasaki-shi Shishi Hensan Shitsu (1938), *Nagasaki-shi shi, tsūkō bōeki hen Tōyō shokoku bu* (A history of the city of Nagasaki, foreign relations and trade edition—the Oriental nations), Osaka: Seibundō Shuppan, p. 86, Ren Hongzhang (1988), *Kinsei Nihon to nicchū bōeki* (Early-modern Japan and the Japanese–Chinese trade), Tokyo: Rokkō Shuppan, pp. 95–106.
65 Nagazumi (1999), *op. cit.*, p. 127.
66 Nagazumi (1990), *op. cit.*, p. 183.
67 Nagazumi Yōko (1992), '17-seiki chūki no Nihon Tonkin bōeki ni tsuite (the Japan-Tonkin trade in the mid seventeenth)', *Jōsai daigaku daigakuin kenkyū nenpō* (Bulletin of the graduate school of the Jōsai University), No. 8, p. 35. Nagazumi (1990), *op. cit.*, p. 129.
68 Coolhaas, *op. cit.*, pp. 290 (21 December 1646), 227 (20 January 1651).
69 Furber, H. (1976), *Rival Empires of Trade in the Orient, 1600–1800,* Minnesota: University of Minnesota Press, p. 232.
70 Nagazumi (1999), *op cit.*, pp. 126, 129.
71 Fujita Kayoko (1999), 'Shohyō Yao Keisuke "Kinsei Oranda bōeki to sakoku" (Book review of "The early modern Dutch trade and Japanese seclusion" by Keisuke Yao)', *Shirin* (Journal of the Society of Historical Research), Vol. 82, No. 6, pp. 162–163.
72 Nagazumi Yōko (1999), 'Tōzai kōeki no chūkeichi Taiwan no seisui (The rise and fall of Taiwan, a junction for the East–West trade)' in Satō Tsugitaka and Kishimoto Mio (eds), *Shijō no sekai shi* (A world history of the markets), Tokyo, p. 355.
73 This conflict began in 1661 and ended in early 1662. Zheng Chonggong used this place as his base for his rebellion against Qing in his attempt to revive Ming. The Qing government ordered the Great Clearance to

enforce a blockade zone between Taiwan and mainland China in order to drive Zheng into isolation (Ren Hongzhang, *op. cit.*, pp. 99–100).

74  Campbell, William, (1903), *Formosa under the Dutch*, London, pp. 455–457.

75  Ōta Katsuya (1992), *Sakoku jidai Nagasaki bōeki shi no kenkyū* (A study of the history of trade in seclusion-era Nagasaki), Kyoto: Shibunkaku Shuppan, pp. 104–105.

76  *Ibid.*, pp. 106–108.

77  Nakada and Nakamura, *op. cit.*, p. 75.

78  'Koshūki (A collection of historical records)', *Tsūkō ichiran*, Vol. 4, p. 304.

79  *Ibid.*, p. 272.

80  'Taisei rei (A large compilation of laws)', 'Nagasaki mushimegane (Nagasaki through a magnifying glass)' in *Tsūkō ichiran*, Vol. 4, p. 273.

81  An article dated 2 July 1668 reports that the Japanese government had issued an order to export gold instead of silver in exchange for imported products (*Jedose en Nagasakisa Ordres beginnende met Anno 1611 tot 1733, Hoge Regering van Batavia No.141, ARA*).

82  Coolhaas, *op. cit.*, Vol. 3, p. 788.

83  Gaastra, *op. cit.*, pp. 465, 475.

## Chapter 2

1  The Historiographical Institute, the University of Tokyo (ed.) (1978), *Diary Kept by the Head of the English Factory in Japan*, Vol. 1, Tokyo: University of Tokyo Press, p. 53. Tokyo Daigaku Shiryō Hensanjo (ed.) (1979), *Igirisu shōkanchō nikki* (Diary kept by the head of the English factory in Japan: Diary of Richard Cocks), Vol. 1 of the Japanese translation, Tokyo: Tokyo Daigaku Shuppankai, p. 79. Nagasaki Ken (ed.) (1966), 'Richādo Kokkusu nikki (Diary of Richard Cocks)', *Nagaski ken shi, shiryō hen 3* (History of Nagasaki prefecture, historical resources edition No. 3), Tokyo: Yoshikawa Kōbunkan, p. 195.

2  Iwao Seiichi (tr.) (1929), *Keigen Igirisu shokan* (Correspondence by the English in 1611–1616), Tokyo: Shunnansha, pp. 514–515.

3  *Ibid.*, p. 537.

4  Nagazumi Yōko and Takeda Mariko (1981), *Hirado Oranda shōkan, Igirisu shōkan nikki* (Diaries of the Dutch factory and the English factory in Hirado), Tokyo: Soshietesha, p. 26.

5  One possible reason for the departure time of returning ships being as late as February was a regulation during the Hirado era which

prevented Dutch ships from departing for at least twenty days after the departure of Portuguese ships from Nagasaki.

6  Katō Ēichi, "Hirado Oranda Shokann no Shougyochobo ni mirareru Nichiran Boeki no Ichidanmen" *Report on the Activities of the Historiographical Institute*, No. 3, (Tokyo: Historiographical Institute, the University of Tokyo, 1968), "1636 nenndo Oranda Shokan no Yushutsunyu Shohin", Report on the Activities of, *op. cit.*, No. 4, 1969, "1637 nenndo Hirado Oranda Shokan Boekihyo", Report on the Activities of, *op. cit.*, No. 5, 6, (1970, 1971).

7  Oskar Nachod (1897), *Die beziehungen der Niederländischen Oostindischen Kompagnie zu Japan im siebzehenten jahrhundert* (The relations between the Dutch East India Company and Japan in the seventeenth century), Berlin: Druck von Pass & Garleb, pp. 208–209.

8  Sumitomo Shūshi Shitsu (ed.), *Senoku sōkō* (Collected records of Izumiya), Vol. 8, Kyoto, p. 13.

9  K. Glamann (1958), *Dutch–Asiatic Trade 1620–1740*, The Hague: Martinus Nijhoff, p. 19.

10  According to the *Diary of Richard Cocks*, gokidō was exported in the second half of the 1610s. It appears for the first time in an article dated 16 February 1616 which states that Cocks had asked Kazariya Tōzaemon in Sakai to procure gokidō (gokodō) for him: 'I got our host Tozaemon Dono to send his man to look out for our goco copp'r, to haue it ready to lade tomorow' (*Diary kept by the head of the English Factory in Japan*, Vol. 1, p, 348; in the Japanese translation, *op.cit.*, Vol. 1p.574). A large part of copper exported by the English was gokidō. Articles about copper exports are found up to March 1618 and become few and far between thereafter.

11  W. Ph. Coolhaas (ed.) (1960–1985), *Generale Missiven van Gouverneurs-Generaal en Raden aan Heren XVII der Oost-indische Compagnie* (Official letters from the governors-general and the committees to the gentlemen XVII of the United East India Company), Vol. 1, 47, The Hague: Martinus Nijhoff, p. 644.

12  *Negotie Journaal 16 Oct. 1634, 22 Oct. 1634, Het Archief van de Nederlandse Factorij in Japan* (Trade Journal 16 Oct. 1634, 22 Oct. 1634, the archive of the Dutch Factory in Japan), No.834, ARA (hereinafter referred to as 'Archief Japan'). *Negotie Journalen 12 Nov.. 1635, Archief Japan*, No. 835, ARA. *Negotie Journalen 2 Feb., 23 Dec. 1636, Archief Japan*, No. 836, ARA.

13 An article dated 20 November 1616 in *Diary of Richard Cocks* refers to 50 picol of *saodō* brought over from Kyoto: 'Echo Dono retorned frō Miako w'th rest of the bar copp'r,being 50 pico' (*Diary kept by the head of the English Factory in Japan,op.cit.,* Vol. 1, p, 351; p. 580 in the Japanese translation, Vol. 1). An article dated 24 November 1616 reads: 'All the rest of our cipp'r was laden abord this day, being 100 *pico.* of bars, & 100 *pico.* of *goco* copp'r' (*Ibid.,* p. 355, *op.cit.,* Vol. 1.p.586).

14 *Negotie Journaal, 19 Jan. 1636, Archief Japan,* No.835, ARA.

15 *Negotie Journaal, 17 Nov. 1636, Archief Japan,* No.836, ARA. The number at the beginning of each entry is the page number for that item in the ledger.

16 Nagazumi Yōko (tr.) (1969), *Hirado Oranda shōkan no nikki* (Diary of the Dutch factory in Hirado), Vol. 3, Tokyo: Iwanami Shoten, p. 505.

17 Katō Eichi (1993), *Bakuhansei kokka no keisei to gaikoku bōeki* (The formation of the shogunate and domain system state and foreign trade), Tokyo: Azekura Shobō, pp. 168–169. Katō (1978), 'Genna, kanei ki ni okeru nichiran bōeki—Sakoku keisei ki ni okeru bōeki gin wo megutte (Japanese–Dutch trade in the Genna and Kanei eras—about trade silver in the formative period of a seclusionist state)' in Kitajima Masamoto (ed.), *Bakuhansei kokka seiritsu katei no kenkyū* (A study of the formation process of the shogunate and domain system state), Tokyo: Yoshikawa Kōbunkan, p. 559.

18 *Negotie Journaal, 22 Oct. 1646, Archief Japan,* No.846, ARA.

19 *Negotie Journaal, 25 Oct. 1649, Archief Japan,* No.849, ARA.

20 *Factuur, 18 Oct. 1651, Archief Japan,* No.775, ARA.

21 *Negotie Journaal, 17 Oct. 1652, Archief Japan,* No.851, ARA.

22 Nagazumi (1969), *op. cit.,* pp. 31–32.

23 Katsu Kaishū (ed.) (1968), *Suijin roku* (A collection of historical resources), Vol. 1, Tokyo: Hara Shobō, pp. 412–413.

24 Yōtarō Sakudō (1958), *Kinsei Nihon kahei shi* (History of Japanese money in the early modern period), Tokyo: Shibundō, pp. 113–114.

25 Nagazumi Yōko (2001), *Shuin sen* (Red seal ships), Tokyo: Yoshikawa Kōbunkan, pp. 144–145.

26 Journals show that coins minted in Sakamoto were exported in large quantities from 1633. For example, the cargo list of the *Venloo* dated 12 December contains 15,420,000 coins (*Negotie Journalen*, 1633/35, *Archief Japan,* No.834. ARA).

27 Tokyo Metropolitan Archives (ed.) (1954), *Tokyo shi shikō, sangyō hen Vol. 4* (Historical materials for the city of Tokyo, industry edition

Vol. 4): Tokyo Metropolitan Archives, p. 198. This source shows that the commencement of this coinage project was recorded in various historical materials.

28 Kuroita Katsumi (ed.) (1981), *Tokugawa jikki* (Official chronicles of the Tokugawa Shogunate), Vol. 3, Tokyo: Yoshikawa Kōbunkan, p. 24.

29 Nagazumi (1969), *op. cit.*, p. 438.

30 *Ibid.*, p. 439.

31 *Ibid.*, p. 444–445.

32 Coolhaas, *op. cit.*, p. 257.

33 Nachod, *op. cit.*, p. 257.

34 Coolhaas, *op. cit.*, Vol. 2, p. 37.

35 Dunlop, H. (ed.) (1930), *Bronnen tot de Geshiedenis der Oostindische Compagnie in Perzie 1611–1638* (Resources for the history of the East India Company in Persia 1611–1638), The Hague: Martinus Nijhoff, p. 610.

36 Coolhaas, *op. cit.*, Vol. 2, p. 60.

37 *Ibid.*, p. 167.

38 Glamann, *op. cit.*, p. 173. Glamann (1953), 'The Dutch East India Company's trade in Japanese copper 1645–1736', *Scandinavian Economic History Review*, Vol. 1, No. 1, p. 55. An article dated 12 December 1642 in the *Generale Missiven* reports on shipments of copper as private trade by a kamer, a section of the VOC. They may be the copper shipments referred to by Glamann. Coolhaas, *op. cit.*, Vol. 1, p. 167.

39 Sakudō Yōtarō (1970), 'Nihon kahei shi gairon (An introduction to the history of Japanese money)' in Honjō Eijirō (ed.), *Dainihon kahei shi* (History of Japanese money), supplementary volume, Tokyo: Rekishi Toshosha, pp. 195–198.

40 Nagazumi (1969), *op. cit.*, Vol. 4 (25 July 1639), p. 219.

41 *Ibid.*, (25 June 1640), p. 356.

42 *Ibid.*, (5 July 1640), p. 358.

43 *Ibid.*, p. 528.

44 *Ibid.*, p. 492.

45 Nagazumi Yōko (1972), 'Hirado han to Oranda bōeki (The Hirado domain and Dutch trade)', *Nihon rekishi* (Japanese history), No. 286, pp. 10–11.

46 Coolhaas, *op. cit.*, p. 184.

47 Dunlop, *op. cit.*, p. 28.

48 *Ibid.*, pp. 134, 217, 264, 278, 433, 480, 500, 501, 509, 542, 610.

49 Kobata Atsushi (1967), *Nihon no kahei* (Japanese money), Tokyo: Shibundō, pp. 209–210. Nachod, *op. cit.*, p. 257. Nagazumi and Takeda, *op. cit.*, p. 104. Yamawaki Teijirō (1960), *Kinsei nicchū bōeki shi no kenkyū*

(A study of the history of the Japan–China trade in the early modern period), Tokyo: Yoshikawa Kōbunkan, p. 77, Note 1. According to this source, Yamawaki drew on Nachod's description.
50  Glamann, *op. cit.*, p. 172.

## Chapter 3

1  K. Glamann (1981), *Dutch–Asiatic Trade, 1620–1740*, The Hague: Martinus Nijhoff, p. 168.
2  *Ibid.*, pp. 167–168. According to Chaudhuri, copper supplies from Japan and Sweden replaced the depleting copper mines of India and filled domestic demand in the mid-seventeenth century. Copper played an important role in India's currency system as well as being an important raw material for the manufacturing of domestic goods. K. N. Chaudhuri (1978), *The Trading World of Asia and the English East India Company, 1660–1760*, Cambridge: Cambridge University Press, p. 206.
3  K. Glamann (1978), 'Nihon dō to 16 seiki yōroppa no pawā poritikkusu (Japanese copper and European power politics in the 16th century)', translated by Yoneo Ishii, *Tōhōgaku* (Eastern studies), No. 56, p. 111.
4  K. Glamann (1953), 'The Dutch East India Company's trade in Japanese copper 1645–1736', *Scandinavian Economic History Review*, Vol. 1, No. 1, p. 60.
5  A. Smith (1937), *An Inquiry into the Nature and Causes of the Wealth of Nations*, New York: Random House, Inc, p. 168.
6  Murakami Naojirō (tr.) (1957), *Nagasaki Oranda shōkan no nikki* (Diaries of the Dutch Factory in Nagasaki), Vol. 2, Tokyo: Iwanami Shoten, p. 94.
7  *Ibid.*, Vol. 1, pp. 217, 248.
8  *Ibid.*, Vol. 2, p. 35.
9  *Ibid.*, p. 39.
10  *Ibid.*, p. 77.
11  *Ibid.*, p. 94. On the 7 September 1646, it read, '[...] petitioned for authorization to export 300,000, 400,000, 500,000 or 600,000 kin of copper [...] told of authorization for as much copper as we desired [...]'.
12  W. Ph. Coolhaas (ed.) (1960–1985), *Generale Missiven van Gouverneurs-Generaal en Raden aan Heren XVII der Oost-indische Compagnie* (Official letters from the governors general and the committees to the board of the VOC), Vol. 2, The Hague: Martinus Nijhoff, p. 297.
13  See Chapter 2 of 'Kinsei shoki no bōeki shōnin (Trading merchants in the beginning of the early modern period) in Suzuki Yasuko (2004), *Kinsei*

*nichiran bōeki shi no kenkyū* (History of the Dutch–Japanese trade in the early modern period), Kyoto: Shibunkaku Shuppan.

14 Sakudō Yōtarō (1970), 'Nihon kahei shi gairon (An introduction to the history of Japanese money)' in Honjō Eijirō (ed.), *Dainihon kahei shi* (History of Japanese money), supplementary volume, Tokyo: Rekishi Toshosha, pp. 195–198.

15 The *Vogelenlank* carried 19,425 kin of 'ongeraffineert off gooykenscoper (unrefined copper or *gokidō*)' at 9.8 tael per picol in 1659. An article in the same year in Kyushu Bunkashi Kenkyūjo Shiryōshū Kankōkai (ed.) (1999), *Nagasaki jikki nendairoku* (The true chronicles of Nagasaki), p. 77, reports a shipment of the same amount of *aradō* (crude copper). 14,935 kin of 'gockjens coper (*gokidō*)' were exported in 1660. Both shipments consisted of *aradō*, also called *gokidō* by the Dutch. 7,676 kin of 'koeck coper' was exported at 11 tael per picol in 1672. An explanatory note about this shipment appears in van Dam, p. (1931), *Beschryvinge van de Oostindische Compagnie* (Description of the East India Company) in F. W. Stapel (ed.), tweede boek deel. 1, The Hague, p. 446; it states that it was a 'name for *itadō* (plate copper)'. 29,000 kin and 1,000 kin of copper described only as 'grof coper (crude copper)' and not identified as *saodō* (bar copper) were shipped on the *Ooievaar* and the *Kalf* respectively in 1660 at the price of 11 tael per picol. In addition, 5,000 kin (11.5 tael per picol) of crude Chinese copper were exported on board the *Nieuw Poort* in 1659, which was purchased as a trade sample for Surat. In 1662, for which no journal of the Dutch Factory is found, *Nagasaki jikki nendairoku* reports that 1,511,160 kin of *saodō* at 11.8 tael per picol and 99,620 kin of *yakidō* at 10 tael per picol were exported. The nature of *yakidō* is not known.

16 Murakami, *op. cit.*, Vol. 2, p. 181.

17 Coolhaas, *op. cit.*, Vol. 2, p. 365.

18 Murakami, *op. cit.*, Vol. 3, p. 230.

19 Nakada Yasunao and Nakamura Tadashi (eds) (1974), *Kiyō gundan* (A collection of records of the Nagasaki region), Tokyo: Kondō Shuppan-sha, pp. 41–42.

20 Shinmura Izuru (ed.) (1928), *Nagasaki kongen ki* (A history of Naga-saki), Kaihyō sōsho (Kaihyō series) Vol. 4, Tokyo: Kōseikaku Shoten, p. 130.

21 Hayashi Fukusai(ed.), *Tsūkō ichiran* (Records of dealings with foreign countries), Vol. 4, (Tokyo: Kokusho Kankokai, 1913) p. 304.

22 'Dō ikoku uri oboechō (shō) (Records of foreign sales of copper [abstract])' in Sumitomo Shūshi Shitsu (ed.) (1989), *Dō ikoku uri oboechō, kōgyō shoyō*

dome, jō saodō chō (Records of foreign sales of copper, records of various mining businesses, records of fine copper bars), Kyoto: Shibunkaku Shuppan, p. 50. Sumitomo Shūshi Shitsu (ed.) (1957), Senoku sōkō (Collected records of Izumiya), Vol. 9, Kyoto, pp. 15–29. Hayashi Fukusai (ed.) (1913), Tsūkō ichiran (Records of dealings with foreign countries), Vol. 4, p. 308. Morinaga Taneo and Ecchū Tetsuya (eds) (1977), 'Kanpō nikki (Kanpō diaries)', Kanpō nikki to hankachō (Kanpō diaries and crime records), Nagasaki: Nagasaki Bunkensha, p. 134.

23  Kobata Atsushi (1968), Nihon kōzan shi no kenkyū (A study of the history of mining in Japan), Tokyo: Iwanami Shoten, p. 6.

24  Sumitomo Shūshi Shitsu (ed.) (1957), 'Dō bōeki kabu kankei shiryō (Materials relating to copper trade license)', Senoku sōkō, Vol. 8 supplement, pp. 2–3.

25  Sumitomo Shūshi Shitsu (ed.) (1985), Nennen chō (Annual records), Vols. 0 and 1, Kyoto: Shibunkaku Shuppan, pp. 37–46. Sumitomo Shūshi Shitsu (ed.) (1989), Dō ikoku uri oboechō, kōgyō shoyō dome, jō saodō chō (Records of foreign sales of copper, records of various mining businesses, records of fine copper bars), pp. 147–150. Sumitomo Shūshi Shitsu (ed.) (1956), Senoku sōkō, Vol. 8, Kyoto, pp. 40–50. Sumitomo Shūshi Shitsu (ed.) (1957), 'Dō bōeki kabu kankei shiryō (Materials relating to copper trade license)', op. cit., p. 2.

26  Oskar Nachod (1897), Die beziehungen der Niederländischen Oostindischen Kompagnie zu Japan im siebzehenten Jahrhundert (The relations between the Dutch East India Company and Japan in the seventeenth century), Berlin: Druck von Pass & Garleb, p. 383.

27  'Nagasaki oboegaki (Nagasaki memoranda)' in Tsūkō ichiran, Vol. 4, pp. 282, 330. 'Kanpō nikki (Kanpō diaries)', op. cit., p. 282.

28  Nachod, op. cit., p. 387.

29  Yamawaki Teijirō (1964), Nagasaki no tōjin bōeki (Chinese trade in Nagasaki), Tokyo: Yoshikawa Kōbunkan, p. 53.

30  Ōta Katsuya (1992), Sakoku jidai Nagasaki bōeki shi no kenkyū (A study of the history of trade in seclusion-era Nagasaki), Kyoto: Shibunkaku Shuppan, p. 304.

31  Imai Noriko (2001), 'Jōkyō, Genroku-ki no dō bōeki to Sumitomo (Copper trade in the Jōkyō and Genroku eras and Sumitomo)', Sumitomo shiryōkan hō (Sumitomo historical archives report), No. 32, p. 5 and Table 2 (p. 6). It was triggered by an entry into the export copper market by the Ashio copper mine.

32  Nakamura Tadashi (1988), Kinsei Nagasaki bōeki shi no kenkyū (A study of the history of the Nagasaki trade in the early modern period),

Tokyo: Yoshikawa Kōbunkan, p. 309. Yamawaki Teijirō (1965), *Nukeni* (Smuggling), Tokyo: Nihon Keizai Shimbunsha, pp. 14–15. Ōta, *op. cit.*, p. 353. Ōta synthesizes preceding studies and concludes that the collection of levies from the copper substitution trade was the underlying motive for the establishment of this system.

33 *Nennen chō, op. cit.*, pp. 146–148.

34 It was revealed by Nagazumi Yōko that Fushimiya Shirobē, a timber merchant in Edo, was a close associate of Yanagisawa Yoshiyasu. Nagazumi (1984), 'Yanagisawa Yoshiyasu to Fushimiya no shiromono-gae (Yanagisawa Yoshiyasu and copper substitution by Fushimiya), *Nihon rekishi* (Japanese history), Vol. 434, pp. 4–6. It was also pointed out by Imai Noriko that Fushimiya possibly had an association with Izumiya, as it once received a contract for a government-owned forest near Betsushi copper mine. Imai, *op. cit.*, p. 22.

35 'Nagasaki tōransen kōeki oboegaki (Records of the Chinese and Dutch sea trade in Nagasaki)', *Hōsei shigaku* (Journal of Hosei Historical Society in Hosei University) (1969), No. 21, p. 26. Niwa Kankichi (ed.) (1975), 'Nagasaki mushimegane (Nagasaki through a magnifying glass)' in *Nagasaki mushimegane, Nagasaki kenbunroku, Nagasaki engiryaku* (Nagasaki through a magnifying glass, records of Nagasaki, abridged history of Nagasaki), Nagasaki: Nagasaki Bunkensha, p. 72. *Tsūkō ichiran*, Vol. 4, p. 348.

36 Nagazumi (1984), *op. cit.*, p. 2.

37 Tokyo Daigaku Shiryō Hensanjo (ed.) (1955), *Tō tsūji kaisho nichiroku* (Diaries of the Chinese interpreters association), Vol. 2, Tokyo: Tokyo Daigaku Shuppankai, pp. 210–211 (7 February 1697).

38 Van Dam, *op. cit.*, p. 534.

39 *Ibid.*, p. 538. Yao Keisuke (1998), *Kinsei Oranda bōeki to sakoku* (The early modern Dutch trade and Japanese seclusion), Tokyo: Yoshikawa Kōbunkan, pp. 79–81.

40 According to van Dam, 437,900 kin of this had been purchased previously. *Op. cit.*, p. 542.

41 Tokyo Daigaku Shiryō Hensanjo (ed.) (1955), *op. cit.*, Vol. 2, p. 289 (22 January 1697). Van Dam, *Ibid.*, p. 542.

42 Sumitomo Shūshi Shitsu (ed.) (1980), *Senoku sōkō*, Vol. 18, pp. 58–59.

43 *Nagasaki jikki nendairoku*, p. 131.

44 Tokyo Metropolitan Archives (ed.) (1962), *Tokyo shi shikō, sangyō hen 8* (Historical materials for the city of Tokyo, industry edition Vol. 8): Tokyo Metropolitan Archives, pp. 834–835. Kobata Atsushi (1966), *Nihon no kahei* (Japanese money), Tokyo: Shibundō, p. 212.

45  Kusama Naokata (1929), 'Sanka zui (A graphic study of the three-tier metal standard)', Vol. 4, in Takimoto Seiichi (ed.), *Nihon keizai taiten* (Compendium of the Japanese economy), Vol. 39, Tokyo: Keimeisha, p. 25.

46  Sumitomo Shūshi Shitsu (ed.), *Senoku sōkō*, Vol. 9, p. 121.

47  *Ibid.*, Vol. 18, p. 100.

48  Kawasaki Eitarō et al. (1960), 'Besshi dōzan (Besshi copper mine)', in Chihōshi Kenkyū Kyōgikai (ed.), *Nihon sangyō shi taikei* (History of Japanese industry series), Vol. 7, Tokyo: Tokyo Daigaku Shuppankai, p. 316.

49  Sumitomo Shūshi Shitsu (ed.) (1980), *Senoku sōkō*, Vol. 18, pp. 170–171.

50  Sumitomo Shūshi Shitsu (ed.) (1987), *Besshi dōzan kōyōchō ichiban niban* (Betsushi copper mine official business records No. 1 and No. 2), No. 2, Kyoto: Shibunkaku Shuppan, pp. 187–190. Sumitomo Shūshi Shitsu (ed.) (1980), *Senoku sōkō*, Vol. 18, p. 143.

51  Copper prices were already high by 1700 due to a strong demand from the *zeniza* and for raw materials for refining in general. Sumitomo Shūshi Shitsu (ed.) (1989), 'Kōgyō shoyō dome (records of various mining businesses)' in Sumitomo Shūshi Shitsu (ed.) (1989), *op. cit.*, p. 205. Sumitomo Shūshi Shitsu (ed.) (1980), *Senoku sōkō*, Vol. 18, p. 151.

52  These were found especially from 1709. According to *Nennen chō*, Vol. 1, the shogunate government ordered copper roof tiles on 24 May 1709; they were given priority over export copper (p. 295). Articles about roof tiles for government use are found here and there in *Nennen shoyō dome niban sanban* (Annual records of business No. 2 and No. 3), No. 2. Sumitomo Shūshi Shitsu (ed.), pp. 3, 8, 56, 58.

53  Kuroita Katsumi (ed.) (1981), *Tokugawa jikki* (Official chronicles of the Tokugawa Shogunate), Vol. 6, Tokyo: Yoshikawa Kōbunkan, p. 671. Osaka Shishi Hensanjo (ed.) (1969), *Osaka hennenshi* (History of Osaka), Vol. 7, Osaka: Seibundō Shuppan, pp. 49–51.

54  Sumitomo Shūshi Shitsu (ed.) (1986), *Nennen shoyō dome niban sanban* (Annual records of business No 2 and No. 3), No. 2, Kyoto: Shibunkaku Shuppan, p. 6. *Senoku sōkō*, Vol. 18, pp. 106–108.

55  *Ibid.*, p. 19.

56  Glamann (1958), *Dutch Asiatic Trade...*, *op. cit.*, pp. 157–158.

57  *Ibid.*, p. 174.

58  *Ibid.*, p. 173.

59  *Ibid.*, p. 173.

60  Coolhaas, *op. cit.*, Vol. 3, p. 114.

61  *Ibid.*, p. 194. The quantity of total exports from Japan in the previous

year was the same as the quantity of shipments to Europe. A further
study is required to ascertain whether this was just a coincidence, or
if 416,000 kin of the total 1.41 million kin exported from Japan were
sent to Asia, with the rest shipped to the Netherlands.

62 *Ibid.*, p. 235. According to this, 570,000 kin were allocated to Asia.
Although the allocation for Europe was greater than that for Asia, a
subsequent passage confirmed that copper sales in Asia took priority
in principle.

63 *Ibid.*, p. 344.

64 *Ibid.*, p. 871.

65 Glamman (1958), *Dutch Asiatic Trade...*, *op. cit.*, p. 174.

66 Glamann (1953), 'The Dutch East India Company's...', *op. cit.*, p. 60.

67 *Ibid.*, pp. 60–62.

68 Coolhaas, *op. cit.*, Vol. 5, p. 68.

69 *Ibid.*, pp. 543, 649, 666, 711, 820, 833.

70 *Ibid.*, Vol. 2, p. 728.

71 *Ibid.*, Vol. 3, p. 173.

72 *Ibid.*, p. 280. 'Two vessels sailed from Tayouan for Persia carrying 155,000
gulden worth of cargos in sugar and copper'.

73 *Ibid.*, Vol. 2, p. 394.

74 *Ibid.*, p. 412.

75 *Ibid.*, Vol. 3, p. 743. In this article, the quantity is described as '15% picol',
which must be a typographical error, and therefore the actual quantity
is unknown.

76 *Ibid.*, p. 764.

77 *Ibid.*, Vol. 4, pp. 696, 726.

78 *Ibid.*, Vol. 3, p. 263.

79 *Ibid.*, pp. 280, 358, 625, 723.

80 *Ibid.*, p. 803.

81 *Ibid.*, Vol. 4, p. 208.

82 An article dated 29 April 1681 reads, 'Japanese copper does not sell very
profitably in Coromandel' (*Ibid.*, p. 436); there was an oversupply as
copper was brought in from various regions (*Ibid.*, p. 446).

83 *Ibid.*, p. 177.

84 *Ibid.*, p. 368.

85 *Ibid.*, p. 627.

86 *Ibid.*, Vol. 4, p. 699.

87 *Ibid.*, p. 726.

88 *Ibid.*, p. 667.

89 Glamann (1978), 'Nihondo to Jurokuseiki no Pawā...', *op. cit.*, p. 21.

90  Coolhaas, *op. cit.*, Vol. 2, p. 624.
91  *Ibid.*, pp. 730, 741.
92  *Ibid.*, Vol. 3, p. 280.
93  *Ibid.*, p. 732.
94  *Ibid.*, p. 809.
95  *Ibid.*, p. 871.
96  *Ibid.*, p. 485.
97  *Ibid.*, p. 548. An article dated 19 March 1683 shows the goods allocated to Southwest Asia in 1681 and 1682.
98  *Ibid.*, Vol. 5, p. 500.
99  Chaundhuri, *op. cit.*, p. 48 shows trade routes in India around 1650.
100  Coolhaas, *op. cit.*, Vol. 3, p. 686.
101  *Ibid.*, pp. 722–723.
102  *Ibid.*, Vol. 4, p. 118.
103  *Ibid.*, p. 396.
104  *Ibid.*, p. 548.
105  *Ibid.*, p. 734.
106  *Ibid.*, Vol. 5, p. 14.
107  *Ibid.*, p. 270.
108  *Ibid.*, p. 363.
109  Under the *Shōtoku shinrei* of 1715, trade restrictions were strengthened and the number of incoming vessels and the payload permitted in one year were stipulated depending on the origin of the vessels. The payload per vessel was limited to 270 kanme across the board in 1749. By then, the number of incoming *okubune* (Chinese vessels from regions to the south of Indochina) had decreased. Suzuki Yasuko (1992), 'Kanen, Hōreki-ki no Nagasaki bōeki kaikaku (Nagasaki trade reforms in the Kanen and Hōreki eras)', *Nihon rekishi* (Japanese history), No. 532, p. 44.
110  Coolhaas, *op. cit.*, Vol. 4, p. 160.
111  *Ibid.*, p. 309.
112  *Ibid.*, p. 399.
113  *Ibid.*, p. 402.
114  *Ibid.*, p. 427.
115  *Ibid.*, p. 661.
116  *Ibid.*, p. 780.
117  *Ibid.*, p. 788.
118  *Ibid.*, Vol. 5, p. 589.
119  *Ibid.*, Vol. 3, p. 334.
120  *Ibid.*, p. 914.

121  *Ibid.*, Vol. 4, p. 94.

122  *Ibid.*, Vol. 5, p. 546.

123  *Nennen shoyō dome niban sanban*, No. 2, pp. 99–100.

124  Shimizu Hirokazu (ed.) (1990), 'Shōtoku shinrei (The new Shōtoku decree)', *Chūō Daigaku ronshū* (Journal of liberal arts of the Chūō University), No. 11, p. 7. The decree is also reported in *Tsūkō ichiran*, Vol. 4, pp. 305–306 and *Tokugawa kinrei kō* (Collection of Tokugawa enactments), Vol. 1, No. 6, p. 630, but neither reports are accurate.

125  'Dō yushutsudaka 1615–1715 (Copper exports 1615–1715)' in *Senoku sōkō*, Vol. 9 supplement.

126  Kuiper, J. F. (1921), *Japan en de Buiten wereld in de 18e Eeuw*, The Hague: Martinus Nijhof, 1921 p. 113.

127  Sumitomo Shūshi Shitsu (ed.) (1986), *Nennen shoyō dome niban sanban* (Annual records of business Vol. 2 and Vol. 3), Vol. 3, Kyoto: Shibunkaku Shuppan, p. 221.

128  Sumitomo Shūshi Shitsu (ed.) (1992), *Nennen shoyō dome yonban jō* (Annual records of business No. 4[1]), Kyoto: Shibunkaku Shuppan, pp. 117, 125. Nagazumi Yōko (1960), 'Osaka dōza (Osaka copper administration agency)', Chihōshi Kenkyū Kyōgikai (ed.), *Nihon sangyō shi taikei* (History of Japanese industry series), Vol. 6, Tokyo: Tokyo Daigaku Shuppankai, p. 410.

129  Morinaga Taneo, Niwa Kankichi (eds) (1973), *Nagasaki jitsuroku taisei* (Compendium of authentic records of Nagasaki), Nagasaki: Nagasaki Bunkensha, p. 222. Kokusho Kankōkai (1913), *Tsūkō ichiran* (Records of dealings with foreign countries), Vol. 4, p. 343.

130  Blussé, J. L. and W. G. J. Remmelink (eds) (1992), *The Deshima Diaries Marginalia 1700–1740*, Tokyo: Institute of Japan–Netherlands, p. 406, ff. 89–91.

131  Kuiper, *op. cit.*, p. 116.

132  Nakada and Nakamura, *op. cit.*, pp. 47–48.

133  'Getsudō kenbunshū (Things seen and heard by Getsudō)' in Kokusho Kankōkai (1913), *Tsūkō ichiran* (Records of dealings with foreign countries), Vol. 4, p. 350.

134  *Tsūkō ichiran*, Vol. 4, p. 350.

135  'Nagasaki Kudari dō kōyōchō (Official records of copper business in Nagasaki)', No. 1, p. 149.

136  'Nagasaki kōyōchō (Official business records of Nagasaki)', Sumitomo Shiryōkan (1997), *Nagasaki kōyōchō goban*, *Nagasaki kōyōchō niban*, *Nagasaki kōyōchō (1714)* (Official business records of Nagasaki No. 5, official business records of Nagasaki No. 2, official business records

of Nagasaki [1714]), Kyoto: Shibunkaku Shuppan, p. 355. The practice of *tashi gin* (silver supplementation) has already been discussed by Imai. Imai Noriko, 'Hōei, Shōtoku-ki no dō bōeki to Sumitomo (The copper trade in the Hōei and Shōtoku eras and Sumitomo)', *Sumitomo shiryōkan hō* (Sumitomo historical archives report), No. 33, pp. 21–24.

137 *Negotie Journalen* 1723/24, *Het Archief van de Nederlandse Factorij in Japan*, No.901, ARA, reports copper export quantities including so-called 'aid' copper.

138 Iwao Seiichi (1980), *Meiji izen yōba no yunyū to zōshoku* (Importation and propagation of foreign horses before the Meiji period), Tokyo: Nichiran Gakkai, p. 50. Kuiper, *op. cit.*, p. 121. Persian horses were imported in 1725 for the first time to fulfill an order from the shogun Yoshimune.

139 Iwao, *op, cit.*, p. 52, Kuiper, *op.cit.*, p. 125.

140 Kuiper, *op. cit.*, p. 120. However, this directive was a confidential document and later revoked.

141 Blussé and Remmelink, *op. cit.*, p. 408, f. 125.

142 *Register van uittreksels uit Patriase Missiven van Heren XVII aan G.G. en Raden, voornamelijk betreffende Japan, 1734–1749*, Archief Japan, No.477, ARA.

143 J. van Goor (ed.). *Generale Missiven*, Vol. 9, The Hague: Bureau der Rijkscommissie voor Vaderlandse Geschiedenis, 1988, p. 776.

144 Kuiper, *op. cit.*, p. 125.

145 Takayanagi Shinzō and Ishii Ryōsuke (eds) (1934), *Ofuregaki Kanpō shūsei* (Collection of official announcements in the Kanpō era), Tokyo: Iwanami Shoten, pp. 940–941. Ōkurashō Kirokukyoku(ed.) (1922), *Nihon zaisei keizai shiryō* (Japan's financial and economic archival materials), Tokyo: Ōkurashō, p. 748.

146 *Nagasaki jitsuroku taisei*, p. 225. *Tsūkō ichiran*, Vol. 4, pp. 343, 354.

147 The shogunate government announced copper export restrictions in 1743. The quota of 500,000 kin has been adopted here, but it varies between historical materials and documents.
   1) 500,000 kin: *Nagasaki jitsuroku taisei*, p. 225. *Nagasaki jikki nendairoku*, p. 200. Kuiper, *op. cit.*, p. 126.
   2) 600,000 kin: Nagasaki Ken (ed.) (1966), 'Nagasaki kaisho gosatsumono (Five-volume books of Nagasaki trade association) in *Nagasaki ken shi shiryō-hen* (History of Nagasaki prefecture, historical resources edition), No. 4: Yoshikawa Kōbunkan, p. 112.
   3) 500,000–600,000 kin: Meiilan, G. F. (1833), *Geschiedkundig Overzigt*

van den Handel der Europezen op Japan (Historical overview of the trade of Europeans in Japan), Verhandelingen van het Koninklijk Bataviaasch Genootschap van Kunsten en Wetenschappen 14 (Proceedings of the Royal Batavian Society of Arts and Sciences 14), p. 160.

148 Sasaki Junnosuke (1957), 'Kinsei san dō seisaku ni tsuite no ichi kōsatsu (A consideration on early modern copper production policies)', Shigaku zasshi (Journal of the historical society), Vol. 66, No. 2, p. 18.

149 1.5 million kin were exported in 1759 because only 700,000 kin were exported in the previous year and the shortfall was exported together with the year's quota of export copper (Nagasaki jikki nendairoku, p. 221).

150 Meijlan, op. cit., p. 185.

151 (1925) 'Taii sho (Collection of abstracts)' in Honjō Eijirō (ed.), Kinsei shakai keizai sōsho (Early modern society and economy series), Vol. 7: Kaizōsha, p. 1.

152 Tsūkō ichiran, Vol. 4, p. 345. Nagasaki jitsuroku taisei, p. 228.

153 For this reason, only 600,000 kin of 800,000 kin was exported in 1765; a total of 1 million kin (the remaining 200,000 kin plus the next year's quota of 800,000 kin) was exported in 1766.

154 In terms of the significance of the establishment of the dōza in the Meiwa era, the procurement of Nagasaki export copper had been the object of attention in the past but now it is clear that there were other aims such as restraining a steep rise in copper prices for domestic sales and relieving copper refineries. Iwasaki, Yoshinori (1995), 'Kinsei dō tōsei ni kansuru ichi kōsatsu (A consideration on copper regulations in the early modern period)', Kyūshū shigaku (Journal of the Kyushu society of historical research), No. 112.

155 Tokugawa jikki, Vol. 10, p. 224. Honjō Eijirō (ed.) (1969), Dainihon kahei shi (History of Japanese money), Vol. 1, Tokyo: Rekishi Toshosha, p. 32. Tsūkō ichiran, Vol. 4, pp. 142–143. 'Taii sho', op. cit., p. 2.

156 'Nagasaki kaisho gosatsumono', op. cit., pp. 112–113.

157 Isaac Titsingh, Numata Jiro(tr.), Nihon Fuzoku Zushi (Illustrations of Japan), Tokyo: Yūshodoshoten, 1970, p. 267.

158 Morinaga Taneo (ed.) (1974), Zoku Nagasaki jitsuroku taisei (Compendium of authentic records of Nagasaki, second series), Nagasaki: Nagasaki Bunkensha, p. 165. Tsūkō ichiran, Vol. 4, p. 346.

159 Krom, N. J. (1941), Gouverneur Generaal Gustaaf Willem van Imhoff (Governor General Gustaaf Willem van Imhoff), Amsterdam: Van Kampen, p. 99. Rhede van der Kloot, M. A. (ed.) (1981), Gouverneur-Generaal en Commissarissen-Generaal van Nederlandsch-Indie

*1610–1888* (Governors general and commissioners general of the Dutch East Indies 1610–1888) The Hague: Martinus Nijhof, pp. 94–95.

160 'Het Oordeel den Gouverneur Generaal G.W. Baron van Imhoff over den Handel met Japan, in 1744 (Considerations of governor general G. W. Baron van Imhoff on the trade with Japan in 1744)', in *Tijdeschrift voor Nederlandsch Indië* (Dutch Indies Review), 1853, deel 1, pp. 317–342.

161 *Ibid.*, p. 333.

162 Kuiper, *op. cit.*, p. 130.

## Chapter 4

1 Kobata Atsushi (1968), *Nihon kōzan shi no kenkyū* (A study of the history of mining in Japan), Tokyo: Iwanami Shoten, pp. 29–30.

2 Yamawaki Teijirō (1975), 'Oranda Higashi Indo Gaisha to Nihon no kin (The Dutch East India Company and Japanese gold)', *Nihon rekishi* (Japanese history), No. 321. Yamawaki (1980), *Nagasaki no Oranda shōkan* (The Dutch factory in Nagasaki), Tokyo: Chūōkōronsha.

3 Nagazumi Yōko (tr.) (1969), *Hirado Oranda shōkan no nikki* (Diary of the Dutch factory in Hirado), Vol. 3, Tokyo: Iwanami Shoten, p. 169, and (1970), Vol. 4, p. 118.

4 *Ibid.*, Vol. 4, p. 431.

5 Murakami Naojirō (tr) and Nakamura Takashi (ed.) (1972), *Batavia jō nisshi* (Diary of the castle of Batavia), Vol. 2, Tokyo: Heibonsha, p. 29.

6 *Ibid.*

7 *Negotie Journaal* 1640, *Het Archief van de Nederlandse Factorij in Japan 1609–1860* (hereafter referred to as '*Archief Japan*'), No.840, ARA.

8 Very few *ōban* coins were exported. Although there is record of the export of 10 *ōban* pieces in 1666 in *Zoku Nagasaki kagami* (The mirror of Nagasaki part two) (Ecchu Tetsuya (ed.), Nagasaki gakkai sōsho Vol. 7 (Nagasaki: Nagasaki gakkai, 1960), p. 37), there is no corresponding record in the trade journal of the Dutch Factory. *Ōban* exports were probably treated by the Dutch as private cargos outside of the regular trade. In any case, *ōban* was not a noteworthy commodity in terms of business as the volume of export was very small.

9 O. Prakash (1985), *The Dutch East India Company and the Economy of Bengal 1630–1720*, Princeton: Princeton University Press, p. 121.

10 *Ibid.*, p. 123.

11 Nagazumi (1970), *op. cit.*, pp. 444–445.

12 *Ibid.*, p. 537.

13 Murakami Naojirō (tr.) (1956), *Nagasaki Oranda shōkan no nikki*

(Diaries of the Dutch Factory in Nagasaki), Vol. 1, Tokyo: Iwanami Shoten, p. 82. The ban was announced again on 14 August (p. 84).

14 K. N. Chaudhuri (1978), *The Trading World of Asia and the English East India Company 1660–1760*, London, pp. 176–178.

15 K. Glamann (1958), *Dutch–Asiatic Trade 1620–1740*, The Hague: Martinus Nijhoff, p. 60.

16. *Ibid.*, p. 58.

17 F. R. G. S. Campbell (1903), *Formosa under the Dutch*, London, pp. 455–457. *Ibid.*, p. 63.

18 Oskar Nachod (1897), *Die beziehungen der Niederländischen Oostindischen Kompagnie zu Japan im siebzehenten jahrhundert* (The relations between the Dutch East India Company and Japan in the seventeenth century), Berlin: Druck von Pass & Garleb, p. 357.

19 Shinmura Izuru (ed.) (1928), *Nagasaki kongen ki* (A history of Nagasaki), Kaihyō sōsho Vol. 4, Tokyo: Kōseikaku Shuppan, pp. 128–129.

20 Kobata Atsushi (1976), *Kingin bōeki shi no kenkyū* (A study of the history of trade in gold and silver), Tokyo: Hōsei Daigaku Shuppan, p. 1.

21 Nakada Yasunao and Nakamura Tadashi (eds) (1974), *Kiyō gundan* (A collection of records of the Nagasaki region), Tokyo: Kondō Shuppansha, pp, 41–42.

22 Hayashi Fukusai (ed.), *Tsūkō ichiran* (Records of dealings with foreign countries), Vol. 4, (Tokyo: Kokusho Kankōkai, 1912), pp. 269–270.

23 Nakamura Tadashi (1988), *Kinsei Nagasaki bōeki shi no kenkyū* (A study of the history of the Nagasaki trade in the early modern period), Tokyo: Yoshikawa Kōbunkan, pp. 268–269. Ōta Katsuya (1992), *Sakoku jidai Nagasaki bōeki shi no kenkyū* (A study of the history of trade in seclusion era Nagasaki), Kyoto: Shibunkaku Shuppan, pp. 92–114.

24 'Dagregister van de factorij te Decima (Diary of the factory in Dejima)', 5 Nov.1664, *Archief Japan*, No.77, ARA.

25 While only the year 1664 was recorded in *Nagasaki kongen ki*, the diary of the Dutch Factory indicates that the date was 11 November. The date in 'Kanpō nikki (Kanpō diaries)' (in Morinaga Taneo, Ecchu Tetsuya (eds) (1977), *Kanpō nikki to hankachō* (Kanpō diaries and crime records), Nagasaki: Nagasaki Bunkensha, p. 117) is 18 September, which is 5 November on the new calendar. Agreement on the export of *koban* was probably reached on this day. However, it was in August according to other historical materials such as *Zoku Nagasaki kagami* (*op. cit.*, p. 37), 'Nagasaki oboegaki (Nagasaki memoranda)' (in *Tsūkō ichiran*, Vol. 4, p. 282) and *Nagasaki ikyō* (Local history of Nagasaki) (Shiba Hideo (ed.) (1943), Tokyo: Sōrinsha, p. 60).

26  *Nagasaki kongen ki*, p. 129. There is a similar passage in 'Nagasaki shū (Nagasaki collection)' (in *Tsūkō ichiran*, Vol. 4, pp. 279–280) with minor differences in wording.

27  The topic of *aidakin* is explained in archival materials such as 'Kaban kōeki meisai ki (Detailed records of the trade with the Chinese and the Dutch)' (in Nagasaki ken (ed.) (1965), *Nagasaki ken shi shiryō-hen* (History of Nagasaki prefecture, historical resources edition), No. 4: Yoshikawa Kōbunkan, p. 276), *Nagasaki kongen ki* (p. 126), *Nagasaki ikyō* (p. 60), *Tsūkō ichiran* (Vol. 4, p. 297), *Nagasaki jikki nendairoku* (The true chronicles of Nagasaki) (Kyushu Bunkashi Kenkyūjo Shiryōshū Kankōkai (ed.)) (1999), p. 91, and *Kiyō gundan* (p. 115).

28  E. Kaempfer, *The History of Japan: Together with a Description of the Kingdom of Siam*, (London: Maicrofilm (International Research Center for Japanese Studies), 1727) Routledge, pp. 360–361.

29  *Nagasaki jikki nendairoku*, p. 81. *Zoku Nagasaki kagami*, p. 33.

30  *Nagasaki jikki nendairoku*, pp. 81–82. *Zoku Nagasaki kagami*, p. 34.

31  *Nagasaki jikki nendairoku*, p. 82.

32  'Kanpō nikki' (*op. cit.*, p. 117) reports that the margin on 500 *ryō* of *koban* in its first year of export was 3 kanme, which was shared equally in Nagasaki. However, *Nagasaki kongen ki* reports that 500 *ryō* were traded at a margin of around 10 monme per *ryō*, which should amount to a total profit of 5 kanme. These variations in the amount of *aidakin* among archival materials are probably due to different interpretations about the domestic market price of gold at the time. For example, *Nagasaki ryakushi* (An abridged history of Nagasaki) (in Nagasaki shi (1925), Nagasaki sōsho 3, p. 60) estimated that the gold price was 60 monme per *ryō*, which was 2–3 monme lower than the estimation in *Nagasaki kongen ki*.

33  'Dagregister van de factorij te Deshima, 2–3. Jul. 1668', *Archief Japan*, No,81, ARA.

34  *Tsūkō ichiran*, Vol. 4, p. 280.

35  'Dagregister van de factorij te Deshima, 1672.5', *Archief Japan*, No,85, ARA. *Nagasaki kongen ki*, p. 130. Ōkurashō Kirokukyoku (1922), *Nihon zaisei keizai shiryō* (Japan's financial and economic archival materials), Tokyo: Zaisei Keizai Gakkai, pp. 633–634.

36  *Nagasaki kongen ki*, p. 130. *Tsūkō ichiran*, Vol. 4, p. 280.

37  Ōta, *op. cit.*, pp. 226–230.

38  *Tsūkō ichiran*, Vol. 4, p. 281. *Nagasaki kongen ki*, p. 132.

39  *Kanpō nikki to hanka chō*, p. 352. *Kiyō gundan*, p. 115.

40  Kuroita Katsumi (ed.) (1981), *Tokugawa jikki* (Official chronicles of the

Tokugawa Shogunate), Vol. 6, Tokyo: Yoshikawa Kōbunkan, p. 238. Honjō Eijirō (ed.) (1925), *Dainihon kahei shi* (History of Japanese money), Vol. 1, Tokyo: Chōyōkai, p. 214 and (1926), Vol. 8, p. 100.

41 *Nihon zaisei keizai shiryō*, pp. 568–569. Takayanagi Shinzō and Ishii Ryōsuke (eds) (1934), *Ofuregakisho Kanpō shūsei* (Collection of official announcements until the Kanpō era), Tokyo: Iwanami Shoten, p. 892.

42 Kobata Atsushi (1967), *Nihon no kahei* (Japanese money), Tokyo: Shibundō, p. 138.

43 Taya Hirokichi (1963), *Kinsei ginza no kenkyū* (A study of the silver mint in the early modern period), Tokyo: Yoshikawa Kōbunkan, p. 148.

44 'Het Oordeel van den Gouverneur-Generaal G. W. Baron van Imhoff over den handel met Japan, in 1744 (Considerations of governor general G. W. Baron van Imhoff on the trade with Japan in 1744)', *Tijdschrift voor Nederlandsch Indie* (Dutch Indies Review), deel.1, p. 236. The purity of *koban* was reported by van Dam and other archival materials, but with minor variations (see notes 46 and 47 in Chapter Six).

45 'Jedose en Nagasakise Ordres beginnende met Anno 1611 tot 1733, 18 Sep 1697 (Orders by the Shogunate in Edo and Nagasaki, 1611–1733)', *Het Archief van Hoge Regering van Batavia* (Archives of the high government in Batavia), No.141, ARA.

46 'Het Oordeel van den Gouverneur-Generaal G. W. Baron van Imhoff over den handel met Japan, in 1744', p. 326. Van Dam reports a similar purity but the loss is estimated at 17.5 percent or 14.5 percent. See van Dam, p. (1927–1954), *Beschryvinge van de Oostindische Compagnie* (Description of the East India Company) in F. W. Stapel (ed.), 7 volumes, The Hague, tweede boek, deel.1, p. 534, and Note 2.

47 Van Dam, *op. cit.*, p. 540.

48 *Ibid.*, p. 534.

49 *Nagasaki jikki nendairoku*, p. 124.

50 W. Ph. Coolhaas (ed.) (1960–1985), *Generale Missiven van Gouverneurs-Generaal en Raden aan Heren XVII der Oost-indische Compagnie* (Official letters from the governors general and the committees to the gentlemen XVII of the United East India Company), Vol. 6, The Hague: Martinus Nijhoff, p. 334.

51 Kuiper, J. F., *Japan en de Buiten wereld in de 18e Eeuw* (Japan and the outside world in the 18th century), The Hague: Martinus Nijhof, 1921, pp. 98–100.

52 Coolhaas (ed.), *op. cit.*, Vol. 6, p. 488. In addition to the export of silver, it appears that the Dutch were considering whether it would be profit-

able to extract silver from the Genroku *koban* as it had a high silver content. *Ibid.*, p. 364.

53  *Ibid.*, Vol. 7, p. 50.

54  *Ibid.*, p. 13.

55  Blussé, J. L. and W. G. J. Remmelink (eds) (1992), *The Deshima Diaries Marginalia 1700–1740*, Tokyo: Institute of Japan–Netherlands, pp. 163–164, ff. 219–226.

56  'Het Oordeel van den Gouverneur-Generaal G. W. Baron van Imhoff over den handel met Japan, in 1744', p. 327.

57  Coolhaas (ed.), *op. cit.*, Vol. 7, pp. 204–205.

58  Shimizu Hirokazu (ed.) (1990), 'Shōtoku shinrei (The new Shōtoku decree)', *Chūō Daigaku ronshū* (Journal of liberal arts of the Chūō University), No. 11, p. 18.

59  Due to frequent re-coinages after the Keichō *koban*, the Dutch used simple descriptions to distinguish between different series of *koban*. The Keichō *koban* was called 'old fine *koban*' or 'old *koban*', the Genroku *koban* was the 'new crude *koban*', the Kenji *koban* was the 'small *koban*' or the 'light-weight *koban*', the Shōtoku and Kyōhō *koban* were 'new large *koban*' or 'double *koban*', and the Genbun *koban*, minted last, was the 'new *koban*'. These could be easily confused in texts due to their simplicity. For example, Yamawaki Teijirō mentions the export of *ōban* from the Kyōhō era in one of his studies about the *koban* trade by the VOC, but this remark is likely to be based on a misunderstanding of the description of the Kyōhō *koban* (Yamawaki [1975], *op. cit.*, pp. 6–7 and Note 46).

60  Coolhaas, *op. cit.*, Vol. 7, p. 590.

61  *Nagasaki jitsuroku taisei*, p. 224. *Nagasaki jikki nendairoku*, p. 187.

62  Blussé and Remmelink, *op. cit.*, p. 469.

63  J. E. Schooneveld-Oostindische Compagnie (ed.), *Generale Missiven van Gouverneurs generaal en Raden aan Heren XVII der Vereigde Oostindische Compagnie*, Vol. 11, The Hague: Bureau der Rijkscommissie voor Vaderlandse Geschiedenis,1997, p. 529.

64  *Ibid.*, p. 658.

65  Kuiper, *op. cit.*, pp. 303–304.

66  Nagasaki Ken (ed.) (1966), 'Nagasaki kaisho gosatsumono (Five-volume books of Nagasaki trade association) in *Nagasaki ken shi shiryō-hen* (History of Nagasaki prefecture, historical resources edition), No. 4: Yoshikawa Kōbunkan, p. 131. And a 1763 entry in *Nagasaki jikki nendairoku* reads: 'An order was issued to export 70,000 kin of copper instead of 1,000 *ryō* of gold *koban* from this year' (p. 227).

67 Perlin, F. (1933), *The Invisible City—Monetary, Administrative and Popular Infrastructures in Asia and Europe, 1500–1900—*, Hampshire: Variorum, p. 229.

68 Arasaratnam, S. (1986), *Merchants, Companies and Commerce on the Coromandel Coast 1650–1740*, Dehli: Oxford University Press, p. 110. Glamann, *op. cit.*, p. 63.

69 Coolhaas, *op. cit.*, Vol. 7, p. 498. However, the purity of the pagoda coin also was different between the northern and southern parts of the Coromandel coast and from year to year (Arasaratnam, *op. cit.*, pp. 294–300).

70 Stapel, F. W. & J. E. Heeres (eds), *Corpus Diplomaticum Neerlando-Indicum* (Corpus of Dutch–Indonesian diplomatic agreements), 6 volumes (The Hague, 1907–1955), Vol. 3, p. 613.

72 O. Prakash (1994), 'Foreign merchants and Indian mints in the seventeenth and the early eighteenth century', *Precious Metals and Commerce*, Hampshire: Variorum, p. 184.

73 Coolhaas, *op. cit.*, Vol. 3, p. 714. A ton of gold is equivalent to 100,000 gulden.

74 Relevant articles in the *Generale Missiven* are listed below:

| | |
|---|---|
| 31 January 1672 | 132,552 gulden of *koban* (Vol. 3, p. 785) |
| 31 January 1673 | *Koban* shipped (Vol. 3 p. 854) |
| 13 November 1673 | 299,880 gulden of *koban* (Vol. 3, p. 884) |
| 8 October 1674 | *Koban* shipped (Vol. 3, p. 921) |
| 17 November 1674 | 3,523 *ryō* (Vol. 3 p. 948) |
| 31 January 1675 | Masulipatam 248,148 gulden of *koban* (Vol. 4, p. 11) |
| 28 February 1675 | *Koban* shipped (Vol. 4, p. 23) |
| 7 February 1676 | 20,537 *ryō* (Vol. 4, p. 92) |
| 13 February 1677 | *Koban* shipped (Vol. 4, p. 160) |
| 13 March 1680 | *Koban* shipped (Vol. 4, p. 382) |
| 19 March 1683 | *Koban* shipped (Vol. 4, p. 548) |
| 31 December 1683 | 4,892 *ryō* (Vol. 4, p. 619) |
| 30 February 1684 | *Koban* shipped from Ceylon (Vol. 4, p. 724) |
| 12 February 1685 | *Koban* shipped (Vol. 4 p. 764) |
| 11 December 1685 | 10,000 *ryō* from Ceylon (Vol. 4, p. 813) |
| 13 March 1688 | *Koban* shipped (Vol. 5, p. 176) |
| 26 March 1691 | *Koban* shipped (Vol. 5, p. 420) |
| 9 February 1693 | *Koban* shipped (Vol. 5, p. 593). |

75 *De Archieven van de Verengde Oostindishe Compagnie* (Archives of the United East India Company), No.2039, ff. 217–2183, ARA.

76 The average loss per *koban* was not included in Heiningen's report. The

figures in the table were calculated by reference to ex-Japanese prices for the purpose of clarifying changes in the loss rate. Glamann argues that the total loss was more than 1.5 million gulden (Glamann, *op. cit.*, p. 69).

77 Coolhaas, *op. cit.*, Vol. 7, p. 303.

78 *Ibid.*

79 The losses incurred in the *koban* trade were reported in the *Generale Missiven* as follows:

    1) Loss rate of 34%: 5 March 1726 (Vol. 8, p. 79, 98), 31 March 1717 (Vol. 8, p. 114)

    2) Loss rate of 38%: 28 December 1731 (Vol. 9, p. 271), 14 February 1731 (Vol. 9, p. 313), 8 February 1732 (Vol. 9, p. 384)

    3) Loss rate of 39%: 6 April 1736 (Vol. 9, p. 727), 14 October 1736 (Vol. 9, p. 766).

80 Glamann, *op. cit.*, p. 69.

81 Coolhaas, *op. cit.*, Vol. 3, p. 689.

82 *Ibid.*, p. 714.

83 *Ibid.*, p. 743.

84 *Ibid.*, p. 785.

85 *Ibid.*, p. 884.

86 *Ibid.*, Vol. 4, p. 8.

87 *Ibid.*, p. 11. 90 per cent of the total amount of precious metals shipped from Batavia to the Dutch Factory in Hougli was in *koban* in 1674. This suggests that the sale of *koban* was quite profitable in Bengal (Prakash (1985), *op. cit.*, p. 132).

88 Coolhaas, *op. cit.*, Vol. 4, p. 69.

89 *Ibid.*, p. 91.

90 *Ibid.*, p. 424. It is thought that the rising purchase price in Japan was one of the reasons for poor *koban* sales in Bengal from 1672 (Prakash (1985), *op. cit.*, p. 132).

91 Prakash (1985), *op. cit.*, p. 137.

92 A large influx of *koban*, which was profitable in Bengal, reportedly caused the decline in the value of gold from 1675. Gaastra, F. S. (1983), 'Exports of precious metal from Europe to Asia' in J. F. Richards, (ed.), *Precious Metals in the Later Medieval and Early Modern Worlds*, Durham: Carolina Academic Press, p. 465.

93 Coolhaas, *op. cit.*, Vol. 3, p; 950. Transactions in the Indonesian Archipelago were conducted in gold, but it appears that *koban* was not so popular in that region.

94 *Ibid.*, Vol. 4, pp. 382, 548, 619, 724, 734.

95  Nagazumi (1969), *op. cit.*, Vol. 4, pp. 404, 413.
96  Coolhaas, *op. cit.*, Vol. 3, p. 614.
97  *Ibid.*, p. 916.
98  Van der Chijs, J. A. (ed.) (1885–1900), *Nederlandsch–Indisch Plakaatboek 1602–1811* (Book of the Dutch East Indies), 17 vols., The Hague, Vol. 2: Landsdrukkerij, p. 563.
99  Coolhaas, *op. cit.*, Vol. 4, pp. 747, 816, Vol. 4, p. 57. It appears that export quantities remained small due to circumstances in Japan during the 1680s, especially the export ban on *koban* imposed by the shogunate from 1685–1686 (Glamann, *op. cit.*, p. 63).
100 According to Kuiper, Batavia came up with an idea in 1729 to remove *koban*-related losses incurred regularly in Southwest Asia out of its books and transfer them to the books of the factory in Japan, issuing a directive to that effect. This reduced the net profit of its Japan Factory to 9–12 per cent but it returned to the 30–50 per cent level after the directive was cancelled three years later (Kuiper, *op. cit.*, p. 117). These *koban*-related losses were incurred by re-minting *koban* into the pagoda and fanum gold coins in Coromandel. According to the *Generale Missiven*, this practice of transferring these losses to the Japan Factory accounts ceased in 1730 (Van Goor, J. (ed.), *Generale Missiven van Gouverneurs-Generaal en Raden aan Heren XVII der Verenigde Ooseindische Compagnie*, Vol. 9, The Hague: Martinus Nijhof, 1988, p. 164).
101 Attman, A. (1983), *Dutch Enterprise in the World Bullion Trade 1550–1800*, Goteborg: Kungl. Vetenskaps och Vitterhets-Samhället, pp. 29–30.
102 Glamann, *op. cit.*, p. 69.
103 Ōno Mizuo (1996), *Edo bakufu zaiseishi ron* (Treatises on financial history of the Tokugawa shogunate), Tokyo: Yoshikawa Kōbunkan, pp. 200–201.

## Chapter 5

1  Nihon Senbai Kōsha (ed.) (1956), *Shōnō senbai shi* (History of camphor monopoly), Tokyo: Nihon Senbai Kōsha, p. 2.
2  Yamada Kentarō (1978), *Kōryō* (Spices), Tokyo: Hōsei Daigaku Shuppankyoku, pp. 146–147.
3  Yamada Kentarō (1964), *Kōryō no rekishi* (History of spices), Tokyo: Kinokuniya Shoten, p. 64.
4  Yamada Kentarō (1942), *Tōa kōryō shi* (East Asian history of spices), Tokyo: Tōyōdō; (1956), *Tōzai kōyaku shi* (History of medicinal spices

in the East and the West), Tokyo: Fukumura Shoten; (1964), *op. cit.*;
(1976), *Tōa kōryō shi kenkyū* (A study of the history of spices in East
Asia), Tokyo: Chūō Kōron Bijutsu Shuppan; (1977), *Kōryō no michi*
(The spice road), Tokyo: Chūō Kōronsha; (1979), *Kōryō hakubutsu
jiten* (Encyclopedia of spices), Tokyo: Dōhōsha; (1978), *op. cit.*; (1980),
*Kōyaku tōzai* (Medicinal spices in the East and the West), Tokyo: Hōsei
Daigaku Shuppankyoku.

5 Miyashita Saburō (1997), *Nagasaki bōeki to Osaka* (Nagasaki trade and
Osaka), Osaka: Seibundō Shuppan.

6 Suzuki Hajime (1934), 'Shōju oyobi shōnō ni tsuite (Camphor tree
and camphor)', *Kagoshima kōtō nōrin gakkō dai 25-shūnen kinen
ronbun shū* (Collected papers commemorating the 25th anniversary
of the Kagoshima college of agriculture and forestry) in Nagasaki
Prefectural Library Archives. Murano Moriharu (1960), 'Satsuma no
shōnō (Satsuma camphor)' in Chihōshi Kenkyū Kyōgikai (ed.), *Nihon
sangyō shi taikei* (History of Japanese industry series), Vol. 7, Tokyo:
Tokyo Daigaku Shuppankai.

7 Hirao Michio (1956), *Tosa han ringyō keizai shi* (An economic history
of forestry in the Tosa domain), Kōchi: Kōchi Shimin Toshokan.
Yamamoto Takeo (1986), 'Tosa no shōnō (Tosa camphor)', *Tosa shidan*
(A historical story of Tosa), No. 171 and (1998), 'Tosa ni okeru shōnō
seisan no suii (Changes in camphor production in Tosa)', *op. cit.*, No.
209.

8 Iwao Seiichi (1940), *Kagoshima ken shi* (History of Kagoshima
prefecture), Vol. 2: Kagoshima Ken and (1958), *Shuin sen bōeki shi no
kenkyū* (Historical study of trade by red seal ships), Tokyo: Kōbundō.
Yamawaki Teijirō (1980), *Nagasaki no Oranda shōkan* (The Dutch
factory in Nagasaki), Tokyo: Chūō Kōronsha.

9 Yamada (1978), *op. cit.*, p. 147.

10 *Ibid.*, p. 149.

11 Doi Tadao, Morita Takeshi and Chōnan Minoru (eds) (1980), *Nippo jisho*
(Japanese–Portuguese dictionary), Tokyo: Iwanami Shoten, p. 794.

12 'Meiji 5-nen shōnō seihō hatsumei no negaisho (An application
concerning the invention of camphor production method in 1872)', in
the possession of the Kagoshima Prefectural Library.

13 Murano, *op. cit.*, pp. 138–139.

14 Yamada (1978), *op. cit.*, pp. 154–155.

15 Abe Keiji (1978), 'Shōnō no seizō to Tei Sōkan (Camphor production
and Tei Sōkan)', *Kikan sanzenri* (Quarterly three thousand leagues),
No. 25, pp. 113–114.

16  Terashima Yoshiyasu (ed.) (1970), *Wakan sansai zue* (Illustrated Sino-Japanese encyclopedia), Vol. 2, Tokyo: Tokyo Bijutsu, p. 1169.

17  Hirase Tessai (1992), 'Nihon sankai meibutsu zue (Illustrated encyclopedia of notable Japanese products)' in Asami Megumi and Yasuda Ken (eds & trs), *Nihon sangyō shi shiryō* (The collected historical materials on Japanese industries), No. 1, Introduction, Tokyo: Kasumigaseki Shuppan, pp. 470–471.

18  Ono Ranzan, *Jūtei honzō kōmoku keimō* (Revised edition botanical classification), Masamune Atsuo (ed.) (1929), Nihon koten zenshū (The collected Japanese classics) Vol. 14, Tokyo: Nihon Koten Zenshū Kankōkai, p. 660.

19  Yamada Tamaki (tr.) (1928), *Tsunberuku Nihon kikō* (Thunberg's travels in Japan), Ikoku sōsho (Foreign country series), Vol. 4, Tokyo: Sunnansha, p. 379, a Japanese translation of C. P. Thunberg (1788–1793), *Resa uti Europa, Africa, Asia, förratta åren 1770–79* (Travels to Europa, Africa, Asia etc. 1770–1779), Upsala. E. Kaempfer and P. F. Siebold did not mention any camphor production methods. Kaempfer, who came to Japan in 1690, wrote a brief comment about camphor in his book: 'the satsuma domain possessed another two provinces in kyūshū; it is next to Fisen in extent, but far superior to it, and indeed to all others in this island, in riches and power, having the best foldiers, and producing a great quantity of camphire' (E. Kaempfer (1727–1728), *The History of Japan*, London: p. 456). Siebold, who arrived in Japan in 1823, wrote, 'Cinnamomum camphora, camphor is produced from this tree in the southern regions of Japan'. (Siebold, Philipp Franz von (1978), *Nippon* (Japan), translated by Nakai Akio and Saitō Shin, Vol. 2, Tokyo: Yūshōdō Shoten, p. 227).

20  Murano, *op. cit.*, p. 145.

21  Nōrin Shō (1933a), *Nihon rinsei shi shiryō (Kagoshima han)* (Historical materials on Japan's forestry (Kagoshima domain)), Tokyo: Chōyōkai, pp. 345, 385–386.

22  Shinmura Izuru and Takenouchi Waka (eds) (1943), *Kefukigusa*, Tokyo: Iwanami Shoten, p. 186.

23  In possession of the Kagoshima Prefectural Library.

24  *Sangoku meishō zue* (Illustrated encyclopedia of the features of the three countries, i.e. Satsuma, Ōsumi, and Hūga), part missing, in possession of Tokyo Daigaku Shiryō Hensanjo. Murano, *op. cit.*, p. 140.

25  'Kagoshima han shōnōsan enkaku (A history of camphor forests in the Kagoshima domain)' in Nihon Senbai Kōsha, *op. cit.*, p. 12.

26  Camphor produced on the Gotō Islands was also exported according
    to the aforementioned travelogue by Thunberg, but no other record
    to that effect has been found so far. If it was in fact exported, the
    volume would have been very small compared with Satsuma camphor.
    Camphor production on the Gotō Islands began to thrive during the
    Meiji period (Suzuki, *op. cit.*, p. 422).

27  Nōrin Shō (1933b), *Nihon rinsei shi shiryō (Kōchi han)* (Historical
    materials on Japan's forestry (Kōchi domain)), Tokyo: Chōyōkai, pp.
    698–699.

28  'Shōnō seizō hō (Camphor production method)' in Takamatsu Toyokichi
    (ed.) (1954), *Kagaku kōgyō zensho* (Chemical industry series), Vol. 4,
    Tokyo: Maruzen Shoten, pp. 229–247. 'Shōnō seizō no hō (Camphor
    production method)' in Asami and Yasuda, *op. cit.*, Vol. 4, pp. 449–466.
    'Shōnō seizō no hō (Camphor production method)' in Yagihashi Shin
    et al. (eds) (1998), *Nihon nōgyō zensho* (Japanese agriculture series), Vol.
    53, Tokyo: Nōsangyōson Bunka Kyōkai, pp. 396–414. The distillation
    method spread nationally from the Meiji period.

29  Nōrin Shō (1933b), *op. cit.*, p. 773.

30  Nichiran Gakkai (ed.) (1989), *Nagasaki Oranda shōkan nikki* (The diary of
    the Dutch Factory in Nagasaki), Vol. 1, Tokyo: Yūshōdō Shoten, p. 310.

31  Nichiran Gakkai (ed.) (1990), *Nagasaki Oranda shōkan nikki* (The diary
    of the Dutch factory in Nagasaki), Vol. 2, Tokyo: Yūshōdō Shoten, p. 17.

32  Oskar Nachod (1897), *Die beziehungen der Niederländischen Oostin-
    dischen Kompagnie zu Japan im siebzehenten jahrhundert* (The relations
    between the Dutch East India Company and Japan in the seventeenth
    century), Berlin: Druck von Pass & Garleb, p. 130. According to Seiichi
    Iwao, 6,000–7,000 kin of camphor were shipped to Siam on the red seal
    vessels in 1619. Iwao (1958), *Shuinsen bōeki shi no kenkyū* (A study of
    the history of the red seal ship trade), Tokyo: Kōbundō, p. 256.

33  Nōrin Shō (1933a), *op. cit.*, p. 6. The 'Kagoshima omawaribumi tome
    (Record of official notices of Kagoshima)' of 1677 also stated that
    camphor was one of the 'goods not to be taken out abroad' (p. 42).

34  Nagazumi Yōko (tr.) (1969), *Hirado Oranda shōkan no nikki* (Diary of the
    Dutch factory in Hirado), Vol. 3, Tokyo: Iwanami Shoten, pp. 16–17.

35  *Ibid.*, p. 542. Nagazumi Yōko (1972), 'Hirado han to Oranda bōeki (The
    Hirado domain and Dutch trade)', *Nihon rekishi* (Japanese history),
    No. 286, p. 5.

36  Nagazumi (1969), *op. cit.*, p. 18.

37  *Ibid.*, p. 360.

38 *Ibid.*, pp. 375, 378, 389. Nagazumi Yōko (tr.) (1970), *Hirado Oranda shōkan no nikki* (Diary of the Dutch factory in Hirado), Vol. 4, Tokyo: Iwanami Shoten, pp. 172, 277, 309.

39 Kagoshimaken Shiryō Kankōkai (ed.) (1973), *Honhan jinbutsu shi* (Who's who of the Satsuma domain), Kagoshimaken shiryōshū (The collected historical materials of Kagoshima prefecture), Vol. 13, Kagoshima.
   • Shimazu Danjō Daihitsu Hisayoshi, a senior retainer from 1634.
   • Niiro Kaga-no-kami Tadakiyo, was not a senior retainer to the lord of the Ōguchi district from 1628.
   • Kawakami Sakon Shōgen Hisakuni, a senior retainer from 1630.

40 Harimaya returned to Hirado with a reply from Satsuma on 27 April. (Nagazumi (1969), *op. cit.*, p. 439) 'Negotie Journaal, 27. Apr. 1637', *Het Archief van de Nederlandse Factorij in Japan*, No.837, ARA.

41 The Shimabara conflict happened in October of that year on the old calendar. Camphor transactions were usually conducted from August to October on the old calendar. The Dutch vessels departed Nagasaki during a period from 20 November to 18 December (4 October to 2 November on the old calendar) in that year (see Table 25). It is therefore unlikely that the failure to procure camphor in this instance was a consequence of the Shimabara conflict.

42 Nagazumi's translation was partially modified with reference to Tokyo Daigaku Shiryō Hensanjo (ed.) (1977), *Oranda shōkanchō nikki* (Diary kept by the head of the Dutch Factory), original text edition Vol. 3, Tokyo: Tokyo Daigaku Shuppankai, p. 342. Nagazumi (1970), *op. cit.*, pp. 164–265.

43 Murakami Naojirō (tr) and Nakamura Takashi (ed.) (1975), *Batavia jō nisshi* (Diary of the castle of Batavia), Vol. 3, Tokyo: Heibonsha, pp. 74–75.

44 Jan van Elseracq, the head of the factory in Japan, ordered 600–700 picol (60,000–70,000 kin) that year (*Ibid.*, p. 96).

45 *Ibid.*

46 *Ibid.*

47 Murakami Naojirō (tr.) (1956), *Nagasaki Oranda shōkan no nikki* (Diaries of the Dutch Factory in Nagasaki), Vol. 1, Tokyo: Iwanami Shoten, p. 220.

48 'Negotie Journaal, 3 Jul', *Archief Japan*, No.843, ARA.

49 Murakami, *op. cit.*, p. 315.

50 *Ibid.*, p. 377.

51 'Negotie Journalen, 20. Nov. 1644', Archief Japan, No.845, ARA.
52 Murakami Naojirō (tr.) (1957), Nagasaki Oranda shōkan no nikki (Diaries of the Dutch Factory in Nagasaki), Vol. 2, Tokyo: Iwanami Shoten, p. 301 (15 June 1650).
53 Murakami Naojirō (tr.) (1958), Nagasaki Oranda shōkan no nikki (Diaries of the Dutch Factory in Nagasaki), Vol. 3, Tokyo: Iwanami Shoten, p. 32 (27 October 1650).
54 It is '6.5 gulden per one hundred kin' in the translation, but it is clear from journal records that it was 6.5 tael (Murakami (1958), Ibid., Vol. 2, p. 300).
55 Ibid., Vol. 3, p. 32.
56 Ibid., p. 75.
57 W. Ph. Coolhaas (ed.) (1960–1985), Generale Missiven van Gouverneurs-Generaal en Raden aan Heren XVII der Oost-indische Compagnie (Official letters from the Governors General and the committees to the Gentlemen XVII of the United East India Company), Vol. 2, The Hague: Martinus Nijhoff, p. 546.
58 Murakami (1958), op, cit., Vol. 3, p. 185.
59 Ibid., pp. 230–231.
60 Ibid., pp. 245–246.
61 Ibid., p. 259.
62 Ibid., p. 304.
63 Ibid., p. 311.
64 Coolhaas, op. cit., Vol. 3, pp. 114–115. 'The medicine' ('dat medicinael' in the original text) means camphor.
65 Ibid., p. 235.
66 'Sappan kinzan torishirabesho (Report on gold mines in the Satsuma domain)' in possession of the Keio University Library. The Yamagano gold mine was discovered in 1640 and mined until a mining ban was issued by the shogunate government because of the Great Famine of Kanei in 1643.
67 Kobata Atsushi (1966), Kōzan no rekishi (The history of mines), Tokyo: Shibundō, pp. 101–102, 131. Ōhashi Hiroshi (1960), 'Kyūshū no kingin kōzan (Gold and silver mines in Kyūshū)' in Chihōshi Kenkyū Kyōgikai (ed.), Nihon sangyō shi taikei (History of Japanese industry series), Vol. 8 Kyūshū region edition, Tokyo: Tokyo Daigaku Shuppankai, pp. 203–210.
68 Nachod, op. cit., pp. 358–359.
69 In the Generale Missiven, Japanese camphor was rarely mentioned after an article that read, 'Camphor from Japan was distributed to Persia,

Surat and Coromandel in 1669' (Coolhaas, *op. cit.*, Vol. 3, p. 665). A
majority of the references to camphor up to around 1674 were about
camphor produced in Baros.

70 Yamada Kentarō (1979), *Kōryō hakubutsu jiten* (Encyclopedia of spices),
Tokyo: Dōhōsha, pp. 237–241. C. J. S. Thompson (1998), *Kōryō bunka
shi* (The mystery and lure of perfume), translated by Yūji Komazaki,
Tokyo: Yasaka Shobō, pp. 42–45.

71 Dunlop, H. (ed.) (1930), *Bronnen tot de Geshiedenis der Oostindische Compagnie in Perzie 1611–1638* (Resources for the history of the East India
Company in Persia 1611–1638), The Hague: Martinus Nijhoff, p. 28.

72 *Ibid.*, p. 118.

73 *Ibid.*, p. 217.

74 *Ibid.*, p. 264.

75 *Ibid.*, p. 509. This record states that the shipment of camphor was part
of the 20,190 catty exported from Japan on board the *Venloo*.

76 'Negotie Journaal, 12. Dec. 1633', *Archief Japan* No.834, ARA.

77 Dunlop, *op. cit.*, p. 589.

78 Coolhaas, *op. cit.*, Vol. 2, p. 206.

79 *Ibid.*, p. 550.

80 Van Dam, P. (1939), *'Beschryvinge van de Oostindische Compagnie*
(Description of the East India Company) in F. W. Stapel (ed.), tweede
boek deel. 3, The Hague: Martinus Nijhoff, pp. 360–361.

81 Coolhaas, *op. cit.*, Vol. 3, p. 665.

82 *Ibid.*, Vol. 4, p. 284.

83 *Ibid.*, p. 364.

84 It is inserted between p. 550 and p. 551 of *Kagoshima ken shi*, Vol. 2.

85 An article dated 24 December 1652 in the *Generale Missiven* reports that
the profit rate of Japanese camphor was about 56 per cent (Coolhaas,
*op. cit.*, Vol. 2, p. 624). However, it was 85.6 per cent in 1652 according
to Table 27. Profit rates calculated from this table are only for reference
purposes because they do not take into account transport and other
costs. The actual rate would be lower than this.

86 *Ibid.*, Vol. 2, p. 300.

87 *Ibid.*, p. 647.

88 *Ibid.*, Vol. 4, 1679, p. 284; 1684, p. 724; 1685, p. 816.

89 *Ibid.*, 1679, p. 284; 1684, p. 724.

90 Murakami and Nakamura, *op. cit.*, Vol. 3, p. 96. 15,000–16,000 pond were
ordered in 1661 (*Ibid.*, p. 237).

91 Coolhaas, *op. cit.*, Vol. 4, p. 486.

92 *Ibid.*, Vol. 2, p. 760.

93  Ibid., Vol. 3, p. 515.
94  It is reported in the *Generale Missiven* that 'Only 10,275 pond of camphor were acquired' (Vol. 6, p. 164). The correct amount should be 10, 375 pond (see Note 10, Table 30).
95  Ibid., p. 222.
96  Ibid., p. 243.
97  Ibid., p. 269.
98  Ibid., p. 334.
99  Ibid., p. 393. In the original text, the unit price is expressed in rixdaalder (rijksdaarder) instead of tael. It has been converted on the basis of '24 rixdaalder or 20.57 tael per 1 picol = 120 pond', as stated in the *Generale Missiven* in 1704. According to this conversion rate, 28 rixdaalder = 24 tael or 35 rixdaalder = 30 tael.
100  Ibid., p. 428.
101  'Negotie Journaal, 26. Oct. 1706', *Archief Japan*, No.886, ARA.
102  Tokyo Daigaku Shiryō Hensanjo (ed.) (1962), *Tō tsūji kaisho nichiroku* (Diaries of the Chinese interpreters association), Vol. 4, Tokyo: Tokyo Daigaku Shuppankai, pp. 112–113.
103  *Tōban kamotsu chō* (Registers of Chinese and European cargos) published in 1969–1970 by Naikaku Bunko.
104  Nagazumi Yōko (ed.) (1987), *Tōsen yushutsunyūhin sūryō ichiran* (A catalogue of exports and imports by the Chinese fleet), Tokyo: Sōbunsha, pp. 256–261. Camphor was still exported from 1718 to 1753, but shipments were infrequent and amounts were small.
105  Coolhaas, *op. cit.*, Vol. 7, p. 154.
106  Ibid., p. 181.
107  Ibid., p. 504.
108  Ibid., p. 474.
109  Nichiran Gakkai (1989), *op. cit.*, Vol. 1, p. 47.
110  Ibid., p. 90.
111  Ibid., pp. 228–234.
112  Nichiran Gakkai (ed.) (1991), *Nagasaki Oranda shōkan nikki* (The diary of the Dutch factory in Nagasaki) Vol. 3, Tokyo: Yūshōdō Shoten, pp. 247–248.
113  The circumstances surrounding the arrival of the British ships are described in detail in Saitō Agu (1922), *Zūfu to Nihon* (H. Doef and Japan): Kōbunkan, Chapters 8 and 9.
114  'Cassa Rekening staat en inventaris 1812/13', *Archief Japan*, No. 1434, ARA., 'Cassa Rekening Anno 1814', *Archief Japan*, No. 1435, ARA. Nihon Senbai Kōsha (1956), *op. cit.*, p. 20.

115 'Sappan kinzan torishirabesho (Report on gold mines in the Satsuma domain)', *op. cit.*

## Chapter 6

1 *De Archieven van de Verenigde Oostindische Compagnie* No.2039, ff. 2178–2183, ARA. This is document No. 1931 of the original colonial archives (*Koloniaal Archief*). While this document is the source of Glamann's table of copper sales in Asia by region, the remaining part of it has not been introduced to the world in detail. K.Glamann, 'The Dutch East India Company's trade in Japanese copper 1645–1736', *Scandinavian Economic History Review*, Vol. 1, No. 1, 1953, p. 54.

2 W. Ph. Coolhaas (ed.) (1960–1985), *Generale Missiven van Gouverneurs-Generaal en Raden aan Heren XVII der Oost-indische Compagnie* (Official letters from the governors general and the committees to the board of the VOC), 8 vols., Vol. 7, The Hague: Martinus Nijhoff, p. 451.

3 *Ibid.*, Vol. 8, p. 125.

4 *Ibid.*, p. 98. The company expected future profits from its trade with Japan based on their calculations, even though profits on copper and camphor shipments to the Netherlands were unknown.

5 Kuiper, J. F., *Japan en de Buiten wereld in de 18e Eeuw* (Japan and the outside world in the 18th century), The Hague, Martinus Nijhoff, 1921, p. 306. Annual profits of the Dutch Factory in Japan were reported in an article dated 31 January 1705 in the *Generale Missiven*; Kuiper's figures are consistent with them but the profit rates are different (Coolhaas, *op. cit.*, Vol. 6, pp. 332–333).

6 Kuiper, *op. cit.*, p. 98.

7 Nagazumi Yōko (1985), 'Shōtoku shinrei to Oranda bōeki (The new law of Shōtoku and the Dutch trade)', in Miyazaki Michio (ed.), *Arai Hakuseki no gendaiteki kōsatsu* (A contemporary study on Hakuseki Arai), Tokyo: Yoshikawa Kōbunkan, pp. 73–74.

8 See Table 20.

9 T. Raychaudhuri (1962), *Jan Company in Coromandel 1605–1690*, Verhandelingen van het Koninklijk Institut voor Taal, Land, en Volkenkunde (Series of the Royal Netherlands Institute of Southeast Asian and Caribbean Studies), deel. 38, The Hague, p. 191. K. Glamann (1958), *Dutch–Asiatic Trade 1620–1740*, The Hague: Martinus Nijhoff, p. 63 (see Chapter Three).

10 Van Dam, P. , *Beschryvinge van de Oostindische Compagnie* (Description

of the East India Company), in F. W. Stapel (ed.), tweede boek deel. 1, (The Hague: Martinus Nijhoff, 1931), p. 534.

11 Camphor was called 'Japansche Campher (Japanese camphor)' up to 1661; the name 'Satsumase Campher (Satsuma camphor)' began to appear in 1662 and the both names coexisted for a while. The latter became the standard name from around 1671.

12 Yamada Kentarō (1956), *Tōzai kōyaku shi* (History of medicinal spices in the East and the West), Tokyo: Fukumura Shoten, p. 35.

13 *Negotie Journaal, Het Archief van de Nederlandse Factorij in Japan*, No. 901, ARA. The total value of the cargo on the Kasteel van Woerden was 519,378 gulden according to a record dated 4 February 1724, including 324,217 gulden of copper, 151,701 gulden of *koban* and 31,544 gulden of camphor.

14 The VOC posted a governor in each region to rule its territories. In around 1685, provinces in which a governor (*Gouverneur*) was stationed included Amboyna, Banda, the Moluccas, Coromandel, Ceylon and Malacca. The Cape of Good Hope, the northern coast of Java, and Makassar were added to the list one century later. A director (*Directeur*: an officer involved in trade) was stationed at commercially important factories such as Bengal, Surat and Persia. Factories in Malabar, the western Sumatra coast, and Bantan were headed by a commanding officer (*commandeur*), while factories in other regions were overseen by a commissioner or a head of the factory (*president* or *opperhoofd*, respectively) (Gaastra, F. S. (1982), *de Geschiedenis van de VOC* (The history of the VOC), Haarlem, pp. 65–66. Wijnaendts van Resandt, W. (ed.) (1944), *De Gezaghebbers der Oost-Indische Compagnie op hare Buiten-Comptoiren in Azië* (Lieutenants of the East India Company at its foreign branches in Asia, Amsterdam). These were very different in nature from the residencies of the governors and directors during the Indonesian colonial period. The number of company employees posted in each region may serve as an indicator of how important that region was at the time. In 1700, there were 2,966 in Ceylon, 514 in Coromandel, 690 in Malabar, 162 in Bengal and 106 in Surat (Gaastra, *op. cit.*, p. 82).

15 According to Raychaudhuri (*op. cit.*, p. 1), Coromandel included the whole of east coast of the Indian Peninsula in a broad sense, from the Godavari River to Negapatam, or Mannar Island. According to Arasaratnam, it covered a broader area in the seventeenth century than in the nineteenth and twentieth centuries, extending from Point Calimere

to Ganjam Port (Arasaratnam, S. (1986), *Merchants, Companies and Commerce on the Coromandel Coast 1650–1740*, Delhi, p. 7).

16 Arasaratnam, *op. cit.*, p. 295.

17 Raychaudhuri, *op. cit.*, p. 196. Coolhaas, *op. cit.*, Vol. 6, pp. 247–248.

18 Arasaratnam, S. (1967), 'The Dutch East India Company and its Coromandel trade 1700–1740', *Bijdragen tot de Taal, Land en Volkenkunde* (Journal of the Royal Netherlands Institute of Southeast Asian and Caribbean Studies), deel. 123, The Hague, p. 332.

19 Coolhaas, *op. cit.*, Vol. 6, p. 248.

20 *Ibid.*, p. 364.

21 *Ibid.*, pp. 396, 398.

22 *Ibid.*, Vol. 7, p. 181.

23 *Ibid.*, p. 497.

24 *Ibid.*, Vol. 6, p. 308.

25 *Ibid.*, p. 867.

26 O. Prakash (1985), *The Dutch East India Company and the Economy of Bengal 1630–1720*, New Jersey: Princeton University Press, p. 140.

27 *Ibid.*, pp. 140, 249. O. Prakash (1986), 'European trade and the economy of Bengal in the seventeenth and the early eighteenth century', J. van Goor (ed.), *Trading Companies in Asia 1600–1830*, Utrecht: HES Uitgevers, p. 22.

28 Coolhaas, *op. cit.*, Vol. 6, p. 134.

29 *Ibid.*, p. 257.

30 *Ibid.*, p. 323.

31 Kyūshū Bunkashi Kenkyūjo Shiryōshū Kankōkai (ed.) (1999), *Nagasaki jikki nendairoku* (The true chronicles of Nagasaki), Fukuoka, p. 139. Niwa Kankichi, Morinaga Taneo (eds), *Nagasaki jitsuroku taisei* (Compendium of authentic records of Nagasaki), (Nagasaki: Nagasaki Bunkensha,1973), p. 220.

32 Coolhaas, *op. cit.*, Vol. 6, p. 428.

33 Bruijn, J. R., F. S. Gaastra, and I. Schoffer (eds), *Dutch–Asiatic Shipping in the 17th and 18th Centuries, 1595–1795*, 3 vols., The Hague: Martinus Nijhof, 1979–1987.

34 Kuiper, *op. cit.*, p. 113.

35 Glamann (1953), 'Dutch East India…', *op. cit.*, p. 55.

36 Coolhaas, *op. cit.*, Vol. 6, pp. 326, 328, 445, 573.

37 Glamann (1953), 'Dutch East India…', *op. cit.*, p. 59.

38 Coolhaas, *op. cit.*, Vol. 6, pp. 93, 549, 560.

39 *Ibid.*, Vol. 6, p. 622.

40 *Ibid.*, Vol. 7, pp. 380, 454, 535, 606.

41  *Ibid.*, Vol. 6, p. 308 (30 November 1709). The amount reported here is 22,000 kisten, which is 2,200,000 kin. This amount has been converted into pond.

42  *Ibid.*, Vol. 7, p. 526.

43  The only available statistical resource on camphor sales in Asia is the sales records of the Surat factory presented by Iwao Seiichi in *Kagoshima ken shi* (The history of Kagoshima prefecture), 1940, Vol. 2, Kagoshima, a photographed version inserted between pp. 250 and 551).

44  Coolhaas, *op. cit.*, Vol. 6, p. 97 (8 January 1700).

45  According to van Imhoff's description, the Keichō *koban* was the 'old *koban*', the Genroku *koban* was the 'new type of *koban*', the Kenji *koban* was the 'small *koban*' and the Kyōhō *koban* was the 'double *koban*' ('Het Oordeel den Gouverneur Generaal G. W. Baron van Imhoff over den Handel met Japan, in 1744 (Considerations of governor general G. W. Baron van Imhoff on the trade with Japan in 1744)', in *Tijdeschrift voor Nederlandsch Indië* (Dutch Indies Review), 1853, deel 1, pp. 326–327). In the *Generale Missiven*, the Keichō *koban* was described as the 'old fine *koban*', the Genroku *koban* was the 'new type of *koban*' or 'new crude *koban*', the Kenji *koban* was the '(new) small *koban*, light *koban*' and the Kyōhō *koban* was the 'large *koban*'. There were no clearly standardized names for *koban* types.

46  'Het Oordeel den Gouverneur Generaal G. W. Baron van Imhoff over den Handel met Japan, in 1744', *op. cit.*, p. 326. Meijlan, G. F. (1833), 'Geschiedkundig Overzigt van den Handel der Europezen op Japan (Historical overview of the trade of Europeans in Japan)', *Verhandelingen van het Koninklijk Bataviaasch Genootschap van Kunsten en Wetenschappen* 14 (Proceedings of the Royal Batavian Society of Arts and Sciences), p. 156. The qualities of the Keichō *koban* and the Genroku *koban* according to the Japanese and Dutch historical resources are as follows.
  1) 'Tokugawa shi kahei ichiranhyō (Currency of the Tokugawa government)' (surveyed by Kōga Yoshimasa, Zōheikyoku (1921), *Zōheikyoku enkaku shi* (Historical records of the mint bureau)).
      Keichō *koban*    84.29 %(1)    86.23 %(2)
      Genroku *koban*   57.37 %(1)    56.41 %(2)
      Official purity (1) and purity based on a number of tests (2).
  2) 'Kyū kahei hyō (Old currency list)' (prepared by Chūzaburō Satō, in Mitsui Takasumi (1973), *Shinkō ryōgae nendaiki kaiken* (New edition chronicled records of money exchange), Vol. 1 resources section, Tokyo: Kashiwa Shobō).

Keichō *koban*      84.29 %

Genroku *koban*      57.37 %

3) 'Edo jidai bakufu kahei ichiranhyō (Currency of the shogunate government during the Edo period)' (Taya Hirokichi (1973), 'Edo jidai kahei hyō no saikentō (Reexamination of the currency in the Edo period)', *Shakai keizai shigaku* (Socio-economic history), 39(3), p. 35.

Keichō *koban*      86.79 %

Genroku *koban*      57.36 %

4) Van Dam, *op. cit.*, p. 534. This document, describing all aspects of the company's activity, was edited by van Dam at the request of the VOC board in 1693 and submitted in 1701.

Keichō *koban*      85.9 % (20 carat 4.5 grain)

Genroku *koban*      55.54 % (13 carat 4 grain)

5) Van Imhoff, 'Het Oordeel den Gouverneur Generaal G. W. Baron van Imhoff over den Handel met Japan, in 1744', p. 326. This is a report presented at the Council of the Dutch East Indies in 1744.

Keichō *koban*      86.29–86.79 % (20 carat 8.5 grain – 20 carat 10 grain)

Genroku *koban*      56.25–56.58 % (13 carat 6 grain – 13 carat 7 grain)

1 carat = 12 grain, 24 carat = 100 % gold.

The export of the Genroku *koban* started from 1697; and its purity had not been tested accurately at the time of submission of van Dam's document. Perhaps this is why the purity is listed as much lower in van Dam's document. Since van Imhoff did not use van Dam's data for reference when he prepared his report, van Dam's figure probably needs further examination. As Taya argues, the purity of the Keichō *koban* was higher than the generally accepted level according to van Imhoff's document. The purity of the Genroku *koban* was lower than the generally accepted level, even though no questions have ever been raised about it. Van Imhoff's figures are close to the figures 'based on a number of tests' in Kōga's survey.

47 See Note 46. 'Het Oordeel den Gouverneur Generaal G. W. Baron van Imhoff over den Handel met Japan, in 1744', *op. cit.*, p. 326. Maijlan, *op. cit.*, p. 156.

48 Oskar Nachod (1897), *Die beziehungen der Niederländischen Oost- indischen Kompagnie zu Japan im siebzehenten jahrhundert* (The relations between the Dutch East India Company and Japan in the seventeenth century), Berlin: Druck von Pass & Garleb, p. 413.

49  'Het Oordeel den Gouverneur Generaal G. W. Baron van Imhoff over
      den Handel met Japan, in 1744', *op. cit.*, p. 326.
50  Coolhaas, *op. cit.*, Vol. 6, p. 901.
51  'Het Oordeel den Gouverneur Generaal G. W. Baron van Imhoff over
      den Handel met Japan, in 1744', *op. cit.*, p. 327.
52  Coolhaas, *op. cit.*, Vol. 7, p. 335.
53  Yamawaki Teijirō argues that it was not the Kyōhō *koban* but the Kyōhō
      *ōban* that was exported from 1721 and that Kuiper's statement about
      *koban* exports was incorrect (Yamawaki Teijirō (1975), 'Oranda Hi-
      gashi Indo Gaisha to Nihon no kin (The Dutch East India Company
      and Japanese gold)', *Nihon rekishi* (Japanese history), No. 321, pp. 6–7).
      Only 8,515 pieces of the Kyōhō *ōban* were produced from 1725 and 1737.
      It had not yet been minted in 1721. It weighed 44.1 monme compared
      with 4.7 monme of the Kyōhō *koban*; it is inconceivable that the *ōban*
      was exported at merely double the price of the *koban*. While the con-
      ventional units of measurement in the Japanese historical documents
      for *ōban* and *koban* were *mai* and *ryō* respectively, *ryō* was the only unit
      used in *Nagasaki jikki nendairoku* after 1721 (from p. 171). Although
      the Kenji *koban* was still circulating in Japan at the beginning of the
      Kyōhō era, the Shōtoku/Kyōhō *koban* had twice the monetary value of
      the Kenji *koban* (Sakudō Yōtarō (1958), *Kinsei Nihon kahei shi* (History
      of Japanese money in the early modern period), Tokyo: Atene Shinsho,
      p. 121). Accordingly, the export of the Kyōhō *koban* at double the price
      of the Kenji *koban* is consistent with the domestic situation at the time.
      The actual export of the Kyōhō *koban* began in 1722, not 1721, perhaps
      because the circulation of the Kenji *koban* was stopped in that year
      (Taya, *op. cit.*, p. 36). Based on the above, it is evident that Kuiper's
      account is correct.
54  'Het Oordeel den Gouverneur Generaal G. W. Baron van Imhoff over
      den Handel met Japan, in 1744', *op. cit.*, p. 327.
55  Coolhaas, *op. cit.* Vol. 7, pp. 590, 598, 644, 685, 699, 747.
56  *Ibid.*, p. 590 (20 January 1722).
57  See Chapter Five.
58  Meijlan, *op. cit.*, p. 158.

# Bibliography for Appendix

Arano Yasunori (1988), *Kinsei Nihon to Higashi Ajia* (Early modern Japan and East Asia), Tokyo: Tokyo Daigaku Shuppankai.

Arano Yasunori and Fujita Kayoko (1996), 'ARA (Het Algemeen Rijksarchief) shozai no Nagasaki shōkan kyūzō no nihongo oyobi chūgokugo bunsho no genjō (The present state of the Japanese and Chinese language documents previously held by the Dutch Factory in Nagasaki presently held by ARA (The Hague National Archive)'. *Nichiran gakkai shi* (Bulletin of the Japan–Netherlands Institute), Vol. 21, No.1.

Arasaratnam, S. (1986), *Merchants, Companies and Commerce on the Coromandel Coast 1650–1740*, Bombay: Oxford University Press.

Arasaratnam, S. (1995), *Maritime Trade, Society and European Influence in Southern Asia, 1600–1800*, Hampshire: Variorum.

Bhattacharyya, S. (1969), *The East India Company & the Economy of Bengal*, Calcutta.

Blussé, J. L. (1986), *Strange Company*, Dordrecht.

Blussé, J. L. (1988), *Otenba Koruneria no tatakai* (Skittish Cornelia's battles), Tokyo: Heibonsha.

Blussé, J. L. (ed.) (1993), *The Deshima Dagregisters their original tables of contents, 1740–1760*, Leiden.

Blussé, J. L. and F. Gaastra (eds) (1981), *Companies and Trade*, Leiden.

Blussé, J. L. and W. G. J. Remmelink (eds) (1992), *The Deshima Diaries Marginalia 1700–1740*, Tokyo.

Blussé, J. L., M. E. van Opstall and Ts'ao Yung-Ho (eds) (1986), *De Dagregisters van Het Kasteel Zeelandia*, Taiwan, Vol. 1 (1629–1641), The Hague; Blussé, J. L., W. E. Milde and Ts'ao Yung-Ho (eds) (1995–2000), Vols. 2–4 (1641–1662), The Hague.

Boxer, C. R. (1965), *The Dutch Seaborne Empire, 1600–1800*, London.

Boxer, C. R. (1988), *Dutch Merchants and Mariners in Asia 1602–1965*, London.

Bruijn, J. R., F. S. Gaastra and I. Schöffer (eds) (1979–1987), *Dutch–Asiatic Shipping in the 17th and 18th centuries*, 3 volumes, The Hague.

Buck, H. de (ed.) (1979), *Bibbliografie der Geschiedenis van Nederland*, Utrecht.

Caron, François (1967), *Nihon dai ōkoku shi* (A true description of the mighty kingdoms of Japan), translated by Shigetomo Kōda, Tokyo: Heibonsha.

Chaudhuri, K. N. (1978), *The Trading World of Asia and the English India Company 1660–1760*, London.

Coolhaas, W. Ph. (1980), *A Critical Survey of Studies on Dutch Colonial History*, The Hague.

Coolhaas, W. Ph. et al. (eds) (1950–1985), *Generale Missiven van Gouverurs-Generaal en Raden aan Heren XVII der Verenigde Oostindische Compagnie* (Official letters from the governors-general and the committees to the gentlemen XVII of the United East India Company), W. Ph. Coolhaas (ed.), Vol. 1–8 (1950–1985); J. van Goor (ed.) Vol. 9 (1988); Vol. 10 is yet to be pubulished; J. E. Schooneveld-Oosterlin (ed.). Vol. 11 (2000), The Hauge.

Davis, D. W. (1961), *A Primer of Dutch Seventeenth Century Overseas Trade*, The Hague.

Doeff, H. (1933), *Herinneringen uit Japan* (Memories from Japan): voor de Haarlem, *Nihon kaisō roku* (Memories from Japan) translated by Agu Saitō (1941), Tokyo; Nagazumi Yōko (2003): Yūshōdō Shuppan.

Dunlop, H. (ed.) (1930), *Bronnen tot de Geschiedenis der VOC in Perzie 1611–1638*, The Hague.

Fujita Kayoko (1999), 'Oranda shiryō kara mita yushutsu gin (Export silver in Dutch historical resources)', Rekishi Bunken Kenkyūkai (ed.), *Iwami ginzan iseki sōgō chōsa hōkokusho* (A comprehensive study report on the former Iwami silver mine site), Vol. 4: Shimane Kyōiku Iinkai.

Furber, H. (1948), *John Company at work*, London.

Furber, H. (1976), *Rival Empire of Trade in the Orient, 1600–1800*, Minneapolis.

Furnivall, J. S. (1939), *Netherlands India, A Study of Plural Economy*, Cambridge; the Japanese version is *Ranin keizai shi* (An economic history of the Dutch India), translated by Minami Taiheiyō Kenkyū Kai (1942), Tokyo.

Meijlan, G. F. (1833), 'Geschiedkundig Overzigt van den Handel der Europezen op Japan (Historical overview of the trade of Europeans in Japan)', *Verhandelingen van het Koninklijk Bataviaash Genootschap van Kunsten en Wetenschappen* (Proceedings of the Royal Batavian Society of Arts and Sciences) 14, Batavia.

Gaastra, F. S. (1973), 'The exports of precious metal from Europe to Asia by the Dutch East India Company', in J. F. Rechards (ed.), *Precious Metals in the Later Medieval and Early Modern World*, Durham.

Gaastra, F. S. (1982), *De Geschiedenis van de VOC* (The history of the VOC), Leiden.

Glamann, K. (1921), *Dutch-Asiatic Trade 1620-1740*, The Hague.

Glamann, K. (1953), 'The Dutch East India Company's Trade in Japanese Copper, 1635-1736', *Scandinavian Econimic History Review*, Vol. 1, No. 1.

Glamann, K. (1978), 'Kinsei no kokusai bōeki to kikinzoku no ryūtsū ni kansuru ichi kōsatsu (A study of international trade and distribution of precious metals in the early modern period)' and 'Nihon dō to jūshichi seiki Yōroppa no pawā poritikkusu (Japanese copper and European power politics in the 16th century)', translated by Yoneo Ishii, *Tōhōgaku* (Eastern studies), No. 56, Tokyo.

Hamashita Takeshi and Kawakatsu Heita (eds) (1991), *Ajia kōekiken to Nihon kōgyōka 1500-1900* (The Asian trading sphere and the industrialization of Japan 1500-1900), Tokyo: Riburopōto.

Harada, Tomohiko (1974), *Nagasaki*, Tokyo: Chūō Kōronsha.

Hayashi, Fukusai et al. (eds) (1913), *Tsūkō ichiran* (Records of dealings with foreign countries), Vols. 4 and 6, Tokyo: Kokusho Kankōkai.

Hirado Shi Shi Hensan Iinkai (ed.) (1998, 2000), *Hirado shi shi* (The history of Hirado city), overseas resources edition II & III, Nagasaki.

Innes, R. (1980), *The Door Ajar*: University Microfilms International.

Ishida Chihiro (1984), 'Kinsei Nichiran bōeki no kisoteki kenkyū (A study of the early modern Japanese-Dutch trade)', *Nagasaki dansō* (Journal of Nagasaki history), 69.

Ishida Chihiro (1985a), 'Dejima bōeki hin no kisoteki kenkyū (A study of trade goods in Dejima)', *Nichiran gakkai shi* (Journal of the Japan-Netherlands society), 19.

Ishida Chihiro (1985b), 'Kinsei chūki Oranda funazumi nimotsu no kisoteki kenkyū (A study of merchandise on Dutch vessels arrived in the middle of Edo period)', *Aoyama Gakuin Daigaku bungaku bu kiyō* (Journal of the college of literature, Aoyama Gakuin University), 27.

Ishida Chihiro (1988), 'Kinsei kōki ni okeru Dejima bōeki hin to sono torihiki katei (Trade goods and the process of transaction in Dejima in the late early modern period)', *Shigaku zasshi* (Journal of the historical society), 97-8.

Ishida Chihiro (1989), 'Oranda sen no yunyū keorimono (Woolen textiles imported by Dutch vessels)', *Chishi to rekishi* (Regional and historical studies), 42.

Ishida Chihiro (1991), 'Edo jidai kōki no Oranda funazumi nimotsu ni tsuite (Merchandise on Dutch vessels in the late Edo period)', *Tsurumi Daigaku kiyō* (The bulletin of Tsurumi University), 28.

Ishida Chihiro (1992), 'Edo kōki ni okeru Ran funazumi nimotsu to sono hanbai (Merchandise on Dutch vessels and their sale in the late Edo period)', *Senseki* (Journal of history), 2.

Ishida Chihiro (1993), 'Edo jidai no sarasa yunyū (The import of cotton in the Edo period)', Nezu Bijutsukan (ed.), *Kowatari sarasa to wa sarasa* (Imported antique printed cotton and Japanese cotton), Tokyo.

Ishida Chihiro (2004), *Nichiran bōeki no shiteki kenkyū* (A historical study of Japanese–Dutch trade), Tokyo: Yoshikawa Kōbunkan.

Ishida Chihiro (2009), *Nichiran bōeki no kōzō to tenkai* (The structure and development of Japanese–Dutch trade), Tokyo: Yoshikawa Kōbunkan.

Israel, J. (1989), *Dutch Primacy in World Trade 1585–1740*, Oxford.

Itazawa Takeo (1940), *Nichiran kōtsū shi wa* (History of traffic between Japan and the Netherlands), Tokyo: Ranryō Indo Sōsho.

Itazawa Takeo (1949), *Nichiran bōeki shi* (History of Japanese–Dutch trade), Tokyo: Heibonsha.

Itazawa Takeo (1959), *Nichiran bunka kōshō shi no kenkyū* (A study of the history of the Japanese–Dutch cultural relations), Tokyo: Yoshikawa Kōbunkan.

Itazawa Takeo (1966), *Nihon to Oranda* (Japan and the Netherlands), Tokyo: Shibundō.

Iwao Seiichi (1947), 'Sakoku jidai ni okeru Nihon bōekihin no hanro (Sales channels of Japanese trade goods in the seclusion era)', *Nihon rekishi* (Japanese history), 2–5.

Iwao Seiichi (1962), 'Kinsei Nihon no kaigai bōeki (Foreign trade by early modern Japan)', *Rekishi* (History), No. 25.

Iwao Seiichi (1973), 'Edo jidai no satō bōeki ni tsuite (Sugar trading in the Edo period)', *Nihon gakushiin kiyō* (Transactions of the Japan Academy), 31.

Iwao Seiichi (1974), *Sakoku* (National seclusion), Tokyo: Chūō Kōronsha.

Iwao Seiichi (1980), *Edo jidai nichiran bunka kōshō shiryōshū 1 Meiji izen no yōba no yunyū to zōshoku* (Collection of materials on the Japanese–Dutch cultural relations in the Edo period 1: Importation and propagation of foreign horses before the Meiji period), Tokyo: Yoshikawa Kōbunkan.

Kaempfer, E. (1727), *The History of Japan*, translated by J. G. Scheuchzer, London; the Japanese version is *Nihon shi* (Japanese history), translated by Tadashi Imai (1973): Kasumigaseki Shuppan.

Katagiri, Kazuo (ed.) (2002), *Nichiran kōryū jinbutsu jōhō* (Japan–Netherlands relations: people and information), Kyoto: Shibunkaku Shuppan.

Katō Ēichi (1968), 'Hirado Oranda shōkan no shōgyō chōbo ni mirareru Nichiran bōeki no ichi danmen (A cross-section of the Japanese–Dutch trade revealed by the trade books of the Dutch Factory in Hirado)', *Tokyo Daigaku shiryō hensanjo hō* (Bulletin of the University of Tokyo Historiographical Institute) 3.

Katō Ēichi (1969), '1636 nen Hirado Oranda shōkan no yushutsunyū shōhin (The goods imported and exported by the Dutch Factory in Hirado in 1636)', *Tokyo Daigaku shiryō hensanjo hō* (Bulletin of the University of Tokyo Historiographical Institute) 4.

Katō Ēichi (1970 & 1971), '1637 nen Hirado Oranda shōkan bōeki hyō (1 & 2) (Statistical tables for trade by the Dutch Factory in Hirado in 1637, 1 & 2)', *Tokyo Daigaku shiryō hensanjo hō* (Bulletin of the University of Tokyo Historiographical Institute) 5 & 6.

Katō Ēichi (1978), 'Genna/Kanei ki ni okeru Nichiran bōeki (The Japanese–Dutch trade in the Genna and Kanei eras)', in Kitajima Masamoto (ed.), *Bakuhansei kokka seiritsu katei no kenkyū* (A study of the formation process of the shogunate and domain-system state), Tokyo: Yoshikawa Kōbunkan.

Katō Ēichi (1980), 'Rengō Higashi Indo Gaisha no shoki kaikei kiroku to Hirado shōkan (The early accounting records of the United East India Company and the Dutch Factory in Hirado)', *Tokyo Daigaku shiryō hensanjo hō* (Bulletin of the University of Tokyo Historiographical Institute) 14.

Katō Ēichi (1981), 'Sakoku to bakuhansei kokka (National seclusion and the shogunate and domain-system state)', Katō Ēichi and Tadao Yamada (eds), *Sakoku* (National seclusion), Tokyo: Yūhikaku Shuppan.

Katō Ēichi (1987), 'Rengō Higashi Indo Gaisha no senryaku kyoten to shite no Hirado shōkan (The Dutch Factory in Hirado as a strategic stronghold of the United East India Company)', Takeo Tanaka (ed.), *Nihon zenkindai no kokka to taigai kankei* (The premodern state and foreign relations in Japan), Tokyo: Yoshikawa Kōbunkan.

Katō Ēichi (1989), '"Kōgi" to Oranda (The "shogunate" and the Netherlands)', Katō Ēichi, Manji Kitajima and Katsumi Fukaya (eds), *Bakuhansei kokka to iiki/ikoku* (The shogunate and domain-system state and foreign territories/countries), Tokyo: Azekura Shobō.

Katō Ēichi (1998), *Bakuhansei kokka no seiritsu to taigai kankei* (The formation of the shogunate and domain-system state and foreign relations), Tokyo: Shibunkaku Shuppan.

*Kenkyō ruiten* (Classified collection of laws), Kyoto: Kyūko Shoin (1984).

*Kinsei shakai keizai sōsho* (Early modern society and economy series), Tokyo: Kaizōsha (1925–1927).

*Kiyō gundan* (A collection of records of the Nagasaki region), Tokyo: Kondō Shuppansha (1974).

Kobata Atsushi (1976), *Kingin bōeki shi no kenkyū* (A study of the history of trade in gold and silver), Tokyo: Hōsei Daigaku shuppankyoku.

Kokuritsu Kōbunsho Kan, *Naikaku bunko kokusho bunrui mokuroku (jō ge)* (A classified catalogue of books in the cabinet library, 2 vols).

Kuiper, J. F. (1921), *Japan en de Buitenwereld in de 18e Eeuw* (Japan and the outside world in the 18th century), The Hague.

Kyushu Bunkashi Kenkyūjo Shiryōshū Kankōkai (ed.) (1999), *Nagasaki jikki nendairoku* (The true chronicles of Nagasaki), Fukuoka: Kyūshū Daigaku.

Kyūshū Daigaku Kyūshū Bunkashi Kenkyū Shisetsu (ed.), *Kyūshū Bunkashi Kenkyūjo shozō komonjo mokuroku 6* (Catalogue of ancient documents in the possession of the Research Institute of Kyūshū Cultural History, Vol. 6).

Kōda Shigetomo (1940), *Shiwa higashi to nishi* (Historical consideration of east and west), Tokyo: Chūō Kōronsha.

Kōda Shigetomo (1942), *Nichiō tsūkō shi* (History of Japan–Europe relations), Tokyo: Iwanami Shoten.

Kōda Shigetomo (1971–1974) *Kōda Shigetomo chosakushū* (Collective works of Shigetomo Kōda), 8 vols., Tokyo: Chūō Kōronsha.

Landwehr, J., P. van der Krogt (ed.) (1991), *VOC: A Bibliography of Publications Relating to the Dutch East India Company 1602–1800*, Utrecht.

Massarella, D. (1990), *A World Elswhere: Europe's Encounter with Japan in the 16th and 17th Centuries*, New Haven.

Matsuda Kiichi (ed.) (1965), *Nichiō kōshō shi bunken mokuroku* (Catalogue of literature on the history of Japan–Europe relations), Tokyo: Isseidō.

Matsui Yōko (2003), '1622 nen ni okeru Nichiran bōeki no tenbō (An outlook of the Japanese–Dutch trade in 1622)', *Tokyo Daigaku shiryō hensanjo hō* (Bulletin of the University of Tokyo Historiographical Institute) 13.

Meilink-Roelofsz, M. A. P. (ed.) (1976), *De V.O.C. in Azië* (The VOC in Asia), Bussum.

Miyashita Saburō (1997), *Nagasaki bōeki to Osaka* (Nagasaki trade and Osaka), Osaka: Seibundō Shuppan.

Morioka Yoshiko (1954), 'Nagasaki bōeki ni okeru kanzei (Tariffs in Nagasaki trade)', *Bunka* (Culture), 18.

Morioka Yoshiko (1962), 'Kinsei shotō ni okeru kiito bōeki (Trade in raw silk in the beginning of the early modern period)', *Rekishi kyōiku* (History education), 10–9.

Morioka Yoshiko (1966), 'Kinsei kōhan ki ni okeru Nasaki bōeki no henshitsu (Changes in Nagasaki trade in the late early modern period)', *Gakushūin shigaku* (Gakushūin historical review), 3.

Moteki Torao (1976), 'Jūshichi seiki shotō Oranda ni okeru kaikei jijō (Accounting practice in the early seventeenth century Netherlands)', *Rikkyō keizaigaku kenkyū* (Rikkyo University economic review), 21.

Murakami Naojirō (1915), *Nihon to Oranda* (Japan and the Netherlands), Tokyo: Nichiran Gakkai.

Murakami Naojirō (1917), *Bōeki shihjō no Hirado* (Hirado in the history of trade), Tokyo: Nihon Gakujutsu Fukyūkai.

Murakami Naojirō (ed.) (1935), *Nagasaki shi shi tsūkō bōeki hen seiyō shokoku bu* (The history of Nagasaki city foreign relations/trade section: Western countries): Nagasaki Shi.

Murakami Naojirō (tr) (1974–1975), *Batavia jō nisshi* (Diary of the castle of Batavia), 3 vols., Tokyo: Heibonsha.

Murakami Naojirō (tr.) (1938–1939), *Dejima rankan nisshi* (Diary of the Dutch Factory in Dejima), 3 vols, Tokyo: Bunmei Kyōkai.

Murakami Naojirō (tr.) (1956–1958), *Nagasaki Oranda shōkan no nikki* (Diaries of the Dutch Factory in Nagasaki), 3 vols., Tokyo: Iwanami Shoten.

Murakami Naojirō (tr.) (1970–1975), *Batavia jō nisshi* (Diary of the castle of Batavia), 3 vols, Tokyo: Heibonsha.

Münsterberg, O. (1896), *Japans Answärtiger Handel von 1542 bis 1854* (Japanese trade from 1542 to 1854), Stuttgart.

Nachod, O. (1897), *Die Beziehungen der Niederländischen Ostindischen Kompagnie zu japan im Siebzehnten Jahrhundert* (The relations between the Dutch East India Company and Japan in the seventeenth century), Berlin; the Japanese version is *Jūshichi seiki Nichiran kōshō shi* (Japan–Netherlands relations in the seventeenth century), translated by Makita Tominaga (1956), Nara.

Nagasaki Bunken Sōsho (Nagasaki document series) (1973–1977), including *Nagasaki jitsuroku taisei* (Compendium of authentic records of Nagasaki) (1973), *Zoku Nagasaki jitsuroku taisei* (Compendium of authentic records of Nagasaki, second series) (1974), *Nagasaki minatogusa* (Records of Nagasaki port) (1973), *Nagasaki kokon shūran jōgekan* (Collection of stories of Nagasaki past and present) (1976) and *Kanpō nikki to hankachō* (Kanpō diaries and crime records) (1977): Nagasaki Bunkensha.

Nagasaki Ken (ed.) (1986), *Nagasaki ken shi taigai koshō hen* (History of Nagasaki prefecture foreign relations edition), Tokyo: Yoshikawa Kōbunkan.

Nagasaki Ken Shi Hensan Iinkai (1974), *Nagasaki ken shi shiryō-hen 4* (History of Nagasaki prefecture, historical resources edition Vol. 4), Tokyo: Yoshikawa Kōbunkan, including 'Nagasaki kaisho gosatsumono (Five-volume books of Nagasaki trade association)' and 'Kaban kōeki meisai ki (Detailed records of the trade with the Chinese and the Dutch)'.

Nagasaki Kenritsu Nagasaki Toshokan, *Kenritsu Nagasaki toshokan kyōdo shiryō mokuroku* (The prefectural Nagasaki library catalogue of local resources) Vol. 1 (1965), Vol. 2 (1966).

Nagasaki Kenritsu Nagasaki Toshokan, *Kenritsu Nagasaki toshokan kyōdo shiryō mokuroku zōka hoi no bu* (The additional and supplementary edition of the prefectural Nagasaki library catalogue of local resources) Vol. 1 (1973), Vol. 2 (1984).

Nagasaki Shi (ed.) (1913), *Bakufu jidai no Nagasaki* (Nagasaki in the Edo period): Nagasaki Shi.

Nagasaki Shiritsu Hakubutsukan (1989), *Nagasaki shiritsu hakubutsukan shiryō mokuroku bunsho shiryō hen* (The Nagasaki city museum resources catalogue-documents edition).

*Nagasaki ikyō* (Local history of Nagasaki), Tokyo: Sōrinsha (1943). *Nagasaki jūkai Kaban yōgen* (Records of Nagasaki, China and Europe), Nagasaki: Nagasaki Junshin Joshi Daigaku (1988).

*Nagasaki kongen ki* (A history of Nagasaki), Tokyo: Kōseikaku Shoten (1928),

*Nagasaki ryakushi* (An abridged history of Nagasaki), Nagasaki Sōsho (Nagasaki series) Vols. 3 & 4: Nagasaki shi (1926).

*Nagasaki shū* (Nagasaki collection), Nagasaki: Nagasaki Junshin Joshi Daigaku (1993).

Nagazumi Akira (1971), *Oranda Higashi Indo Gaisha* (The Dutch East India Company), Tokyo: Kondō Shuppansha.

Nagazumi Yōko (1970), 'Hirado Oranda shōkan nikki wo tōshite mita Pancado (Pancado through the diary of the Dutch Factory in Hirado)', *Nihon rekishi* (Japanese history), 260.

Nagazumi Yōko (1972), 'Hirado han to Oranda bōeki (The Hirado domain and the Dutch trade)', *Nihon rekishi* (Japanese history) 286.

Nagazumi Yōko (1977), 'Oranda bōeki no tōgin to shakunyūkin (Investments and borrowings in the Dutch trade)', *Nihon rekishi* (Japanese history), 351.

Nagazumi Yōko (1979), 'Oranda shōkan no wakini bōeki ni tsuite (Unofficial trading by the Dutch Factory)', *Nihon rekishi* (Japanese history) 379.

Nagazumi Yōko (1985), 'Shōtoku shinrei to Oranda bōeki (The new law of *Shōtoku* and the Dutch trade)', in Miyazaki Michio (ed.), *Arai Hakuseki no gendaiteki kōsatsu* (A contemporary study on Hakuseki Arai), Tokyo: Yoshikawa Kōbunkan.

Nagazumi Yōko (1986), 'Tsūshō no kuni kara tsūshin no kuni e (From a trading nation to an information nation)', *Nihon rekishi* (Japanese history), 458.

Nagazumi Yōko (1990), *Kinsei shoki no gaikō* (Diplomacy in the beginning of the early modern period), Tokyo: Sōbunsha.

Nagazumi Yōko (1991), 'Jūshichi seiki no Higashi Ajia bōeki (The East Asian trade in the seventeenth century)', in Hamashita Takeshi and Kawakatsu Heita (eds), *Ajia kōekiken to Nihon kōgyōka 1500–1900* (The Asian trading sphere and the industrialization of Japan 1500–1900), Tokyo: Riburopōto.

Nagazumi Yōko (1992), 'Jūshichi seiki chūki no Nihon Tonkin bōeki ni tsuite (The trade between Japan and Tonkin in the mid seventeenth century), *Jōsai Daigaku Daigakuin kenkyū nenpō* (Annuals of Josai Graduate School of Economics), 8.

Nagazumi Yōko (1994), 'Kaisha no bōeki kara kojin no bōeki e (From company trade to private trade)', *Shakai keizai shigaku* (Socio-economic history), 60–3.

Nagazumi Yōko (1999), 'Tōzai kōeki no chūkeichi Taiwan no seisui (The rise and fall of Taiwan, the hub of the entrepot trade between east and west), Tsugutaka Satō and Mio Kishimoto (eds), *Shijō no chiiki shi* (Regional history of the market), Tokyo: Yamakawa Shuppan.

Nagazumi Yōko (2000), 'Jūhachi seiki no bōeki suitai to Roshia sekkin (Declining trade and closer ties with Russia in the eighteenth century)', *Nichiran kōryū yonhyaku nen no rekishi to tenbō* (400 years of the Japanese–Dutch relations: the history and the future), Tokyo: Nichiran Gakkai.

Nagazumi Yōko (2002), *Shuin sen* (Red-seal ships), Tokyo: Yoshikawa Kōbunkan.

Nagazumi Yōko (tr.) (1969–1970), *Hirado Oranda shōkan no nikki* (Diary of the Dutch factory in Hirado), 4 vols., Tokyo: Iwanami Shoten.

Nagazumi Yōko (tr.) (1985), 'Konrāto Kurāmeru no Kyoto sanpu nikki (Coenraad's diary of visit to Kyoto)' *Kirishitan kenkyū* (Historical studies of Christianity), No. 25.

Nagazumi Yōko and Takeda Mariko (1981), *Hirado Oranda shōkan Igirisu shōkan nikki* (Diaries of the Dutch Factory and the English Factory in Hirado), Tokyo: Soshietesha.

Nakada Yasunao (ed.) (1977), *Kinsei taigai kankei shi ron* (Studies of the early modern history of foreign relations), Tokyo: Yūshindō Shuppan.

Nakada Yasunao (1984), *Kinsei taigai kankei shi no kenkyū* (A study of the history of foreign relations in the early modern period), Tokyo: Yoshikawa Kōbunkan.

Nakada Yasunao (ed.) (1999), *Kinsei Nihon taigai kankei bunken mokuroku* (Catalogue of documents on foreign relations of early modern Japan), Tokyo: Tōsui Shobō.

Nakamura Tadashi (1989), *Kinsei Nagasaki bōeki shi no kenkyū* (A study of the history of the Nagasaki trade in the early modern period), Tokyo: Yoshikawa Kōbunkan.

Nakamura Tadashi (2000), *Kinsei taigai kōshō shi ron* (Studies of the early modern history of foreign relations), Tokyo: Yoshikawa Kōbunkan.

Nakamura Tadashi (ed.) (1997), *Sakoku to kokusai kankei* (National seclusion and international relations), Tokyo: Yoshikawa Kōbunkan.

Nichiran Gakkai (ed.) (1980), *Edo bakufu kyūzō ransho sōgō mokuroku* (A comprehensive catalogue of Dutch books previously held by the Edo shogunate), Tokyo.

Nichiran Gakkai (ed.) (1984), *Yōgaku kankei kenkyū bunken yōran* (A general survey of research papers on Western learning), Tokyo: Nichigai Associates.

Nichiran Gakkai (ed.) (1989–1999), *Nagasaki Oranda shōkan nikki* (The diary of the Dutch factory in Nagasaki) 1801–1823, 10 vols., Tokyo.

Nichiran Gakkai (ed.) (2001), *Nichiran kōryū yonhyakunen* (400 years of Japan–Netherlands relations), Tokyo: Nichiran Gakkai.

Nihon Kobunka Kenkyūjo (ed.) (1974), *Oranda fūsetsusho no kenkyū* (A study of Dutch reports), Tokyo: Yoshikawa Kōbunkan.

*Nihon keizai sōsho* (Japanese economy series), Tokyo: Nihon Keizai Sōsho Kankōkai (1914–1917).

*Nihon keizai taiten* (Compendium of the Japanese economy), Tokyo: Keimeisha, Tokyo (1928–1929).

*Nihon zaisei keizai shiryō* (Japan's financial and economic archival materials), Tokyo: Zaisei Keizai Gakkai (1922–1925).

Numata Jirō (1947), *Dejima*, Tokyo: Taika Shobō.

Numata Jirō (1964), 'Edo jidai no bōeki to taigai kankei (Trade and foreign relations in the Edo period)', *Nihon rekishi* (Japanese history), Vol. 13, Iwanami Shoten.

*Ofuregaki shūsei* (Collection of official announcements), Tokyo: Sōbunsha (1934–1941).

Okada Akio (1936), 'Kensetsu ki no edo bakufu ni yoru gunjuhin no yunyū ni tsuite (The import of military supplies by the construction-era shogunate government)', *Shakai keizai shigaku* (Socio-economic history), 6–9.

Okada Akio (1937), 'Kinsei ni okeru shikagawa no yunyū ni kansuru kenkyū (A study of buckskin imports in the early modern period)', *op. cit.*, 7–8.

Okada Akio (1939), 'Kinsei ni okeru shuyō na yunyū busshi ni tsuite (Major imported goods in the early modern period)', Shigakukai (ed.), *Tōzai kōshō shi ron* (Historical studies of east-west relations), Vol. 1, Fuzanbō.

Okada Akio (1983), *Okada Akio chosakushū* (Collective works of Akio Okada) III, Kyoto: Shibunkaku Shuppan.

Okamoto Yoshitomo (1932), *Nagasaki kaikō izen ōhaku raiō kō* (A study of visiting European ships before the opening of Nagasaki port), Tokyo: Nittō Shoin.

Okamoto Yoshitomo (1936), *Jūroku seiki nichiō kōtsū shi no kenkyū* (A study of the history of traffic between Japan and Europe in the 16th century), Tokyo: Kōbunsō.

*Oranda ni okeru Ajia Oseania kankei shiryō shozai mokuroku* (The catalogue of locations of historical resources relating to Asia and Oceania in the Netherlands) (1982).

Ōta Katsuya (1980), *Nihon bōeki shi no kenkyū (kinsei)* (A study of the history of Japanese trade (early modern times)), Tokyo: Tachibana Shoin.

Ōta Katsuya (1992), *Sakoku jidai Nagasaki bōeki shi no kenkyū* (A study of the history of trade in seclusion-era Nagasaki), Kyoto: Shibunkaku Shuppan.

Ōta Katsuya (2000), *Nagasaki bōeki* (Nagasaki trade), Tokyo: Dōseisha.

Ōtsuka Hisao (1947), *Kabushiki gaisha hassei shi ron* (A study of the history of the joint stock company), 2 vols., Tokyo: Chūō Kōronsha, also (1969), *Ōtsuka Hisao chosaku shū* (Collected writings of Ōtsuka Hisao), Vol. 1, Tokyo: Iwanami Shoten.

Prakash, O. (1984), *The Dutch Factories in India 1617–1623*, New Delhi.

Prakash, O. (1985), *The Dutch East India Company and the Economy of Bengal 1630–1720*, New Jersey.

Prakash, O. (1994), *Precious Metals and Commerce*, Hampshire.

Raben, R. and H. Spijkerman (eds) (1992), *The Archives of the Dutch East India Company 1602–1795*, The Hague.

Reid, A. (1988), *Southeast Asia in the Age of Commerce 1450–1680*, New Haven.

Rocher, R. (ed.) (1997), *Private Fortunes and Company Profits in the India Trade in the 18th Century*, Hampshire.

Roessingh, M. P. H. (ed.) (1964), *Het Archief van de Nederlandse Factorij in Japan 1609–1860*, The Hague.

Roessingh, M. P. H. (ed.) (1982–1983), *Sources of the History of Asia and Oceania in the Netherlands*, Part I, up to 1796, Part II, 1796–1949, München, New York, London, Paris.

Saitō Agu (1922), *Zūfu to Nihon* (H. Doef and Japan), Tokyo: Kōbunkan.

Shimada Ryūto (2006), *The Intra-Asian Trade in Japanese Copper by the Dutch East India Company during the Eighteenth Century*, Leiden: Brill.

Shimizu Hirokazu (1976), 'Sakoku jidai no bōeki sen ni tsuite (Trade ships during the seclusion period)', *Tōkei* (Statistics), 27–9.

Shimizu Hirokazu (1979), 'Nukeni kō (A study of smuggling)', *Chūō Daigaku bungaku bu kiyō* (Annuals of the faculty of letters, Chūō University), 92.

Shimizu Hirokazu (1985), 'Nichiō kōshō no kigen (The origin of the Japan–Europe relations)', *Chūō Daigaku hyakushūnen ronbunshū (bungaku bu)* (Collected monographs commemorating the centenary of the Chūō University (faculty of letters)).

Shimizu Hirokazu (1990), 'Kanei sakoku rei wo megutte (The Kankei edicts of seclusion)', *Nihonkai chiiki shi kenkyū* (The study of the history of Japan sea region) 10.

Shinano, Kōzō (1984a), *Kinsei Nichiran bōeki kō* (A study of the history of early modern Japanese–Dutch trade), Tokyo: Bōekino Nihonsha.

Shinano Kōzō (1984b), *Oranda Higashi Indo Gaisha* (The Dutch East India Company), Tokyo: Dōbunkan.

Shinano Kōzō (1988), *Oranda Higashi Indo Gaisha no rekishi* (History of the Dutch East India Company), Tokyo: Dōbunkan.

*Shōhō jiroku* (Official notices and decrees in the Shōho and Hōreki eras), 3 vols., Tokyo: Gakujutsu Shinkōkai (1964–1966).

Siebold, P. Fr. Von (1832–1852), *Nippon: Archivzur Beschreibung von Japan und dessen Neben- und Schutzländern Jezo mit den Süldichen Kurilen, Sachalin, Korea und den Liu-Kiu Inseln*, Leiden; the Japanese version is *Nihon kōtsū bōeki shi* (The history of foreign relations and trade of Japan) (1929), Tokyo: Ikoku Sōsho.

Sumitomo Shiryōkan (ed.) (1985), *Sumitomo shiryō sōsho* (Sumitomo historical resource series), Kyoto: Shibunkaku Shuppan.

Sumitomo Shūshi Shitsu (ed.) (1951–1983), *Senoku sōkō* (Collected records of Izumiya) 20 vols., Kyoto: Sumitomo Shūshi Shitsu.

*Taisei rei* (A large compilation of laws) Kyoto: Kyūko Shoin (1982).

Takase Kōichirō (1977), *Kirishitan jidai no kenkyū* (A study of Christianity in feudal Japan), Tokyo: Iwanami Shoten.

Takase Kōichirō (2002), *Kirishitan jidai no bōeki to gaikō* (Trade and diplomacy at the time of Christianity in feudal Japan), Tokyo: Yagi Shoten.

Takeno Yōko (1979), *Han bōeki shi no kenkyū* (A study of the history of trade by feudal domains), Kyoto: Minerva Shobō.

Thunberg, C. P. (1788–1793), *Resa uti Europa Africa, Asia, förratta åren 1770–79* (Travels to Europa, Africa, Asia etc. 1770–1779), Upsala; the Japanese version is Yamada Tamaki (tr.) (1928), *Tsunberuku Nihon kikō* (Thunberg's travel in Japan): Ikoku sōsho.

*Tokugawa jikki* (Official chronicles of the Tokugawa house), Tokyo: Yoshikawa Kōbunkan (1940–1976).

*Tokugawa kinrei kō* (A study of Tokugawa interdicts) (1959–1960).

Tokyo Daigaku Shiryō Hensanjo (1969), *Nihon kankei kaigai shiryō mokuroku* (The catalogue of Japan-related overseas historical resources), No. 14, Tokyo.

Tokyo Daigaku Shiryō Hensanjo (ed.) (1963–1964), *Nihon kankei kaigai shiryō mokuroku 1–4: Oranda koku shozai bunsyo (1–4)* (The catalogue of Japan-related overseas historical resources 1–4: documents in the Netherlands (1–4)), Tokyo.

Tokyo Daigaku Shiryō Hensanjo (ed.) (1974–2003), *Oranda shōkanchō nikki* (Diaries of the head of the Dutch Factory) original text edition 10 vols., (1976–2001), translation edition 9 vols., Tokyo: Tokyo Daigaku Shuppankai.

Tokyo Daigaku Shiryō Hensanjo, *Tokyo Daigaku Shiryō Hensanjo shashin chō mokuroku* (The Historiographical Institute, The University of Tokyo, photographic archive catalogue).

Tokyo Daigaku Shiryō Hensanjo, *Tokyo Daigaku Shiryō Hensanjo tosho mokuroku dainibu wakansho shahon* (The Historiographical Institute, The University of Tokyo catalogue Vol. 2, Japanese and Chinese manuscripts).

*Tokyo shi shi kō sangyō-hem* (Historical materials for the city of Tokyo, industry edition): Tokyo Shi (1935–1989).

Tsuji Zennosuke (1930), *Kaigai kōtsū shi wa* (A history of international traffic), Tokyo: Naigai Shoseki.

*Tō tsūji kaisho nichiroku* (Diaries of the Chinese interpreters association) 7 vols., Tokyo Daigaku Shuppankai (1944–1968).

*Tōban kamotsu chō* (Registers of Chinese and European cargos) 2 vols., Tokyo: Naikaku Bunko (1970).

'Tō ran sen kōeki oboegaki (Records of the Chinese and Dutch sea trade in Nagasaki)', *Hōsei shigaku* (Journal of Hosei Historical Society in Hosei University), Nos. 20–21, 23–24.

Van Dam, P. (1927–1954), *Beschrijvinge van de Oost-Indische Compagine* (Description of the East India Company), F. W. Stapel and C. W. Th. van Boetzelaer van Asperen en Dubbeldam (eds), 7 volumes, The Hague.

Van Goor, J. (ed.) (1986), *Trading Companies in Asia 1600–1830*, Utrecht.

Van der Chijs, J. A. (1867), *Neêrlands Streven tot de Openstelling van Japan voor de Wereldhandel*, (The Netherlands' commitment to the opening of Japan to the world trade), Amsterdam.

Van der Chijs, J. A. (ed.) (1885–1900), *Nederlandsch-Indisch Plakaatboek 1602–1811* (Proclamations in the Dutch East Indies 1602–1811), 17 volumes, Batavia, The Hague.

Van der Chijs, J. A. (ed.) (1887–1931), *Dagregisters, gehouden op het Kasteel Batavia 1624–1682* (Diary of the Castle of Batavia 1624–1682), 31 volumes, Batavia, The Hague.

Van der Velde, P. and C. Vialle (eds) (1995), *The Deshima Dagregisters their original tables of contents 1760–1780*, Leiden.

Wakamatsu Masashi (1990a), 'Nagasaki kaisho no setsuritsu ni tsuite (The founding of the Nagasaki trade association)', *Rekishi* (History), 74.

Wakamatsu Masashi (1990b), 'Nagasaki tōjin bōeki ni kansuru bōeki rigin no kisoteki kōsatsu (A study of trade profits relating to the Chinese trade in Nagasaki)', *Tōhoku Daigaku fuzoku toshokan kenkyū nenpō* (Annual research report of the Tōhoku university library), 23.

Wakamatsu Masashi (1992), 'Kinsei zenki ni okeru Nagasaki chōnin to bōeki (Townspeople of Nagasaki and trade in the first half of the early modern period)', in Nobuo Watanabe (ed.), *Kinsei Nihon no toshi to kōtsu* (Cities and transport in early modern Japan), Tokyo: Kawaide Shobō Shinsha.

Yamawaki Teijirō (1971), 'Nagasaki Oranda shōkan no kaikei chōbo (Accounting books of the Dutch Factory in Nagasaki)', *Nihon rekishi* (Japanese history), 272.

Yamawaki Teijirō (1975), 'Oranda Higashi Indo gaisha no tainichi kiito bōeki (Raw silk trade with Japan by the Dutch East India Company)', *Nihon rekishi* (Japanese history), 321.

Yamawaki Teijirō (1976a), 'Nagasaki bōeki ron—Orand shōkan no satō bōeki wo megutte—(A study of Nagasaki trade—sugar trading by the Dutch Factory), *Rekishi kōron* (History review), 5, Yūzankaku Shuppan.

Yamawaki Teijirō (1976b), 'Oranda sen no yunyū orimono (Textiles imported by the Dutch fleet)', *Nihon rekishi* (Japanese history), 332.

Yamawaki Teijirō (1978), *Kaigai kōshō shi* (History of foreign relations), Tokyo: Hōsei Daigaku Tsūshin Kyōiku Gakubu.

Yamawaki Teijirō (1980), *Nagasaki no Oranda shōkan* (The Dutch Factory in Nagasaki), Tokyo: Chūō Kōronsha.

Yamawaki Teijirō (1995), *Kinsei Nihon no iyaku bunka* (The medical and pharmaceutical culture of early modern Japan), Tokyo: Heibonsha.

Yamawaki Teijirō (2002), *Kinu to momen no edo jidai* (Silk and cotton in the Edo period), Tokyo: Yoshikawa Kōbunkan.

Yanai Kenji (1959), *Nagasaki*, Tokyo: Shibundō.

Yanai Kenji (ed.) (1988), *Sakoku Nihon to kokusai kōryū* (Japan in seclusion and international relations), 2 vols., Tokyo: Yoshikawa Kōbunkan.

Yanai Kenji (ed.) (1998), *Kokusai shakai no keisei to kinsei Nihon* (The formation of international society and early modern Japan), Tokyo: Nihon Tosho Sentā.

Yao Keisuke (1998), *Kinsei Oranda bōeki to sakoku* (Early modern Dutch trade and Japanese seclusion), Tokyo: Yoshikawa Kōbunkan.

Yukutake Kazuhiro (1986), '1641 nen no Nichiran bōeki ni okeru "torihiki" ni tsuite ("Transactions" in the Japanese–Dutch trade in 1641)', *Chūō shigaku* (Chūō historical society), 9.

Yukutake Kazuhiro (1988–1990), 'Dejima Oranda shōkan no kaikei chōbo (The accounting books of the Dutch Factory in Dejima)', *Chūō shigaku* (Chūō historical society), 11–13.

Yukutake Kazuhiro (1990a), 'Oranda Higashi Indo Gaisha no Nihon muke shōhin sentei ni tsuite (Selection of trade goods for Japan by the Dutch East India Company)', *Nichiran gakkai shi* (The journal of the Japan–Netherlands society), 28.

Yukutake Kazuhiro (1990b), 'Sakoku taiseino kansei to Nichiran bōeki (The completion of the seclusion regime and the Japanese–Dutch trade)', *Chūō Daigaku daigakuin kenkyū nenpō* (Annuals of the Chūō University graduate school), 19.

Yukutake Kazuhiro (1992), 'Dejima Oranda shōkan no kaikei chōbo (The accounting books of the Dutch Factory in Dejima)', *Shakai keizai shigaku* (Socio-economic history), 57–6.

'Tō ran sen kōeki oboegaki (Records of the Chinese and Dutch sea trade in Nagasaki)', *Hōsei shigaku* (Journal of Hosei Historical Society in Hosei University), Nos. 20–21, 23–24.

# Personal name and trade name index

Abe Bingo-no-kami 42
Arai Hakuseki 190

Baba Saburō 48
Baba Saburōzaemon 48
van der Bel 91
Brouwer, H. 27

Caron, F. 101
Chaya Kyōka 71
Chaya Shinkurō 40
Cocks, R. 27, 222
Couckebacker, N. 39, 44, 134
Colijn, P. 159
Cromwell, O. 193

Daigaku 42
Daizen 42
Doeff, H. 154–154
Doi ōi-no-kami 42
Doi Jōho 31
Durven 89

Fushimiya Shirobē 71–72, 228

Harimaya Kurōzaemon 134–135,
    246
Hartsingh, C. 99
van Heyningen, R. 120, 159, 161,
    171, 187–188, 240
Hirano Tōjirō 40
Hiranoya Sakubei 133
van Houten, A. 186

Izumiya 28, 69, 74, 89, 228
van Imhoff, G. W. 96, 113, 186, 188,
    194, 253
Inoue Chikugo-no-kami 48–49,
    100–101

Jourden, J. 27

Kaempfer, E. 103
Kawakami Sakon Shōgen Hisakuni
    134, 246
Kazariya Tōzaemon 222
Kōno Gonemon 20
Koeckebakker 11
Kuiper, J. F. 117
Kurokawa Yohei 102–103

Laurense, C. 133–134

Makino Takumi-nokami
    Nobushige 44
Matsudaira Izu-no-kami
    Nobutsuna 42, 44–45
Matsudaira Jinzaburō 20–21
Matsudaira Sadanobu 96
Matsura Iki-no-kami 42
Muller, A. 99

van Neijenroode, C. 39
Niiro Kaga-no-kami Tadakiyo 134,
    246

Oda Nobunaga 98

# Subject and geographical name index

*17-seiki nichiran kōshōshi* 22

accountant general 159
*aidakin* 20, 103, 110, 112–113, 237
*aitai* (direct dealings) period 138
Akita 10, 91, 95 *see also* "copper mine"
America 17, 192
Amsterdam 17, 192–193
Anglo-Dutch War 75–76
annual export quota system 145, 156
Antwerp 17, 192
Arabia 102, 139
arrival of the British ship 249
Ashikaga shogunate 98
Asia Minor 102
Asian market 17, 77, 119

Bantan 83–85, 122, 251
Batavia 4, 19, 30, 32–37, 39, 43, 48, 52–65, 83, 100, 111, 114, 120, 122–125, 135–136, 140, 143–144, 153–154, 159, 179–182, 187, 241
governor general in Batavia 101, 114, 123, 134, 145, 179, 194 *see also* "governor general of the Dutch East Indies"
Battle of Plassey 97
Bengal 19, 24, 61, 76–78, 80–81, 83, 100, 114, 119, 122, 141, 159, 161–162, 164–169, 173, 176–177, 183, 193, 241, 251
Bengali raw silk 100 *see also* "silk"

*Beschryvinge van de Oostindische Compagnie* 110, 150
Besshi 95 *see* "copper mine"
Britain/British 2–3, 13, 17, 75, 192–193 79, 84–85, 96–97, 152–154, 156, 176–177, 187, 193–194
British East India Company 97
British merchant 176
British trade in India 153
British vessel 84
English Factory 2
*Bronnen tot de Geshiedenis der Oostindische Compagnie in Perzie* 45

camphor 70, 115, 117, 126, 159–160, 170–172, 176–179, 183–185, 187, 193–194, 245–246, 249, 251
camphor merchant 131, 135
camphor price 135, 138, 144–145, 152, 156
camphor production 131–135, 138, 145, 245
camphor production technology/method 128, 156, 244
camphor sales 134, 140, 169, 172, 177–178, 253
camphor substitution system 151
camphor tree 127, 129–130, 135, 136
expansion of the camphor trade 152
Tosa camphor 127
Chinese camphor 127